God's Presence

In 2011, Frances Young delivered ı ⌐ıı Lectures in Oxford to great acclaim. She offered a systematic tneology with contemporary coherence by engaging in conversation with the fathers of the church – those who laid down the parameters of Christian theology and enshrined key concepts in the creeds – and exploring how their teachings can be applied today, despite the differences in our intellectual and ecclesial environments. This book results from a thorough rewriting of those lectures in which Young explores the key topics of Christian doctrine in a way that is neither simply dogmatic nor simply historical. She addresses the congruence of head and heart, through academic and spiritual engagement with God's gracious accommodation to human limitations. Christianity and biblical interpretation are discussed in depth, and the book covers key topics including creation, anthropology, Christology, soteriology, spirituality, ecclesiology and Mariology, making it invaluable to those studying historical and constructive theology.

FRANCES YOUNG previously served as Edward Cadbury Professor of Theology, Dean of Arts, and Pro-Vice-Chancellor at the University of Birmingham. She is the author of *The Making of the Creeds* (1991), *Biblical Exegesis and the Formation of Christian Culture* (1997) and *Brokenness and Blessing* (2007). She is co-editor of *The Cambridge History of Early Christian Literature* (with Lewis Ayres and Andrew Louth, Cambridge, 2004) and the first volume of *The Cambridge History of Christianity* (with Margaret M. Mitchell, Cambridge, 2006).

CURRENT ISSUES IN THEOLOGY

General Editor:
Iain Torrance
Princeton Theological Seminary

Editorial Advisory Board:

David Ford   *University of Cambridge*
Bryan Spinks   *Yale University*
Kathryn Tanner   *University of Chicago*
John Webster   *University of Aberdeen*

There is a need among upper-undergraduate and graduate students of theology, as well as among Christian teachers and church professionals, for a series of short, focussed studies of particular key topics in theology written by prominent theologians. *Current Issues in Theology* meets this need.

The books in the series are designed to provide a 'state-of-the-art' statement on the topic in question, engaging with contemporary thinking as well as providing original insights. The aim is to publish books which stand between the static monograph genre and the more immediate statement of a journal article, by authors who are questioning existing paradigms or rethinking perspectives.

Other titles in the series:

Holy Scripture   John Webster
The Just War Revisited   Oliver O'Donovan
Bodies and Souls, or Spirited Bodies?   Nancey Murphy
Christ and Horrors   Marilyn McCord Adams
Divinity and Humanity   Oliver D. Crisp
The Eucharist and Ecumenism   George Hunsinger
Christ the Key   Kathryn Tanner
Theology without Metaphysics   Kevin W. Hector
Reconsidering John Calvin   Randall C. Zachman

The cover image, created by Silvia Dimitrova, depicts the loving friendship of Jesus for Lazarus understood as a person with learning disabilities, a novel motif (see pp. 19–22) of particular significance for the integration sought in this theological project. Lazarus' chariot doubles as wheelchair and symbol of heavenly ascent, while the building stands both for the daily home-building of his carers, Martha and Mary, and one of the many mansions in the Father's house. The tree of life represents Lazarus' resurrection, which is still to come, and also the way in which trees fascinate one whose sense of the world is limited. The composition's implicit sphere, broken only by Christ's stepping down to earth to touch our lives, is the traditional iconographic symbol of God's perfection and encompassing presence.

FRANCES YOUNG

God's Presence

A Contemporary Recapitulation of
Early Christianity

CAMBRIDGE
UNIVERSITY PRESS

CAMBRIDGE
UNIVERSITY PRESS

University Printing House, Cambridge CB2 8BS, United Kingdom

Cambridge University Press is part of the University of Cambridge.

It furthers the University's mission by disseminating knowledge in the pursuit of education, learning and research at the highest international levels of excellence.

www.cambridge.org
Information on this title: www.cambridge.org/9781107038370

© Frances Young 2013

This publication is in copyright. Subject to statutory exception and to the provisions of relevant collective licensing agreements, no reproduction of any part may take place without the written permission of Cambridge University Press.

First published 2013
Reprinted 2014

Printed in the United Kingdom by T. J. International Ltd, Padstow

A catalogue record for this publication is available from the British Library

Library of Congress Cataloguing in Publication data
Young, Frances M. (Frances Margaret)
God's presence : a contemporary recapitulation of early Christianity / Frances Young.
    pages   cm. – (Current issues in theology)
"The Bampton Lectures for 2011."
Includes bibliographical references and index.
ISBN 978-1-107-03837-0 (hardback)
1. Theology – History – Early church, ca. 30–600.   2. Church history – Primitive and early church, ca. 30–600.   I. Title.
BR118.Y695   2013
270.1 – dc23   2013009536

ISBN 978-1-107-03837-0 Hardback
ISBN 978-1-107-64278-2 Paperback

Cambridge University Press has no responsibility for the persistence or accuracy of URLs for external or third-party internet websites referred to in this publication, and does not guarantee that any content on such websites is, or will remain, accurate or appropriate.

Contents

Preface

This book is the fruit of a long-standing dream. Some thirty years ago, when I had completed the first edition of *From Nicaea to Chalcedon*,[1] I felt tooled up to produce what I then conceived as a *Theology of the Fathers*, somewhat on the model of theologies of the New Testament. But that idea stimulated the question as to what exactly such a thing might be. Did it mean an exercise in strictly historical reconstruction? Or would it be a hermeneutical exercise in retrieval or appropriation, or some kind of dialogue between theology then and now? One thing I was clear about – that I wanted to explore theological argument in a historically responsible way, rather than pursue the so-called development of doctrine. Circumstances over the years meant that this project was left for the so-called leisure of retirement, though meanwhile attempts were made to scope what might be involved, and ideas were tried out in various papers, lectures and talks along the way, excerpts being incorporated into the text of this book.[2] Now, in the aftermath of the second edition of *From Nicaea to Chalcedon*, this dream was realized in the Bampton Lectures for 2011. Each chapter in the book corresponds to one lecture, but here considerably more material is presented than could be delivered on any occasion.

I am grateful to the Bampton Electors for providing the opportunity, and for their encouragement and hospitality. I acknowledge

---

[1] *From Nicaea to Chalcedon: A Guide to the Literature and its Background* (London: SCM Press, 2010).

[2] Key papers have been collected and republished in *Exegesis and Theology in Early Christianity* (Farnham: Ashgate Variorum, 2012).

with thanks invitations to deliver series of lectures at King's College, London and New College, Edinburgh, in which ideas were developed and tested out; neither the F. D. Maurice Lectures nor the Croall Lectures have been published, but both were significant steps towards what is now here. The enterprise of dialogue with the fathers was anticipated at a more popular level in the Sarum Theological Lectures, published as *Brokenness and Blessing: Towards a Biblical Spirituality*,[3] though that work focussed on key themes rather than doctrines.

The encouragement of my erstwhile colleague, David Ford, and his willingness to read the draft of each chapter, was vital in keeping my nose to the grindstone, as was the expectation of certain Oxford friends, notably Andrew Teal, Paul Joyce and Sister Barbara June of the Convent of the Incarnation. The profound influence of Jean Vanier will be frequently evident in the following pages. My thanks to such supportive friends.

But there are two particular persons without whom none of this would have been possible, Arthur, and Bob, my husband and fellow-carer. Neither of them can know or understand how profound has been their contribution, and the least I can do is dedicate this volume to them.

---

[3] *Brokenness and Blessing: Towards a Biblical Spirituality*, Sarum Theological Lectures for 2004 (London: DLT, 2007).

Acknowledgements

Grateful acknowledgement is made to the following for permission to abstract material from earlier publications: Cambridge University Press for '"Creatio ex nihilo": A Context for the Emergence of the Christian Doctrine of Creation', *SJT* 44 (1991), 139–51; Church House Publishing for 'Christian Scripture and the "Other"' in Michael Ipgrave (ed.), *Scriptures in Dialogue: Christians and Muslims Studying the Bible and the Qur'an Together*, a record of the seminar 'Building Bridges' held at Doha, Qatar, 7–9 April 2003 (2004); Éditions Beauchesne for 'The God of the Greeks and the Nature of Religious Language' in W. R. Schoedel and Robert Wilken (eds.), *Early Christian Literature and the Greek Intellectual Tradition*, Festschrift for R. M. Grant, Théologie Historique 53 (1979); Koninklijke Brill NV, Leiden, for 'Adam and Anthropos: A Study in the Interaction of Science and the Bible in Two Anthropological Treatises of the Fourth Century', *VC* 37 (1983), 110–40; and 'The Church and Mary', *Ecclesiology* 5 (2009), 272–98; Peeters, Leuven, for 'Christology and Creation: Towards an Hermeneutic of Patristic Christology' in T. Merrigan and J. Haers (eds.), *The Myriad Christ* (2000), pp. 191 205; 'Creation and Human Being: The Forging of a Distinct Christian Discourse', *SP* 44 (2010), 335–48; and 'God's Image: "The Elephant in the Room" in the Fourth Century?', *SP* 50 (2011), 57–71; SCM Press for *From Nicaea to Chalcedon*, (2nd edn, 2010), pp. 116 27 on 'Macarius'; SPCK for 'From Analysis to Overlay: A Sacramental Approach to Christology' in David Brown and Ann Loades (eds.), *Christ: The Sacramental Word: Incarnation, Sacrament and Poetry* (1996), pp. 40–56; St Vladimir's Seminary Press for 'Inner Struggle: Some Parallels between the Spirituality of John Wesley and the Greek Fathers', in S. T. Kimbrough, Jr (ed.), *Orthodox and Wesleyan Spirituality* (2002); and 'The "Penultimate" Nature of the Church – the *Eschaton* Is Not Yet!' in S. T. Kimbrough, Jr (ed.), *Orthodox and Wesleyan Ecclesiology* (2007), pp. 199–211; T&T Clark, Continuum Books, for '*Theotokos*: Mary and the Pattern of Fall and Redemption in the Theology of Cyril of Alexandria' in Thomas G. Weinandy and Daniel A. Keating (eds.), *The Theology of St Cyril of Alexandria: A Critical Appreciation* (2003), pp. 55–74; and 'Hermeneutical Questions: The Ordination of Women in the Light of Biblical and Patristic Typology' in Ian Jones, Janet Wootton and Kirsty Thorpe (eds.), *Women and Ordination in the Christian Churches: International Perspectives* (2008); the *Australian Biblical Review* for 'Allegory and Atonement' in the *Australian Biblical Review* 35 (1987), Special Issue in Honour of Professor Eric Osborn, 107–14; the Ecclesiastical History Society and Boydell and Brewer Ltd for 'Naked or Clothed? Eschatology and the Doctrine of Creation' in Peter Clarke and Tony Claydon (eds.), *The Church, the Afterlife and the Fate of the Soul*, Studies in Church History 45 (2009); the Methodist Publishing House for 'University Sermon for the Tercentenary of the Birth of John Wesley', *Epworth Review* 31 (2004), 44–51; the Methodist Sacramental Fellowship for *Presbyteral Ministry in the Catholic Tradition or Why Shouldn't Women be Priests?* (1994); and 'The Materialism of the Christian Tradition', *Bulletin* No. 138 (Epiphany 2011), 4–10. Many thanks also go to Rev. Dr. Andrew Teal, Chaplain, Pembroke College, Oxford, for compiling the index to this volume, with the assistance of Chris Long.

Abbreviations

ACW	*Ancient Christian Writers*, New York: Newman Press
ANCF	*Ante-Nicene Christian Fathers*, Edinburgh: T&T Clark
ARCIC	The Anglican-Roman Catholic International Commission
CCL	*Corpus Christianorum Series Latina*, Turnhout: Brepols
CSCO	*Corpus Scriptorum Christianorum Orientalium*, Leuven: Peeters
CSEL	*Corpus Scriptorum Ecclesiasticorum Latinorum*, Vienna: Kommission zur Herausgabe des *CSEL*
CWS	*Classics of Western Spirituality*, New York: Paulist Press
DLT	Darton, Longman & Todd
ET	English Translation
FC	*Fathers of the Church*, Washington, DC: Catholic University of America Press
GCS	*Die Griechischen Christlichen Schriftsteller*, Berlin: Akademie Verlag
HTR	*Harvard Theological Review*
JECS	*Journal of Early Christian Studies*, Baltimore: Johns Hopkins University Press
JEH	*Journal of Ecclesiastical History*, Cambridge University Press
JSNT	*Journal for the Study of the New Testament*
JTS	*Journal of Theological Studies*, Oxford University Press
LCC	*Library of Christian Classics*, London: SCM Press
LCL	*Loeb Classical Library*, London: Heinemann/Cambridge, MA: Harvard University Press

MIT	Massachusetts Institute of Technology
NPNF	*Nicene and Post-Nicene Fathers*, London: Parker
NS	New Series
NT	New Testament
OECT	*Oxford Early Christian Texts*, Oxford University Press 1971
PG	*Patrologia Graeca*
PTS	*Patristische Texte und Studien*, Berlin: de Gruyter
SC	*Sources Chrétiennes*, Paris: Les Éditions du Cerf
SJT	*Scottish Journal of Theology*
SP	*Studia Patristica*
VC	*Vigiliae Christianae*, Leiden: Brill
WCC	World Council of Churches

Introduction

My intention in this book is to cross boundaries within the discipline of theology in a search for integration. The key topics of Christian doctrine are explored in a way neither simply dogmatic nor historical; rather this is a stab at a systematic theology which has contemporary coherence, but is informed, not by the usual dialogue with contemporary philosophers or theologians, but rather by engagement with the theology of the early church fathers who laid down the parameters of Christian theology and enshrined key concepts in the creeds.

Appropriation of theology from the past necessarily starts by adopting a historico-critical approach to reading extant work – it cannot simply be the exposition of tradition as if tradition could straightforwardly be adopted without question in a totally different intellectual context, as was recognized in Maurice Wiles' programme of 'doctrinal criticism'. On the other hand, we are ourselves constrained by our post-Enlightenment, post-modern mind-sets, and the possibility must be entertained that thinkers of the past might challenge the unquestioned assumptions which inform present conceptual frameworks. Being as true as possible to texts from the past, while also being true to ourselves, may be described as 'ethical reading'.[1] This requires balance between reception and distance, between critique and respect, acknowledging both kinship and otherness. In this respect the aim is a kind of ecumenism over

---

[1] See my articles, 'The Pastorals and the Ethics of Reading', *JSNT* 45 (1992), 105–20; 'Allegory and the Ethics of Reading' in Francis Watson (ed.), *The Open Text* (London: SPCK, 1993), pp. 103–20.

time, a respectful listening to the theological commitments of those with whom we share an identifiably common faith but in very different circumstances.

To make sense of things means being coherent in our terms, while letting perspectives from other worlds contribute, as they prove to ring true or provide maps and guides which clearly cover the same terrain, even if out of date. What I offer, then, is a conversation in which the interests and anxieties of myself and my contemporaries influence the selection and reading of past texts, yet allow sometimes strange ideas to contribute to shaping our own understanding. So I endeavour to expound patristic theological argument and insights with empathy and sensitivity to context, then to explore how this material might contribute to constructing a theological position which is tenable by someone like myself in the circumstances of today. Two points inform this undertaking:

- Texts (whether classical or canonical) potentially have a future, and may become transformative.
- Theology is an exploratory rather than an explanatory discipline – 'faith seeking understanding'.

Though largely shaped as hermeneutical engagement with the intellectual, moral and spiritual reasoning of the fathers, this study bears testimony to a theological journey through modernity and post-modernity. The struggle with modernity shaped the minds of my generation, which has then been faced with the questions of post-modernity – the breakdown of a common rationality in the face of pluralism, the cry for justice in the midst of an unjust century. We cannot avoid the challenges of racism, religious traditions other than Christianity, feminism and disability issues, any more than previously the challenge of science, psychology and sociology. We occupy a particular place in the history of thought and culture. Yet the principal focus of my scholarship has been texts from a different world, a pre-modern world where such matters were never considered. So, my aim is integrity and integration, a systematic theology of an unusual kind, covering the standard *topoi* but not in a standard way, and embracing other aspects of my experience too:

- ecclesial life: the search for an understanding of theology that can affirm and celebrate different histories, relationships and identities, including the ministry of women, within an ecumenical horizon
- public life: the search for an understanding of Christian theology which is robust enough to discern the presence of God in a post-Christian, pluralist society, within a globalized world dominated by science and technology, and on a planet subject to humanly induced climate change
- personal life: from long, and sometimes desperate, searching for answers to the discovery that questions of theodicy cease to engage as over forty years of caring for a profoundly disabled son gives privileged access to the deepest truths of the Christian religion.

As a systematic theologian I need to make sense of all my experience. If that seems ambitious, my only response can be affirmation of the amazing journey made through the months of pulling together the material presented here. It has indeed been an experience of integration for which I am heartily grateful.

Integration also involves, in my case, daring to include writing in less academically conventional registers. To describe theology as second-order discourse is to fix it in a critical and reflective mode foreign to the ethos of patristic theology, which was never divorced from prayer and the life of the church. So, a prelude to each chapter offers a collection of snapshots whose purpose is to earth the topic in the everydayness of language and living; and two other genres appear, both of which I would defend as creating discourse more directly appropriate to theology than propositions philosophical or historico-critical:

(1) A postlude to each chapter offers some of my own poetry. Poetry is surely not 'second-order' reflection on discrete

primary experience. Rather, in the gift of images, symbols and other figures of speech, along with the constraints of form, a kind of creative spirit enables the generation of elusive yet direct insight (or *theōria*) into truths that transcend logocentric rationality.[2] Language is necessarily the medium of theology, but theology can never be reduced to language – appropriate language always points beyond itself. In the mid-twentieth century, when linguistic philosophy dominated the intellectual scene, the status of religious language was a key issue. But the fact that religious language does not straightforwardly work in the same way as everyday, or even scientific, language was well recognized already by the church fathers, who knew that languages are multiple and translation from one language to another is indicative of its accidental rather than essential relationship with the things to which it refers. Trained in rhetoric, they knew that, even in the same language, the same thing can be said in many different ways, that language constantly points beyond itself and that language is inadequate to theological task.[3] Ephrem the Syrian discerned a parallelism 'between God's two incarnations, first into human language when "He put on names" in Scripture, and then the Incarnation proper';[4] since God was incarnate, or rather inscribed, in words – in types and symbols and metaphors which point beyond themselves, he found poetry the most satisfactory medium for his theology. Ephrem's precedent justifies the poetic postludes.

(2) But the primary genre of theological discourse must be preaching. Surely it is no accident that so much extant patristic material is in the form of sermon or homily; furthermore, theological affirmation in the context of liturgy is surely performative, and not merely descriptive, reflective or second order. Accordingly,

---

[2] See Chapters 4 and 6.   [3] See Chapter 8.
[4] Sebastian Brock, *The Luminous Eye: The Spiritual World Vision of St Ephrem* (Rome: CIIS, 1985, republished Cistercian Publications, 1992), p. 32.

each chapter contains some material attributed to 'the preacher'. This trope allows for the inclusion of story, symbol, illustration, even personal testimony, as well as examples of how scripture comes alive through insight and application to the realities of experience. It therefore lies at the very heart of this enterprise.

Each of the eight chapters might stand alone as an essay on a particular theological topic, yet together they provide a consistent overview of the subject. Recurring motifs shape the over-arching theological perspective:

- a reading of the Bible as essentially a transformative text, the Creator God being presented in scripture as constantly at work to bring order out of chaos, good out of evil, and inviting human actors into this activity
- the inadequacy of the 'Craftsman' or Demiurge analogy for God's creativity (with attendant consequences for 'intelligent design')
- the sense of 'creatureliness' as a fundamental constituent in theological reasoning in the Christian tradition, as well as in liturgical and ethical responses to life's giftedness
- the wisdom of intellectual humility: the limitations of created intelligence, human language and conceptuality – the potential for idolatrous language and conceptuality – the *hybris* of attempts at theodicy – the privilege of 'liminal' experiences and utter weakness as access to the deepest theological insights
- the apparent will of the transcendent God to accommodate the divine self to the human level, to work through particularities and the constraints of history, paradoxically exercising power through weakness
- the sacramental perspective which seems to shape and unite the incarnation, the scriptures as Word of God, the eucharist, the church, enabling the discernment of the Creator through the creation, of the Spirit in ordinary, physical dailiness, of God in God's human image and the human community of the Body of Christ

- *corruptio optimi pessima* – fall and redemption as an over-arching narrative that rings true to the way the world is, with all its ambiguities, and the way human persons experience their innermost selves and actions
- the inseparability of truth, beauty and goodness
- true love as without power or possessiveness – *apatheia/* detachment as essential to love, and the fundamental significance of that for understanding God's *oikonomia*, as well as human response to the love commandments in contemplation and action
- the significance of facing the 'other' for theological, ethical and spiritual transformation
- the 'otherness' of God – we know something of God through the divine activities, but not the divine essence – God's utter transcendence yet universal *episcopē* – the paradox of God's concurrent absence and presence
- the mystery of the Trinity as the all-embracing, overflowing wisdom of divine love.

1 | From pondering scripture to the first principles of Christian theology

Prelude

The child is gripped by stories in a children's Bible; the teenager puts the book on the same shelf as *Grimm's Fairy Tales*.

The archaeologist explores ancient sites, while the expert deciphers inscriptions in ancient scripts, construes unearthed texts in ancient languages and notes telling parallels to the biblical literature.

The student learns Greek and Hebrew, and encounters a world distant in time, geography, language and culture; the scholar analyses style, notes *aporiai* in the text, probes questions about origin and redaction, date and provenance, authenticity and historicity.

The apologist struggles with scientific and moral challenges to the Bible's wisdom and veracity; the fundamentalist reverses the priorities, asserting the Bible's authority over against human ideas.

The theologian seeks to make sense of God and the universe, of human nature and human life, of history and human behaviour, in the light of contemporary knowledge about the way things are, as well as the Bible and the traditions of Christian doctrine.

The simple believer memorizes key words to guide action and shape prayer; the preacher picks up the lectionary, seeking to relate the texts to liturgy and life . . .

* * *

The preacher[1] opens the Bible at the Gospel lection for the Sunday eucharist, Mark 9.30–7: Jesus is teaching his disciples in private that

---

[1] Preparing for worship on 20 September 2009.

the Son of Man is to be handed over to be killed, and three days later will rise again. Then, in Capernaum, Jesus asks what the disciples were arguing about on the way; they are silent because they had been discussing who was greatest. Jesus' response is to sit down, observing that anyone who wants to be first must make themselves last and servant of all; and, taking a child in his arms, he adds, 'Whoever receives a child like this in my name, receives me; and whoever receives me, receives not me but the One who sent me.'

The preacher turns to the lection appointed from the Old Testament, Proverbs 31.10–31, the description of the good wife; then to the epistle, James 3.13–4.3. With these three passages read together for the first time, and in the context of the approaching liturgy, a fresh reading emerges that enables discernment of the Word of God for congregation and preacher on this unique and sacramental occasion. The scriptures offer wisdom, wisdom that upturns the high-mindedness and ambition of human cultures, placing value instead on the little child; on modesty and love of peace rather than rivalry and claims to truth; on the woman and her everyday provision of life's necessities, such as food and clothing; on Christ's willingness to be handed over to death for the sake of new life. What the Word of God evidently intends (its *skopos* or aim) is a kind of 'trans-valuation', a wisdom that will initiate transformation in the congregation, as those who hear come to discern the reality of God's presence in life's everyday ordinariness, its struggles, its suffering, even its tragedy and death. This is a Word destined to be fully focussed in the bread and wine of the eucharist, ordinary yet extraordinary, pointing beyond itself, to Christ and the new life made possible by his sacrifice.

The homily begins to shape itself. It would begin with a modern parable, showing how the place where we find redemption is in the ordinary everyday. William Trevor's *Love and Summer*, a poetic evocation of the everyday routines of mundane existence on a farm and in a country town in Ireland, would provide this. The woman in Proverbs 31 and the women characters in the novel reflect one another in different ages and circumstances. Ordinary goodness and a kind of peace is captured in regular habits; yet a potential time-bomb is thrown in with the chance meeting of two young people and the slow, unintentional development of a clandestine love affair. The young man is working through long-term disappointment in love and, even before the affair begins, is all set on selling up and leaving Ireland for good; while the woman is experiencing love for the first time and soon begins to dream of going with him. But her guilt is palpable – she's an orphan, brought up by nuns, sent to be a maid for a widowed farmer, who married her.

The penultimate day comes. She buys a hold-all and supplies of food for the house to be abandoned, then arrives home to find things in unaccustomed disarray. The door is jammed. She fears her husband has shot himself, but it's only a fallen welly-boot. He's overwhelmed by something. She dreads the possibility that he's heard gossip. Gradually it comes out – a confused local has sought him out and said things which caused his distress. His widowhood was the result of an accident – he'd backed the tractor and wagon over his former wife and his child. He interprets what's been said as public suspicion that he'd done it on purpose, because his wife had been with another man.

> In the silent kitchen it came coldly to her that the tragedy of the man who had taken her into his house was more awful by far than love's denial . . . And it came coldly, too, that the truth she yet might tell to draw the sting of his agony would cause more suffering than she could inflict, more than any man who had done no wrong deserved.[2]

Next day she doesn't leave after all; she helps her husband with a chore in the farmyard. He acknowledges she made it easier for him – she's helped to defuse his fear. Her lover, as he departs, hints at his own guilt, and the likelihood that, without meaning to, he would have destroyed her if she'd come with him. He says two significant things: 'People run away to be alone', and 'He saved you. That old

---

[2] William Trevor, *Love and Summer* (London: Viking/Penguin, 2009), p. 198.

man.'[3] Thus the story subverts the expectations of the modern novel. Instead of the joys of romantic love and fulfilment, the value of ordinary, unromantic faithfulness to the everyday is celebrated.

For the epistle of James that gentleness is wisdom, wisdom from above that is willing to yield, full of mercy and good fruits, without partiality or hypocrisy, righteousness sown in peace. And the upturning of expectations is found in the Gospel, too – the little child, the sufferings of Christ.

After drawing out the truths in those lections, the sermon would tell another story. The preacher's severely disabled son, Arthur, would be present, as usual, in the congregation; she would recall a time when he was present for evening prayers with the Othona community. The old stone chapel was the kind of place which would stimulate him into incoherent noise, fascinated by the echo. The prayer leader had planned to spend the time in silence, but knew it was impossible; so he said, 'We will create silence by singing Psalms' – Arthur is quiet and listens to music. With guitars and flutes, one Psalm after another was sung, in the 'Othona' version. Psalm 131 went like this:

> I am too little, Lord,
> To look down on others.
>
> I've not chased great affairs
> Nor matters beyond me.
>
> I've tamed my wild desires
> And settled my soul.
>
> My soul's a new-fed child
> At rest on the breast.
>
> My brothers, seek the Lord,
> Both now and for ever.

[3] *Ibid.*, pp. 205–6.

As the Psalm was sung, it seemed as if Arthur became the Christ-figure in the midst of the community. The distance between the Gospel and the present was collapsed.

$$* * *$$

I Pondering scripture

To collapse that distance might be described as the homiletic imperative. The Bible is the one thing held in common among all those groups who claim the name Christian. In every century, in every place, in every church of whatever tradition, the homily or sermon has been the principal locus of theological exploration. Whether generated by the lectionary, or part of a sequence on a particular biblical book, or emerging from the demands of a particular occasion or situation, always the discernment of God's word for the moment is rooted in the reading of scripture, and scripture inspires discernment of God's way of addressing present contingencies. In other words, theology grows out of engagement with scripture in such a way as to create meaning for the particular people gathered together for liturgy. The reading of the Bible fosters a sense of identity and community, which issues in a particular way of life, which may challenge societal norms. To get a sense of the diversity yet consistency of homiletic outcomes we shall eavesdrop on some preaching and reflection from the fourth century and the twenty-first century.

1.1 Basil, Homily 8: In Time of Famine and Drought

It's the year 368, and famine is stalking the highlands of central Turkey, the Roman province of Cappadocia. Basil's starting-point in *Homily* 8[4] is the prophet Amos: he sees the same evils in his own

---

[4] Greek text: Migne, *PG* 31.303–28; ET: Appendix to Susan R. Holman, *The Hungry are Dying* (Oxford University Press, 2001).

day as Amos was addressing, and the same need for repentance. Graphically he describes the drought:

> ... we lack the basic necessities of life; we are new Israelites seeking a new Moses and his marvellous, effective rod in order that stones, being struck, might supply the needs of a thirsting people and clouds might drop down manna, that strange food.

Basil fears that without repentance the people of his region may become a 'new narrative of famine and judgement'. To capture the situation a Gospel saying is subverted: 'the labourers are many and there is little harvest'. The preacher returns to Amos, quoting 4.7– 8. From this text he deduces that God sent these calamities as a consequence of 'our' turning away and indifference. God is like a father disciplining children for their own good.

Basil notes how the consequences of famine are exacerbated by hoarding and the search for profit. He urges repentance, like that of the Ninevites in response to Jonah. A collage of biblical allusions leads to the plea to examine 'our lives . . . both as individuals and as a community'. He then confronts the objection that God must lack either power or goodness, given that these disasters happen. He urges hope in God, turning first to Elijah, depicting him as a hermit on a high mountain receiving bread from ravens, then to Moses and the people in the desert, surviving for forty years without farming. The congregation should follow Job's example and remember the apostolic saying, 'In everything give thanks.'

Recalling the widow whose cruise of oil never failed while she shared with Elijah, Basil exhorts his hearers to share with the beggar, even if they have but one loaf. A harrowing description of what starvation is like is followed by allusions to the Gospel; the implied parable of the sheep and the goats suggests God's criteria for judgement – the stingy will be handed over to the fire before all other sinners. Basil even suggests that the philanthropy of the Hellenes (pagans) puts Christians to shame. We should emulate the first

Christians who had all things in common, he suggests, pointing to the fact that there are many examples of brotherly love in the Old and New Testaments, and dwelling particularly on the stories of Joseph. The sermon ends by returning to the theme of God's ultimate judgement.

In this example we may observe:

- the rich way in which Basil draws on scripture as the fundamental resource for interpreting theologically the exigencies of the moment and discerning a wisdom that translates into practical action
- the enculturation of Basil's address, as he uses rhetorical techniques and builds in quotations and examples from scripture as orators would from the classics
- the counter-cultural challenge in his modifications to the usual services (*leitourgia*) rendered by the community's leading prosperous citizens: (i) the clientele is widened to include the destitute, the non-citizen, those to whom there was no obligation arising from the usual patron–client reciprocal exchange of late antique society; (ii) the motivations are shifted from the pursuit of earthly *doxa* (reputation, glory) to the benefits of accepting God's discipline in hope of present help and future salvation.

Thus the imperatives of scripture enable the potential transformation of individuals and society within a particular locality at a particular time in a particular culture and era.

1.2 The Gregories on care for the poor

Round about the same time, though not directly associated with the famine of 368, Basil's friend, Gregory of Nazianzus, and Basil's younger brother, Gregory of Nyssa, preached sermons on care for the poor.[5] Both may have been speaking in support of Basil's project to

---

[5] Gregory of Nazianzus, *Oration* 14: Greek text: Migne, *PG* 35.857–909; ET: Brian E. Daley, *Gregory of Nazianzus* (London: Routledge, 2006). Gregory of Nyssa, *On Loving*

build a refuge for the destitute, which was completed in 372. The two homilies of Gregory Nyssen seem dependent on the long sermon of the other Gregory, and they evidence features similar to Basil's homily in terms of the transformational interaction of scripture with current societal norms, though with interesting new features. Compared with Basil, both tend to use the New Testament a great deal more, and their message is focussed more on human solidarity and salvation in Christ; they also draw on then current medical theory, since they focus on the doubly poor – those whose economic status results from sickness and disability. Certain key themes will be distilled, cross-referencing both Gregories: Scripture; imitating God; human solidarity; and Christ as poor.

Scripture

As observed in Basil's homily, collages of scriptural examples and texts draw the listener into scripture and its transformational dynamic, while allusive use of language makes the rhetoric both biblical and encultured. The opening section of Nazianzen's *Oration* 14 provides a good illustration: preacher and listeners, described as themselves beggars and needy of divine grace, may become 'rich in God's Kingdom' by 'breaking spiritual bread for the poor'. Gregory then embarks on the typical rhetorical ploy of listing virtues, the climax celebrating love as the greatest commandment and love of the poor as its most excellent form. The suggested exemplar of each virtue is drawn from scripture. Abraham models faith, Lot and Rahab hospitality, David self-control, Elijah, John the Baptist and Peter frugality. Solitude and silence are seen in Elijah's Carmel, John's desert and Jesus' mountaintop – indeed, remarkable are the occasions when Jesus is named as exemplary: he appears as an example of brotherly love, of *philanthrōpia*, asceticism, prayer, watching,

---

the Poor. Greek text in W. Jaeger *et al.*, *Gregorii Nysseni Opera* 9.1 (Leiden: Brill, 1967); ET: Holman, *The Hungry are Dying*, Appendix.

chastity and virginity, humility, poverty and contempt for money. The citations indicate that his incarnation – his readiness to become human, humbling himself and taking the form of a slave, and being born of a virgin – is just as exemplary as his fasting and conquest of temptation; and the demonstration of his *philanthrōpia* is by appeal to the fact that he created humankind for good deeds.[6]

Imitating God

Exemplars are to be imitated, and to imitate Christ is to imitate God. To imitate God is above all to serve the poor. God is love, and nothing other than mercy is more proper to God, 'before whom mercy and truth march as escorts', and to whom mercy is to be offered as a sacrifice in preference to justice. In Greek *eleēmosynē* (mercy) had come to refer to almsgiving, just as 'charity' did in Latin and English. Gregory observes that 'you have received the gift of sharing God's mercy from God himself' and enumerates God's kindnesses to humanity in all the gifts of human existence: creation, the products of the earth, the skill to raise crops, food, crafts, laws, civilized society, family, to name but a few of his list. For him responsible stewardship means imitating the even-handedness of God, rather than hoarding or over-consumption; it means imitating God's highest and first law, which makes the rain fall on the just and sinners, and makes the sun rise equally on all,[7] lavishing necessities on all rather than burying treasure and refusing to share surpluses. So one becomes 'a god to the unfortunate by imitating the mercy of God' – for 'a human being has no more God-like ability than that of doing good'.

Gregory of Nyssa likewise indicates that it is God 'who in the first instance manifests the divine self as author of good and phil-anthropic deeds', citing the creation of the earth, the rhythm of the seasons, the provision of seed, and so on, as pointing to God as the original designer of good deeds, nourishing the starving, watering

[6] Ephesians 2.10.   [7] Matthew 5.45.

the thirsty, clothing those who are naked. Furthermore, God eases our sicknesses, providing herbs and medicines, hot springs and mineral waters. 'Each letter of the Bible teaches us to imitate our Saviour and Creator'; 'mercy and good deeds are works God loves; they divinise those who practice them and impress them into the likeness of goodness, that they may become the image of the Primordial Being'.

Human solidarity

The appeal to human solidarity is particularly striking in the second homily from Gregory of Nyssa. His hearers are not to 'consider as strangers those beings who partake of our nature'; they are not to walk on the other side like the priest and the Levite, 'who passed by on the road without the least compassion for the unfortunate man whom the robbers had come and left for dead'.[8] Gregory describes people with all kinds of terrible malady causing disfigurement and the slow decomposition of bodily parts, admitting that they are scarcely recognizable as human beings, but they are not to be shunned, he says. He contrasts the act of the Lord who 'became man for you and put on this stinking and unclean flesh . . . in order to effect a total cure of your ills by his touch', with 'you, who share the nature of this brokenness' and even so 'flee your own race'.

> Don't you know who it is who lives in this condition? Man born in the image of God, entrusted with the governance of the earth and rule over all creatures, here so alienated by sickness that one hesitates to recognize him.

> They may have 'lost the form', but 'remember who they are . . . human beings in no way distinct from the common nature.' All have the same birth, the same need for food and drink, the same physical make-up and all will 'return to the dust'. So . . . it is beautiful for the

---

[8] Luke 10.30–7.

soul to provide mercy to others who have fallen on misfortune. For all humanity is governed by a single nature.

Gregory Nazianzen, too, despite graphic depiction of their ostracism from society, driven away because of pollution, yet unable to survive except as parasites, desperate for pity and attention to satisfy basic necessities, still identifies them as kindred, human beings made in the image of God as much as the people hearing his sermon – indeed they might even:

> preserve that image better than we, even if their bodies are corrupted; they have put on the same Christ in the inner person, and have been entrusted with the same pledge of the Spirit; they share in the same laws as we do, the same scriptural teachings, the same covenants and liturgical gatherings, the same sacraments, the same hopes. Christ died for them as he did for us, taking away the sin of the whole world; they are heirs with us of the life to come, even if they have missed out on a great deal of life here on earth; they have been buried together with Christ and have risen with him; if they suffer with him, it is so they may share his glory.

Christ as poor

But the real trans-valuation comes when Christ is discerned not just in the 'top-down' philanthropy of the congregation, but rather in the poor and the lepers themselves. This was an age when there was much debate about what it meant to be made in God's image; many rejected the idea that the image is seen in the body, not only in principle since God is incorporeal, but also because of the abhorrence of associating God with an Ethiopian, a leper, a cripple or a blind man, let alone 'an ailing man squatting to perform his necessities'.[9] So it is particularly striking when Nazianzen presents the idea that it

---

[9] See Chapter 4.

is Christ who is received and served in the act of assisting the poor, including those suffering from the 'sacred disease' (that is, leprosy).

Gregory of Nyssa likewise urges his hearers not to despise the sick 'stretched out on the ground as if they merit no respect'; they 'bear the countenance of our Saviour'. Nazianzen, however, more consistently links the theme of human solidarity with being in Christ: all share the nature of embodied beings. He and his hearers should care for their neighbours' bodies as for their own:

> for we are all one in the Lord, whether rich or poor, whether slave or free, whether in good health of body or in bad; and there is one head of all, from whom all things proceed: Christ.

Love of the poor involves 'receiving Christ as guest' and 'sharing our goods with Christ'. Like Basil, he alludes to the parable of the sheep and the goats, but Gregory notes that condemnation comes 'because they have not cared for Christ through the needy'. So his final exhortation is:

> Let us take care of Christ while there is yet time; let us minister to Christ's needs, let us give Christ nourishment, let us clothe Christ, let us gather Christ in, let us show Christ honor . . . Let us give this gift to him through the needy . . . so that . . . they may receive us into the eternal tabernacle, in Christ himself, who is our Lord, to whom be glory for all ages. Amen.

With these examples we confirm earlier observations about the rich way in which scripture functions as the fundamental resource for interpreting current issues theologically, and for discerning a wisdom that translates into practical action, potentially transforming individuals and society. The process involves identifications between people contemporary with the preacher and those in scriptural texts or narratives, collapsing the time gap and reading one in terms of the other,[10] as when Gregory of Nyssa paints a lively picture of

---

[10] See my paper, 'John Chrysostom on I & II Corinthians', *SP* 18 (1986), 1.349–52.

the wealthy gourmands lying on magnificent couches with richly embroidered hangings at silver tables, while 'a myriad of Lazaruses sit at the gate'; they are 'the beloved of Christ'. This is hardly the only time that Lazarus has inspired a telling identification – we turn to our twenty-first-century example.

1.3 Jean Vanier on John 11

Preaching is a live event; yet it is through written records that we have access to fourth-century preaching. Jean Vanier's reflections on the Gospel of John[11] were first delivered in a TV series, but the written form remains a way of eavesdropping. One reviewer of the book said he had learned nothing new – maybe an understandable comment, yet peculiarly insensitive to the way in which Vanier's pondering of scripture draws the reader into the text and enables a transformation of outlook and, potentially, of behaviour. This is commentary in the homiletic tradition, *lectio divina* rather than scholarship. Vanier likens the Gospel of John to a mine of precious stones, from which he has extracted a few, others many more: 'there is such life and wisdom contained in this Gospel that no one person can discover or hold on to it all'. One precious stone is found in his treatment of chapter 11. 'This is the first time in the Gospel of John that we hear of Jesus' love for individual people', notes Vanier. Cross-referencing Luke's Gospel, he observes that the family's home in Bethany is called the 'home of Martha', not the home of Lazarus. In Luke, Lazarus is not present, while in John's Gospel 'Lazarus is present but never speaks and is never described'.

> Lazarus seems to be a 'nobody',
> except to his sisters and Jesus, who love him deeply.
> He seems to be at the centre of the family,

[11] Jean Vanier, *Drawn into the Mystery of Jesus through the Gospel of John* (Toronto: Novalis, 2004).

living with his two unmarried sisters.
As I read all this I cannot help but come to the conclusion,
which of course comes from my experience in l'Arche
with people with disabilities,
that Lazarus has a handicap and probably a serious one.
The word *asthenés* can imply this.
Were the two sisters unmarried in order to look after him?
The words of his sister, 'the one you love is sick',
seem to me significant.
To me, these words imply
'the one that you visit and bathe,
the one you love with tenderness and affection,
is in danger of death'.
This is of course only a supposition.

The particular, special love that Jesus had for Lazarus and his family is brought out in meditation on the conversations first with Martha and then with Mary. Vanier contrasts the serene way Jesus had spoken about death earlier and his highly emotive reaction at this point. Explaining the Greek words used, he comments:

It is difficult to translate the Greek verbs *embrimáomai* and *tarássō*;
I have translated them as 'shuddered' and 'agitated'.
Embrimáomai is a word filled with emotion;
it can mean 'groaning' and can even be used for a horse snorting!
Tarássō can mean agitated, anguished, troubled.
Jesus shudders, he is in anguish, he gives out a cry of pain.
It is clear that Jesus is living something hard to describe.
Jesus is generally serene and peaceful . . .
Here we see something else: Jesus in emotional pain.
Something seems broken in him.
Never have we seen Jesus so profoundly human.

In John's Gospel the miracle of Lazarus' raising is the last straw for the Jewish authorities and leads directly to the decision that Jesus must die. Vanier reflects:

So here, in front of Mary, he is torn between
his love for her, his desire to respond to her call,
and the inner certitude that if he does respond,
he will be condemned to death.
It is this inner tension that seems to provoke his shuddering,
this deep disturbance within him, and his tears.

Jesus acts to give Lazarus life at the cost of his own; this 'nobody' becomes somebody with a very special significance.

The profound insight that Lazarus might be a person with learning disabilities, with whom Jesus had a special relationship quite different from that which he had with others, including his disciples, might also explain the curious fact that the parable of Dives and Lazarus in Luke's Gospel is the only parable anywhere in the Gospels where a character is named. Did Jesus rub home the lesson of the parable by naming the beggar after a similarly disabled person whom he nevertheless loved in a very special way, so overturning the normal valuation placed on such 'nobodies'?

That possibility goes beyond Vanier's text, but in his own way he offers a critique of that 'normal valuation' by exploiting the generally acknowledged symbolic levels of understanding in John's Gospel and identifying his readers with Lazarus. 'Are there not parts in each one of us that are dead?' he asks.

We judge and condemn and push people down,
wanting to show that we are better than they.
We refuse to listen to those who are different and so we hurt them.
All these destructive acts have their origin in all that is dead within
   us,
all that creates a stench in the hidden parts of our being,
which we do not want to look at or admit.

Like Martha we may cry out that it is too dirty and smells too bad, but Jesus calls us by name:

We can then rise up, a bit more whole and holy,
With the Spirit of Jesus in us . . .
We can let the light of Jesus penetrate all the darkness within us . . .
The story of Lazarus is the story of each one of us.

So we are drawn into the mystery of the Gospel of John and challenged towards a profound inner transformation which will then affect the world around us. As in the preaching of the Cappadocian bishops, so here there is enculturation, in this case, a post-Freudian awareness of our hidden depths. There is an empathetic entering into the story and identifying with the characters, but at the same time there is an explicit awareness of how the interpreter's context informs the reading of scripture, provoking surprising insight into its potential meaning. What we have called the homiletic imperative is the driving force. Some might be tempted to regard aspects of Vanier's interpretation as allegorical or merely subjective. Yet more than once he appeals to the original Greek in an attempt to discern the deeper implications of the text itself; and there is awareness of the role of the story in the Johannine Gospel as a whole, as well as of the Lucan parallels. These moves reflect modern biblical scholarship. How, then, does this 'homiletic imperative' relate to what has come to be called the 'traditional historico-critical method' and post-modern reaction to it?

II Biblical scholarship: Re-evaluating the historico-critical method

II.1 Biblical criticism

The scholar picks up the Greek Testament and details the tantalizing coincidences and discrepancies between the Gospel of John and the other Gospels. The facts, enumerated so often, are painstakingly re-examined. The questions that arise are such as these:

- Why do we find sayings word-for-word the same but set in different stories in different locations?

- Why are there no parables of the kind found in the synoptics?
- Why is Jesus found in Jerusalem several times but in the synoptic Gospels only at the time of the passion?
- What really happened? How can we reconstruct a biography of Jesus on the basis of this evidence?
- Where did John's Gospel come from? What are its sources?
- What was this Gospel-writer intending to say in putting together this particular account of Jesus?

The scholar reviews solutions proposed by earlier scholars and begins to refine them, or frame better ones. There is much reading between the lines, much research into the historical context from which the texts come, much speculative theory about the transmission of tradition prior to anything being written, much reconstruction of earlier drafts or documents, and much argument about the dependence of one text on another. The scholar endeavours to be 'objective' in making these assessments. Such is the 'professional' biblical scholarship, often now erroneously called 'traditional', current from early in the nineteenth century until the late twentieth century, and still predominating in academic publications.

The scholar focuses on chapter 11, noting the historically more plausible sequence of events in the synoptics. That the authorities proceeded against Jesus because he caused a commotion in the Temple at a time of mass pilgrimage is far more likely than the Johannine suggestion that the final straw was the raising of Lazarus, an event whose account presents the historian with further difficulties:

- There are layers of symbolic meaning in a narrative that is a 'sign' of the saying 'I am the resurrection and the life.'
- There is the oddity of Jesus' deliberate delay in responding to the message about Lazarus' illness.
- The story, like the other miracle-stories in John, emphasizes the extreme nature of the event, in that, according to belief at the time, the body had been in the tomb long enough for decomposition to set in.

- The story has a curious relationship with the parable of Dives and Lazarus in Luke, which ends with the words, 'even if one should rise from the dead they shall not believe'. Indeed, by providing a potential seed for the imaginative development of a theologically significant but implausible miracle, that relationship reveals the crux of the problem. Conclusions tend towards the sceptical.

So what is the scholar committed to Christian faith to do with these questions? Exegesis of the Gospel easily becomes an exercise in apologetics, finding plausible ways of explanation to counter scepticism. This may lead to significant insights into the nature of the Gospel – even the scholarship of the early church noted that:

> last of all, John, perceiving that the external facts has been made plain in the gospels, being urged by his friends and inspired by the Spirit, composed a spiritual Gospel.[12]

Indeed, one significant theory about John's Gospel is that it grew from a series of 'homilies'[13] on oral material similar to that collected in the synoptics; so what is recorded here is reflection on the significance of Jesus, rather loosely based on traditions about his life and teaching. The emphasis on factuality and historicity, driven by the demands of modern apologetic, prioritizes categories foreign to the text itself. Such observations may help to bridge what many have experienced as a huge gap between scholarship and the exegetical needs of the preacher.

However, for many the gulf still yawns, and so the last forty years or so have seen challenges mounted to the historico-critical method, with new methods championed. John Barton's robust defence of

---

[12] Clement of Alexandria, quoted by Eusebius, *Church History* VI.14: Greek text: E. Schwartz (ed.), *Die Kirchengeschichte: Eusebius Werke II*, GCS; ET: G. A. Williamson, *Eusebius: The History of the Church from Christ to Constantine*, rev. edn, A. Louth (Harmondsworth and Baltimore: Penguin, 1989).

[13] Barnabas Lindars, *The Gospel of John*, New Century Bible (London: Oliphants, 1972).

modern biblical criticism[14] against post-modern caveats suggests that the challengers have misconceived what lies at its root. He asserts its fundamental interest in the 'plain meaning' of the text; the sort of questions listed above do not constitute the primary aim of the critical method, he suggests, but rather arise out of it, the primary aim being to attend to what the text actually says and not read alien meanings into it. What Barton perhaps underestimates is the extent to which the various post-modern critiques stem from the fact that large numbers of students have actually experienced biblical criticism as the kind of thing here characterized (or in his view caricatured). Be that as it may, Christian theology in the twenty-first century clearly requires viable principles for scriptural interpretation. The following sections sketch a position honed over the author's scholarly career, discussed in previous publications, and reached not only by pondering trends in literary theory and hermeneutics, but also the genuinely 'traditional' exegesis of the fathers.[15] In the end there is much in common between Barton's position and my own, though we develop the matter somewhat differently; rather than appealing to the 'plain meaning', I would prefer to speak of the 'philological method' as establishing appropriate constraints on the meaning of the text; and I would be more sympathetic to claims that texts have multiple levels of meaning.

[14] John Barton, *The Nature of Biblical Criticism* (Louisville, KY and London: Westminster John Knox, 2007).

[15] See, e.g., *Meaning and Truth in 2 Corinthians*, with David Ford (SPCK, 1987); *The Art of Performance: Towards a Theology of Holy Scripture* (London: DLT, 1990); 'The Pastorals and the Ethics of Reading' *JSNT* 45 (1992), 105–20; 'From Suspicion and Sociology to Spirituality: On Method, Hermeneutics and Appropriation with Respect to Patristic Material', *SP* 29 (1997), 421–35; *Biblical Exegesis and the Formation of Christian Culture* (Cambridge University Press, 1997); 'Towards Transformational Reading of Scripture', with Jean Vanier, in Craig Bartholomew, Scott Hahn, Robin Parry, Christopher Seitz and Al Wolters (eds.), *Canon and Biblical Interpretation* (Bletchley: Paternoster Press, 2006).

11.2 The future of the text

The historico-critical method, with its concern for objectivity, has been accused of focussing on past meaning – being 'archaeological', it fails to deliver present meaning. Hermeneutical theory attempts to grapple with that issue, emphasizing the point that significant or classic texts transcend their origins, having not just a past but a future. Meanwhile literary theory has stressed the fact that an author has no control over the text once it is published – a text may take on new meanings never imagined at the time of writing. Reception-history easily demonstrates that texts take on different meanings as different questions are asked of them: so, for example, the fathers looked to biblical texts to resolve issues about the relation between Father and Son, while modern readers confronted the texts with questions about miracles and creation. For post-modern readers, however, the potential future of the text has proved ambiguous – the Bible may foster liberation in all kinds of ways for all kinds of oppressed persons, but it has also provided warrant for slavery and patriarchy with its 'texts of terror'. The future of the text is significant in its consequences – texts create worlds; but it may be that the ambiguities of that future actually reinforce the importance of the historico-critical method in that biblical texts are seen, through its application, to be demonstrably earthed in particular cultures of the past from which later readers in a different cultural setting may need to distance themselves, discovering the 'otherness' of the text. Then that 'otherness' might also present counter-cultural challenges which may come to constitute the surprising Word of God to a new situation. We saw something like this happening in the preaching of the Cappadocians.

11.3 Presuppositions in exegesis

The historico-critical approach to interpretation rests on modernist presuppositions, so the idea of treating it as the only proper way to interpret scripture is challenged – it is not appropriate to make judgements about pre-critical interpretation from a position of superiority. No reading is without presuppositions: as we discern the ways in which Origen's exegetical approach was encultured, so we acknowledge that the historico-critical programme bears similar marks of enculturation. For modernity puts a premium on factuality as constituting truth, espouses a detective-model of investigation for reconstructing the past from available evidence, and adopts evolutionary or developmental models as a heuristic tool, by contrast with the Platonism of Origen and others in the early church. But is it true that this recognized enculturation means the whole method is to be dismissed? To use this as a way of espousing so-called 'literal reading' – the counter-cultural assumption that the Word of God is exactly coterminous with the words of the human authors of the various writers of the scriptures – is fraught with problems, and is itself encultured in its insistence on one-to-one correspondence between verbal statements and historical facts. The fathers recognized that God accommodated the divine word to the human level not only in the incarnation, but also in the human language of the scriptures, which necessarily used types and symbols to speak of what transcends everything in the created order. This accommodation to the limited realm of human understanding, with its risks, with the potential for distortion in transmission, with its own inevitable particularity within a particular language, culture and time, is all the more evident if the questions raised by the historico-critical method are respected. The scriptures, like Christ, are in two natures – the flesh and inadequate human words both reveal and conceal the true Word of God. So exegesis is necessary; it has to be explanatory – but it also needs to be adventurous and exploratory.

II.4 Literary approaches and literary theory

Literary methods, some claim, have superseded the historico-critical method. Yet all interpretation has been influenced by literary reading.

The fathers adopted and adapted the methods of interpretation used by rhetoricians and philosophers in their day. The historico-critical method was itself indebted, among other things, to the nineteenth-century literary aim to 'think the author's thoughts after him', exploring the author's biography, historical circumstances, influences, etc., in order to realize that. Structuralist and post-structuralist interpretations followed contemporary trends in literary theory. The so-called literary approach, focussing on genre, plot and character, narratology and other such features simply continues a historic process of using for the scriptures the techniques developed to interpret other literature. However, sacred texts are surely not quite the same as novels, and the lone reader imagining himself, or losing herself, in a world created by the text is perhaps not quite the right model, any more than the lone specialist scholar in the library. Even individual readers belong to interpretative communities, with traditions of reading. The interpretation of scripture as scripture takes place in the community gathered for worship. Here the text finds its proper 'future' meaning, as in the homiletic examples considered above. Still, drawing the hearer or reader imaginatively into the text is important – what was accomplished by the fathers through typology and allegory may be facilitated by literary analysis, including its historico-critical aspects.

Literary theory articulates key elements in the process of reading. By hindsight we can now see that modernity put over-riding emphasis on the original meaning and the *author*'s intention; while structuralism focussed on the *text* itself – the meaning inscribed in its structure and built into its language, a meaning which might go beyond whatever the author might have had in mind; and reader-oriented criticisms turned attention to the *reader*'s inevitable input into the interpretation of the text – until the text is read it is just marks on a page without meaning as such. But surely each claim needs to be modified in the light of the others. For what got lost in this discussion was any sense that a written text is a form of communication, and communication necessarily involves more than one party. Ancient rhetorical theory explored the interaction of speaker and audience, recognizing that three things were involved in the process of persuasion or the generation of *pistis*, often translated 'faith', but here meaning 'conviction'. First, the *logos*, the argument or story, has to be plausible; secondly, the *ēthos*, the character and lifestyle, of the speaker has to be reliable; and thirdly, the response (*pathos*, suffering or emotion) of the audience has to be receptive. This analysis would suggest that it is simply not possible to privilege author, text or reader, because it is the interaction of all three that is essential to the creation of meaning.

That an act of communication requires such a triangular relationship is evident when one considers something like a letter addressed to particular recipients by some correspondent, such as Paul. Problems arise when subsequent readers become interlopers on the exchange and have available only half of the conversation. Then it is the historico-critical method which enables such readers to take seriously the gap between themselves and those to whom the letter was sent. They may seek information so as to understand the text as its original readers did, but they will never actually stand in their shoes. There is value in trying to understand the original dynamic and circumstances of the communication, but now another dynamic is operative, the triangular interaction between the epistle as scripture, the congregation as audience and the Holy Spirit as author. Each of these communication triangles needs to inform the other. What is striking about the homilies of John Chrysostom, the most famous preacher of late antiquity, nicknamed the Golden-mouth, is the way in which he imaginatively makes his own the pastoral rhetoric of Paul's address to his congregation, noting how he now offers comfort and encouragement, now warnings, so that there is an empathetic collapsing of the gap between the two triangles.[16] Not for nothing did the fathers suggest that the reader has to be inspired in order to understand the inspired text. Nevertheless, the reader's

---

[16] See 'John Chrysostom on I & II Corinthians'.

inspiration is enhanced by being informed, by taking seriously the historico-critical reconstruction of the original circumstances as an aid to understanding.

The 'death of the author' undermined the idea that the reader is in dialogue with the text: the speaker–hearer relationship was rejected as an analogy for the author–reader interaction. But the triangular relationship suggested above means that a reader has to respect both text and author, and to keep returning to what is there in the text to check whether the assumed meaning is justified by what is actually stated. This modifies the so-called hermeneutical circle, turning it into a progressive spiral of interaction. This is what it means to read ethically, and it clearly involves 'dialogue' of a sort. Ethical reading also implies dialogue through recognizing difference: the hermeneutic of suspicion and of differentiation is an aspect of serious rather than superficial engagement.

II.5 *The constraints and potential of language*

By insistence on the original languages, the historico-critical method, it is said, creates experts and cuts ordinary people off from the Bible. Yet the danger of reader-oriented interpretations is the implication that a reader may make the text mean anything they like, a common charge against the allegory of the fathers. Language carries constraints within itself – it is possible to *mis*understand, and language teachers mark real mistakes. The philological method has always lain at the heart of commentary, which began as *scholia* explaining problem words, identifying figures of speech or construing unclear sentence-structures. Here the historico-critical method is in direct continuity with the fathers, especially those like Jerome who went behind translated versions to the original Hebrew and Greek. In the case of translated texts, the issue of language, and what may be regarded as appropriate exegesis of the linguistic configuration of the text, means that some readers are bound to be more competent than others. Responsible interpretation requires the philological dimension of the historico-critical method.

On the other hand, multiple translations alert us to the fact that there is never one single expression that exactly and exclusively represents the original. Besides, language is 'infinite' – meaning is often not constricted. Especially in poetry, a reader may discern meaning which was not consciously envisaged by the author, and this applies to all language that is metaphorical, parabolic or visionary. The fathers' emphasis on discerning figures of speech and thereby penetrating to deeper meanings remains important. The image of a fountain was applied to scripture – no one should think that they have exhausted it when they have taken a drink that satisfies their own needs.[17] Exegesis, then, is not simply explanatory but also exploratory.

Language is always changing, and subtle shifts in meaning are especially likely in the case of the idiosyncratic expressions of an 'in-group'. Commentators in late antiquity had to explicate the archaic Homeric dialect, often using cross-reference to establish the characteristic Homeric meaning of words which remained in use. So too Christian commentators on the scriptures would gather lists of cross-references to show the biblical meanings of Septuagint Greek – translationese, influenced by the Hebrew or Aramaic original. They would also indicate the specifically Christian connotations of the language of the scriptures, again by collecting specimen texts from across the whole spectrum of the Bible. The historico-critical approach produced dictionaries of the Bible, an essentially similar undertaking; and while 'intertextuality' puts cross-referencing into a broader literary framework, it clearly draws on the same recognition that language and literature belong to particular traditions with their own 'internal' influences. So the historico-critical method belongs within a wide spectrum of exegetical techniques.

---

[17] Ephrem Syrus; see Chapter 8 for full quotation.

II.6 Canonical reading

The historico-critical method came to be seen as too analytical, constantly searching out differences between biblical books and sources behind the existing texts. Reaction began with the redaction-critical impulse to look at the editorial end-product of, for example, a particular Gospel, but even this left the New Testament, let alone the whole Bible, speaking with a plurality of voices. Canon-criticism arose as counter-challenge to this. Campaigning against the historico-critical dissection of scripture, it sought to read the whole Bible as a single text, the meaning of each different perspective being modified by its incorporation into the whole. But, to discern the shift in meaning effected by the text becoming part of the canon, the method was parasitic on historico-critical analysis. Besides, which canon? Different canons are accepted by different churches – not to mention the Hebrew Bible of the Jews. Furthermore, in practice, history demonstrates that scripture by itself does not generate a unified viewpoint. Augustine regarded 'Love God and love your neighbour' as the 'content' of scripture and the criterion by which everything in scripture was to be judged and interpreted. The historico-critical enterprise raised the question of the 'canon-within-the-canon' – in other words, asked which bits of this diverse, and sometimes contradictory, library provide the key to reading it as a whole.

Long before Augustine, there was recognition that scripture on its own can be misread – Irenaeus knew that gnostics used the same texts but set them in a different framework. Christian reading of scripture, as distinct from literary or historical reading, emerges from incorporation into an interpretative community shaped by the rule of faith. The rule of faith inscribed in the creeds is a summary of scripture, but it is not a straightforward précis. It is a quite specific selection of the significant highlights that make up the over-arching story that Christians tell to give meaning to human life, and define their identity. Only this 'external' key can produce appropriate canonical reading within the Christian tradition, and indeed advocates of a canonical approach presuppose the common rule of faith passed down in the mainstream tradition of the church.

Stress on the unity of the Bible is important, but it may suppress its distinct voices and the richness of the particularity of God's communication at different times with different persons and communities in different eras and cultures. It is precisely this diversity which enables analogies to be drawn between particular situations addressed in the scriptures and those confronted in other cultural contexts. Alongside the rule of faith we need the full variety of voices brought to light by analytical and critical engagement with their provenance – in other words, the historico-critical method.

II.7 Conclusions

A number of vital points emerge from this survey:

- It is important to distinguish between reading the Bible as literature, significant as it is among the world's classics, and reading it as scripture within the Christian community – there are different interpretative communities which properly approach the texts from different standpoints.
- The historico-critical method, by privileging the original languages of the Bible, both provides appropriate constraints on meaning and also enhances the potential for a rich reading of the biblical texts, especially as it creates sensitivity to the limitations and potential of language and its figures of speech.
- Within the Christian community the historico-critical method has an important role in reinforcing certain fundamentals of Christian theology – namely, that the material world of human history, with its risks and failings, is the arena in which the Word of God is nevertheless mediated.
- However, a 'thick' reading of scripture involves a multiplicity of approaches for discerning past, present and potential meanings, to which literary theories contribute alongside Christian traditions

of worship and spirituality in which the Bible is read publicly and homiletically.

- The Bible, read ethically and not just historically, invites the Christian community to ponder its meaning for present and future, to allow the communication of God's Word beyond the confines of its historical origins – for, listening to the text, the congregation hears the offer of transformation and the challenge to change.
- The Bible's meaning is generated by interaction with other things that go to make up Christian identity, such as the rule of faith, the life of worship, and current issues concerning Christian belief and lifestyle. This is what drives the homiletic imperative. It also challenges the doctrine of *sola scriptura*, for the complexities of its reception and interpretation require other 'first principles' to be engaged in interaction with scripture.

III The first principles of Christian theology

When Origen wrote his treatise, *On First Principles*,[18] he produced what is in effect the first attempt to articulate a theological system or, as he put it, a 'single body of doctrine'. What he was aiming to do in his own context has been much debated: was he providing a typical philosophical textbook from a Christian perspective? Or was he mainly concerned to tease out the principles of scriptural interpretation? Maybe the title (*Peri Archōn*) was cleverly ambiguous,[19] implying an exposition of the basic elements of scriptural interpretation alongside Christian engagement with the topics of 'physics'.

Origen's preface would seem to support this conclusion, though it is difficult to be sure exactly how and where the word '*archē*' is used, since the original Greek doesn't survive. Origen begins with the

---

[18] Text: P. Koetschau *et al.* (eds.), *GCS*; ET: G. W. Butterworth (London: SPCK 1936, reprinted Gloucester, MA: Peter Smith, 1973).

[19] Joseph W. Trigg, *Origen: The Bible and Philosophy in the Third-Century Church* (London: SCM Press, 1983), pp. 91–2.

words and teaching of Christ; for him that includes Moses and the prophets. He notes that many who profess to believe have conflicting opinions about substantial matters, not just trivia. So a definite rule is needed, and he finds that canon in the tradition handed down from the apostles. The grounds for what the apostles taught, he says, were left to be investigated by those who have the gifts of the Spirit – particularly the graces of language, wisdom and knowledge. He rehearses the plainly set-out teachings of the apostles in what is a recognizable version of the rule of faith, indicating that some things not spelt out there need further investigation. The contents of scripture are the outward forms of certain mysteries and the images of divine things; the church accepts this, he claims, though the inspired meaning is not recognized by all, only by those gifted with the grace of the Holy Spirit in the word of wisdom and knowledge. The climax of his discussion states that anyone wanting to construct a connected body of doctrine 'must use points like these as elementary and foundation principles', and then 'by clear and cogent arguments discover the truth about each particular point', so producing 'a single body of doctrine'.

These 'first principles' seem to be foundations on which theology is built. For Origen they include *scripture* and *tradition*, examined in the light of *reason* inspired by the wisdom of the Holy Spirit. Thus he anticipates the tripartite foundation of theology to which appeal is commonly made in the Anglican tradition; Methodism would add *experience*. Our consideration of what it means to ponder scripture would seem to lead to a similar conclusion. Each of these 'first principles', on whose interaction the theological enterprise rests, invites some further explication:

- *Scripture* was the starting-point for Origen, as it is for those in the Protestant tradition. Given the central place accorded to scripture in all forms of Christian worship, the same can surely be said about Orthodox, Catholic or Pentecostal theology. But biblical interpretation cannot be univocal; its interpretation involves interaction with what its readers/hearers bring to the table: presuppositions, cultures, traditions, experience, frameworks of understanding – theological and otherwise. A single, definitive meaning for all time cannot be established, nor even a common 'Christian' meaning without interpretative keys supplied by the tradition in the context of the believing community; even there, multiple insights alone make it possible for particular persons or communities to drink from the fountain and have their thirst quenched – hence the homiletic dimension which ideally allows scripture to be heard afresh time and again. This constant replenishment is possible because the language of scripture points beyond itself, and generates the response of worship.

- *Tradition*, like scripture enshrined in worship, provides the context and criteria for scripture's homiletic interpretation. Origen recognized the fundamental importance of the rule of faith, the core elements handed down from the apostles, which acted as a foundation for Christian identity as well as for scriptural hermeneutics. We might see tradition as a kind of ecumenism over time, enabling the recognition of Christian identity across different ages and in different environments. Major Christian doctrines held in common across the denominations emerged through argument and deduction from scripture, communal decisions having been made at key moments in history when scripture's ambiguities needed clarifying. For example, if the results of the historico-critical method are taken as conclusive, the Christian concept of God as Trinity belongs to the 'future' of the text; but tradition indicates that for 'mainstream Christianity' it is at the core of theological identity and at the heart of liturgy. This demonstrates that even though appeals to tradition often assume it is fixed and incontrovertible, living tradition continually gets modified in relation to fresh insights as scripture is read in new intellectual and cultural contexts. It interacts with the other 'first principles' and does not stand alone, any more than scripture can.

- *Experience* – non-Methodists may baulk a little at 'experience' being made an explicit 'first principle'. Given that it is associated with the 'warmed heart' and 'conversion' in the evangelical sense, it might appear to be far too individual and subjective to be taken seriously. It is clear, however, that the response of inspired and committed believers is what has produced living exemplars of the transformation which lies at the heart of the scriptural message – saints, in other words. 'Experience' is what enables people to enter into the biblical text and be changed. Furthermore, experience includes being part of the worshipping community, so that the individual's response is not simply subjective, but in accord with the communal response of the Body of Christ. This 'principle' means that tradition and scripture are not simply remote and allegiance to them nominal, but that the whole person, within the whole community, set in a particular contemporary culture and a particular life-history, is fully committed and engaged and open to transformation in mind, heart and material lifestyle – in other words, to *metanoia* (change of mind, repentance) – by encounter with Christ through scripture and through becoming incorporated into the church. Origen's endeavour to communicate Christian faith to people at various stages of spiritual development was fully in accord with this principle that what is required is a person's responsiveness at the appropriate level and then advancement in spiritual understanding, experience and action.
- *Reason* implies that the theological enterprise involves making rational sense of things, using the intelligence that God has given us: *fides quaerens intellectum*. Origen insists on the fact that language, wisdom and knowledge are among the gifts of the Spirit, associating these gifts with teasing out the higher meaning of scripture, and investigating both the grounds for the tradition and those aspects which were not spelt out fully by the apostles. True, his attempt to spell out Christian theology led at a later date to his condemnation as a heretic, his speculations

37

becoming suspect as subsequent arguments refined responses to new questions. Historico-critical reassessment, while rehabilitating his essentially orthodox intention, has tended to regard him as a Platonist, thinking through his Christian ideas in terms of current philosophy so as to provide a reasoned account. But Origen also challenged Platonism[20] from the perspective of scripture and tradition. He used his reason to distinguish between philosophical ideas that rang true to the way things seemed to be and those that did not. In the early church there was always a tendency to criticize philosophy for its production of many conflicting opinions (its *haeresēs*), and to scorn heretics for being too easily carried away by the claims of philosophy – just as in our time conservative believers have tended to vilify the 'liberal' views of those who have attempted to make sense of Christianity within the rational framework of modernity. But serious engagement with questions of truth cannot avoid using reason to identify where to challenge contemporary intellectual culture and where to take account of its reasonable analysis of the way things are. Theological thought has always involved using the mind to make sense of scripture, tradition and experience, including the implicit and explicit rational frameworks of understanding that are currently operative. We cannot but take account of science, and the workings of language, culture and society, as they impinge on the Christian account of things. We cannot but address inconsistencies within scripture and incoherence within traditions of theological exposition – critical reason often contributes to a process of purification. Indeed, the church fathers were very clear that the biggest problem with philosophies and heresies was their tendency to cultivate intellectual arrogance. The true theologian has to go through a process of moral and intellectual stripping, an *askēsis* of the mind, which in humility acknowledges that the subject-matter of theology transcends the capacities of created human reason. It is rational to

---

[20] Mark Edwards, *Origen against Plato* (Aldershot: Ashgate, 2002).

accept the limits of human rationality. To define God is to reduce God to the size of the human intellect. Wisdom requires recognition that knowledge and understanding are not an achievement but a gift, a grace of the Holy Spirit, as Origen stated; and the greatest theologians are precisely those who approach the task with a wisdom that springs from humility and love.

IV Theology, exegesis and preaching

We have explored what it means to ponder scripture within the life of the church, and so progressed to a consideration of the first principles of Christian theology. We have found that scripture cannot stand alone – always there is a hermeneutical process in which the same interacting principles undergird its interpretation as those found at the root of the theological enterprise. Tradition, experience and reason interact with scripture in determining how the Christian community understands life and lives it. For this reason the homily, based on scripture and delivered in the context of worship, should be regarded as the principal locus of creative, theological engagement – which takes us back to where we began: the preacher, taking up the Bible and opening at the Gospel lection set for the following Sunday, pondering . . .

The preacher, this time, had been asked to preach in what was then known as Mental Handicap week. As the parent of a son born with profound learning disabilities, the preacher would speak out of experience – indeed, the pressure of the occasion would inspire an initial breakthrough, from the struggle to maintain faith despite the family's predicament, to seeing this as gift, as privileged access to the deepest truths of Christianity. Scripture, tradition, reason and experience would be intertwined in the proclamation of the Gospel as the proper Christian response to the problems of theodicy.

The preacher began with reflection on John 9 – the man blind from birth. The challenge was to make sense of the opening discussion with the disciples: 'Who sinned, this man or his parents?' they asked. 'Neither', was Jesus' reply – 'he was born blind so that God's works might be revealed in him.' The preacher's anger boiled up: why should this adult have lived years of disability just so Jesus could wave a magic wand and display his power? This was no answer to the question how you could go on believing in a good Creator God when something had gone so wrong in the creation of a new human being . . . But deeper reflection, facilitated by hours of reading and re-reading the text in Greek with students, set the particular story in the wider context of the Gospel as a whole. It was told as a sign that Jesus is the light of the world, the light that darkness could not grasp,[21] the light that in the end did not wave a magic wand but entered into the very depths of the darkness of the world's 'gone-wrongness' on the cross – for in this Gospel, the cross is the 'hour of glory', to which the whole narrative moves. So God in Christ took responsibility for all the 'gone-wrongness', sin and suffering alike, and by entering it and bearing it, transformed it. Theodicy questions were overtaken by this twist on the doctrine of atonement, and the seed of renewal was born. It would germinate not only the sermon for this occasion, but also prayers of thanksgiving and the fruits of the Spirit in the challenge of everyday life.

* * *

Postlude: pondering the passion

Seven Words in Seven Sonnets

An empty space becomes the stage of life,[22]
Filled with the play of weeping without end.
Drama requires the bitter pill of strife.
So women weeping for sons and lovers tend

---

[21] John 1.5.

[22] Inspired by Peter Brook, *The Empty Space* (London: Penguin Modern Classics, 2008; first published 1968).

Their graves. Weeping for innocent victims slain –
The first-born in Egypt, Bethlem's toddler sons –
Resounds in the Gulag. Torture's twisting pain
Exhilarates. There's fun in games with guns.
There is no consolation for Rachel's grief.
There is no Messianic peace but a sword.
Women weeping, weeping without relief.
Daughters of Zion, do not weep for the Lord.
Weep for yourselves and your children. 'Father, you
Forgive them; they know not what they do.'

The woman weeps, weeps at the foot of the cross.
What a waste of a life – what promise bites the dust!
What purpose, meaning or sense is there in this loss?
Is it enough to reflect what must be must?
'Woman, behold your son. Your mother, son,'
He rasps, and harsh the voice of reality:
'It's no good clinging to me, woman, I'm done.
Mother instead my beloved community
That's in the world not of the world, but new.
Woman, my hour has come. Don't cling to me.'
Her human anguish he cannot thus subdue.
Love possessively clings to empathy.
Love proves itself by seeming most distressed,
And yet – the pain of joy pierces her breast.

The weeping of a father for a son
Lain on the altar as a sacrifice.
The agonizing cry, 'Thy will be done' –
No explanation ever could suffice.
The drama's climax is his isolation,
Deserted by crowds, betrayed, denied,
Friendless, alone, he faces desolation.
In ultimate abandonment he died.
Why, O my God, O why? Face to face

With the dark horror of humanity
A cry of desperation puts his case,
'Why, O God, hast thou forsaken me?'
So where was God? A strangely present absence,
Weeping, emptying out the divine essence.

'I thirst', he cries, for vinegar and gall.
The way he takes is a kind of destiny,
Entering a deep abyss on behalf of all,
The struggle patterned on ancient prophecy.
The king of the Jews plays out the testing role
Of victim exposed to the people's enemies,
Exposed to judgment, cut to the very soul.
The people play out unconscious destinies –
They part his garments, casting lots. They wag
Their heads at him, deriding him, and rave,
'Come down from the cross.' His limbs begin to sag.
'He saved others, himself he cannot save.'
'He trusts in God, let him deliver him.'
The answering darkness is a silence grim.

'It's finished.' The joy of fulfilment fills full up
To the point of choking. The curtain's rent in twain.
The audience rises, applauds, lifting the cup
Of celebration on high, its cheeks tears stain.
'I, if I be lifted up, will draw
Everyone to myself in this moment of glory.'
After each curtain call a call for more –
No one dare let go this spacious story,
This passionate actor acting out a passion,
Performed by submission, controlling events
By loss of control, and apparently perdition.
The stench of death makes incense breathing scents,
Slaughter sacrifice and death new life.
Atonement requires the bitter pill of strife.

The play demands the spaciousness of God,
An emptying of God that's no retreat
From bearing stigmata, scars slashed by the rod
Which empties human pride of self-conceit;
The weeping of a king riding an ass
Yearning like a hen to mother her chicks;
The hooligan act of human hate en masse
Stringing him up exposed on two crossed sticks.
The way of paradox his destiny:
Ironical judgement judges the judge of all
And judged itself is made a mockery.
The violence and innocence appal.
God's empty space alone transcends our limit.
'Father, into thy hands I commit my Spirit.'

So what's it about – this strange drama dispensed
In emptiness – this strange king not a king,
Judge not a judge, offender without offence?
Why does this passionate suffering action bring
Catharsis, despite its ambiguity?
Weeping and fear, involvement and dread,
The deep darkness of shared identity,
A chill tingling creeping over the head
And cold tremors shivering down the spine
Bring strange purgation. It's holy mystery
That intimation of sin line by line,
Disclosure of corporate corruptibility,
A powerful catalyst of hope should be –
'Today in paradise you'll be with me.'

2 | From cosmology to doxology: reading Genesis alongside Plato and Darwin

Prelude

Basil the Great noticed that the first word God spoke was 'Let there be light.'[1]

'And there was *light*.' The musicians capture this outburst of brilliance in an eruption of scintillating sound, and at a performance of Haydn's *Creation* the audience sits up; for this moment is the genesis of amazement.

The scientist, fascinated by light, explains its paradoxical behaviour as both particle and wave, tracing another stage in that sequence of discoveries by which the speed of light, travelling across the cosmos, revealed the depth of space and time which shrinks the history of humankind to a speck in the vast story of the universe – science is as much the genesis of wonder as a claim to comprehension.

The cosmologist finds that all that's made visible by light is exceeded by dark matter, known through its powerful effects mathematically demonstrated, and then discovers the cosmic microwave background radiation which is the 'afterglow of creation', 'an echo, as it were, of the "explosion" that initiated the universal expansion', commonly known as the 'big bang';[2] while the biologist notes that life itself depends on light through photosynthesis.

Arthur now stares at the pattern of light and shade falling through the slats of a Venetian blind, now looks up at the complex tracery

[1] *Hexaemeron* II.7.
[2] Martin Rees, *Before the Beginning: Our Universe and Others* (London: Simon and Schuster, 1997; The Free Press, 2002), pp. 53–7.

of dark branches of trees against the light sky, now creates his own version, lifting his hand with the fingers open to look through them to the bright world beyond, eyes wide with wonder.

The photographer goes into the wilderness to paint with light: 'I rarely set out with the sole intention of photographing a landscape or a mountain,' he writes.[3] 'My primary purpose is to photograph light which – like a language to a writer – is the means of my creative expression.' Powerful images he discovers at dawn or sunset, in oblique light, which enhances the colour and deepens the patterns of shade.

The artist explains how she found herself struggling to catch the glory of light; while praying she had a 'loud thought': 'Paint in the dark places.' This she did, and the light glowed. She discovered the icon-writer's insight, that the light of transfiguration is revealed against the dark depths of divine reality. This glory is the genesis of awe.

* * *

I Cosmology and creation

The ancient philosopher, like the biblical book of Genesis, speculated that, at the origin of all things, light was separated from darkness. Philosophy was the genesis of objective observation and deduction.[4] Cosmogonical myths gave way to the search for a simple underlying *archē*, an explanation of the world that needs no explanation, a first cause having priority both in time and in power. An early suggestion was water, which obviously exists in solid, liquid and gaseous forms. That idea led to more complex theories about opposites in interaction, about the universe consisting in eternal process or repeated cycles with no ultimate beginning. Where Greek

---

[3] Colin Prior, *Scotland: The Wild Places* (London: Constable, 2001), p. 56.
[4] For exposition and discussion, see M. R. Wright, *Cosmology in Antiquity* (London and New York: Routledge, 1995); on *archē*, see p. 167.

philosophy canvassed the eternity of the universe, the Bible spoke of God as the originator of created order. Cosmology was bound to be an area where the earliest Christian theology confronted the prevailing culture; and once again in the twenty-first century, it has become a significant bone of contention. It might be thought that the theology of the fathers of the church, with their pre-scientific understanding of the universe, would have nothing to contribute. Yet I shall argue that their approach puts long-standing disputes, like that between creation and evolution, into helpful perspective, and potentially reintegrates explanatory theories with amazement, awe and wonder so as to produce appropriate wisdom about our place in the cosmos.

1.1 *The beginning*

1.1.1 Basil

Basil's nine homilies on the six days of creation (*Hexaemeron*)[5] demonstrate how the homiletic imperative drove interpretation of Genesis. His opening words draw attention to the good order of the visible world, an indication that its formation could not be spontaneous, as some imagined, but must draw its origin from God. Moses' account is significant because he spent forty years contemplating nature in the desert. For Basil, the fact of a beginning implies an end – the universe is finite and time-bound, not co-eternal with its Creator. Its beginning happened in an instant, and it is continuously sustained by the Creator's power. The visible world points beyond itself to the invisible through its beauty, for finite 'bodies' of all kinds indicate by their grandeur some conception of the infinite, divine Being. This is what philosophers miss by their inherent atheism.[6]

---

[5] Greek text: Amand de Mendietta and S. Y. Rudberg (eds.), *Basilius von Caesarea: Homilien zur Hexaemeron*, *GCS*; ET: *NPNF* and *FC*.

[6] Wright, *Cosmology*, pp. 165–6, notes that Plato saw cosmologists as atheists – assuming 'the cosmos arose from elemental masses as a result of the workings of chance and their own nature'.

Basil states that he eschews allegory;[7] when the scripture says 'water' or 'grass', it means water and grass. However, his homiletic approach constantly draws moral lessons. So what did he mean by claiming to avoid allegory? Evidently he meant that the subject was the creation of the concrete material world, not some spiritual universe; yet embodiment in this created order was intended to have a transcendent outcome. This world came into being not by chance but through God's will and purpose to school us into knowledge and love of God. Genesis does not tell us everything; for example, the creation of the four elements (then held to be the basic constituents of everything) is not mentioned, nor are cosmological puzzles solved, such as how the earth is held in position or what shape it is. The elements must be implicit in the general statement about the creation of heaven and earth, while the solution to other perplexing questions is simply not necessary for our perfection.[8] Wonder, awe and amazement at nature should lead to worship not of the creature but the Creator.[9]

For Basil, then, Genesis is a summary account of the sheer gift of finite existence, a doxological invitation rather than a full philosophical or scientific exposition of origins. Not that his homilies fail to utilize contemporary ideas about the natural world – indeed, they are exploited to generate the wonder, amazement and awe that feeds into worship. The knowledge Basil assumes is now outdated: we no longer think that everything depends on the interaction of those four elements, earth, air, fire and water, nor do we believe that mud produces eels.[10] Thus his work is a salutary warning against the temptation to accommodate current scientific thinking to Genesis and *vice versa*. Indeed, he makes the point himself that no system of philosophy has remained firm, each being overtaken by its successor. What Basil clarifies is this: Genesis requires us only to accept

---

[7] *Hexaemeron* III.9, IX.1.   [8] *Ibid.* I.6, 7, 10; IX.1.
[9] *Ibid.* I.2, 6, 10, 11.   [10] *Ibid.* IX.2.

the simple fact of a beginning,[11] and that has profound theological consequences.

1.1.2 Augustine

Augustine's first exposition of Genesis sought to counter attempts by the dualist Manichaean sect, to which he had once belonged, to undermine the single, creating cause implied by the Genesis text.[12] One question the Manichees posed was 'In what beginning?' – 'If God made heaven and earth in some beginning of time, what was he doing before he made heaven and earth?' Augustine replied by referring to John's Gospel: 'in the beginning' means 'in Christ', named 'the beginning' elsewhere in scripture.

Later Augustine made several attempts to engage with what he called the 'literal meaning' of Genesis. Like Basil, he intended 'literal' to signify an intelligible account of the *fact* of creation by God, not to insist on the word-for-word correspondence of Genesis to reality – one well-known conundrum lay in the question how the six days could be ordinary days when the sun was not created until the fourth. Augustine sought to understand 'what really happened', assuming that Genesis was never intended to provide a full scientific analysis.[13] He too recognized that Genesis leaves much unclear. 'The obscure mysteries of the natural order, which we perceive to have been made by God, the almighty craftsman, should rather be discussed by asking questions than by making affirmations.'[14]

In his final attempt, *The Literal Meaning of Genesis*, Augustine takes it for granted that questions are more appropriate than solutions;

[11] See further Andrew Louth, 'The Six Days of Creation According to the Greek Fathers' in Stephen C. Barton and David Wilkinson (eds.), *Reading Genesis after Darwin* (Oxford University Press, 2009), p. 49.
[12] Latin texts of Augustine on Genesis: D. Weber (ed.), *De Genesi contra Manichaeos, CSEL*; J. Zycha (ed.), *De Genesi ad litteram liber imperfectus* and *De Genesi ad litteram, CSEL*; ET: Edmund Hill, *Saint Augustine: On Genesis* (New York City Press, 2002).
[13] Hill, *Augustine*, p. 158.   [14] *Unfinished Literal Commentary* 1, 1.

'God does not work by time-measured movements . . . but by the eternal and unchanging, stable formulae of his Word, co-eternal with himself, and by a kind of brooding . . . of his equally co-eternal Spirit.' We must 'never think in a literal-minded, fleshly way of utterances in time throughout the days of divine works.' He rebukes wilful ignorance of human knowledge

> about the earth, about the sky, about the other elements of this world, about the movements and revolutions or even the magnitude and distances of the constellations, about the predictable eclipses of moon and sun, about the cycles of years and seasons, about the nature of animals, fruits, stones and everything else of this kind.[15]

Such wilful ignorance can only bring Christianity into disrepute. He fears aggressive defence of what scripture seems to say, which may turn out to be a case of 'championing our own cause rather than that of the scriptures'. Questions, on the other hand, are essential to the never-ending search for the depth of the Trinitarian mystery beyond matter, place and time: how after all could God say in time, 'Let there be light' – it would not literally be the 'utterance of a voice'? The text must be understood in a way appropriate to the eternal, transcendent God. Despite its organization in six days, the first account of creation in Genesis 1 actually 'tells of the first moment of creation, in which a single creative act of God called all things into existence in an inchoative state', while what we now understand as the second account in Genesis 2 'no longer describes an event on the threshold between time and eternity, but an event in time'.[16]

Augustine recognizes, like Basil, that much is passed over in silence; for the Spirit speaking through scripture only wanted to teach what would contribute to salvation.[17] So the literal meaning of Genesis is not in the surface of the text, but is uncovered by probing

---

[15] *Literal Meaning* I.19, 39.   [16] Hill, *Augustine*, p. 160.   [17] *Literal Meaning* II.9, 20.

its implications, through theological questioning, through bringing it into association with human knowledge of the way the cosmos is. Neither Basil nor Augustine were afraid of what was for them contemporary science.[18] The primordial light, brought into being prior to the creation of sun and moon, cannot have been just light perceptible by physical senses. The words are signs; yet what the text signifies is that creation was 'a "happening" *par excellence*', a 'completely unique and incomparable event that does not take place within history but instead is the basis of time and history'.[19] As such it is an absolute 'singularity', a unique peculiar beyond the reach of human science or conceptuality, beyond expression in human language. This absolute beginning is literally 'beyond physics' – beyond even a meta-physic which seeks only the fundamental principles of the natural order.

1.1.3 Appropriation?

Now such discussion of the 'beginning' still has theological implications. The 'steady-state theory' is the modern equivalent of the ancient philosophical preference for the eternity of the universe, a view which has 'a deep philosophical appeal – the universe existed, from everlasting to everlasting, in a uniquely self-consistent state'.[20] But with the discovery, among other things, of the cosmic microwave background radiation, scientific cosmology moved to the theory of the 'big bang'. That might seem congenial to those committed to the biblical insistence on a 'beginning'. It is tempting to speak of 'the initial energy that loved the world into being';[21] but, warned by Basil and Augustine, we should be careful not to wed Genesis to the

---

[18] Cf. Louth, 'Six Days of Creation', p. 53. [19] Hill, *Augustine*, p. 159.
[20] Rees, *Before the Beginning*, p. 43. Cf. Wright, *Cosmology*, p. 1.
[21] James Macmillan, speaking in the series *Sacred Music* (BBC TV, 2010).

physics of a particular era.[22] In various ways scientists are already going behind the 'big bang'.[23]

'Even though we can trace the evolution of our universe back to when it was only a second old',[24] all that current scientific evidence shows is that this applies to ***this*** cosmos:

> What's conventionally called 'the universe' could be just one element – one 'atom', as it were – in an infinite ensemble: a cosmic archipelago. Each universe starts with its own big bang.[25]

If conditions must have been set exactly right at our 'big bang' for the emergence of conscious, intelligent beings able to observe their environment and deduce the character of their own universe (the so-called anthropic principle), that need not be the case for other universes.

> Some cosmologists speculate that new 'embryo' universes can form within existing ones. Implosion to a colossal density (around, for instance, a small black hole) could trigger the expansion of a new spatial domain inaccessible to us.[26]

There are on-going questions, new puzzles, known unknowns and unknown unknowns.

Interpreted by the fathers, Genesis invites us neither to devise some artificial integration with current physics, nor to deny its findings or its fascination. Science, its data, its assured results and the philosophical enquiries generated by science – all have the same status *vis à vis* theology as the hypotheses, questions and knowledge

---

[22] Cf. Francis Watson in 'Genesis before Darwin: Why Scripture Needed Liberating from Science' in Barton and Wilkinson, *Reading Genesis after Darwin*, p. 24; he suggests that '"Darwin" will represent the liberation of the biblical text from its captivity to the natural sciences.'

[23] Stephen Hawking and Leonard Mlodinow, *The Grand Design: New Answers to the Ultimate Questions of Life* (London: Bantam Press, 2010); BBC TV Horizon programme, 11 October 2010, 'What Happened before the Big Bang?'.

[24] Rees, *Before the Beginning*, p. 2 f.   [25] *Ibid.*, p. 250.   [26] *Ibid.*, p. 253 f.

about the natural world which Basil and Augustine both challenged
and embraced. As the Astronomer Royal puts it:

> Despite all we are learning about our cosmic environment, I don't
> think the interface with philosophers and theologians is, in principle,
> any different from what it was in Newton's day.[27]

In the last analysis the theological claim about the beginning is of
a different order altogether from the discernment of the 'big bang'
through analysis of astronomical evidence. It is truly incomparable,
beyond replication, utterly beyond time and space, rooted in the
ultimate first principle, the will of God to create something other
than the divine self, and to create that other something from nothing.

1.2 Creatio ex nihilo

1.2.1 The first Christian 'doctrine'

Augustine indicates that the Manichees' objections to Genesis
included the question, 'How did God make heaven and earth in the
beginning if the earth was already there invisible and shapeless?' The
question reveals how persistent the view was that Genesis assumed
the prior existence of formless matter, creation meaning God's formation of existent things from pre-existent stuff. Augustine was clear:
that was not what really happened. Rather God made all things from
nothing; that is, the material from which God made things was itself
made from absolutely nothing by God.[28] The craftsman analogy is
inadequate because the carpenter needs wood, the silversmith silver,
and so on, while it is sacrilege to suggest that the Almighty God
needs anything at all. So when Genesis says, 'In the beginning God
made heaven and earth', it implicitly refers to the formless matter
which God made from nothing – the seed of everything, as it were.
Augustine would eventually prefer the view that formless matter is

---

[27] *Ibid.*, p. 164.   [28] Augustine, *On Genesis against the Manichees*, 1.3–10.

only prior as source, not 'prior in time to things formed from it, since they are both created simultaneously together'.[29] These questions interest him, but they are variations above the fundamental ground that God created out of nothing everything that is.

Basil also assumes the position that God created out of nothing, with the same argument. The Creator is not like an artisan with pre-existing material: matter and form came into being together at God's behest, and there can be no dualism, with matter as an opposing principle.[30] God did not create just half of everything, but produced the substance with the form, each being in need of the other for real existence. Neither Basil nor Augustine gives high priority to this debate – it was long established as Christian teaching. The arguments used betray engagement with Platonism and the need to read Genesis in distinction from that philosophical position.

This stance goes back at least to the second century, though probably not explicitly articulated until then.[31] Apparent anticipations in 2 Maccabees 7.28, Romans 4.17, Hebrews 11.3 and *Hermas* 1.1.6, provided scriptural warrant, but were probably not themselves explicit rejections of pre-existent matter. That it was possible to read Genesis in terms of God shaping pre-existent, formless stuff is proved not only by Augustine's reference to the Manichees' hostile question, but by other intriguing facts: (i) Genesis appears to be understood that way by the Wisdom of Solomon, Justin Martyr, Athenagoras and Hermogenes, and probably also Philo and Clement of Alexandria; and (ii) Jewish commentators of the Middle Ages, notably Rashi, understood the text as meaning, 'In the beginning, *when* God created . . . ', so as to harmonize the first verse with the chaotic primitive

---

[29] *Literal Meaning* 1.15, 29.   [30] *Hexaemeron* 11.2–3.

[31] Cf. my article, '"Creatio ex nihilo": A Context for the Emergence of the Christian Doctrine of Creation', *SJT* 44 (1991), 139–51 for fuller discussion and references; and Gerhard May, *Creatio ex Nihilo: The Doctrine of 'Creation out of Nothing' in Early Christian Thought* (ET: A. S. Worrall, Edinburgh: T & T Clark 1994; original German edn, 1978). For an opposing argument see J. C. O'Neill, 'How Early is the Doctrine of *creatio ex nihilo*?' *JTS NS* 53.2 (2002), 449–65.

state of the earth described in the second verse. The Rabbis generally condemned speculation about creation, the only example suggesting otherwise being a discussion recorded in Midrash Genesis Rabbah between Gamaliel II and, significantly, a philosopher. Greek philosophy provided the context in which creation out of no-thing rather than some-thing was explicitly articulated.

The clearest statement is found in Tertullian, writing against the Christian Platonist, Hermogenes. Hermogenes, like Philo and Justin, correlated Genesis with Plato's *Timaeus* and took the myth literally[32] – that is, they understood Plato to speak not of the eternal relationship between mind, matter and form, but to describe an initial creative act by the demiurge imposing form on a pre-existing material substrate. Against this, Tertullian stated that God neither created out of the divine self, for then everything would be divine, nor out of eternal existing matter, or there would be a second eternal first principle; if neither out of God's self nor out of some-thing, it must have been out of no-thing.

Tertullian was not the first to make that move. Justin's pupil, Tatian, asserted that God was alone, and matter is not, like God, without beginning – it was brought into existence by the one who alone framed all things. Theophilus of Antioch criticized Plato for regarding matter as uncreated and therefore equal to God, arguing for God's unique *monarchia* – a word which ambiguously carried the notion not only of 'sovereignty' but 'sole first principle'. Theophilus also argued against the craftsman analogy – a human artisan creates out of pre-existent material, so there is nothing remarkable about God doing likewise; the power of God is evident in the creation of whatever God wants *ex ouk ontōn* – out of the non-existent. Irenaeus insisted that the sole cause of creation is God's goodness and love, resisted speculations about how God created, rejected the idea of

---

[32] Wright, *Cosmology*, p. 178, notes that Aristotle took the *Timaeus* literally, and offered criticism, going for 'steady state' rather than a 'beginning'.

previously existing matter and asserted that God simply called things into existence as they are.

Such formulations reflect resistance to the temptation to equate the chaos of Genesis with the conception expressed in these words of Plutarch:

> For creation does not take place out of what does not exist at all but rather out of what is in an improper or unfulfilled state, as in the case of a house or a garment or a statue. For the state that things were in before the creation of the ordered may be characterised as 'lack of order' (*akosmia*); and this 'lack of order' was not something incorporeal or immobile or soulless, but rather it possessed a corporeal nature which was formless and inconstant, and a power of motion which was frantic and irrational.[33]

The Christian position was grounded in God's absolutely uncontested priority. Yet the formula 'out of nothing' was a daring thing to espouse in a culture where 'nothing comes from nothing' was a commonplace, taken to imply that anything coming from nothing was a sham – it could have carried anti-materialist implications of a docetic kind. Indeed, some have, unconvincingly, explained those anticipations of the formula *ex ouk ontōn* in terms of an eschatology which saw the world as unreal and passing away.[34]

Yet 'nothing' does have a slippery sense: to say '*there is* nothing' allows it to take on the character of a quasi-something indeed, 'non-being' could be applied to that pre-existent stuff which only had

---

[33] *On the Creation of the Soul in the Timaeus* 1014B; quoted John Dillon, *The Middle Platonists* (London: Duckworth, 1977), p. 207.

[34] Arnold Ehrhardt, *The Beginning: A Study in the Greek Philosophical Approach to the Concept of Creation from Anaximander to St John* (Manchester University Press, 1968).

potential and no real existence as something until formed. 'Infinity' was also applied to matter, the word having similar disturbing ambivalences – pre-existent matter was infinite in being indefinite, having no boundaries, form or definition. In Greek philosophy infinity was not associated with the divine – to capture divine transcendence Irenaeus spoke of God containing all things while being uncontained; he had to avoid suggesting that God was indefinite, while ensuring that the transcendent God was not an object within the created order. God was easily entwined with the cosmos[35] as the first cause of motion, as in Aristotle and the *De Mundo*, or identified with the immanent *logos* or fire, the first principle of the material cosmos, as for the Stoics. But none of this was true to the scriptures. Ultimately Christianity would affirm the 'otherness' of the Creator over against everything made 'out of nothing', while maintaining the reality and goodness of the physical creation as the work of transcendent divine goodness – a novel cosmological position, affirmed over against platonizing interpretations of the world and of the book of Genesis.

So God did not produce the creation out of the divine self, or everything would be divine (pantheism does not belong to traditional Christian theology); nor did God form the world from pre-existent stuff, or God would have a rival, eternal first principle (dualism does not belong to traditional Christian theology). God's will was simply to create, and God was powerful enough just to bring into being anything God chose. So everything in creation, integrated as matter and form, body and soul, had its being as sheer gift, and as such would be redolent of the Giver.

1.2.2 The implications for God's creativity

The idea of creation out of nothing, together with a non-docetic affirmation of materiality, had significant consequences. (i) It broke

[35] Wright, *Cosmology*, pp. 178 ff.

the hold of 'necessity' and 'chance', substituting the notion of a created order with its own rationality, so ultimately permitting the rise of modern science;[36] furthermore, it de-sacralized nature, allowing its utilization, even exploitation, for human benefit through technology. (ii) It exerted significant pressure on the articulation of Christian doctrine. It should probably be described as the first Christian doctrine to be formulated by engaging reason informed by contemporary philosophy in interaction with the scriptures; and subsequently influenced Christology, Trinitarianism and the Christian sense of what it means to be human. But the immediate question is this: has the doctrine of creation *out of nothing* yet had its full impact on Christian claims about God's creation of the world?

The point to consider is how much further the critique of the craftsman analogy needs to go. 'The Creation is an abandonment,' wrote Simone Weil.[37] 'Creation is abdication.' 'God has emptied himself.' 'The apparent absence of God in this world is the actual reality of God,' she says. What she meant was that if the eternal, infinite God were to create something other than the divine self, it would be necessary for God to 'withdraw', allowing 'space', as it were, for something other than God to be. Doubtless this spatial metaphor is inappropriate to the divine: as the fathers so often emphasized, we speak of what we cannot know in inadequate and limited human language and conceptuality. But another inadequate image might be that of a loving parent letting a child take risks so as to mature and become herself. There is love and self-emptying involved. Weil pursues the potential coherence between creation and cross: 'Not only the Passion but the Creation itself is a renunciation and sacrifice on the part of God.' Jesus cries out, 'My God, my God, why hast thou forsaken me?' and Godforsaken-ness constitutes the creature's

---

[36] Stanley L. Jaki, *Creator and Cosmos* (Edinburgh: Scottish Academic Press, 1980); T. F. Torrance, *Divine and Contingent Order* (Oxford University Press, 1981).

[37] Quotations from *Gateway to God* (David Raper (ed.), London: Collins/Fontana, 1974), pp. 48, 54, 55 and 80 ff. Cf. John F. Haught, *God after Darwin* (Boulder, CO: Westview Press, 2000), p. 112.

existence and freedom to be itself.[38] 'If God did not abandon them, they would not exist. His presence would annul their existence as a flame kills a butterfly.'

If God, who contains everything without being contained, has to let 'nothingness' be so that something other than God might come into being, then God's creativity is hardly comparable to human creativity: '"My thoughts are not your thoughts, nor my ways your ways," says the Lord.'[39] We need a critique not just of the craftsman analogy, but of all 'demiurgic' accounts of God's creation, including intelligent design. '*God is not an alternative to science as an expla-nation . . .* [God] is the ground of all explanation.'[40] God might be a significant inference, arising from a response of worship to the giftedness of existence; but the reserve of the Rabbis and of Irenaeus is required. If we speak of God holding the whole world in his hands, then the shaping touch of the potter's hands at the wheel, though scriptural, needs qualifying; better would be the delicate distance required to contain a butterfly without damaging it. Containing, yet uncontained, the infinite God emptied the divine self in a creative act of self-constriction – something like that might describe the begin-ning of the finite, time-bound universe, astonishingly brought into being out of nothing. Cosmology gives way to wonder, and wonder to doxology.

II Creation and evolution

II.1 The monarchy of God and the problem of evil

II.1.1 From the second century to Basil and Augustine

The conclusion that creation is 'out of nothing' was driven by the need to affirm God's *monarchia*. God's *monarchia* justified attacks

---

[38] Cf. Haught, *God after Darwin*, p. 39.   [39] Isaiah 55.8.
[40] John C. Lennox, *God's Undertaker: Has Science buried God?* (Oxford: Lion, 2007), p. 47.

on polytheism, idolatry, the myths of the gods, and philosophies based on chance and fate. As the emperor Constantine would argue in his *Oration to the Saints*,[41] there needs to be a single sovereignty over creation, otherwise there would be chaos among the elements, and harmony would be destroyed by jealousy and ambition; the fact that there is a universal order is proof that everything is under the providential care of one superior power – discord among heavenly powers would produce confusion on earth. God's providential management of everything implied the accountability of every creature; God's judgement, even of the secrets of the heart, meant the universe had a moral structure which one flouted at one's peril.

Basil and Augustine inherited these traditions. Basil's homilies celebrate the harmony of the cosmos and the providential purposes of God evident in creation. Philosophers missed the fact that an intelligent cause presided at the birth of the universe, some attributing its origin to the elements, or imagining that atoms form the nature of the visible world, others reckoning the world co-eternal with God, or giving it a double origin by suggesting matter was there for the Creator to act upon.[42] But Moses shows how God thought up the whole thing, creating matter in harmony with the form God wished to give it. God made everything beautiful, forming the different parts in one perfect accord, and making a harmonious symphony result from the whole.[43] Darkness is not evil, nor evil's personification in perpetual struggle with God's goodness;[44] nor is evil to be attributed to God. Basil admits that evil exists, but will not treat it as some thing – an essence; rather, it is a condition of soul opposed to virtue – each of us is the first author of our own evil. The affirmation of the goodness and harmonious perfection of the cosmos

---

[41] Greek text: I. A. Heikel (ed.), *Das Leben Konstantins: Eusebius Werke I*, *GCS*; ET: S. G. Hall and Averil Cameron, *Eusebius: The Life of Constantine* (Oxford: Clarendon Press, 1998).

[42] *Hexaemeron* I.2; II.2. [43] *Ibid.* I.7. [44] *Ibid.* II.4.

thus posed the problem of evil. God's *monarchia* had to be affirmed against certain odds.

The same issue was the more pressing for Augustine, as he challenged the Manichaean dualism he had once espoused.[45] Darkness is not some thing, but rather absence of light, just as silence is not a thing, but lack of sound. God could not be said to have made the darkness. For Augustine, evil was simply absence of good, and goodness greater than what simply serves human interests. His opponents ask what use are all those animals God created, especially those that are pernicious and dangerous. Augustine suggests that they are beautiful to their maker who has a use for them all in the management of the whole universe. He confesses he has not the slightest idea why mice and frogs were created, or flies or worms. But he suspects that it is because of our sins they seem to be against our interests, and that they have a use in punishing us, testing us, or stimulating us to seek a better life, freed from worries and anxieties. God saw that all things together were very good – the whole is more beautiful than the parts, like the human body or a well-delivered speech. All are good insofar as they exist, since God made all things good, the whole being a perfect whole which God, its founder and author does not for one moment cease to administer in a completely just regime.[46] God's *monarchia* is affirmed not simply as a cosmological principle but a moral one.

In the *Unfinished Literal Commentary on Genesis*, affirmation of creation's goodness appears second only to *creatio ex nihilo*. Evils are not part of nature, but are either sin or its punishment. There is nothing evil about fire, for example, but we get burned by it as our sins justly deserve. God did not make darkness, which is an absence or nothing, but God did divide the light and darkness since the lacks or absences have their place in the total pattern of things designed

---

[45] *On Genesis against the Manichees* I; see 4, 7, 9, 15, 16, 21, 25 and 32 for points in this paragraph.

[46] *Ibid.* II.29, 43.

and controlled by God, just as moments of silence are introduced into music and contribute to the sweetness of the whole song; or, in pictures, shadows mark out the more striking features. Augustine argues that God, though not the source of our vices, is in control as regulator of sin. There is beauty in all things together as ordered by God, light and darkness representing what God makes and what God regulates.

By the *Literal Meaning of Genesis*, Augustine is clear that the initiating act of creation (Genesis 1) was one simultaneous action whose potential is unfolded in historical time, and that God is still at work, governing all development by providence. He challenges those who see providence in the ordering of the regular heavenly bodies while regarding the lower regions as the plaything of chance and fortuitous upheavals. Just as the seed contains all that is necessary for the tree, so everything required for the actual cosmos was present when God created all things simultaneously, and now God is at work steering and guiding everything by regulatory activity.[47] Augustine subsumes what seems evil to human beings within the over-arching goodness of the whole, allowing that God manages and controls moral evil, despite being not in any way responsible for originating it.

11.1.2 Appropriation?

Both Basil and Augustine were sure of God's providential *monarchia* and the harmony of the whole of creation, confident that, for things that would seem to challenge this, there must always be a higher explanation. Post-Enlightenment thinkers have not been so sure, modernity foregrounding the problems of theodicy and through science providing explanations which bracket out God. My suggestion is that a re-appropriation of patristic perspectives could both reveal the theological impoverishment within which post-Enlightenment debates have been conducted and permit scientific discoveries about

---

[47] *Literal Meaning* v.21–3, 42–4.

life on earth to be embraced as offering liberation from the tight constrictions of theodicy.

II.1.2.1 *From an impoverished theology to the absence of God*

> From harmony, from heavenly harmony,
> > This universal frame began.

So wrote Dryden; while Addison could proclaim that 'the spacious firmament on high'

> . . . publishes to every land
> The work of an Almighty hand.

This might seem like the cosmic harmony of Basil and Augustine, but, as Charles Taylor pointed out,[48] what was celebrated was an 'impersonal order' in which the laws of nature and the laws of society were providentially set up by a benevolent but remote Deity for the benefit of humanity. As the Age of Reason slipped into the Age of Wonder,[49] this Deity became even more remote, given the deep space revealed by Herschel's telescopes and the deep time implicit in the geological perspectives of Hutton and Lyell.

The remote Deity became more and more absent and in the end unnecessary. As a potential ordinand Darwin[50] had read Paley on natural theology and the evidences of Christianity, and Pearson on the creed. As a result he understood theology as a framework of intellectual ideas, a set of propositions deduced from evidence. When his own researches led him to question those propositions, his mind demanded a kind of proof which is simply not possible. As for so many in the modern age, the argument about God was reduced to a narrow debate about the first cause, about explanation of the

---

[48] Charles Taylor, *A Secular Age* (Cambridge, MA: Harvard University Press, 2007).

[49] Richard Holmes, *The Age of Wonder: How the Romantic Generation Discovered the Beauty and Terror of Science* (London: Harper Press, 2008).

[50] Nick Spencer, *Darwin and God* (London: SPCK, 2009).

cosmos. Darwin felt no great loss when he ceased to believe – he had never had a deep sense of God or the possibility of transcendence. If the seventeenth-century clergyman, Gilbert White, had earlier been able to delight in God's creation through his pioneering observations of the natural world, a century later Darwin's detailed cataloguing of different natural specimens and precise scrutiny of variations within species would lead him to a gradual letting go of ideas about intelligent design because the evidence did not add up. Evolution as such was not religiously disturbing – it had long been in the air; rather, it was the notion of natural selection, a proposed mechanism explaining how the spectrum of interconnected creatures that made up the tree of life could have evolved from a single origin in deep geological time, thus making God otiose.

Subsequently developments in physics and the theory of evolution have progressed to the point where the dominant assumption of the culture is that scientists will eventually explain everything. Clearly there have been real advances in human knowledge. Scientists know that the earth is 4,600 million years old, that it is 3,500 million years since life began, and that the sun will die in 5,000 million years; they can give a plausible account of how we got here in entirely naturalistic terms, and predict that in 100 million years there will be precious little trace of our brief presence here in the geological record.[51] True, there are uncertainties, on-going controversies, possibly even extraordinary accidents. The nucleus of the complex cell (required for living creatures other than bacteria) probably did not form through gradual evolution but through 'a rare and fortuitous event', while its 'tendency to collect DNA and to recombine it in the endless constellations of the magical world around us' was also accidental. So 'this world of marvels, it seems, springs from two deep accidents'.[52] But 'accidents' do not come out of the blue:

---

[51] Jan Zalasiewicz, *The Earth after us* (Oxford University Press, 2008).

[52] Nick Lane, *Life Ascending: The Ten Great Inventions of Evolution* (London: Profile Books, 2009), p. 117.

absolute randomness does not seem to be the case – some things are more likely to happen, and some things have happened more than once in the evolutionary process – eyes have evolved more than forty times independently.[53] Natural selection ensures that only favourable mutations spread, and there is 'stratified stability': atoms, molecules, bases, amino acids, proteins, cells, simple animals, then sophisticated ones.

> The stable units that compose one level or stratum are the raw mate-rial for random encounters which produce higher configurations, some of which will chance to be stable . . . Evolution is the climbing of a ladder from simple to complex by steps, each of which is stable in itself.[54]

Chaos theory finds underlying patterns in complex, apparently chaotic and random phenomena: chance and necessity are con-stantly interacting in physics as in evolution, and there is no reason for attributing 'accidents' to the direct hand of God – the 'God of the gaps'.[55] 'Darwin knew nothing of genes, but it is the fine structure of genes, more than anything else, that has eliminated all the distasteful gaps from the Darwinian view of the world.'[56] A coherent scientific account of how we evolved can in principle be offered, an account which belongs wholly within the natural 'laws' empirically traceable through scientific research and mathematical calculation.

---

[53] I owe these observations to a conversation with a biologist colleague, and to Francisco Ayala, *Darwin's Gift to Science and Religion* (Washington, DC: John Henry Press, 2007), especially pp. 77, 145.

[54] Jacob Bronowski, *The Ascent of Man* (London: BBC Publications, 1973; paperback London: Macdonald Futura, 1981), p. 218, summarizing his own position.

[55] Michael Ruse, *Can a Darwinian be a Christian? The Relationship between Science and Religion* (Cambridge University Press, 2001), pp. 64–6.

[56] Lane, *Life Ascending*, p. 97.

Will human scientific discovery eventually reach its limits in principle?[57] The chances are, surely, that new discoveries will always pose new questions. Scientific understanding may never be 'final', but it is a mistake to think it merely 'relative', or the construct of the investigators' interpretative community. Real outcomes have been produced by real discoveries. Discoveries are exhilarating and generate, not just *hybris*, but wonder – it is like standing on the top of a huge mountain, filled with a sense of achievement but also suddenly brought down to size by the view of snowy peak after snowy peak filling the horizon in all directions. But whether discovery goes on or reaches its limits, we are bound by nature, while God is beyond nature.

Darwin's uncertainties about God were rubbed home by a certain humility of mind, reinforced by his own theories. The ape had a brain adapted to know what was necessary for survival; the human brain was the same, though more sophisticated – in other words, adapted for survival, not for dealing with issues like God. Darwin, unlike Dawkins,[58] was agnostic rather than aggressively atheist. An element of agnosticism is an appropriate theological stance, since creatures, deeply integrated into the created order and limited by their creatureliness, can hardly know all there is to know. Claims to truth must always be tinged with recognition of finitude and fallibility. Human wisdom remains transient and open-ended because finite, and Darwin's humility of mind is more appropriate than a sense of mastery. A degree of agnosticism is characteristic of the church fathers, who consistently affirmed the otherness of God, recognizing that infinity, or lack of definition, necessarily implied inability to grasp such a Being. I shall claim that, despite the power of scientific explanation and the profound differences of intellectual context, the fathers have things to say that could re-enrich the perception of who or

[57] Russell Stannard, *The End of Discovery* (Oxford University Press, 2010).
[58] Richard Dawkins, *The God Delusion* (London: Bantam, 2006).

what God is and lift the debate from its narrowed and impoverished parameters. First, however, we retrace our steps, and consider that other factor in the eclipse of God, theodicy.

II.1.2.2 *Anthropocentrism, theodicy and the importance of wilderness*

The 'Providential Deism'[59] of the eighteenth century generated the problem of theodicy. John Wisdom's famous parable of the invisible gardener captures anxieties about a natural world that lacks evidence of order:

> Two people return to their long-neglected garden and find, among the weeds, that a few of the old plants are surprisingly vigorous. One says to the other, 'It must be that a gardener has been coming and doing something about these weeds.' The other disagrees and an argument ensues. They pitch their tents and set a watch. No gardener is ever seen. The believer wonders if there is an invisible gardener, so they patrol with bloodhounds but the bloodhounds never give a cry. Yet the believer remains unconvinced, and insists that the gardener is invisible, has no scent and gives no sound. The sceptic doesn't agree, and asks how a so-called invisible, intangible, elusive gardener differs from an imaginary gardener or even no gardener at all.[60]

The anthropocentric universe, set up for the benefit of humanity, faced the moral challenge of innocent suffering: devastating natural disasters, from the Lisbon earthquake of 1755 to the tsunami of 2008, have repeatedly challenged belief in God. People have cried out, 'Why?', or asked specific questions, such as my own: 'How can I go on believing in a good Creator God with a purpose for each human being when 2 per cent of births produce offspring with profound disabilities – including my Arthur?'

[59] Taylor, *A Secular Age*, chapter 6.
[60] John Wisdom, 'Gods' in *Wisdom, Philosophy and Psychoanalysis* (Oxford: Blackwell, 1953).

For Darwin, too, the general slipped into the personal: Paley's watchmaker was no match for his anguish over the loss of his daughter, which reinforced his gradual realization that the universe is not harmonious, good and beautiful – there was the problem of sheer waste and suffering in his competitive picture of the survival of the fittest, though Tennyson's famous observation that nature is 'red in tooth and claw' pre-dated Darwin's publications. Moral sensitivities were aroused, and precluded acceptance of trials and tribulations within some kind of transcendent meaning and purpose.

Religion was deeply affected by this anthropocentric turn; believers found themselves obliged to explain their beliefs in humanist, this-worldly terms, apologetics repeatedly struggling with the theodicy issues. But what Darwin potentially did was to challenge at root that anthropocentrism. He recognized that all life is a continuum of which we are part – a point ever clearer with advances in understanding DNA. This holistic, indeed ecological, perspective – the outlook that respects the being of all things whether they impinge on us beneficially, detrimentally or not at all – can diffuse some of the theodicy issues and encourage an appreciation of the integrity and harmony of a whole which transcends its parts.[61] After all, tsunamis are generated by the very geological forces now thought to be responsible for the origin of life,[62] and that is just one example. What we perceive as good or bad is so closely intertwined as to belong to a single 'geotapistry'. This kind of thing is found time and time again: natural disasters arise from characteristics of the earth, like volcanoes and rainstorms, which are vital for its chemical balance; some bacteria may cause ill-health, but bacteria were responsible for oxygenating the atmosphere, so making animal life possible, and without bacteria in guts food would not be digested.

Indeed, reflection on the food chain again gives us pause. Life depends on the consumption of other life, the stuff of life constantly being recycled, a process which can either be viewed as death-dealing

---

[61] Ayala, *Darwin's Gift*.   [62] Lane, *Life Ascending*, chapter 1.

and destructive or as constitutive of the surging diversity of living growth. Death is part of life, a prerequisite for the constant recycling that produces abundance. 'Only death makes multicellular life possible' – 'true multicellular life can only be achieved by cells "prepared" to subsume themselves entirely to the cause' and cancer reveals 'the impossibility of cellular life when cells do their own thing'.[63] Should we be focussing on 'waste' or fecundity? Surely the four horsemen of the Apocalypse (war, famine, pestilence and plague) are the natural mechanisms for keeping humankind in ecological balance with the rest of nature – our cleverness in thwarting them may yet bring its own apocalypse. Indeed, over-population might be compared to an invasive mould upsetting the planet's ecosystem.

The anthropocentric take on things struggles for a theodicy, but what about a perspective humbled by the wondrous ways in which we are ourselves integrated into the natural order, with DNA sequences similar to the malaria parasite! Again, given that reproduction involves the unzipping and recombining of DNA's double helix, with potential for positive but also negative mutations, our very individuality derives from a process with possibly ambiguous outcomes. Natural selection is a 'force for stability', in that it allows for the retention of positive changes, 'while more serious errors or alterations miscarry, literally'.[64] But not always – so proper development of the embryo or foetus occasionally misfires, with life-changing effects. 'Accidents' of various kinds produce conjoined twins, or the chromosomal abnormalities of Down's syndrome, or the microcephaly and brain damage consequential upon intra-uterine deprivation of oxygen – the condition which caused my son, Arthur, to be born with profound learning disabilities. Sparrows fall to the ground, but, according to the saying of Jesus, never without God.[65] It is the way things are.

Such reflections alert us to the perils of anthropocentrism and the search for the kind of order in creation that we expect from our

---

[63] *Ibid.*, p. 267. [64] *Ibid.*, p. 37. [65] Matthew 10.29.

point of view. From this limiting perspective arises failure to appreciate our deep integration into the web of biochemical interactions and balances. From this humanist viewpoint comes the question whether this is the best of all possible worlds. John Wisdom's parable suffers from the assumption that an ordered garden is better than wilderness – a typically eighteenth-century idea. Since then there's been increasing appreciation of the rugged and the wild, wilderness embodying 'sublimity'.[66]

> In terms of aesthetic values, the new mathematics of fractal geometry brought hard science in tune with the peculiarly modern feeling for untamed, uncivilised, undomesticated nature. At one time rain forests, deserts, bush, and badlands represented all that society was striving to subdue. If people wanted aesthetic satisfaction, they looked at gardens.[67]

Beautifully documented in Macfarlane's book, *Mountains of the Mind*, is the story of how mountains, viewed for centuries as hostile and dangerous, began to capture the imagination, while a second haunting book of his explores the search for wilderness in our increasingly crowded island.[68] Poetically he brings out the 'otherness' of wilderness – the busy life which goes on without us, the way in which wilderness beautifies the derelict land of post-industrial sites: 'the sheer force of ongoing organic existence, vigorous and chaotic'; 'this wildness was ... about luxuriance, vitality, fun'; nature takes over when we are gone: 'the ivy will make it back and unrig our flats and terraces, as it scattered Roman villas'.[69] In the long run the short period of human dominance will scarcely leave a trace.[70]

---

[66] Taylor, *A Secular Age*, pp. 336 ff.
[67] James Gleick, *Chaos: The Amazing Science of the Unpredictable* (London: Heinemann, 1988), p. 117.
[68] Robert Macfarlane, *Mountains of the Mind: A History of a Fascination* (London: Granta, 2003) and *The Wild Places* (London: Granta, 2007).
[69] Macfarlane, *Wild Places*, p. 316.   [70] Zalasiewicz, *The Earth after us*.

This shift in attitude has had practical consequences in increasing commitment to the preservation of the fast-diminishing wilderness, the conservation of disappearing habitats for wildlife, even the return of predators to areas where they were long since eliminated for the sake of human flourishing. Since time immemorial the lion has been celebrated as king of beasts, the eagle as lord of the skies; for most of human history, people have respected and loved creation for its own awe-inspiring sake, without getting too hung up about theodicy. It was in the wilderness that the people of the Bible met God, and it was to the wilderness that early Christian ascetics turned for spiritual renewal in the monastic movement of the fourth and fifth centuries. A terrifying environment in which they met demons, it was also where they found God.[71] Stories of wild animals befriending and protecting lone monks conjured up pictures of paradise and new creation. Basil, you recall, thought Moses' account of creation should be taken seriously because he had spent forty years contemplating nature in the desert.

Such re-evaluation of our place in creation could permit appropriation of the patristic perspective and help us to move beyond defensiveness against 'atheists, wielding theodicy like a club'.[72] Theodicy proves to be a kind of blasphemy, reducing the Creator to a watchmaker fine-tuning creation for our benefit alone. We have allowed our developing understanding of the universe, coupled with our anthropocentrism, to challenge God rather than ourselves. Like Job, we protest and try to put God on trial, but then we are reminded by Darwin, as well as the church fathers and ultimately Job himself, that this is something we may never presume to do – we are but creatures. It is in the Bible that we read:

I said in my heart with regard to human beings that God is testing them to show that they are but animals. For the fate of humans and

[71] Andrew Louth, *The Wilderness of God* (London: DLT, 1991).
[72] Taylor, *A Secular Age*, p. 278.

the fate of animals is the same; as one dies, so dies the other. They all have the same breath, and humans have no advantage over the animals; for all is vanity. All go to one place; all are from the dust, and all turn to dust again.[73]

11.2 Anagogy through beauty and goodness

11.2.1 Basil and Augustine

Basil and Augustine would have approved neither the remote God of deism nor a 'God of the gaps'. The whole creation pointed to the Creator, yet in a veiled manner. They recognized the demanding process needed in order to gain insight into the transcendent God.

The Christian tradition had long combined sharp critical analysis, born of opposition to all kinds of idolatry and mental projections, with acceptance of a language of powerful symbols and signs, to be found in scripture and in nature, which point beyond themselves.[74] The divine must be 'infinite, not merely in the sense that one cannot give an exhaustive account of it, but in the sense that one cannot analyse it into parts and that it has no boundary and is therefore without form or name'. So 'how could that be spoken of which is neither genus, nor differentia, nor species, nor individual, nor number, and on the other hand is neither accident nor that to which accident pertains?' God 'is not to be understood by scientific demonstration, for this depends on prior and more readily known principles, and there is nothing prior to the Unoriginated' – the first principle [75] God, then, is not an object alongside other objects, and no human conceptuality is adequate for such a being. The critical process had to be absolutely radical, and to reach any knowledge of God, however dim, this asceticism of mind had to be accompanied by strict

---

[73] Ecclesiastes 3.18–20.   [74] See Chapter 8.
[75] Clement of Alexandria, *Stromateis*. v.12.81–2. Greek text: O. Stählin, L. Früchtel and U. Treu (eds.), *Stromateis*, *GCS*. ET: *ANCF* and *FC*.

asceticism of the body. Yet in the teeth of such principled agnosticism Christian theology affirmed that God had accommodated the divine self to the limitations of human language and our creaturely existence, both in scripture and in the incarnation, an accommodation which necessarily involved symbolism – metaphor and type that pointed beyond itself. The way of synthesis and the way of analogy provided constructive processes of enlarging as well as purifying human conceptuality so as to reach some inkling of the divine through contemplation of what God has made, its truth, beauty and goodness. So the creation, like scripture, points beyond itself – there is more than meets the eye, and contemplation can follow the way of anagogy, or ascent, from physical beauty and goodness to some sense of divine goodness and beauty.

In his *Hexaemeron* Basil constantly uses anagogy to lift the vision from the wonders of creation to a sense of the Creator's presence. Genesis states that God saw that each creation was good, and this allows Basil to emphasize its beauty – not just the beauty in the eye of the beholder, for what God esteems beautiful is the capacity of a thing to fulfil its divinely intended purpose.

> A hand, an eye, or any portion of a statue lying separate from the rest, would look beautiful to no-one; but if each is restored to its proper place, the beauty of proportion, until now almost unperceived, would strike even the untutored eye. Yet the artist, before uniting the parts of his work, distinguishes and recognises the beauty of each of them, thinking of the object he has in view.

With that analogy Basil suggests how it is that scripture depicts the supreme artist praising each of his works and, when the work is complete, accords praise to the whole together.[76] The sea is good, not just because it is lovely to watch its brightness and the moving tints of purple and azure produced by its ruffling in the wind, but because it is the source of all the moisture of the earth, filtering through

---

[76] *Hexaemeron* III.10.

underground waterways, vaporized by the sun's warmth and falling as rain, collecting water again from rivers, and facilitating communication and trade.[77] Each thing created indicates ineffable wisdom, and Basil wants his congregation to recognize 'grandeur even in the smallest objects', so 'redoubling your love for the Creator'.[78]

> If sometimes on a bright night, whilst gazing with watchful eyes on the inexpressible beauty of the stars, you have thought of the Creator of all things; if you have asked yourself who it is that dotted heaven with such flowers . . . if sometimes, in the day, you have studied marvels of light, if you have raised yourself by visible things to the invisible Being, then you are a well-prepared auditor.

He continues, 'If we are penetrated by these truths, we shall know ourselves, we shall know God, we shall adore our Creator.' Again he says:

> If the sun, subject to dissolution, is so beautiful, so grand, so rapid in its movement, so invariable in its course; if its grandeur is in such perfect harmony with and due proportion to the universe, if by the beauty of its nature, it shines like a brilliant eye in the middle of creation, if finally, one cannot tire of contemplating it, what will be the beauty of the Sun of Righteousness?

The climax of Basil's homily on the sun and moon[79] is an exhortation to find from them 'a still higher idea of their Creator'. Compared with their author, 'the sun and moon are but a fly or an ant'; 'the whole universe cannot give us a right idea of the greatness of God; and it is only by signs, weak and slight in themselves, often by the help of the smallest insects and of the least plants, that we raise ourselves to him'.

Augustine uses a similar analogy to Basil's dismembered statue, emphasizing the beauty and goodness of the whole:

---

[77] *Ibid.* IV.6.   [78] *Ibid.* V.8–9.   [79] *Ibid.* VI.

Every beauty, after all, that consists of parts is much more admirable in its totality than in any of its parts. Take the human body, for example; if we admire the eyes alone or the nose alone or the cheeks alone or the head alone, or the hands and feet alone, and if we admire all the other parts one by one and alone, how much more the whole body on which all its parts, each beautiful by itself, confer their particular beauties? If by contrast a beautiful hand, which in the body was admired even on its own, is separated from the body, not only does the hand itself forfeit its proper grace, but the other parts also are rendered unsightly without it. Such is the force and power of completeness and unity, that many things, all good in themselves, are only found satisfying when they come together and fit into the whole. The universal, the universe, of course, takes its name from unity.

If only the Manichees would consider these points, they would 'praise God the author and founder of the whole universe'.[80]

Like Basil, Augustine sees signs of God's wisdom in the minutest of creatures – even the grubs that infest garbage, rotten fruit and corpses, not to mention the sores on living bodies. To observe them is to wonder at these tiny creatures, with such sharp senses, and be 'more amazed at the agile flight of a fly than at the stamina of a sturdy mule on the march; and the co-operative labours of tiny ants strike us as far more wonderful than the colossal loads that can be carried by a camel'.[81]

Augustine, however, has a sense of creation's dynamism: the initial act of creation sets up a 'living system destined to grow toward beauty and order', or potentialities, 'latent powers of development in created things', which are then unfolded in time as things change and creatures succeed one another in a beautiful tapestry. There is both completeness and incompleteness in God's creation. The purposes

[80] *On Genesis against Manichees* 1.21, 32 (ET: Hill, *Augustine*, p. 60); cf. *Literal Meaning* III.37.
[81] *Literal Meaning* III.22.

of God are implicit in that process, hidden yet discernible, regular but non-deterministic – 'there is a real history of interaction between Creator and creation, so that miracle is not "against nature".[82]

11.2.2 Appropriation?

With advances in biochemistry and particle physics, we may agree that the minuteness of things is as extraordinary as the vastness of deep space and time. Given evolution, we may also agree that there is completeness and incompleteness, potentiality and development in creation. But surely the universe as understood by science precludes the patristic inferences. And isn't the God who 'withdraws' so remote that creation can hardly display God's wisdom, as they thought? Alongside the reflections of Basil and Augustine we place three proposals for moving from the scientific understanding of the universe to a sense of God.

11.2.2.1 The 'anthropic' principle

Some appeal to the fact that 'a world containing men is not just any old universe, "specified at random" so to speak, but it has to have a particular character in its basic laws and circumstances'.[83] Speculations about a multiverse, writes Polkinghorne, are 'not physics but, in the strictest sense, metaphysics. There is no purely scientific reason to believe in an ensemble of universes.' Stephen Hawking[84] would beg to differ, but Polkinghorne regards it as 'a possible explanation of equal intellectual respectability', indeed 'greater economy

[82] Rowan Williams on 'Creation' in Allan D. Fitzgerald, *Augustine through the Ages: An Encyclopedia* (Grand Rapids, MI: Eerdmans, 1999), referring to *Literal Meaning* VI.14.25.

[83] John Polkinghorne, *One World – The Interaction of Science and Theology* (London: SPCK, 1986), p. 58.

[84] Hawking and Mlodinow, *The Grand Design.*

and elegance', to posit that this fine-tuning arises because of 'the will of a Creator who purposes that it should be so'.

> The world that science describes seems to me, with its order, intelligibility, potentiality and tightly-knit character, to be one that is consonant with the idea that it is the expression of the will of a Creator, subtle, patient and content to achieve his purposes by the slow unfolding of process inherent in those laws of nature which, in their regularity, are but the pale reflections of his abiding faithfulness.[85]

If this seems to resort to the God of the gaps, objectors should note that the appeal is not to a 'gap' but to the character of the totality, and is therefore parallel to the patristic appeal to the harmony and beauty of the whole.

This position is buttressed by two further observations: (i) the striking fact that mathematics, an abstract intellectual construct of human minds, turns out to unlock the physical workings of the universe, an intelligibility that demands an explanation,[86] the best being that 'the Reason of the Creator . . . establishes the common ground for an observed rationality of the world and the experienced rationality of our minds';[87] and (ii) realization that God is not a cause among causes or an object among objects, but the 'guarantor of [physical] law' whose 'role is to sustain the world in being'.[88] As Swinburne put it: 'I am not postulating a "God of the gaps" . . . I am postulating a God to explain why science explains.'[89] 'Far from science abolishing God, it would seem that there is a substantial case for asserting that it is the existence of a Creator that gives to science its fundamental intellectual justification,' concludes Lennox.[90]

II.2.2.2 *Information*

Some appeal to the difficulty of explaining the origin of life and the complexity of living organisms. The chance of DNA emerging is a bit

---

[85] Polkinghorne, *One World*, p. 80.   [86] *Ibid.*, p. 46.   [87] *Ibid.*, p. 79.
[88] *Ibid.*, p. 66.   [89] Quoted by Lennox, *God's Undertaker*, p. 47.   [90] *Ibid.*, p. 61.

like monkeys typing Shakespeare – it could only happen in an infinite universe; and DNA itself may be compared to a computer program, far more advanced than any software so far created – indeed, the DNA in a human genome contains 7 billion bits of information, and it could 'be argued that the molecular biology of the cell shows the same order of fine-tuning [seen] in connection with physics and cosmology'.[91]

> The existence of complex specified information, therefore, provides a substantial challenge to the notion that unguided natural processes can account for life and makes scientifically plausible the suggestion that an intelligent source was responsible.[92]

'Information and intelligence are fundamental to the existence of the universe and life and . . . were involved from the beginning.'[93]

But to appeal to God as the intelligent in-putter is surely another case of the God of the gaps. Or is it? This is not a case of reducing God to the explanation of a gap in knowledge which might one day be closed, but rather drawing an inference from the fundamental nature of the whole, its mathematical intelligibility and fine-tuning, its character as information. A similar argument could surely be made from 'chaos theory', which showed that 'disorder was chan-nelled . . . into patterns . . . A realm lies there of forms to explore, or harmonies to discover.'[94] 'Systems too complex for traditional mathematics could yet obey simple laws',[95] and this 'disorderly behaviour of simple systems acted as a *creative* process', generating:

> complexity. richly organised patterns, sometimes stable and some-times unstable, sometimes finite and sometimes infinite, but always with the fascination of living things.[96]

> Our feeling for beauty is inspired by the harmonious arrangement of order and disorder as it occurs in natural objects – in clouds,

[91] *Ibid.*, p. 147.   [92] *Ibid.*, p. 164.   [93] *Ibid.*, p. 167.
[94] Gleick, *Chaos*, pp. 152–3.   [95] *Ibid.*, p. 307.   [96] *Ibid.*, p. 43.

trees, mountain ranges, or snow crystals. The shapes of all these are dynamical processes jelled into physical form, and particular combinations of order and disorder are typical for them.[97]

This kind of observation could well occasion the patristic anagogy from the beauty and harmony of the cosmos to transcendental Beauty itself.

11.2.2.3 Emergence

Scientific investigation has a tendency to reductionism. However, it is one thing to say 'we are all made of the ashes of dead stars'[98] and quite another to conclude that we are *only* atoms, or that mind is *simply* 'the epiphenomenon of brain'.[99] There are different levels, and as one moves from sub-atomic particles to chemical combinations, living cells, complex organisms, human consciousness and so on, each whole is clearly more than its parts[100] – there are 'emergent' phenomena. No extra component is added, yet 'what happens at a higher level is not completely derivable from what happens on the level beneath it'.[101] The behaviour of slime mould provided an intriguing clue: most of the time its life is spent as 'thousands of distinct single-celled units, each moving separately from its other comrades'; but 'under the right conditions' the 'myriad cells' coalesce into a 'single larger organism'.[102] Something similar happens in swarms of starlings, bees or locusts, in the self-organizing capacity of ant colonies and human cities – through feedback mechanisms individuals become part of a larger whole with its own patterns of behaviour. For Basil and Augustine, the beauty of the whole is what

---

[97] *Ibid.*, p. 117.   [98] Polkinghorne, *One World*, p. 56.

[99] *Ibid.*, p. 92; cf. Lennox, *God's Undertaker*, chapter 3.

[100] Polkinghorne, *One World*, p. 86; cf. Ross Thompson, *Holy Ground: The Spirituality of Matter* (London: SPCK, 1990).

[101] Lennox, *God's Undertaker*, p. 56.

[102] Steven Johnson, *Emergence* (London: Penguin, 2001), p. 13.

points beyond itself; similarly it can be said that 'reality is multi-layered unity', and to 'deny one of the levels' is 'to do less than justice to the richness of reality'. So:

> part of the case for theism is that in God the Creator, the ground of all that is, these different levels find their lodging and their guarantee. He is the source of connection, the one whose creative act holds in one the world-views of science, aesthetics, ethics and religion, as expressions of his reason, joy, will and presence.[103]

These three proposals are suggestive, but risk remaining somewhat 'demiurgic'.[104] God can neither be an explanatory first cause deduced from the evidence of the natural world, nor an intervening cause in the process of evolution.[105] Evolutionary theory which sees the whole thing as in some way self-determining is theologically coherent with the point made earlier – that God's creativity must involve a kind of withdrawal, a kind of 'letting be'. But does this mean a God even more remote than deism? Simone Weil would not approve such a deduction from her thought:

> God's creative love which maintains us in existence is not merely a superabundance of generosity, it is also renunciation and sacri-fice ... His love maintains in existence, in a free and autonomous existence, beings other than himself ... It is by an inconceivable love that he comes down so far as to reach them ... The Creation itself is a kind of passion. My very existence is like a laceration of God, a laceration which is love.[106]

---

[103] Polkinghorne, *One World*, p. 97.

[104] See above 1.2.2; 'demiurgic' implies there are residual traces of the 'craftsman' analogy.

[105] Haught, *God after Darwin*.   [106] Weil, *Gateway to God*, pp. 80 ff.

She is not alone in seeing that the cross challenges the theistic notion of the all-powerful Creator. In *God after Darwin*, John Haught suggests that 'reflection on the Darwinian world can lead us to contemplate more explicitly the mystery of God as it is made manifest in the story of life's sufferings, the epitome of which lies for Christians in the crucifixion of Jesus'.[107]

The affirmation of the Bible and the fathers would be that the God who lets be does not let go, but is continually engaged. That engagement will concern us as we move into exploration of the human story. But already things may be said in relation to the created universe as a whole. If God contains without being contained, as Irenaeus said, God must be an encompassing presence. There would be no creation at all without God's constant will to uphold in being something other than the divine self, to grant existence and life, to maintain the harmony of the cosmos through a loving providence which is intimately engaged with, possibly in some way regulating and directing,[108] yet not coercive of, the whole amazing process. The cosmological argument fails because it reduces God to an explanation; the cosmological *insight*, on the other hand, lets us see how creation points beyond itself.[109]

God's presence is inevitably ambiguous and hidden, since God's absolute 'otherness' can be mediated only through what is other than God; and that is entirely consistent with the character of the God who wills to become incarnate in a truly human being.

> If there is a God he is a hidden God. He does not make himself known unambiguously in acts of transparent significance . . . this elusive character seems necessary in One whose infinite presence totally disclosed would overwhelm our finite being.

---

[107] Haught, *God after Darwin*, p. 46.
[108] Cf. Augustine above. Maybe Lennox's position, in *God's Undertaker*, is pertinent to this sense of continuous engagement with physical and natural processes. See further, Chapter 8.
[109] Polkinghorne, *One World*, p. 79.

While God is in his essential nature eternal and unchanging, his act of creation and his love for his creatures implies a self-limiting and a self-emptying – a kenosis, as the theologians say – by which he allows the vulnerability implicit in the creative act to impinge upon him.[110]

So it takes discernment to worship the Creator rather than the creature; much religious devotion is doubtless offered to idols, man-made gods and human projections. The true God transcends the cosmos and attracts creatures towards transcendent truth, beauty and goodness through the truth, beauty and goodness immanent in the harmony of the cosmos. That is what Augustine would have affirmed, and surely so may we.

> In order for the world... to undergo a genuine self-transcendence in its evolution, a God of love would concede to the world its own autonomous principles of operation... This "self-distancing" of God, however, is in no sense apathy but, paradoxically, the most intimate form of involvement... God is nothing like the otiose and remote first cause of deism; for it is out of a longing to relate deeply to the world that God foregoes any annihilating "presence" to the world. This... is the very condition of dialogical intimacy... The God of self-giving compassion is in fact the only God that normative Christian faith can claim legitimately ever to have encountered.[111]

If we move beyond every kind of demiurgic picture of God's creativity, if we avoid the temptation to rescue God by consigning divine activity to the gaps in our explanations, then we may again wonder at the harmonious whole which has come into being out of nothing and explore the subtle ways in which God is mediated to us through creation, despite not being an item within it, or a

---

[110] *Ibid.*, pp. 26, 34. Cf. Haught, *God after Darwin.*
[111] Haught, *God after Darwin*, p. 114.

cause intertwined with it, or even an explanatory hypothesis. We may humbly recognize that we have ape-like brains, with limited capabilities, and can only speak of transcendent mysteries through inadequate analogies.

We might also find the analogy of the lyre-player more appropriate than Paley's watchmaker. When you hear music, suggested Gregory Nazianzen, you start to wonder about the one who made or plays the lyre, the one who conjures such beauty from the physical stuff of wood and cat-gut. This captures imaginatively God's constant creative playing on instruments graced with existence, though like all analogies it has its deficiencies: Gregory, like Paley, was after all admiring the clever way the lyre was put together. But the lyre was not a mechanism, intelligently designed and left to work on its own. A musical instrument is dead unless its musical life is called into existence by the sensitive touch of the musician enabling transcendence of the wood and cat-gut. The music seems to emerge from nothing, constituting time and then unfolding in time, with ever greater complexity, yet always with extraordinary beauty, from the first pure note to fugues and symphonies of the most intricate harmony.[112]

Arthur listens to the music as he looks through his fingers at a world of light and shade – his face enraptured.

* * *

Doxology in the wilderness

The preacher begins:

The opening chapters of Genesis don't begin to cover everything the Bible says about creation. The passages read today from Job, Revelation and Matthew,[113] together with Psalm 8, point us in directions other than the old struggles over creation and evolution.

---

[112] For an intriguing exploration of these points, see Arthur Peacocke and Ann Pedersen, *The Music of Creation* (Minneapolis: Fortress, 2006).

[113] Job 38.1, 4–7, 16–18; Revelation 21.1–7; Matthew 6.25–34.

First, we're put in our place. 'When I look at the heavens, the moon and the stars you've established', we sang, 'what are we human beings that you are mindful of them, mortals that you care for them?'; and the Lord answered Job out of the whirlwind: 'Where were you when I laid the foundation of the earth? . . . Is it by your wisdom that the hawk soars?' At first sight this is no answer to Job's searching questions, no solution to his desperate struggle to grasp how his fate can be reconciled with God's justice. But that reaction assumes the book is about the problem of suffering. Suppose it's not. Suppose its purpose is to celebrate loyalty which is not self-interested, trust which transcends reward, loving God for God's sake. And what if the final chapters are an invitation to love creation for its own sake, irrespective of human interest?

Come with me to the wilds of the Okavanga Delta. Our African guide walks in front through the bush. Suddenly he stops and urges us back. After a bit we turn and ask, 'What's the problem?' He points to some waving branches: 'Elephant!' We'd been dangerously close. We set out down wind and give it a wide berth. Back in camp, we see an elephant splash across the channel of water.

All night the call of the nightjar, the bark of hyena, the sound of roaring lion. Early next morning we walk miles tracking lion, but the cats are elusive. We find fresh elephant dung, and nervously take a circular route back. And the next 24 hours are similar. We hear hippo grunting, and our guide poles the dugout away fast in the other direction. We spot buffalo grazing, and avoid the area. We go in search of the leopard we've been hearing, but see nothing but wildebeest and leaping buck, lechwe and impala.

We were in one of the last places in Africa where you can still have experiences similar to the old explorers'. For safety we were dependent upon traditional skills – tracking, observation, caution, keeping the fire alight all night. We didn't see much game, but slid through long grassy meadows in a punt on a level with frogs and dragonflies, spiders' webs and waterlilies. It was a rich paradise. Yet always the *frisson* of the wild, the edge of insecurity . . .

This was amazing – the kind of experience Westerners rarely have. We were little and vulnerable in a stunningly beautiful but potentially threatening world. There was something awesome about just being there. Even so we were cushioned compared with our hunter-gatherer ancestors: we had tinned food and tin-openers, we had insect-repellant and anthisan. We escaped the dreaded malaria and sleeping-sickness, but on return appreciated antibiotics to deal with our tick typhus. And we would escape, flying dramatically over the swamp and seeing the giraffe far below.

This was a salutary reminder of what the human condition really is in the context of creation, and how wrong-headed so many of our protests at life's hardships are. In the bush you don't question the right of the elephant to charge or the lion to pounce on its prey – the world you inhabit is not something over which you have control, but one where you seek the wisdom to cope with its challenges. It's a majestic world to be respected, to be loved for what it is, a world of wonder that exhilarates even as it terrifies.

It never crosses your mind that God ought to make things easy. Any power which took control of that environment would destroy it. If it is to be what it is, it has to be let be. Power corrupts: divine omnipotence might be demonic. Isn't God to be glorified for letting the paradoxical paradise of this wilderness be itself, dangers and all? And isn't that just what Job learned: after all his protests, confronted with the wonders of God's creation and made to feel very small, made to respect nature for nature's sake, he's ashamed of his narrow, self-pitying attitude to God's miraculous gift of existence. Face -to- face with the Creator, Job's questions faded away.

So we too are put in our place and called to doxology – that praise which comes from sheer awe at the extraordinary context in which we find ourselves. Scientific discoveries enhance that sense of littleness and awesome wonder, for they enlarge our cosmic perspectives and set us within a surging mass of endlessly novel life-forms in ecological interaction with one another. How could we presume to put things to rights from our own limited perspective? We are but vulnerable creatures in the midst of an utterly amazing cosmos.

Second, we're pointed towards the future. The Bible is a book of promise. Revelation 21 picks up words from the prophet Isaiah: 'I am about to create new heavens and a new earth . . . Be glad and rejoice for ever in what I'm creating.'[114] 'I am about to do a new thing', cries God, gasping and panting in labour pains, 'Can't you see it?'[115]

God's purposes call us into a new future, or, to put it another way, God's future comes to meet us, drawing us to ever greater fulfilment. The potential for novelty to emerge is hinted at by life's prolific fecundity over the millennia revealed by evolutionary biology. Someone put it like this: 'the fifteen billion years of cosmic evolution now appear in the perspective of faith to have always been seeded with promise . . . and bursting with potential for surprising future outcomes'.[116] Nature's creative profligacy matches the sheer overflow of God's grace seen in Christ and the Spirit. 'In Christ we are a new creation', says Paul;[117] 'the creation waits with eager longing for the revealing of the children of God', and is in labour to bring new things to birth.

What exactly that means for creation as a whole is impossible to predict, but maybe clues to a new world can be spotted if we return to the African wilderness. On foot through open spaces and patches of bush, our guide focussed on symbiosis, like the termite hill and the tamarisk tree – the termites build their hill under the tree for shade, while the roots of the tree are kept moist by the water brought up by the termites to cement their construction; the tree also gets nutrients from the mound, as do elephants who gouge it out to eat. Another day the guide pointed out a fungus that grows on a particular kind of bush and deters animals

114 Isaiah 65.17–18.
115 Isaiah 43.19, with allusion to 42.14.   116 Haught, *God after Darwin*, p. 115.
117 References to 2 Corinthians 5.17; Romans 8.18, 22.

from browsing on it while it is young; but when the mature tree is out of reach it loses the fungus. Collaboration unconsciously emerges.

It seems an utterly unrealistic dream, Isaiah's vision of the wolf lying down with the lamb, the leopard with the kid, the calf and the lion and the fatling together, with a little child leading, as the cow and the bear graze, their young lying down together and the lion eating straw like an ox. Yet it captures a sense that the creation has not yet reached its fruition. It signposts a future in which we're not autonomous individuals, but communities, part of a cosmic harmony which points towards something bigger than ourselves. Anticipation of that future stimulates the hope that is in us and calls us forward into visions that transcend what we normally regard as possibilities.

Third, the Bible suggests that creation was not a one-off event: for Psalm 104 it is not just about the origin of the universe, while Genesis 1.2 implies that the Spirit of God constantly moves over the chaos creatively. Debates about Genesis get hung up about origins and causes, as if it was meant to answer scientific questions. *Yes*, the Genesis story *was* meant to establish God's priority. The motif of chaos probably arose as a kind of rationalization of ancient Near Eastern mythologies in which the creating god struggled with Leviathan; but here God *creates* sea monsters – the dragon is reduced to a creature. God's priority is established, but priority points to transcendence.

Creation is about the ongoing dependence of the universe on its Creator. Jesus invites us to look at the birds of the air, who 'neither sow nor reap nor gather into barns, and yet your heavenly Father feeds them', to consider the lilies of the field, who 'neither toil nor spin, yet I tell you, even Solomon in all his glory was not clothed like one of these', to note that not a single sparrow falls to the ground 'without your Father'.[118] Even when God seems absent, withdrawn or uncaring, God is present, if elusive.

---

[118] Matthew 10.29.

Back for a moment to a night-drive in the wilderness: an elusive leopard frozen in a distant bush, staring at the spot-light, one eye green, one orange. Gripped in eye-contact, I stared back for minutes in the strangest of encounters, until it slunk away. For me it became a paradoxical sign – a sign of God's elusive presence, a sign of God's penetrating eyes, glimpsed in the darkness, seeing right into our depths. An early Christian bishop once wrote:

> Nothing escapes the Lord's notice – indeed, even our hidden secrets are present to him. So let us act in everything we do as if he were dwelling within us, so that we may be his temples and he may be our God within us.[119]

What is really at stake in the Bible is God's on-going purposes, and our involvement in them. To humanity, crowned with glory and honour, God meant to delegate pastoral responsibility for the earth and all its creatures – the word so often translated as 'dominion' means something like 'shepherd'. Humankind, created on the same day as land animals, has the same breath as other creatures; yet as God's image on earth, humanity is meant to be God's representative or co-worker, the steward of creation, contributing to the process of change and renewal, the emergence of novelty – yet more beauty, truth and goodness. Thanks be to God. Amen.

* * *

Postlude

Emergence

Nothing comes from nothing – yet
    A little something God let be.

---

[119] Ignatius, *Ephesians* 15.3.

Nothing comes from nothing – yet
 Black holes within deep space and time
  Suggest a singularity.

Nothing comes from nothing – yet
 In oceans' depth volcanic vents
  Produced life's biochemistry.

Nothing comes from nothing – yet
 From nothingness came all that is
  In such profuse diversity
  With microbes, monkeys, mice and me
  Evolving branches of life's tree
  Because in generosity
  God limited infinity
  Allowing otherness to be.

Nothing comes from nothing – yet
 Existence like a gift unwrapped
  Makes evident dust's pregnancy.

Nothing comes from nothing – yet
 Amidst the desert nothingness
  On Moses' mount God spoke to me
  The still small voice of prophecy
  Transfigured rock revealed the key
  Unlocked the little mystery
  Of sacredness in ordinary
  And God's own physicality.

Some observations

Imagination blinks at dazzling snow,
At nature's royal icing glaciate,

Whose drifts compacted hard can excavate
A U-shaped valley. Such a fluted flow
Is not mere decoration, just for show.
Terrible is this tool, honed to create
Living environments for a future date.
Gleaming white above, deep down below
The fractured ice is weirdly navy-blue.
And in that colour time's deposit rests
While motion's slowed. For old yet ever new,
Eternal snows adorn the mountain crests
And inch by inch towards the sea they glide
Reducing human life to time's aside.

Imagination contemplates the greens,
A subtle, natural colour-chart, unmatched
By human imitation. Hillsides patched
With fields of several shades are startling scenes,
Missed by the casual glance. Attention means
A look of deep attachment, yet detached,
An objectivity with feeling matched.
The distant gaze reverts: an old tree leans.
The ancient mosses lining greenish bark
And variegated tints of new green leaves
Shade into one another, light to dark,
With deepest tones where dark-green ivy weaves.
Lowered the eyes caress the rich green sod.
Such passionless passion is the love of God.

Imagination gazes at the flowers,
At nature's colour-trials on sketch-pad daubed,
Impressionistic beauty, light absorbed
In variations played by spattered showers.
But transience and frailty speed the hours.
A wounded world by death and darkness flawed

Is symbolized in wreaths and ashes poured.
Yet over tragedy transcendence towers
And intuition knows the painter's hand;
Analysis of form reveals the art
Whereby within the chaos strokes were planned.
Imagination's insight fires the heart
And love dispels the ambiguity
As overall design chants unity.

A sudden movement at once catches the eye.
Was it a bird, a mouse, an old dead leaf?
Nature intrigues and baffles, from mighty massif
To minute microbe or transient butterfly.
Surrealist creatures implausibly live and die,
Unnatural natural beings, beyond belief.
A swarm of life lives hid in the Barrier Reef,
For aeons quaintly secreted – wonder why?
Strange such wealth of living undiscerned,
This ecological equilibrium
That even now, seeing, we have not learned
To see amazingly. Can praise be dumb?
Is consciousness the crowning apex of all?
Or intimation of supernatural call?

Imagination listens to the birds,
To nature's unsurpassed symphonic choir.
From dawn to dusk their voices hardly tire.
The cuckoo heralds hope in minor thirds.
The lark ascends, transcending earth-bound herds;
Celestial sounds pour down from higher and higher.
These messengers on wings with notes of fire
Achieve communication without words.
Peace on the earth, their harmony evokes.
The corncrake rasps; the blackbird's warning cry

Shatters the dream – for peace is but a hoax
Without the pain of judgment. Self must die
And rise above itself, should it aspire
To join the counterpoint of Abel's choir.

3 | From creation to re-creation: nature and the naked ape

Prelude

The minister leads in the coffin, intoning the traditional texts:

- I am the resurrection and the life, saith the Lord: he that believeth in me, though he were dead, yet shall he live: and whoso liveth and believeth in me shall never die.[1]
- We brought nothing into this world and it is certain we can carry nothing out. The Lord gave and the Lord hath taken away: blessed be the name of the Lord.[2]

The grandmother is the first to hold the new-born infant in her arms. Gazing at the tiny face, she hears the child named with her own name, the maiden name of the baby's great-great-grandmother, a given name for four generations. She's awed by the continuities of generations, their dying and birthing.

The cyclists crash down the gears and pedal fast up the steep little rise, eyes caught by the dark mist of bluebells in the wood glimpsed through the hedge. On the way they've heard the squawk of a pheasant, birds chattering in woods and larks singing above fields; they've seen a meadow of cowslips, ramsons in verges, primroses on banks, blackthorn in hedges, delicate carpets of wood anemones and the purple faces of violets. Exercise induces deep breathing, a racing pulse and the biochemistry of euphoria; the sheer physical joy of living produces insistent beats of heartfelt praise – earthed in belonging to the natural order.

---

[1] John 11.25–6.   [2] I Timothy 6.7; Job 1.21.

The gardener waters the flowers; he roots out weeds and piles them on the compost heap where they'll become fertiliser for these blooms. In a hidden corner he husbands a wild patch of nettles to encourage bees and butterflies – a little nook of managed wilderness.

The bereaved family listens to Brahms' German Requiem, tears welling as words and music sink into their hearts:

- Blessed are they that mourn, for they shall be comforted. Those that sow in tears shall reap in joy . . . [3]
- Behold, all flesh is grass, and all the goodliness of man is as the flower of the field; the grass withereth and the flower thereof decayeth . . . But the word of the Lord endureth for ever . . . joy and gladness shall be their portion, and tears and sighing shall flee from them.[4]
- Lord, make me to know the measure of my days on earth, to consider my frailty, that I must perish . . . man passeth away like a shadow . . . But the righteous souls are in the hand of God, nor shall pain nor grief come nigh them.[5]

People say it with flowers.

* * *

Philosophy has debated human nature since antiquity. The church fathers[6] both embraced and challenged ancient philosophy, incorporating into their theological perspectives the theories of ancient medicine in particular. It would seem implausible that such

---

[3] Matthew 5.4; Psalm 126.5–6.

[4] I Peter 1.24–5; James 5.7.   [5] Psalm 39.5, 6, 7, 8; Wisdom 3.1.

[6] This chapter incorporates material from three previously published articles of mine, where fuller references and discussion may be found: 'Naked or Clothed? Eschatology and the Doctrine of Creation' in Peter Clarke and Tony Claydon (eds.), *The Church, the Afterlife and the Fate of the Soul*, Studies in Church History 45 (Woodbridge: Boydell and Brewer, 2009); 'Adam and Anthropos: A Study in the Interaction of Science and the Bible in Two Anthropological Treatises of the Fourth Century', *VC* 37 (1983), 110–40; 'Creation and Human Being: The Forging of a Distinct Christian Discourse', *SP* 44 (2010), 335–48.

pre-scientific thought would have anything to contribute at a time when anthropology and neuroscience are dramatically advancing understanding of what it means to be human. Yet again I shall argue that the fathers approached the subject with their own counter-cultural perspective informed by biblical theology, and that their approach has significant things to suggest to theologians in the present very different context.

This chapter will explore human nature so far as possible without reference to the fall. That distinctively Christian insight is the pre-requisite for the Christian story of redemption and will figure later. Other perceptions, sometimes shared with those of other faiths or none, are also crucial to any conception of humanity and its place in the cosmos.

I Creation and resurrection

Striking is the way early Christian literature links creation with resurrection, often treating the eschatological promises as intended from the beginning. In patristic argument, the beginning of the cosmos implied its end, thus challenging the notion of its eternity. Against the cosmic cycles of Stoicism, early Christianity learned to affirm the linearity of history, and against the 'otherworldliness' of both Platonism and gnosticism, human embodiment. Both emphases find their basis in a sense of creatureliness which admits the possibility of re-creation. The affirmation of resurrection underlined the essential physicality of human nature and may have contributed to the doctrine of creation out of nothing. Could it be that focussing on the ultimate destiny of humankind throws significant light on its fundamental nature?

1.1 Making the connection

Creation and resurrection are already connected in 2 Maccabees 7. In the face of his potential martyrdom, the mother begs her son to recognize that God made heavens and earth and all creation, and human beings too. The context concerns God's power to bring life out of death, and birth is called in as a parallel mystery;[7] in other words, fear can be dismissed because God brought you into existence when you did not exist *as you* before, and can therefore restore that existence if you put your hope and trust in God. This text, often taken to refer to creation out of nothing and certainly read that way later, actually says nothing about the presence or absence of a material substrate; rather, it is entirely compatible with human creation 'out of clay', as in Genesis 2. Similarly in Romans 4, the focus is not creation as such, but the connection between creation and resurrection. Paul speaks of 'those who share the faith of Abraham' in the God 'who gives life to the dead and calls into existence the things that do not exist'. But the thrust of his argument is that Abraham believed that God could bring life out of death – for:

> he did not weaken in faith when he considered his own body, which was already as good as dead . . . or when he considered the barrenness [i.e. *nekrōsis* or deadness] of Sarah's womb.[8]

Some second–century writers, such as Justin Martyr and Athenagoras, assume that God as Creator imposed form on a material substrate – there was not yet an unambiguous doctrine of creation out of nothing.[9] Athenagoras is especially pertinent, since he provides us with the first treatise on the subject of resurrection.[10] Disbelieving opponents, he argues, need to demonstrate that God, despite being Creator, either cannot or will not restore dead bodies so as to reconstitute the human beings which were before. The original creation of bodies shows that God's power suffices for their

---

[7] 2 Maccabees 7.23.   [8] Romans 4.19.   [9] See Chapter 2.

[10] *Pace* W. R. Schoedel, Introduction to *Athenagoras: Legatio and De Resurrectione*, *OECT*, following R. M. Grant, 'Athenagoras or Pseudo-Athenagoras?' *HTR* 47 (1954), 121–9. See L. W. Barnard, *Athenagoras: A Study in Second-Century Christian Apologetic* (Paris: Éditions Beauchesne, 1972) for a critique of the case against authenticity.

resurrection; if God first gave them form when they did not exist before, he can just as easily raise them up after their dissolution.[11]

2 Maccabees and Paul used creation as encouragement to faith in God even in the face of death; now this author turns that into a philosophical defence of resurrection. Whatever the objection raised, such as what happens to those eaten by wild animals or turned into fish food after drowning, Athenagoras trumps it with the power and wisdom of the Creator. The apparent crudities of collecting every bit of matter which had belonged to each body is finessed by the notion of a body transcending what is known in our present existence. Yet without the composition of soul and body you would not have a human being; so even a transformed human being must be such a composite.[12] Resurrection thus reflects back on the nature of human being from the beginning – the idea that the naked soul[13] is the real human, which is only temporarily embodied, is ruled out. The connection is developed further as God's reason for creating human beings is considered. It was not from God's own need – it was for humanity's sake and out of God's wisdom and goodness. God 'decreed an unending existence to those who bear his image in themselves, are gifted with intelligence and share the faculty for rational discernment'. The two parts, soul and body, are receptive to the appropriate changes, 'including, along with the other changes affecting age, appearance or size, also the resurrection'.[14] Resurrection is taken to be 'transformation for the better', or 'survival in an incorruptible form'.

All the arguments offered to confirm the resurrection spring from the same basic idea, namely the origin of human beings in the act of creation.[15] This treatise maps out recurring topics in patristic discussion:[16] it affirms the goodness of materiality; it insists that the

---

[11] *On the Resurrection* 2–3.   [12] *Ibid.* 15.   [13] Cf. 2 Corinthians 5.1–6.

[14] *On the Resurrection* 12.   [15] *Ibid.* 18.

[16] E.g. Tertullian, *On the Resurrection of the Flesh*; Cyril of Jerusalem, *Catechetical Homily* 14; Gregory of Nyssa, *On the Making of Humankind*, etc.

union of body and soul constitutes a created human person; and it demonstrates that hope of resurrection played a part in Christian characterization of human nature.

Tatian makes the same connection, now reinforced by explicit affirmation of creation out of nothing. God was definitely alone, he asserts.[17] Matter is not, like God, without beginning; it was brought into existence by the One who framed all things. 'On this account', he says, 'we believe that there will be a resurrection of bodies': even if all trace of one's physical existence were to be obliterated by fire, or dispersed through waters, or torn in pieces by wild beasts, nothing can stop the creative power of God restoring one to the original pristine condition. Here is utter rejection of the immortality of the soul,[18] for the notion of the soul's immortality is incompatible with the doctrine of creation. The soul is mortal; yet it is possible for it not to die. It dies, dissolved with the body, if it does not know the truth; but, united with Spirit, it ascends. In other words, the creative activity of God is at the root of any afterlife. And this involves another corollary: conscious of the complexity of human nature, Tatian underlines the inability of the soul to be by itself without the body – both reach dissolution in death, and neither can rise without the other. Body and soul belong together, and after death may be reconstituted by the Creator God who created them together in the first place.

Tatian,[19] then, espoused the notion of *creatio ex nihilo*, and asserted its bearing on resurrection. In the *Epistle to Rheginos* (or *Treatise on the Resurrection*)[20] found in the Nag Hammadi library, the consequences of losing that connection can be observed. While the Lord

[17] *Oration to the Greeks* 5, 6; Greek text edited and translated by Molly Whittaker, *Tatian, Oratio ad Graecos and Fragments*, OECT.
[18] *Ibid.* 13.
[19] Cf. Theophilus of Antioch, *To Autolycus* I.4 and 7; II.4. Greek text edited and translated by Robert M. Grant, *Theophilus of Antioch Ad Autolycum*, OECT.
[20] ET: Malcolm L. Peel in James Robinson (ed.), *The Nag Hammadi Library in English* (Leiden: Brill, 1977), pp. 50–3.

'existed in flesh', it claims, he lived 'where you remain', a place which 'I call "Death"!' He:

> raised himself up, having swallowed the visible by the invisible, and gave us the way of our immortality.

This is the spiritual resurrection which swallows up the psychic in the same way as the fleshly.

The question is posed, 'What is the resurrection?' The answer is: 'It is always the disclosure of those who have arisen.' The appearance of Moses and Elijah in the transfiguration narrative is used as proof that the resurrection is no illusion. Rather the world is an illusion; the resurrection is the 'revelation of what is, and the transformation of things, and a transition into newness'. Described as 'permeated with Valentinian symbols and imagery', this work appears to spell out the views of those criticized in 2 Timothy 2.18 for asserting that 'the resurrection has already occurred'.[21] Its epistolary genre, its language and allusions, make this seem a Christian text, but redemption is escape from matter and creation is never mentioned – the connection has been lost.

The argument with gnostics about the goodness of the material creation involved creation, incarnation and resurrection – they hung together. Tertullian's treatise *On the Resurrection of the Flesh* shows how he saw the connections. From both heathen and heretic alike comes invective against the flesh, he asserts,[22] offering an alternative view – of the glory of the flesh, created by God out of nothing, redeemed in Christ and to be resurrected. He sees the resurrection as the basis of the whole Christian position; and his cross-references to other treatises, *Against Marcion* and *On the Flesh of Christ*, indicate his awareness of how these doctrines cohere. This is what underlies my claim that resurrection had something to do with the emergence of the doctrine of creation out of nothing. It

---

[21] Peel, Introduction to *The Nag Hammadi Library in English*, p. 50.
[22] *On the Resurrection* 4.

would be impossible to demonstrate a linear connection: Athenagoras apparently affirms one without the other, and the doctrine's basis lay in the arguments against alternative cosmogonies discussed previously.[23] But Tertullian, the first to set out those alternatives and reject them in favour of *creatio ex nihilo*, also saw how incarnation and resurrection hang together with God's act of creation from nothing. Spiritual interpretations of resurrection were heretical in Tertullian's view. The rejection of anti-materialist positions and the assertion of creation out of nothing surely derived their punch from faith in the physical resurrection of Christ and the promised general resurrection.[24]

When we turn to the fourth century, we find the connection between creation and resurrection powerful in modifying the Platonic tendencies of Christian thinkers like Gregory of Nyssa and Augustine.

1.2 Gregory of Nyssa

In his work *On the Making of Humankind*,[25] Gregory of Nyssa indicates that creation and resurrection were both alike within God's purposes for humankind from the beginning – eschatology is not simply a reversal of the fall. The distinction between God and everything else is fundamental;[26] God is immutable, but created nature cannot exist without change – for its very passage from non-existence to existence is a kind of motion and change. But this mutability is not negative:[27] if God's power is sufficient to bring things into existence from nothing, then the transformation of this creation is also within divine power. Gregory's spirituality expressed itself in terms of eternal *epektasis* and progress, taking mutability positively in a way that

---

[23] See Chapter 2.
[24] Cf. Irenaeus, also opposing gnostic heresies, in *Against Heresies*. Text: A. Rousseau and L. Doutreleau (eds.), *Irénée de Lyon: Contre les hérésies*. SC. ET: *ANCF* and *ACW*.
[25] Greek text: Migne, *PG* 44; ET: *NPNF*.
[26] *On the Making* xvi.10, 12.   [27] *Ibid.* xxiii.5–xxv ff.

was arguably unprecedented. Scholarship has tended to relate this to his positive evaluation of God's infinity;[28] maybe 'creation out of nothing' was an equally important driver. Emerging out of nothing human beings were to be oriented towards an ever-new future and be capable of endless self-transcendence.

So discussion of human destiny[29] begins with the inherent mutability of creatures, the great thing being that humankind will not stay settled in evil. Paradise will be restored, along with the grace of God's image. Our hope, he says, is for something beyond anything we can envisage. When the full complement of human nature has reached its predetermined measure, then, says Gregory,[30] the trumpet of the resurrection will sound, awaken the dead and transform to incorruptibility those still alive, as well as those who have been raised – so that the weight of the flesh is no longer heavy, and its burden no longer holds them down to earth, but they rise up through the air to be with the Lord.[31] This scriptural hope Gregory associates with world re-formation.[32] He challenges those who deny the resurrection alongside those who suggest that matter is co-eternal with God. Just as the power of the divine will is sufficient cause for things to have come into being out of nothing, so there is nothing improbable in referring world re-formation to the same power. Creation out of nothing and resurrection are acts of a kind, mutually supporting each other in challenging philosophical assumptions, such as, nothing comes from nothing, or the soul's liberation is to be released from the body.

Still, despite the evidence of scripture, he faces those who doubt such a thing is possible even for God, pressing awkward cases like those consumed in fire or eaten by wild beasts, or ship-wrecked

---

[28] E.g. E. Mühlenberg, *Die Unendlichkeit Gottes bei Gregor Von Nyssa* (Göttingen: Vandenhoeck and Ruprecht, 1966); R. E. Heine, *Perfection in the Virtuous Life* (Cambridge, MA: Philadelphia Patristic Foundation, 1975).

[29] *On the Making* XXI.   [30] *Ibid.* XXII.6.

[31] Here Gregory exploits 1 Corinthians 15.51–2 and 1 Thessalonians 4.17.

[32] *On the Making* XXIII–IV.

sailors devoured by fish.[33] Of course death means dissolution, Gregory acknowledges; the elements return to the elements, earth to earth, moisture to water. But what is possible to God must not be judged by the limits of human capacity or imagination. Body and soul were brought into being together, and this wholeness is to be restored in the resurrection. In exploring human formation and re-formation, Gregory is clear that a human being is a psychosomatic unity. His picture of how the dissolved particles of the body are imprinted with an identity and reconstituted by the soul's knowledge of them might seem quasi-scientific – indeed a parallel with modern notions of the persistence of DNA has been drawn.[34] But the fundamental drive is to affirm God's creativity.

In the dialogue *On the Soul and the Resurrection*,[35] Gregory's sister, Macrina, like Socrates, discusses the nature of the soul on her deathbed. She roundly rejects its immortality as pagan nonsense – we find here the same complex, psychosomatic whole as in *The Making of Humankind*. To treat death simply as the dissolution of this complex being is dismissed: creation proclaims the Creator, and reconstitution is less problematic than the initial creation from nothing. Here Gregory introduces discussion of the emotions,[36] identifying them as growths, somewhat like warts, on the soul's thinking part. In the re-formation of human nature which is the resurrection, all this will be stripped away so that there will be nothing to impede contemplation of the beautiful, nothing to prevent participation in the good, both identified with God. The soul will know its own nature

---

[33] *Ibid.* xxv–vi.

[34] Vasiliki Limberis, 'Resurrected Body and Immortal Flesh in Gregory of Nyssa' in *Jesus Christ in St Gregory of Nyssa's Theology*, Minutes of the Ninth International Conference on St Gregory of Nyssa, Athens 7–12 September 2000 (Athens: Eptalophos, 2005), pp. 515–28.

[35] Greek text in W. Jaeger *et al.*, *Gregorii Nysseni Opera* (Leiden: Brill, 1960–); ET: Catherine Roth, *On the Soul and the Resurrection* (Crestwood, NY: St Vladimir's Seminary Press, 1993).

[36] On emotions/passions, see Chapter 6.

as God's image, and will behold the original beauty reflected in her own beauty.[37] Assimilation to the divine is to make our own life a copy of the Supreme Being – despite the utter difference between the transcendent unknowable divine and the created nature of human being. To one purified of emotions and negative habits, love alone will remain, Gregory's vision melding Platonic motifs with Paul's hymn to love in 1 Corinthians 13.

The resurrection body, despite being woven from the very same particles of matter which now weigh us down, will be restored to us with a brighter and more entrancing beauty, its threads worked up into something more subtle and ethereal. For the soul still wrapped in earthly passions there will be agonized struggle when God is drawing it to the divine self and scraping the foreign matter off by main force – the analogy with metal dross being purified in fire creates the impression of a Platonic version of hell. But Gregory soon makes it clear that the Platonic idea of the pre-existent soul dragged down into the material world is inconsistent with the notion of God as the Creator of the whole universe out of nothing. Nature and scripture alike point to the hope that in the resurrection we are born again in our original splendour.

Thus Gregory of Nyssa demonstrates how deep the connection was between creation and resurrection, and how, despite Platonism, *creatio ex nihilo* made the union of body and soul essential to humankind, a creature made and redeemed by God for life eternal.

1.3 Augustine of Hippo

So does the work of Augustine. His thinking in the final book of the *City of God*[38] is clearly indebted to this tradition, though developed in

---

[37] See Chapter 4.

[38] *City of God* XXII, though earlier books, e.g. X, XIII, XX and XXI, anticipate some of the material. Latin text: B. Dombart and A. Kalb (eds.), *De Civitate Dei*, CCL. ET: Henry Bettenson, in *Pelican Classics* (Harmondsworth: Penguin, 1972).

his own inimitable way, with much reference to scripture, along with asides targeted at Platonists. Their views he thought should logically lead to Christian truth, but they assert that 'escape from any kind of body is an essential condition for our happiness', whereas Christians affirm that 'this body will be incorruptible and immortal and will present no obstacle to that contemplation by which the soul is fixed on God'.[39]

Augustine's understanding may be captured in the following points:

- Created existence itself is the most powerful testimony for belief in the physical resurrection of Christ, the coming resurrection to the new age of humankind and the immortality of the body.[40] God's promises are to be relied upon, God being the originator of creation, with all its marvels and surprises,[41] and creation's goodness being rooted in God.[42]
- There is resurrection of the soul from the death of irreligion and wickedness to righteousness and faith here and now – a resurrection of mercy. The second resurrection is of judgement; anyone not wanting to be condemned then, must rise up in the first. The resurrection to come is of bodies; through fire their corruptible elements will perish, and by a miraculous transformation their substance suited to our immortal bodies.[43] Objections to the idea that bodies and material flesh could belong to heaven are dismissed – you cannot set limits to God's power, as if God were unable to make bodies capable of dwelling in the heavens.[44]
- The classic problems of people being consumed by wild beasts or fire, or drowned, or born with defects receive the classic answer: nothing is beyond the resources of the Creator. The original substance of the person will be re-used rather as an artist re-uses or re-mixes material to produce a work without defects. The almighty Artist can correct all disharmony and distortion, while retaining

---

[39] *Ibid.* x.29.　　[40] *Ibid.* xxii.4, 24.　　[41] *Ibid.* xxii.1–3.
[42] *Ibid.* xi.24.　　[43] *Ibid.* xx.6, 16.　　[44] *Ibid.* xxii.4, 11.

the marks of the glorious wounds of the martyrs. The same flesh
will arise, re-formed as a spiritual body, the grace of which Augustine cannot describe because he has had no experience of it.[45]

- Other quibbles designed to derail resurrection – such as, 'What
about abortions or miscarriages?' or 'What will be the height and
size of the resurrection body?' – are met by appeal to the apostolic
statement that we shall all attain to the stature of the full maturity
of Christ.[46] To reach that stature and be shaped in his likeness refers
not so much to literal size as to the inner person and the condition
of immortality.[47] No weakness will persist; sexual differentiation
will, though there will be no lust or childbirth, so the female
organs will be part of a new beauty arousing praises of God 'for
his wisdom and compassion, in that he not only created out of
nothing but freed from corruption that which he created'.[48] The
Body of Christ is what is meant by perfect humanity – so the
gradual building up of the church is what will find fulfilment at
the resurrection.[49] When Augustine attempts a description,[50] it is
of a society in heaven, which is genuinely a body politic, at peace
and bound in the closest possible harmony, where God is the goal
of all longings, and 'we shall see him for ever, love him without
satiety and praise him without weariness'.

This position is remarkable. Augustine's first instinct was to place
sensible and material reality well below the intellectual in the hierarchy of existence, treating it as a drag downwards, and arguing in
Platonic fashion for 'the indestructibility of the soul as a philosoph-
ically evident truth',[51] rooting the soul's immortality in its creation
in the image of God and natural kinship to the transcendent world

---

[45] *Ibid.* XXII.12–14, 19–20.   [46] *Ibid.* XXII.12.   [47] *Ibid.* XXII.15.
[48] *Ibid.* XXII.17.   [49] *Ibid.* XXII.18.   [50] *Ibid.* XXII.30.
[51] Brian E. Daley, *The Hope of the Early Church* (Cambridge University Press, 1991),
p. 142. See also Daley, 'Resurrection' in Fitzgerald, *Augustine through the Ages*; other
entries on 'Soul', 'Body' and 'Anthropology' helpfully trace Augustine's developing
views.

of truth and beauty. In the 390s he could suggest that being 'raised a spiritual body', as Paul suggested in 1 Corinthians 15, implied a lack of material flesh and blood, given the words 'flesh and blood will not inherit the Kingdom of God'.[52] Later, however, he speaks of spiritual flesh.[53] Over the years he alluded to resurrection in sermons and other ecclesiastical writings, but not until the *City of God* did he fully set out the Christian critique of Platonism and explore the integration of soul and body as the ultimate human reality to be realized at the resurrection.[54] But now Augustine's vision, despite all the oddities and speculations which discussion of bodily resurrection keeps raising, is fully informed by the power of God the Creator so to transform the whole person that the goal of the original creation is realized, beyond time in eternity.

1.4 Appropriation?

Nowadays cultural pressures have turned attention away from our ultimate destiny to survival in this world. With massive reaction against the 'otherworldliness' of 'pie-in-the-sky-when-you-die', death, endlessly postponed by the successes of medical science, has become the taboo subject, though, paradoxically, popular sentiments about souls going to heaven persist, along with vague beliefs in reincarnation. It must seem perverse to suggest that this ancient connection between creation and resurrection might be of significance in our context. Yet my contention is that, for Christians, reflection on the ultimate destiny of humanity genuinely clarifies fundamental aspects of human being in the here and now.

To some extent I am anticipated by David Kelsey's work, *Eccentric Existence.*[55] Like Gregory of Nyssa he recognizes that the fulfilment

---

[52] 1 Corinthians 15.50.   [53] *City of God* xxii.21.
[54] I am indebted to the work of my graduate student, Rowena Pailing, for demonstrating the exceptional character of the *City of God* in this respect.
[55] David Kelsey, *Eccentric Existence: A Theological Anthropology*, 2 vols. (Louisville, KY: Westminster John Knox Press, 2009).

of God's promises for humanity is not simply a reversal of the fall but rather the outworking of God's creative intention. He challenges the 'binary structure' of theology: nature v. grace, law v. gospel. For him there are three poles to be considered, and these three, the protological, eschatological and soteriological, all express different ways in which humanity is related to the Trinitarian God. This interesting turn in systematic theology comes after a period which produced various theologies of hope, and Kelsey's treatment owes much to a reading of scripture that emphasizes realized eschatology; but he finds inadequate theologies of hope focussed on this-worldly liberation. So rehabilitation of resurrection proves vital.

What then might be clarified by the connection between creation and resurrection? First, it reinforces the sheer giftedness of human existence. Students of the Bible have long been invited to distinguish between the resurrection of the body and the immortality of the soul, the latter being foreign to the biblical texts and read into them under Platonic influence – we noted Tatian's parallel rejection of the soul's immortality. Yet in popular parlance dualism reigns.[56] With reference to persons with profound learning disabilities a nun once said in my hearing, 'You can see the soul peeping out of their eyes.' A woman whose life spanned the twentieth century was heard to say, after suffering a stroke in her nineties, 'I've had enough of this old body.' The Cartesian distinction between mind and body allows us to treat bodies, distinct from the 'real person', as mechanisms to be medically fixed. Somehow this 'real person' is supposed to transcend the body and exist in its own right. What the link between creation and resurrection does is to challenge that persistent intuition from a quite fundamental theological perspective. Life depends on the Creator; renewed life will likewise depend on God's will to re-create. Existence is not a right, but sheer gift. That should transform attitudes to life, and how it is lived, here and now.

---

[56] Hence the need for Nancey Murphy's book, *Bodies and Souls, or Spirited Bodies?* (Cambridge University Press, 2006).

The second implication is the sanctity of bodies, and of human beings as embodied persons. Speculation about the resurrection body has never been very edifying. Parallel to those patristic assertions about bodies eaten by sea monsters is the report of a sermon heard in the 1920s which depicted the resurrection in terms of the severed limbs of soldiers, wounded in World War I, flying through the air to be joined up together again. It is probably wise to remain agnostic. Yet there is a necessary connection between our physical constitution and our personality. Not for nothing did the fathers speak of the martyrs retaining the scars of their wounds; nor is it insignificant that stories of the resurrected Christ show him appearing with the wounds in his hands, his feet and his side. What has been experienced in this life shapes our being, and we would not be ourselves if the promise that sorrow and sighing will cease meant that past suffering, or even past limitation, would be entirely superseded.

Arthur's limited experience, limited above all in ability to process the world external to himself, is a crucial element in who he is, in his real personhood. An ultimate destiny in which he was suddenly 'perfected' (whatever that might mean) is inconceivable – for he would no longer be Arthur but some other person. His limited embodied self is what exists, and what will be must be in continuity with that. There will also be discontinuities – the promise of resurrection is of transcendence of our mortal 'flesh and blood' state. So there's hope for transformation of this life's limitations and vulnerabilities, of someone like Arthur receiving greater gifts while truly remaining himself. Perhaps the transformation to be hoped for is less intellectual or physical advance and more the kind of thing anticipated in the present when the fruits of the Spirit are realized in relationships.

For, meanwhile, the promise of resurrection makes his limited, embodied being sacred, here and now. This is one of the great insights of the L'Arche communities: beauty is perceived in damaged bodies. Arthur's carers share the L'Arche experience when feeding him and preparing his twisted and impaired body for bed. In the everydayness of attending to bodily functions, eating and defecating, washing and dressing, touching and caressing, the sanctity of bodies is acknowledged, in a context in which their transformation is not through miracles, but through the recognition of God's love and power in mutual need. It's no accident that washing one another's feet has been developed as a paraliturgy in the L'Arche communities; for here in community bodily dependence on one another is sanctified, and a shift in values enabled – away from individualism, dominance, competitiveness, to community, mutuality. At a meeting at L'Arche some years ago, some 'wise sayings' emerged:[57]

> Community means you never suffer alone.
> What is really human is the capacity to ask for help, and that is the gift of the unlikely givers.
> *Moi-même tout seule pas capable* (me alone can't do it).
> I smile, therefore you are.

Indeed, the third important observation is the social or corporate dimension of human being. We belong to one another quite fundamentally – the utter dependence of someone like Arthur testifies to the illusion of autonomy. The resurrection is not just about the discrete individual but, as Augustine recognized, about the community which is the body of Christ, or the city of God. That, too, should affect our understanding of human life on earth. Again the L'Arche communities provide a sign of our interdependence, our need for mutuality, of the giving and receiving at the heart of relationships, of the possibility of sensing the presence of God in the gaze of a person with Down's syndrome. The link between creation and resurrection enables the discernment of human values, such as love, joy, peace, patience, kindness, generosity, faithfulness, gentleness and self-control,[58] as fruits of the Spirit and anticipations of God's future in the present.

[57] Frances Young (ed.), *Encounter with Mystery: Reflections on L'Arche and Living with Disability* (London: DLT 1997), p. xi.
[58] Listed in Galatians 5.22–3 as fruits of the Spirit.

Finally, resurrection presupposes mortality and essential creatureliness, so challenging the perennial human tendency to create
hubristic accounts of what we are, then to act on our apparent superiority to other creatures. The modern pursuit of 'superman' needs
to be offset by a rediscovery of finitude, of respect for nature and of
'doxological gratitude'[59] for the present life we have been given, with
all its vulnerabilities and its inevitable end in death.

II The human creature among creatures

II.1 *The distinctiveness of humankind*

Augustine, in his unfinished 'literal' commentary on Genesis, notes[60]
that 'man was made on the same day as the beasts', observing all are
land animals. However, 'in other cases God said *Let it be made, and it
was made*, while here God said *Let us make*'; Augustine deduces that
the Holy Spirit wished to suggest the superiority of human nature.
This is reinforced by 'Let us make man in our image and likeness',
which refers to 'the innermost and principal element in humanity',
that is, 'the mind', or rational nature.[61]

> It is from this element, after all, which holds the leading place in
> human nature, which separates it from that of the brute beasts, that
> the worth of the whole human being is to be reckoned. The other
> things in us, though beautiful in their kind, are still common to us
> and animals, and therefore are to be prized cheaply.

Augustine acknowledges that there may be a physical representation
of this difference in that 'the human body is constituted to stand erect'
and look up to the sky, while 'the bodies of other animals . . . are laid
out prone on their bellies', but he is a bit wary, not wanting to suggest
that the *body* is some kind of image of the incorporeal divine being.

---

[59] A key phrase in Kelsey, *Eccentric Existence.*
[60] *Unfinished Literal Commentary* 16, 55–6, 60.   [61] Cf. Chapter 4.

Augustine's second attempt at a 'literal' commentary on Genesis reaches similar overall conclusions.[62] Focussing on the authority given to humankind over all other creatures, fishes, birds and land animals, he sees this as:

> giving us to understand . . . that it was in the very factor in which he surpasses non-rational animate beings that man was made to God's image. That, of course, is reason itself, or mind or intelligence.

Conflating Ephesians 4.23–4 and Colossians 3.10 so as to associate the renewal of the mind with renewal according to the image of him who created him, Augustine argues that this 'makes it plain enough just in what part man was created to God's image – that it was not in the features of the body but in a certain form of the illuminated mind'.

Parallel but not identical moves were made by Gregory of Nyssa as he completed Basil's *Hexaemeron* with his own study of the creation of humankind. He opens by describing humanity as the greatest wonder of the world, the human creature alone being made like God. Creation as a whole was prepared for humankind, who was to be its ruler. Genesis 1.26 indicates the unique nature and status of humankind within the created order: the autonomous soul can exercise sovereignty because it is in the image of the sovereign of all. God is mind, word, love, all-seeing and all-hearing; in humanity these divine capacities are imitated.[63] Gregory turns to the differences between humanity and other creatures, adopting a number of ancient philosophical commonplaces: uprightness, lack of defence from cold and predators, dexterous hands. These demonstrate human capacity to tame creatures providentially adapted to serve them. Moses' order of creation, beginning with the vegetative and ascending *via* the beasts to rational beings, is confirmed by the fact that there are three orders of soul: the nutritive, the sensitive and the intellectual. The highest order of bodily life is found in humanity, which combines all

[62] *Literal Meaning* iii.20, 30.   [63] *On the Making* i–v.

these forms of soul.[64] 'Since man is a rational animal, the instrument of his body must be made suitable for the use of reason.'[65]

Gregory scorns pagan writers who call humanity a *micros cosmos* – a mini-universe; that is to dignify the human with the attributes of a gnat or a mouse.[66] The greatness of humankind lies not in likeness to the created world, but in being the image of the Creator. But how can this mortal, passible, short-lived being be the image of one who is immortal, pure and everlasting? Gregory distinguishes Genesis 1.26 from Genesis 1.27: the intellectual element, humanity like to God, preceded the 'irrational' which is characterized by its polarization into male and female – sexuality was a concession to the fallen state of humanity which God foreknew. In spite of seeing humankind as the crown of creation, in spite of describing the human body as perfectly adapted for the operations of mind,[67] Gregory is unhappy about the things shared with animals. Human being is two-fold, the mean between the divine, incorporeal nature and the irrational life of animal creatures, with a tendency to be dominated not by the rational soul but the irrational passions shared with the beasts. Even the intellect can be dragged down and made brutish, though this is not the ultimate destiny of human beings.

The crucial point for Gregory is that human beings, composed of 'lower' and 'higher' elements, have to make choices between carnal pleasures and spiritual perfection. Yet the human creature was made for royalty: his 'purple' is virtue, his 'sceptre' immortality, his 'crown' righteousness.[68] His royal prerogative is autonomy, his own will his ruler. Created last as king and freely pursuing his own ends, the human being is the image of the one who rules over all.

Exegesis of Genesis led Gregory and Augustine to make such comments on the distinctiveness of human nature within the order of creation. From the same period comes a more formal treatise on the

---

[64] *Ibid.* VII–IX.   [65] *Ibid.* VIII.8.   [66] *Ibid.* XVI.   [67] *Ibid.* VII–IX.   [68] *Ibid.* IV.

nature of humanity from Nemesius of Emesa.[69] This is a summation of ancient reflection on what it means to be human, reporting the views of various philosophers and theologians and purporting to arrive at a Christian synthesis. Here are standard commonplaces: 'Laughter is a peculiar mark of man's being,' and 'It is peculiar to man to learn arts and sciences.' The truly distinguishing characteristic is, of course, rationality. Humanity is set on the boundary between the phenomenal and the intelligible, so indicating the unity of creation and the interlinking of every order of reality. Proofs from observation of nature demonstrate that there is no clear division between the inanimate, the nutritive, the animal and the rational orders of creation; and this proves that the whole universe is the creation of one God. Nemesius acknowledges the authority of Aristotle, while observing, as Gregory had done, that this justifies the order of the Mosaic narrative. Further scriptural texts indicate that humanity lies on the border between the rational and the irrational. The crucial link in the hierarchy of created orders of being, humankind is a *micros cosmos*, bearing the image of the whole creation in its own nature by its very combination of the intellectual and physical, Nemesius here differing from Gregory. Like Gregory, however, he regards the natural world as created for human benefit, and affirms human pre-eminence among creatures in skills and authority. A link in the hierarchy, humankind is distinguished, not just from animals, but from other rational creatures such as angels. So among the 'choice prerogatives' which 'are shared by no other creature' are these:

> Man only, on repenting, can gain forgiveness; and only man's body, though mortal, is immortalized. This privilege of the body is for the soul's sake. So likewise, the soul's privilege is on account of the body, for it is only man, among rational beings, that has this unique

[69] Nemesius, *On the Nature of Humankind:* Greek text: M. Morani (ed.), *Nemesius: De Natura Hominis* (Leipzig: Teubner, 1987); ET: W. Telfer, *Cyril of Jerusalem and Nemesius of Emesa, LCC.*

privilege of claiming forgiveness by repenting. Neither demons nor angels repent and are forgiven.[70]

So Nemesius, too, adopted the eschatological perspective and wedded it to his view of humanity as the one creature compounded of corporeal and incorporeal.

II.2 Body and soul: the composite constitution of human nature

The fathers, adopting the classic positions of antique philosophy, took it for granted that a human being was composed of soul and body. The opening words of Nemesius' treatise capture this consensus. 'General consent' is 'that the soul deserves more regard than the body, and that, indeed, the body is only an instrument employed by the soul', the proof of this being death: once the soul has left, 'the body lies completely still and passive, just like a workman's tools after he has gone away and left them lying'. Nemesius' main interest was humanity's place in the universe and the experience of making moral decisions, but he realizes that these matters require an understanding of the human constitution, a complex subject.

So the bulk of his work treats various ways of analysing the components which make up a human being and their various functions: first the soul, then its relationship with the body, then the body and the elements of which it is composed, then sense-perception, the imagination, the functions of the intellect and the different capacities of soul, then passions and the irrational soul, nutrition, respiration, generation, and so on. He reviews a wide range of options from the pre-Socratic philosophers to his own time, and then gives his own view, often that of Galen. The soul's nature and the manner of its union with the body were matters not easily resolved. Nemesius reviews the following questions: is the soul corporeal or incorporeal? Is the soul real – that is, a substance? Or is it harmony

---

[70] *Ibid.* 7.

or temperament or 'form' of the body? What is the origin of the soul? Is there more than one kind of soul – rational and irrational, for instance? Are there many individual souls, or is there one 'world-soul'? Nemesius concludes, on the basis of Plato's arguments, that the soul is incorporeal and immortal, yet affirms in the end: 'for us the sufficient demonstration of the soul's immortality is the teaching of Holy Scripture, which is self-authenticating because inspired by God'.[71] So, unlike modern commentators (or indeed Tatian), Nemesius thinks the immortality of the soul is scriptural doctrine which contrasts with the views of Aristotle, the Stoics and Galen. Yet the soul is no simple entity[72] – it has rational and irrational parts, and the interaction of the various faculties of soul with each other and the body are sometimes conscious, sometimes unconscious. The irrational is partly susceptible to reason's control, partly not. The elements (earth, air, fire and water) constituting the body have an effect on human temperament, and emotion provides the driving force of action. Thus, 'passions' are necessary to human life (a corrective to the widespread ascetic emphasis on *apatheia*);[73] there are good as well as evil passions, and pleasures are necessary and natural to the good life which is directed towards divine learning and the virtues.[74] Only in the light of this complex analysis of human being can conclusions be drawn about human responsibilities and moral potentialities. Human behaviour is affected by temperament, upbringing and habit; but humankind has free will to make choices in certain spheres, and ideally rationality should be in control.

While Nemesius' underlying conception is that a human being has a footing in two orders of reality, his physiological statements presuppose a psychosomatic unity:

> Whatever movement takes place by the operation of nerves and muscles involves the intervention of soul, and is accomplished by an act of will.[75]

---

[71] *Ibid.* 19.   [72] *Ibid.* 34.   [73] Cf. Chapter 6.
[74] *Nature of Humankind* 36–9.   [75] *Ibid.* 43.

Soul provides the *energeia* in respiration: panting and sobbing accompany moments of grief, and soul keeps respiration going during sleep, since it is essential for human life. So the physical and the psychical are intimately woven together. Thus:

> a living creature is composed of soul and body; the body is not a living creature by itself, nor is the soul, but soul and body together.[76]

This picture of the soul pervading the body is remarkably similar to our conception of the central nervous system.

How to give an account of this union is the thing which Nemesius finds most puzzling[77] – he sticks to the dichotomist view rather than a more complicated one (a trichotomist analysis in terms of body, soul and spirit) simply because that would make the union even more problematic. The union is a puzzle because there are no natural analogies. Normally what comes together to form a single entity is made completely one only if the constituents undergo change. So how is it possible for body and soul to be united without the body losing its corporeity or the soul ceasing to be incorporeal and self-subsistent? Juxtaposition is not a true unity. So, having ruled out juxtaposition and mixture, Nemesius adopts the Platonic view that the soul 'puts on' the body. Intelligibles can unite with things adapted to receive them and, without undergoing change, remain unconfused while in union. The soul is united to the body through 'sympathy' – the whole living being 'sympathizes . . . as if one thing'. The soul, itself incorporeal, is yet in every part of the body, giving it life and movement, while also being transcendent, that is, not confined to some portion of space (the evidence for this is dreams). The soul is said to be in the body, not because it is located in it, but because of its habitual relation of presence there.

Nemesius provides the most systematic Christian appraisal of the human constitution, and he not only defends the compound unity of the human being during life on earth, but also speaks of the body

---

[76] *Ibid.* 49.   [77] *Ibid.* 20–2.

being 'immortalized' – a 'privilege of the body' which is 'for the soul's sake'.[78] Resurrection meant for him, as for others considered earlier, that human nature would be reconstituted as a complex being, body and soul. A similar account is found in Gregory of Nyssa's *On the Making of Humankind*. His treatment is more exegetical, but he too draws on contemporary philosophy to describe human anatomical functioning and the relationship of bodily activities with the motivating power of soul.[79] The mind works through sense-perception, though it is impossible to identify the location of soul with any particular organ. He treats tears and laughter, sleep and dreams; and then in a long final section summarizes a mass of information about respiration, the functions of the heart, liver and brain, the natural combinations of heat and cold, moist and dry, which constitute the body, and so on. That the power of soul is interwoven with the body is established truth, but beyond rational conception. His account of the unity is very similar to that of Nemesius, again inviting comparison with our view of the central nervous system:

> the root cause of our constitution is neither a soul without a body, nor a body without soul, but that from ensouled and living bodies, our nature is generated at the first as living and ensouled being.[80]

For all that, Gregory thinks that, while one may speak of the nutritive and sensitive aspects of soul, really the word 'soul' should only be properly applied to the intellectual.[81] The soul finds perfection in what is rational; mind may use the body as a musical instrument perfectly adapted to express its music, but mind itself is invisible and incorporeal. Beauty, goodness, intellect – these are the Platonic notions which Gregory dwells upon; and these are the characteristics he sees reflected in the divine image in humanity; 'likeness to God', a phrase from Plato's *Theaetetus*, had long been correlated with Genesis 1.26–7. Gregory is less than happy with the 'animal nature'

---

[78] *Ibid.* 7.   [79] *On the Making* IX–XIII.   [80] *Ibid.* XXX.
[81] *Ibid.* XV.1–2. Cf. V, IX, XI, XII.9–11, XVII–XVIII.

of humankind, suggesting that the two-fold nature means we have a choice, to be like the angels or like the beasts; in the end the needs and desires of the flesh – for food, for sex – will be transcended. Yet he recognizes the essential constitution of humankind as composite, and the reconstitution of that compound character is affirmed as humanity's destiny.

II.3 A patristic contribution to contemporary debate?

II.3.1 Defending the soul

Serious theological anthropology long since abandoned the soul–body dichotomy. Pannenberg wrote in the 1960s:

> there is no independent reality of a 'soul' in contrast to the body, just as there is not a body that is merely mechanically or unconsciously moved. Both are abstractions. The only reality is the unity of the living creature called man.[82]

Kelsey's theological anthropology likewise eschews resort to the soul–body dualism, consigning it to pre-modern theology and indicating how it is problematic. He treats the human creature as a 'personal living body' rather than as an embodied soul, citing the:

> incommensurability of the theoretical frameworks in which pre-modern and modern cultures describe and explain inorganic and organic matter, the nature of life and what happens in death.[83]

Biblical criticism has demonstrated that, contrary to the reading of Nemesius and Gregory, scripture does not give authority to the soul–body analysis; indeed, the Hebrew Bible does not support anything like the separable soul of Platonic philosophy. Theologians

---

[82] Wolfhart Pannenberg, *What is Man? Contemporary Anthropology in Theological Perspective*, ET: Duane A. Priebe (Philadelphia: Fortress Press, 1970; German original 1962).
[83] Kelsey, *Eccentric Existence*, p. 37.

must surely start by taking seriously the way in which scripture is now read, rather than respecting assumptions which reflect the 'Hellenizing' of the Gospel, and then engage with the understanding of human nature current in our post-Cartesian, post-Darwinian, post-Freudian world.

Such a procedure would, in fact, follow the same method as the fathers, who engaged with the best knowledge of their own time and faced the challenge of bringing that together with what scripture seemed to mean when read in their context; but that very parallel reveals the necessary provisionality of theological proposals. There might be a danger that, by accepting that the soul–body dichotomy is out of date, theologians just let the scientific position go by default, laying theology open to an avowedly non-metaphysical position such as that of Don Cupitt – is it really true that naturalism is the only possible stance and 'after Darwin religion must reconcile itself to this earth'?[84] It must be worth enquiring what the patristic talk of soul enabled, and whether that should be retrieved. In antiquity 'soul' implied recognition that each of us is, and is not, entirely identified with the body which we 'inhabit', with its needs and cravings, even its limitations to a particular place and time. The 'I' that remembers, makes decisions and hopes, as well as feeling hungry or lost, experiences itself as both being a body and having a body. Whatever our concept of human nature, it must be able to account not only for our self-consciousness and morality, but also that sense of transcendence. So what we need to consider is the work that the ancient analysis in terms of body and soul actually did.

In fact abandonment of the soul is by no means universal, either at the popular or the philosophical level. Keith Ward provides good reasons for not being too hasty. What he fears is that:

> the sense of moral obligation, and of the uniqueness of the human soul in responding to it, will disappear in the rising tide of realization

[84] Don Cupitt, *Only Human* (London: SCM Press, 1985), p. 56.

that human beings are without purpose, without uniqueness, without future, in a world originating by chance and ruled by necessity.[85]

Against Nietzsche and Freud, he affirms the significance of conscience, freedom and responsibility. Against Darwinism and behaviourists, he exposes the reductionism implied by chance mutation or determinist cause-and-effect, appealing to consciousness and introspection. Against sociobiology and the presumption of nothing but social conditioning, he points to the purposive action of rational beings by contrast with animal instinct and impulse, and draws out the uniqueness and dignity of each subject within society. Against mechanistic theories of brain activity and the pervasive analogy with computers, he observes that 'the most important characteristic of the soul is its capacity for transcendence', 'its ability to stand outside the physical processes that generate it':

> It is distinguished, not by being quite different in kind from its material environment, but by reflecting and acting in that environment in a more conscious goal-oriented way.[86]

> The transcendence of the soul is its self-determination towards the true, the beautiful and the good.[87]

To believe in the soul is:

> to believe that man is essentially a subject, a centre of consciousness and reason, who transcends all objective analysis, who is always more than can be defined, predicted or controlled. In his essential subjectivity, man is a subject who has the capacity to be free and responsible – to be guided by moral claims, to determine his own nature by response to those claims.[88]

All of this, Ward believes, is only secured by belief that:

---

[85] Keith Ward, *Defending the Soul* (London: Hodder and Stoughton, 1992), p. 131.
[86] *Ibid.*, p. 142.   [87] *Ibid.*, p. 144.   [88] *Ibid.*, p. 119.

The God who is the spirit of compassion and love is a God who gives us, and requires of us, freedom and the awesome power of self-determination in relation to absolute standards of moral goodness.[89]

Ward's primary concerns, however, are voiced by others without his interest in defending God or 'soul' language – Kenan Malik, for example, a writer with a background in neurobiology and psychology, who writes:

> Alone among terrestrial matter, human beings are both subject, and object. We are biological, and hence physical, beings, and under the purview of biological and physical laws. But we are also conscious beings with purpose and agency, traits the possession of which allow us to understand the kind of creatures we are and to design ways of breaking out of the constraints of biological and physical laws. We are, in other words, both inside nature and outside it.[90]

Drawing on a wide range of disciplines – the social sciences, history and philosophy – Malik shows that human attributes and behavioural patterns are both 'naturally given' and 'socially constructed'.[91] Materialist philosophers have not, in his opinion, discovered a fully materialist way of describing the human mind: 'insofar as they portray the human being as a natural machine, so they have discarded the human being as a conscious subject'.[92] Furthermore, that conscious subject only makes sense of itself insofar as it 'lives in and relates to a community of thinking, feeling, talking beings'. Humans are 'symbolic creatures, with language, self-awareness and a social existence'.[93] Language is public, and so, in

---

[89] Ibid., p. 116.

[90] Kenan Malik, Man, Beast and Zombie: What Science Can and Cannot Tell us about Human Nature (London: Phoenix, 2000), p. 339.

[91] Ibid., p. 45.   [92] Ibid., pp. 50–1.

[93] Ibid., pp. 219–20. Cf. Mary Midgley, Beast and Man: The Roots of Human Nature (Sussex: Harvester, 1978; rev. edn. Abingdon: Routledge, 1995; reissued 2002, reprinted 2010).

some sense, is the mind, he suggests: 'what we know is embodied not just in our brains', for 'the ascription of meaning is a social process, not an individual one'. Most people will have some idea what DNA is, but only biologists have a clear representation of what the composition and function of the molecule DNA actually is. So meaning is given by 'knowledge distributed . . . through society'.[94] This is reminiscent of the ancient speculation that there is a kind of universal soul which transcends the souls embodied in individual persons.

For Malik, as for Ward, the most crucial aspect of mind is the capacity of human beings to make moral choices.[95] The problem with naturalism is that it encourages people to see themselves as victims of fate – it is 'all in the genes', people think, or 'evolution explains things like violent behaviour'. But human beings can learn to control impulses. Malik deploys as an analogy a description of John Wayne taking control of a team of runaway horses in the film *Stagecoach*: the self is like a cerebral John Wayne, he suggests – the maturing brain 'learns to control itself, and it is that process of self-control that we call the self'. Intriguingly, his analogy re-plays the Platonic tripartite soul, reason, the charioteer, controlling the emotions, the impulsive and reactive horses that impel human action. 'Soul' and 'body' may be 'abstractions', but they also illuminate the ambiguous experience of being human, of being a self-reflective subject with moral agency. Modern discussion cannot avoid reflecting the debates of antiquity.

Yet is this 'subject' the same as the 'soul'? At first sight it might appear that the ancient soul–body dichotomy has simply morphed into the Cartesian dualism of mind and matter, with the problem of the union of two entities remaining. However, the real 'I' became the immaterial, thinking subject with a capacity to manipulate and control physical entities – Descartes essentially treated the body as a machine. This sovereign subject or autonomous individual, able to create its own destiny, is a far cry from the fathers' conception of rationality as a transcendent or cosmic reality in which human

---

[94] *Ibid.*, pp. 327–8.   [95] *Ibid.*, p. 363.

beings participate; and, as Malik observed, 'the question of how the transcendent soul acted upon the physical body became replaced by the question of how the immaterial mind could arise out of fleshly material'.[96] Transmuted into the mind–brain problem, the search for an explanation of how the physical organ produces consciousness turned the problem upside-down compared with the puzzle as presented in the philosophical discussion of antiquity.

For meanwhile Darwin had focussed attention on humankind as belonging to the same 'tree of life' as all other living creatures, and reduction of the mind to brain functions seemed increasingly appropriate, given the similarities between animal brains, animal behaviour, animal use of tools, animal socialization, etc., and human equivalents. The soul defended by Ward is not only nearer to Descartes' 'mind' than the 'soul' of the fathers, but also emerges from the processes of physical evolution:

> The soul is not an alien intrusion into a mechanistic world. It is the culmination and realization of the principles that dimly inform what we call 'matter' at every stage of its existence. Yet, in that culmination, it is able also to transcend the material.[97]

He contrasts this with the notion of soul as 'a complete spiritual thing, with its own personality', which then God has to attach to some physical body, the soul having 'a purely external relationship to the body'. For:

> the biblical account is that man is a truly physical entity, touched with God's spirit. It is *this holistic entity* that knows and thinks and decides; yet this entity is more than electrons or chemicals or genes or psychological states or social roles.[98]

Essentially, then, Ward adopts the same idea of emergence as Malik, and the same non-dualist position as theologians who reject 'soul' language. Is there any difference between his position and

[96] *Ibid.*, p. 37.   [97] Ward, *Defending the Soul*, pp. 142–3.   [98] *Ibid.*, p. 147.

that of Pannenberg and Kelsey? The grounds for rejecting dualism, both scientific and philosophical, are effectively argued by Nancey Murphy:

> *The physicalist thesis is that as we go up the hierarchy of increasingly complex organisms, all of the other capacities once attributed to the soul will also turn out to be products of complex organisation, rather than properties of a nonmaterial entity.*[99]

> If we discard the concept of soul as unnecessary, this is not to discard higher human capacities, but rather to open ourselves to wonder at the fact that creatures made of the dust of the ground have been raised so high.[100]

Each theological treatment in the end refers to the Christian tradition of physical resurrection, so admitting, like the fathers, that dualism, though the most prevalent view over centuries of Christian reflection, hardly provides an adequate account of the human creature. All talk of emergence, of the continuities between our physical, psychological, moral and spiritual being. The physicalist position offers an important critique of the elitism and individualism inherent in Cartesian dualism, while essentially converging with the more complex patristic analysis explored earlier – did we not find their treatment of the soul remarkably like our understanding of the central nervous system?

11.3.2 Human distinctiveness

Both Ward and Malik, writing in the 1990s, treat animals by contrast with humanity as subject to instinct, or 'zombies'. Neither took account of the work of Mary Midgley, who already in the 1970s had begun her book, *Man and Beast*, with the words:

---

[99] Murphy, *Bodies and Souls*, p. 57; italics original.   [100] *Ibid.*, p. 146.

We are not just rather like animals; we are animals. Our difference from other species may be striking, but comparisons with them have always been, and must be, crucial to our view of ourselves.

However complex our nature, she suggests, 'our dignity arises *within* nature, not against it', and we should not 'feel our dignity threatened by our continuity with the animal world'.[101] She provides a list of the special marks of humankind, which noticeably overlaps with suggestions made in antiquity: 'conceptual thought and reason, language, culture, self-consciousness, tool-using, productivity, laughter, a sense of the future'. She treats these as a non-exhaustive cluster – indeed, someone who had all those characteristics 'but none of the normal human affections' would be classed as 'inhuman',[102] while studies of animals show that using tools, language and even a certain practical intelligence are present in a less complex form in non-human creatures. Social bonds structure animal lives, especially those who care for their young; '*communication, and therefore intelligence, develops only where there are these long-standing deep relationships*'.[103] Speech, rationality and culture have simpler pre-human forms. Midgley refuses to be reductive – life is not simply about survival, and creatures have divergent and conflicting desires; genes, sociobiology[104] and neurology cannot short-circuit the conceptual questions about motives, ethics and consciousness.

Since Midgley, research in neuroscience and evolutionary psychology has demonstrated the significance of animal cognition and sociability as precursors of more sophisticated human versions. Yet the issues remain far from resolved. A prolific contributor, Raymond

---

[101] *Beast and Man*, pp. 187–8. For a post-modern take on this continuity, see Joanna Bourke, *What It Means to be Human: Reflections from 1791 to the Present* (London: Virago, 2011).

[102] *Ibid.*, p. 198.   [103] *Ibid.*, p. 265; italics original.

[104] As Midgley completed her first draft, E. O. Wilson published *Sociobiology: The New Synthesis* (Cambridge, MA: Harvard University Press, 1975).

Tallis[105] contests the materialist reductionism that identifies mind with brain, emphasizing human intentionality and morality over against blind cause-and-effect, and tracing the contradictions inherent in the attempt to explain consciousness as simply brain events. He characterizes the mind in terms of the human constructed world of politics, science, literature and religion, deploring the idea that biology can take over all other disciplines. He insists that, though we are animals, it does not follow that:

> I am "just an animal" . . . Every seemingly animal need or appetite – for food, water, warmth – is profoundly changed in humans. We appropriate the biological givens and subordinate them to distinctively, uniquely human ends.[106]

In an earlier meditation entitled *Michelangelo's Finger: An Exploration of Everyday Transcendence*,[107] he highlighted the distinctiveness of the human ability to point, building up from that an account of how we alone 'interact on an illuminated stage that is built up out of mutual acknowledgement': pointing presupposes another's point of view, another's need to know, the hidden existence of another mind, of realities not in our immediate purview, and the possibility of teaching and learning, not just imitating. For the retired medical doctor, Tallis, an avowed humanist and atheist, education, morality and the humanities need defending against the reductionism of popular writers like Dawkins and Dennett.[108] However, while demonstrating ever more clearly the continuities between humans

---

[105] Raymond Tallis, *Aping Mankind: Neuromania, Darwinitis and the Misrepresentation of Humanity* (Durham: Acumen, 2011).

[106] *Ibid.*, p. 149.

[107] Raymond Tallis, *Michelangelo's Finger: An Exploration of Everyday Transcendence* (London: Atlantic Books, 2010).

[108] Richard Dawkins, *The Selfish Gene* (Oxford University Press, 1976), *The Blind Watchmaker* (Harmondsworth, Penguin, 1988) and *The God Delusion*; D. Dennett, *Darwin's Dangerous Idea: Evolution and the Meaning of Life* (New York: Simon and Schuster, 1995) and *Consciousness Explained* (Harmondsworth: Penguin, 1992).

and animals,[109] biologists themselves repudiate extreme reductionist accounts, particularly in two contentious areas.

The first concerns social learning and cognition.[110] In the 1990s there emerged 'convincing experimental demonstrations of true learning by imitation in animals'. It took a 'long and complex process to establish' the 'acquisition of adaptive behaviour', but there are some convincing examples.[111] Behaviour is not just in the genes but also in response to the environment. So animals cannot simply be regarded as instinct-driven. Despite 'the apparently unique complexity and yet great adaptive utility' of human cognition, there is real potential for understanding humans by the investigation of:

> other species with cognitive complexity approaching ours, which in addition to great apes may include some other monkeys, some cetaceans, parrots, and corvids . . . Our interpretation of the evidence is that human cognition mainly evolved to acquire and manage cumulative cultural traditions.[112]

Yet, 'humans outperform animals, in most of the respects where comparison may be made', and 'the faculties of the human mind are characterized by new properties, such as verbal language and context-free thought, that couldn't easily be reduced to their prerequisites.' In other words, 'simple reductionism fails'.

---

[109] See R. E. M. Dunbar and Louise Barrett (eds.), *The Oxford Handbook of Evolutionary Psychology* (Oxford University Press, 2007); Robin Dunbar, *How Many Friends Does One Person Need? Dunbar's Number and Other Evolutionary Quirks* (London: Faber and Faber, 2010).

[110] See Cecilia M. Heyes and Bennett G. Gale, Jr (eds.), *Social Learning in Animals: The Roots of Culture* (San Diego, London, etc.: Academic Press, 1996); and Cecilia M. Heyes and Ludwig Huber (eds.), *The Evolution of Cognition* (Cambridge, MA: The MIT Press, 2000).

[111] Introduction to *Social Learning*, pp. 4 and 6.

[112] P. J. Richerson and R. Boyd, 'Climate, Culture and the Evolution of Cognition' in *Evolution of Cognition*, p. 344.

The second point concerns empathy. Biology seemed to 'justify a society based on selfish principles,'[113] since natural selection pre-supposed competitive self-interest. Many now accept, however, that the 'selfish gene' metaphor is tricky because it slams together 'two levels that biologists work so hard to keep apart': 'what drives evo-lution and what drives animal behaviour' are not the same thing, and 'the animal kingdom is full of traits that evolved for one reason but are also used for others'. So even if 'offering assistance to others evolved to serve self-interest, which it does if aimed at close rela-tives or group mates willing to return the favour', that 'doesn't mean that humans or animals only help one another for selfish reasons'. A growing collection of case-studies and observations shows that empathy is found among many animals which live in social groups, and especially among primates. Indeed:

> according to the social brain hypothesis, the advantage gained by understanding others' behaviour and intentions constituted a major driving force behind the primate brain evolution.[114]

Social relationships in their complexity stimulated the 'theory of other minds', as well as language.

In *Dependent Rational Animals*,[115] Alasdair McIntyre brings together two questions: 'Why is it important for us to attend to, and to understand what human beings have in common with mem-bers of other intelligent animal species?' and 'What makes attention to human vulnerability and disability important for moral philoso-phers?' Pre-linguistic capabilities in animals are 'preconditions for human rationality' and 'require us to think of the relationship of human beings to members of other intelligent species in terms of a

[113] Frans de Waal, *The Age of Empathy: Nature's Lessons for a Kinder Society* (London: Souvenir Press, 2009), p. x. Quotations in the rest of this paragraph from *ibid.*, pp. 40–5.
[114] *Oxford Handbook*, p. 173.
[115] Alasdair McIntyre, *Dependent Rational Animals: Why Human Beings Need the Virtues* (London: Duckworth, 1999).

scale or spectrum'.[116] The developing child moves across that spectrum as it learns. But human beings are vulnerable – indeed, there is a scale of disability on which we all find ourselves, and acknowledgement of dependence is the key to independence.[117]

McIntyre's exploration of the virtues of acknowledged dependence is profoundly significant for understanding the human condition, and doubly pertinent to reflection on the humanity of persons, like Arthur, whose development has been damaged. Arthur's pre-linguistic cognition is evidently less sophisticated than that of primates – indeed of other creatures too – as reported in scientific studies. It is hard to gauge how much he understands: there's been considerable difference of opinion among those who have loved and cared for him. He clearly recognizes places, faces and routines and, insofar as he responds to a mirror, probably has the basic prerequisites for a sense of self; but so do primates. He perhaps understands pointing, but never points himself. The first thing the human baby does is to smile: Arthur smiles and laughs, interacting with people he knows and loves; and music he invariably attends to. Responding to singing and imitating the intonation of language, he clearly belongs to the human species. We naturally presume that he is, and indeed that babies are, conscious, but what do we mean by consciousness?

Debate rages about the evolution of cognition, consciousness and culture. Dogs and cats 'respond similarly to humans to stimuli that afford us pleasure and pain', which 'suggests that they, like us, are conscious in the sense they experience feelings'. For some investigators, however, only the acquisition of language makes possible a sense of self as subject, and such a 'self concept is necessary for the experience of feelings'. There is 'evidence that associative learning may proceed in humans without conscious awareness, and that babies do not form consciously accessible memories before they acquire

[116] *Ibid.*, p. 57.   [117] *Ibid.*, p. 85.

language and construct a self'.[118] Nor is the child fully *self*-conscious before acquiring 'theory of mind', which happens no sooner than the age of 4 or 5. Arthur is a long way from reaching this – we know he recognizes people and places, but does he remember?

So should we attribute consciousness to Arthur? He must lie somewhere on a somewhat uneven spectrum of cognitive competences, compounded by his brain's less than average size and his failure to achieve developmental milestones at the usual age, this resulting in acquired physical disabilities. Even if some miracle could now provide him with a normal brain, he would not be 'normal', since he has missed out on forty and more years of learning experience. His personality is deeply affected by damage to his physical being – for he is a psychosomatic whole. Yet he bears the marks of 'transcendence' as any other human person does, held as he is within social networks and larger cultural frames. In rejecting as pre-modern the fathers' understanding of the human person as composite, Kelsey found himself obliged to affirm the 'mystery' of each personal living body. That core mystery was surely what the fathers were trying to capture with their talk of a person as an ensouled body or an embodied soul. Against idealist philosophers, and like contemporary naturalists, they were clear that humankind was a creature within the natural world which God had created, but this was somehow a special creature.

Suppose Gregory of Nyssa had been faced with the post-Darwinian question, 'Apes or Angels?' He would surely have answered, 'Both'. Indeed, neither the fathers nor the Bible itself provide endorsement for rejection of the notion that humankind belongs to the natural order; Augustine, remember, observed that humanity was created on the same day as other land animals, and the preacher in Ecclesiastes mused that God tests human beings to

---

[118] Euan M. Macphail, 'The Search for a Mental Rubicon' in *Evolution of Cognition*, p. 269.

show that they are but animals.[119] They were, of course, clear that we are not mere animals, naked apes with exceptional intelligence but no soul.

So, in our post-Cartesian, post-Darwinian world, what legacy might be salvaged from the patristic discussion? The principal benefit might be a balanced perspective, informed by patristic theological priorities. Modern philosophical and scientific discussions have inherited a tension between reductionism and exaggerated humanism. Painting with a very broad brush and acknowledging the complexities, we could say that what we now need is a mean between the Enlightenment tendency to over-estimate the superiority of human rationality and the tendency of naturalism to treat our whole being, personal and social, as explicable through biochemistry and evolutionary theory. And we need it urgently if we are to take moral responsibility for the effects of being the most successful species on earth. Ecological disaster, over-population and climate change scarcely suggest that humankind has been the royal steward of creation that the Bible and the fathers thought was the human vocation. Accepting our own creatureliness is perhaps the spiritual shift required.

III Creatureliness and the doxological imperative

III.1 The creatureliness of humankind

What did it mean to become conscious of oneself, of humanity in general, of the whole universe including the spiritual world, as being essentially creatures of the one true God, Maker of heaven and earth? It meant the transformation of the otherwise Platonic discourse of certain fourth-century fathers, Eastern and Western, and the forging of a distinctive Christian spirituality.

---

[119] Ecclesiastes 4.18–20. See Chapter 2.

The climax of Augustine's *Confessions* is a discussion of creation. Quite why lengthy explorations of memory, time and eternity, and an exposition of Genesis 1 appear at the end of a work, two-thirds of which is plausibly described as the first autobiography, is somewhat puzzling. My suggestion is that throughout Augustine was working out the implications for human being of *creatio ex nihilo*.

The opening words suggest a re-reading of the first book in terms of a reflection on creatureliness. Humanity, 'a little piece of your creation', is stirred to praise, 'because you have made us for yourself, and our heart is restless until it rests in you'. 'For Plotinus (6.7.23.4) the soul finds rest only in the One', noted Chadwick;[120] but 'the One can make no choices; it causes without creating, presides without governing, superabounds without love'.[121] By contrast Augustine invokes a God who causes as Creator and Lord of heaven and earth:

> You are God and Lord of all you have created. In you are the constant causes of inconstant things.[122]

He tells of his own birth and early years as a way of celebrating his existence and the gifts given him by God. Thus, the first book may be read as a meditation on the miracle of existence, and the paradox of a God who is 'deeply hidden yet most intimately present', without whom nothing would exist.[123]

Themes from Book I are taken up in that final book: 'You made me and, when I forgot you, you did not forget me.' Augustine has shown how God exerted pressure on him and continues to do so, constantly calling him further on the journey towards the divine self. 'To you I owe my being and the goodness of my being,' he affirms. This utter dependence on God for existence is reinforced by the reflection that neither physical matter nor the spiritual creation would exist unless

---

[120]   Henry Chadwick, ET of *Confessions* in World's Classics (Oxford University Press, 1992), Introduction, p. 3.

[121]   Edwards, *Origen against Plato*, p. 61.   [122]   *Confessions* I.vi(9).   [123]   *Ibid.* I.iv(4).

God had made it; nothing has any claim on God. The climax affirms *creatio ex nihilo*:

> Your works praise you that we may love, and we love you that your works may praise you. They have a beginning and an end in time, a rise and a fall, a start and a finish, beauty and the loss of it . . . They are made out of nothing by you . . . You made . . . the beauty of the world from formless matter – and both simultaneously so that the form followed the matter without pause or delay.[124]

Coming from nothing is precisely what produces instability and restlessness. Augustine may distinguish in classic Platonic style between the changeable and the changeless, but the thrust has shifted. A creature, inherently changeable because it has changed from nothingness into something, must keep changing in the right direction. Augustine's story, like that of the whole human race, is one of restless wandering and being brought back on track by God's providential promptings. According to Sirach 18.1, God created everything at once, but Genesis records things in a particular order, so revealing the hidden plan whereby order emerges from chaos, and saints from sinners. That the story of creation is the story of redemption justifies figural reading of Genesis 1 in terms of new creation in Christ – creation is not just a one-off event, but something that happens within time and in response to God's loving providence. Without the Word creation is inchoate and unformed; it needs to be conformed to the Word:

> by whom it was made, more and more to live by the fount of life, to see light in his light, and to become perfect, radiant with light and in complete happiness.[125]

Augustine understands himself, then, as a creature brought into being by the Creator God to whom he prays, and also as integrally part of what has been described as 'a living system destined to grow

---

[124] *Ibid.* XIII.xxxiii(48).   [125] *Ibid.* XIII.ii(3)–iii(5).

toward beauty and order, even if this beauty and order is not at any given moment apparent'.[126] Acceptance of vulnerability and mutability, in response to the creative and providential action of a God who freely loves, distinguishes Augustine's self-understanding from the intellectual mysticism of Neoplatonism, for all its surface similarities.

Those similarities he acknowledges by telling of his intellectual formation and his struggles with the problem of evil. The books of the Platonists rescue him from the Manichaean position.[127] He discovers that evil is not a substance. Sounding like a Platonist, he writes (as usual, addressing God), 'the further away from you things are, the more unlike you they become'; heaven is 'close to you', while the 'earth' is 'close to being nothing'.[128] But the implicit correlation of evil with nothingness confirms that for Augustine the creative power of God is constantly at work bringing things out of nothingness into existence, bringing order out of chaos, and good out of evil, redeeming what wanders restlessly and gets corrupted because of its inherent changeability – it is all of a piece. Creatureliness and corruptibility do not exclude goodness. The totality of creation is good, though finite, time-bound and in need of grace, indeed in need of the completion offered by the incarnation. The incarnation is what Augustine famously confessed he did not find in the Platonists, and the incarnation is indispensable to God's creative purpose because the cause of things is not descent from the One, but ascent from nothingness by the power of God's creative Word.

There is, then, a deep connection between Augustine's reassessment of the problem of evil and his discovery of what it means to be created. The doctrine of creation 'out of nothing' is fundamental to his rejection of Manichaeism and his journey beyond Platonism. The *Confessions* tells the story of this intellectual journey, but the point of the story is to celebrate what it means to be a creature in the process of being formed according to the will of the Creator.

---

[126] Rowan Williams, 'Creation' in Fitzgerald, *Augustine through the Ages*, p. 252.
[127] *Confessions* vii.ix(13)–xx(26).   [128] *Ibid.* xii.vii(7–9).

The presence of the final three books confirms that. The work as a whole is about knowing God, as also being known by God,[129] being naked before the God who is the physician of one's most intimate self, and responding to that God of mercy and grace both daily and through the course of one's life. Augustine's distinctive spirituality is rooted in creatureliness; his reflections throughout the *Confessions* are shaped by creation out of nothing.

The Cappadocians anticipated the moves traced in Augustine's *Confessions*. From *creatio ex nihilo* Gregory of Nyssa[130] deduces that, while God is immutable, created nature cannot exist without change – for its very passage from non-existence to existence is a kind of motion and change. So his spirituality expresses itself in terms of the eternal *epektasis* of an essentially limited creature. Humankind is set in the context of a creation that God calls good, an integral part of it and there to enjoy and appreciate it.[131] That had been a central theme of Basil's *Hexaemeron*. Indeed, *creatio ex nihilo* not only shifted perspective on human being itself, but also on the natural world. It stimulated that amazement and rejoicing in the beauty and harmony of the creation which is the really striking thing about the *Hexaemeron* – its tone of sheer wonder at creation, its affirmation that nothing is superfluous or wrong or out of place, everything contributing to the rich tapestry of the created order and its beauty.[132] The development of this creation spirituality is grounded in the assertions that God is the sole source (a dualism with matter, or indeed with evil, is absolutely ruled out),[133] and that this wonderful reality, created out of nothing, is finite.[134] Of Basil's work Gregory Nazianzen affirmed:

> Whenever I take his *Hexaemeron* in hand and quote its words, I am brought face to face with my Creator; I begin to understand the rationale of creation; I feel more awe than ever I did before.[135]

[129] 1 Corinthians 13.12.   [130] *On the Making* xvi.10, 12.   [131] *Ibid.* 11.
[132] E.g. *Hexaemeron* i.11; iii.10; vii *passim*; etc. Cf. Chapter 2.
[133] *Ibid.* 11.   [134] *Ibid.* i.3.   [135] *Oration* 43.67.

The Cappadocians appreciated the nature of humankind as a creature within creation, a creature which would be reconstituted at the resurrection as a finite creature ever progressing in its doxological response to the Creator.

Augustine also celebrated the natural creation in his works on Genesis,[136] making parallel claims about the beauty and harmony of the whole. In the *City of God*, he claims that the nature of things in itself, without regard to our convenience or inconvenience, gives glory to the Creator.[137] In his celebration of divine generosity in Book XXII, the sheer beauty and utility of the natural creation figures, as well as the wonderful fashioning of the human body. Despite his reputation for a pessimistic view of human nature focussed on the fall of Adam and original sin,[138] there are three features of the *City of God* which to my mind demonstrate that *creatio ex nihilo* and a sense of creatureliness remained a foundational impetus to Augustine's thinking about human being.

The first is his focus on worship; as in the *Confessions*, prayer and praise are fundamental. The true God is to be worshipped rather than false gods, on the grounds that this God is the Creator of all that is, indeed the Creator of the soul itself. Giving thanks for existence and life, celebrating the good things in human life, appreciating the wonders of the human body and of nature as a motive for praise, recognizing the blessings God bestows through creating and transforming human creatures – all this reaches its climax in the final picture of eternal felicity, rest and peace in the city of God.[139]

The second is the implicit parallel between the *City of God*'s history of the whole human race and the *Confessions'* individual story. Images of wandering, of exile and of pilgrimage are pervasive, reflecting the restlessness depicted in the *Confessions*. Augustine writes:

> There is only one unchanging Good; that is the one, true, blessed God. The things he made are good because they were made by him;

---

[136] See Chapter 2.   [137] *City of God* XII.4, 5.   [138] See Chapter 5.
[139] *City of God* IV.30; V.11; VII.5, 28, 30–1; XXII.24, 30.

but they are subject to change, because they were made not out of his being but out of nothing.[140]

Failure to adhere to God is a perversion in the rational nature – for, though changeable, it was created to obtain blessedness by adherence to the unchangeable God. The long history of the two cities illustrates the two tendencies: to turn away from God to self-love, and to allow God's grace to renew and transform.

The third feature is eschatology. The very fact of creation out of nothing is the guarantee that God's promises will be fulfilled.[141] What is needed is not escape from the body but an imperishable body. The removal of defects will 'arouse the praises of God for his wisdom and compassion, in that he not only created out of nothing but freed from corruption that which he created'. 'We cannot keep silent about the joy of our hope, because of the praise due to God.'[142]

III.2 Towards retrieval?

The doctrine of creation was a crucial factor in forging a distinctively Christian discourse, reflecting a distinctively Christian sensibility in relation to nature, alongside a distinctively Christian spirituality in relation to God. These, surely, are attitudes we need to retrieve, recovering the sense that creatureliness and finitude are constitutive of human being and, as Augustine shows, the basis of thanksgiving and confession.

We need to reclaim this perspective on nature and our place within it as fundamentally Christian. Christianity has been blamed for treating nature as created for the good of humanity, for justifying human dominance and exploitation on the basis of Genesis 1.28–9, and for promulgating the superiority of humanity to the rest of the animal creation. Humanity has frightening, if often unintended, domination over the planet's ecosystems; if the consequences of

---

[140] *Ibid.* XII.1.　　[141] E.g. *Ibid.* XXI.7, 8; XXII.11. Cf. I.3 above.　　[142] *Ibid.* XXII.17–26.

the indiscriminate human spread of plants and animals to alien environments were not enough of a warning, we are now faced with human-induced climate change. Ironically, the more the human race has acquired awareness of its insignificance in the perspective of deep space and time, the more it has dominated this planet and the less it has been mindful of its integral place in the created order. We see, yet don't see; and our very seeing implies the perspective of external observer – a dualism even after Darwin. Nature, the wild, the animal kingdom, has been treated as a parallel world, apart from human society, and ripe for exploitation.

The fathers understood humanity to be in a kingly position in relation to the rest of the created order, which at first sight might seem to endorse not merely anthropocentrism, but also that dominion over the earth which justified exploitation of natural resources for human ends. However, this is to read the fathers in the light of colonialism, capitalism and the pursuit of ever-expanding economic growth. Their overall outlook was different. Royal rule meant responsibility and stewardship – the conventional model was a somewhat paternalistic philosopher-king. The move towards properly managed wilderness in national parks and reserves, with appropriate respect for the ecology and balance of a region's natural systems, might seem more in line with the thinking of the fathers.

Darwin should be seen as having done a service to Christian anthropology by restoring us to our proper place in creation. Mary Midgley helps us to appreciate this. Challenging scientific reductionism, she criticizes the anthropocentrism of Enlightenment philosophers like Kant; and accepting that we 'are members of a vulnerable species', observes that we are also 'receptive, imaginative beings, adapted to celebrate and rejoice in the existence, quite independent of ourselves, of the other beings on this planet'.

We need the vast world, and it must be a world that does not need us; a world constantly capable of surprising us, a world we did not program, since only such a world is the proper object of wonder.[143]

She quotes Job 38 and 41 at some length, and deplores the kind of humanism which, smelling religion, deprives us of this wonder. Thus, with the aid of a humanist philosopher, we revisit from an anthropological angle the doxological theme of the previous chapter.

Midgley reminds us of the essential vulnerability of the human creature as part of this natural order. Throughout nature there is fragility and vulnerability – indeed, of all species, the naked human is one of the most fragile and vulnerable; yet theodicy has become the prime issue for theism. The lack of concern with this problem in Christian writings from past centuries is striking. Ordinary people in earlier centuries suffered – indeed, high infant mortality, brief life expectancy, inability to alleviate many medical conditions, epidemics and unrelieved famine meant they suffered far more than most people now troubled by the theodicy question. Why was the atheist critique not so powerful in past centuries? Part of the answer must lie in the reality of living precariously, close to nature, which was as awe-inspiring as it was sustaining: the fear of the wolf haunts European legend and literature. People knew they were small and vulnerable; so they depended on God. The fathers recognized that human beings belong to a context dominated by changes and chances, hurt and death, and, accepting the human condition as creaturely, vulnerable and mortal, were concerned with finding the wisdom to face and cope with the hardships of life. Moderns have been offended by them.

For me, a shift from struggling with theodicy was facilitated by discovering a profound thanksgiving for Arthur, and enjoyment of relationship with him for his own sake. Doxology in the everyday, thanksgiving for the sheer gift of existence – these are the potential gifts of patristic theology. Humanity, the fathers affirm, is no exception to the general order of creation but subject to the mortality

---

[143] Midgley, *Beast and Man*, p. 349.

and vulnerability of all the rest of the natural world, and necessarily limited; yet, oriented to God, receiving life as gift, learning how to relate in love to all that God has made, allowing the fruits of the Spirit to mature in everyday life, humankind not only points beyond itself as God's image on earth, but is also fitted to receive God's promise of new life.

* * *

Wisdom in weakness

The preacher begins:[144]

When God created, according to Genesis 1, God said, 'let there be light', and there was light. Later he put lamps in the sky, the bigger one to reign over the day, and the smaller one to reign over the night – we call them the sun and the moon. Lamps in the ancient world were simple pots made of fired clay, filled with oil and a wick stuck through the spout. So, in biblical times, light to chase away darkness came in earthenware vessels.

When God created, according to Genesis 2, he took dust, dampened it into clay and shaped a human figure – archaeologists have found little earthenware figurines all over the Middle East, and the storyteller probably had them in mind. God first fashioned the clay figure, then breathed life into it – so the man became a living being.

These two moments in the biblical creation-stories provide clues to what Paul meant when he wrote, 'We have this treasure in clay pots.'[145] Light and life constitute this treasure, and it is contained in the equivalent of common clay jars, our human bodies. What I'll suggest is that the experience of knowing and

---

[144] Adapted from the address given to the L'Arche International General Assembly at Swanwick in 2002.

[145] 2 Corinthians 4.7.

loving people with learning disabilities also provides clues to Paul's meaning.

In the biblical world pots were used to store basic commodities like grain and oil. But they were also used to hide precious things – money, jewels – treasure of all sorts, sometimes books. In Egypt in the 1940s at Nag Hammadi pottery jars full of religious books were found by peasants digging for fertilizer. People stored things they cared about in common clay pots. When Paul says, 'we have this treasure in clay pots', he may imply a contrast with expensive gold or silver containers, so reinforcing the ordinariness of his image. Treasure is secreted in the everyday – it is not far away at the proverbial end of the rainbow, an unattainable dream, nor the object of a long quest, as legend would have it. No – we have this treasure, present, in ordinary clay pots. The treasure is light and life, God's life contained in the clay pot, God's image in ordinary human being.

In this letter Paul discusses his own vocation. Our reading began with him pointing away from himself to Christ. 'For we do not proclaim ourselves: we proclaim Jesus Christ as Lord and ourselves as your slaves for Jesus' sake.' He goes on:

> For it is the God who said, 'Let light shine out of darkness', who has shone in our hearts to give the light of the knowledge of the glory of God in the face of Jesus Christ.

Paul refers back to creation, then points to the face of Jesus as the place where we see the glory of the Creator God, who not only breathed life into human beings, but through Jesus has shone light into peoples' hearts. This light implies wisdom: wherever the word 'treasure' appears in the Greek Bible which Paul knew, it refers to wisdom, and in Colossians, Christ is described as the one in whom are hidden 'all the treasures of wisdom and knowledge'.[146]

So the treasure is light and life and wisdom, hidden in clay, in ordinariness, in our vulnerable and fragile bodies. Clay pots are

[146] Colossians 2.3.

expendable; cheap, and thus easily replaced, as they need to be, because they are easily shattered; and, once broken, are not reparable. Mostly that's true of our mortal bodies.

In the Modern Western world, people forget the limitations and vulnerability of human life. The success of medical science has done so much to ensure that our ills are cured, our brokenness repaired and the expectation of life prolonged, that most people live as if everything should be perfect. Suffering and death, disfigurement and disability seem uncomfortable. The cult of sport exposes perfect bodies and encourages their development through training – aiming to be gold and silver vessels rather than clay pots, we might say. Women are seduced into emulating the exposed perfect bodies of those ideal models whose images are all around us in the media.

This is where L'Arche comes in. Because here beauty is perceived in damaged bodies. The presence of treasure within brokenness is acknowledged, and the sanctity of vulnerable and fragile bodies.

You see, if you put a lighted candle in a clay pot, it's only when it's broken that the light is exposed!

Paul used this image to reinforce the contrast between God's power and human weakness:

> We have this treasure in clay jars, so that it may be made clear that this extraordinary power belongs to God and does not come from us. We are afflicted in every way, but not crushed; perplexed but not driven to despair; persecuted, but not forsaken; struck down, but not destroyed; always carrying in the body the death of Jesus, so that the life of Jesus may also be made visible in our bodies.

Paul wants us to realize the paradox – the broken body of the crucified Christ is where light and life, wisdom and beauty are to be found. And it is the broken, vulnerable, clay pots of our bodies which bear testimony to God's power, God's glory, light, life and wisdom hidden in the ordinariness of fragile clay jars.

When liberation theologians read their Bibles they see God on the side of the poor. They hold out hopes of changing the world, ending poverty, fulfilling the Magnificat – bringing down the powerful and lifting up the lowly, filling the hungry with good things and sending the rich empty away. They offer theologies of hope for the oppressed and marginalized. In important ways, L'Arche shares that perspective. People with learning disabilities are poor in terms of life's gifts and talents, not to mention their social exclusion, economic deprivation and, often, lack of human relationship and love. Like liberation theologians, L'Arche knows that charity is patronizing.

But in important ways L'Arche challenges liberation theologies. For the poverty of people with learning disabilities is simply not removable, at least not by human agency. People with learning disabilities are born that way, or become that way through incurable brain damage. L'Arche reminds us of the limits of human capacity to put things right. It obliges us to confront the vulnerability of human creatureliness and the false ideology of trying to turn this life into a perfect paradise.

How, then, is God on the side of these 'poor' people? Hope lies not in the removal of their condition, but in another dimension. Assistants in L'Arche discover that through difference is revealed something deeply significant about our common humanity, and about God's presence. In communion and community, there is a contemplative waiting on God with one another, which is far removed from political activism or patronizing charity, a mutual respect which embraces weakness, vulnerability, even death. All are vulnerable and in need of salvation, and in mutuality grace is imparted to each, each giving and receiving as we accord dignity to one another.

We have this treasure in clay pots. Clay pots are easily shattered, but brokenness reveals the treasure within – the light and life and wisdom of God which we receive through Christ. So we are always *carrying in the body the death of Jesus, so that the life of Jesus may also be made visible in our bodies.* God's presence is recognized in mutual dependence. In the ordinary everyday business of living together, the divine image is discerned, secreted in ordinary clay pots – that's the L'Arche experience which chimes with Paul's climax:

> Yes, everything is for your sake, so that grace, as it extends to more and more people, may increase thanksgiving, to the glory of God. Amen.

* * *

Postlude

Bodily Awareness

Physical I was made.
Physical I am.
I feel I am just
Physical.

Lying in a bath,
Soaking up the warmth,
Strained body relaxed,
Soothed, caressed and nursed.
Blood tingling in every vein,
Joy tingling in every nerve,
Thanks mingling with every thought.

Lying in a bath,
Breathing in hot steam,
Weary muscles relieved,
Torn flesh cleansed and healed.
Milk tingling in swollen breasts,
Joy tingling in every nerve,
Thanks mingling with every thought.

Lying in a bath,
Revelling in new birth,
Purged of pain's assault,
Reintegrated self.
Love tingling in every pore,
Joy tingling in every nerve,
Thanks mingling with every thought.

Physical I was made.
Physical I am.
I feel I am just
Physical.
I glory in being
Physical.
Within the physical
I taste the spiritual.

From Age to Age

Erosion exposes the contours of loss
    and creates canyons deep in the soul
    where swirl the deeps of daily grind
    that gouge out peace.

For beauty hides in habitual clouds
    and in layered sediments laid in the self
    where fossils of feeling are petrified
    which rains release.

The chant of waters washing out hurts
    and thunders echoing long in the heart
    dissolves the dust of familiar fears
    and doubts decrease,

As the strata spattered with autumn's dress
    and the clinging life, like clasping hands,

are freshened by the clarity
of hope's increase.

For truth's deferred in time's decay,
in the bedrock's vulnerability,
as eternity's incarnated in change
beyond decease.

To Another

I think, and therefore I am:
In the deep dark well of an inturned self,
Where echoes are hollow,
Existence is burden.

You smile, and therefore I am:
In the lightening sky of the dawning day,
Attention grasped
By being that's other,
Existence is birdsong.

I smile, and therefore you are:
In the afternoon, in communion, we
Together smile
And all's worthwhile.
The rainbow beauty of smiles through tearfulness
Can focus flickering flames of hopefulness,
Despite the gathering evening shades.
With sparks of light
At dead of night,
Existence is bonfire!

4 | From image to likeness: incarnation and *theōsis*

Prelude

The mirror reflects a perfect image but back to front; while the xerox-machine turns out a pile of copies that are identical, multiple images indistinguishable from the original.

The artist produces an image which, however faithful a representation of the subject, is necessarily other; while the portrait-painter surveys her work, searching for the touch that would deliver the sitter's authentic essence.

The caricaturist demonstrates that 'similarity is not essential to likeness',[1] an alien shape suggesting the image of a particular individual; while the cartoonist captures the comical reflection of the dame in her dog.

The image-maker endlessly modifies computer designs; while the photographer adjusts the illumination to produce telling highlights and shadows, manipulating the picture further through the process of development and printing.

The politician is artfully made up, then trained in self-presentation to create a positive image; while the sculptor of old would gently tap the chisel and smooth the high cheek-bone to perfect a likeness appropriate to the regal status of the model.

The dictionary spells out the ambiguities and potential range of meaning:

---

[1] Iain McGilchrist, *The Master and his Emissary: The Divided Brain and the Making of the Western World* (New Haven and London: Yale University Press, 2009), p. 304, quoting E.H. Gombrich and E. Kris, *Caricature* (Harmondsworth: Penguin 1940).

image, likeness: a statue: an idol: a representation in the mind: a picture in the imagination or memory: an appearance: that which very closely resembles anything: a type: the figure of any object formed by rays of light reflected or refracted: a metaphor or simile: *public image* – the picture in the minds of most people of what, e.g., a political party stands for.

The iconoclast insists that scripture prohibits images and the divine cannot be represented in finite form; while the icon-writer creates an image which enables the worshipper to see through the traditional form to its transcendent archetype.

The exegete discerns types and images, patterns and parables across the panorama of scripture; while the poet creates images through figures of speech, like a prophet, stimulating fresh vision through symbol and metaphor.

The priest offers the eucharistic elements as material representations of the body and blood of Christ, and the church recognizes the image of Christ in the lived lives of the saints.

* * *

Imago Dei

The preacher reflects on the assumption that it is the mind or soul which is in God's image. This interpretation inevitably carries negative implications for those perceived to be intellectually inferior – women, slaves, persons with disabilities. There are, of course, examples of positive acceptance of intelligent persons with physical disabilities, such as Didymus the Blind who was nick-named the See-er because he saw more profoundly than those with physical sight. But the intellectualizing tradition is elitist, and also dualist, excluding those who challenge the dualist analysis by the very fact that their incapacities profoundly affect their entire personality.

Taken to mean that each is made in God's image, this also conspires with modern individualism, encouraging people to assert their rights no matter what their race, religion or impairment. This may enhance dignity and respect for those who are not white, male, able-bodied and intelligent, but such individualism tends to exacerbate the prejudice that, since we're made in God's image, we should all be perfect. Failure to reach notional perfection is then problematic. How can this person, who has physical or mental defects, be made in God's image?

The preacher returns to the biblical text. In Genesis Adam represents the whole human race – the very name means humankind. Adam was made in the image of God, but this was marred by disobedience, classically known as the fall. So glib talk about everyone being made in God's image needs countering with sensitivity to the corporate nature of that image, as well as awareness that all have fallen short of God's glory.[2] Paul's epistles show how crucial the parallel is between Adam and Christ. In Christ we are a new creation, and, as in Adam all die, so in Christ all will be made alive. Adam is the 'old man', Christ the 'new man',[3] and all of us (male and female) are in Adam and potentially in Christ,[4] both being in some sense corporate figures. Christ is the true image of God – the image of God in Adam (the old humanity) was marred. It's in Christ that we're in God's image. Being in Christ is being in the body of Christ, a corporate reality – for a body is made up of many members, all of whom bring different contributions to the whole.[5] Indeed, those body bits we are ashamed of and cover up[6] are indispensable, and the weak are to be especially honoured. This is a physical image – and the physical reality was that in his bodily existence Christ was abused, disabled and put to death. Some aspects of God's image in Christ can only be reflected in the church by the full inclusion and honouring of those who have bodies that are likewise impaired.

Then the preacher remembers hearing Jean Vanier say that Mother Theresa spoke of repulsion, compassion and wonderment. She recalls

---

[2] Romans 3.32.   [3] Romans 5; 2 Corinthians 5.17.   [4] Romans 7; 1 Corinthians 15.22.
[5] 1 Corinthians 12; Romans 12.   [6] See the Greek of 1 Corinthians 12.23.

passing through that sequence on successive visits to the original L'Arche community in France – first, embarrassment at her own *repulsion* when sitting opposite Edith at the dinner table, slobbering her food and wine down her front; then *compassion*, when she sat with Edith on the sofa during evening prayers, endeavouring to constrain her self-abuse; finally, *wonderment*: she'd happened to visit again when Edith had just died. At the wake, person after person gave testimony to what Edith had meant to them. Then she went to the chapel where Edith was laid out, surrounded by flowers and candles, still and at peace; in prayer with others she was overcome with *wonderment*. That kind of discernment is what allows recognition of God's image and likeness in human living and being.

From these reflections the preacher feels confident a sermon will emerge.

* * *

In the patristic period, tensions surrounded the notion of God's image, including:

- different perceptions as to what constituted God's image in humankind – whether it was to be identified with the mind or soul, or the body, or the whole person, or virtue, or what
- different ideas about what might be the principal capacity resulting from human creation in God's image: rationality, freewill, sovereignty, or something else
- different estimates of how exclusively or inclusively the human race might be said to be in God's image
- different approaches to whether 'image' and 'likeness' meant the same thing, how far the 'image' was granted in the beginning or fully realized only at the consummation, whether it was lost or merely marred in the fall
- different Christological understandings whether the image belonged to the incarnate Christ or the transcendent Logos, and, in the latter case, what kind of resemblance between Father and Son was implied.

In the fourth century a comprehensive model emerged which resolved some of these tensions, while integrating three biblical motifs: the prohibition of images; the identification of humankind as the locus of God's image; and the recognition of Christ as God's true image. Association of these three motifs generated Nicene theology, with its emphasis on the divinization of humanity. This complexity we'll explore fully before turning to questions of appropriation.[7]

I Made according to God's image

1.1 The homily, On That Which is According to the Image[8]

Scripture is like a mirror in which we see ourselves – otherwise, we remain ignorant of what and why we are, suggests the homilist. Genesis 1.26 demonstrates that God created humankind directly and with deliberation; but 'In what sense are we according to the image of God?' The author attacks those who deduce from the text that God is the same shape as ourselves, that there are eyes in God and ears, a head, hands, feet with which to walk, a behind on which to sit – for it says in scripture that God sits.[9] Such suggestions are blasphemous. God's image has nothing to do with our bodily shape.

> The human body is different in youth and in old age, different in health than in sickness, different in fear than in happiness . . . How then can what is changing be like the unchanging?

---

[7] This chapter draws some material from my article 'God's Image: "The Elephant in the Room" in the Fourth Century?', *SP* 50 (2011), 57–71.

[8] Two homilies on the human creation appear to be Basil's, though never found with the *Hexaemeron*'s nine homilies in the manuscript tradition; in some manuscripts they are anonymous or attributed to Gregory of Nyssa. Greek text: Alexis Smets and M. van Esbroek (eds.), *Basile de Césarée: Sur l'origine de l'homme: Homélies* x *et* xi *de l'Hexaémeron*, *SC*; ET: Nonna Verna Harrison, *St Basil the Great: On the Human Condition* (Crestwood, NY: St Vladimir's Seminary Press, 2005).

[9] E.g. Psalm 46.5.

To solve the puzzle, attention is directed to the words that follow, 'let them rule the fish'. The ruling principle is the superiority of reason. It is the 'inner human being' which is according to God's image;[10] 'I' am not identified with my hand; rather the hand is mine, and 'I am the rational part of the soul.' Human dominance over fish, wild beasts, birds, reptiles shows the superiority of reason. 'The passions are not included in the image of God, but reason is master of the passions'; for, 'where the power to rule is, there is the image of God'. The moral is that to 'throw away your own dignity' by allowing the passions to enslave you is to renounce 'the nobility of your own nature'.

Soon attention is drawn to the difference between Genesis 1.26 and 1.27:[11] why does the latter say only 'according to the image' when the former has said 'according to our own image and likeness'? Every detail of scripture is important, and the difference must be significant. 'By our creation we have the first, and by our free choice we build the second', for 'by free choice we are conformed to that which is according to the likeness of God'.

> In giving us the power to become like God, he let us be artisans of the likeness to God, so that the reward for the work would be ours. Thus we would not be like images made by a painter . . . For when you see an image exactly shaped like the prototype, you do not praise the image, but you marvel at the painter. Accordingly, so that the marvel may become mine and not another's, he has left me to become according to the likeness of God.

What it means to be 'according to the likeness' is demonstrated by cross-referencing the sermon on the mount, 'Be perfect as your heavenly Father is perfect', and 'For he makes his sun rise upon evil and good, and he sends rain upon just and unjust.'[12]

---

[10] *According to the Image* 7, cross-referencing 2 Corinthians 4.16.
[11] *Ibid.* 15–16.   [12] Matthew 5.48, 45.

If you become ... brother-loving and compassionate, you are like God. If you forgive your enemy from your heart, you are like God. If as God is toward you, the sinner, you become the same toward the brother who has wronged you, by your good will from your heart toward your neighbour, you are like God.[13]

So, 'as you have that which is according to the image through your being rational, you come to be according to the likeness by undertaking kindness'. The likeness is left incomplete, precisely so that 'you may complete yourself'. Christianity is 'likeness to God as far as is possible for human nature'. The hearers are encouraged to receive baptism,[14] women deliberately included – 'male and female he created them' according to Genesis 1.27. Women are not to use their weakness as an excuse, because that applies only to the body, not the soul; when have men been able to equal women's patience, or imitate women's vigour in fasting, toiling in prayer, abundance of tears or readiness for good works?

1.2 Antecedents and challenges

Few will be surprised to learn that the inclusion of women in God's image was contested:

> Diodore, Chrysostom and Theodoret ... liked to cite Paul's statement that man *qua* male "is in the image and glory of God but woman is the glory of man" (I Cor. 11.7). The most they would affirm is that women are "images of the image".[15]

By contrast, Clement of Alexandria had asserted that sexual differentiation applies only to this world, human God-likeness being incorporeal. With combined reference to Colossians 3.11 and Galatians 3.28, Clement underlined that all – barbarians, Greeks, slaves,

[13] *According to the Image* 17.   [14] *Ibid.* 18.
[15] Frederick G. McLeod, SJ, *The Image of God in the Antiochene Tradition* (Washington, DC: Catholic University of America Press, 1999), p. 191.

children and women – are capable of attaining wisdom in Christ; 'woman shares man's spiritual and moral nature by being God-like human being, *anthropos*, in her rational soul'.[16] A hierarchical relationship is admitted, though 'women can imitate men's moral headship by dominating inferior bodily appetites'. The homily outlined above follows this tradition: the interior human being, or intellect, is created in God's image, 'male and female' designating a difference restricted to the body, and on the spiritual level both man and woman have the same capacity to imitate God, so achieving virtue.

Origen is the most obvious antecedent. *On First Principles* displays the same assumption that it is the incorporeal soul or mind which was made in the image and likeness of God,[17] and also the same distinction between image and likeness,[18] based on the same observation that Genesis 1.27 differs from 1.26. This:

> points to nothing else but this, that man received the honour of God's image in his first creation, whereas the perfection of God's likeness was reserved for him at the consummation.

For Origen, 'the purpose of this was that man should acquire it for himself by his own earnest efforts to imitate God'. The 'possibility of attaining perfection was given in the beginning through the honour of the "image"', but the perfect likeness was to be 'conferred on us in proportion to the perfection of our merits'.

This Alexandrian distinction between image and likeness, perhaps already suggested by Irenaeus, was dropped by Athanasius and Gregory of Nyssa, while Augustine was directly critical of the distinction – 'likeness' is after all inherent in 'image'.[19]

---

[16] Kari Elisabeth Børresen, 'God's Image, Man's Image? Patristic Interpretation of Gen. 1,27 and I Cor. 11,7' in Børresen (ed.), *The Image of God: Gender Models in Judaeo-Christian Tradition* (Minneapolis: Fortress Press, 1995), pp. 194 ff.

[17] *First Principles* II.x.7, xi.3; III.i.13.   [18] *Ibid.* III.vi.1.

[19] *Unfinished Literal Commentary* 16, 57–8.

1.3 Epiphanius on the Audians

The opposite approach to Genesis 1.26 can be seen by turning to Epiphanius.[20] He, and later Theodoret,[21] attest a heretical group called the Audians, followers of one Audius, who came from Mesopotamia and was supposedly condemned at the same council as Arius. Theodoret accuses the Audians of immoral practices, but Epiphanius describes Audius as a purist who challenged lax standards in the church – indeed Epiphanius has considerable respect for him and his ascetic companions, regarding their way of life as admirable and their position entirely orthodox except for one small point – they:

> stubbornly declare that the gift of being in his image which God granted Adam applies to his body . . . "Since scripture has said <that God made> man from the earth," says Audius, "see how it has said with perfect truth that the entire earthy part is 'man'. Therefore it said earlier that the earthy part of man will itself be in the image of God."

Theodoret confirms this from another angle:

> He understood the Divine Being to have a human form, and conjectured it to be enveloped in bodily parts; for Holy Scripture frequently describes the divine operations under the names of human parts.

It is unclear, then, whether an anthropomorphic concept of God, or a reading of Genesis 1.26 in the light of Genesis 2, was the fundamental issue.

Epiphanius focusses on the stubbornness and ignorance of someone trying to decide in which part of a human being God's image is located because of 'the many conflicting ideas of this text which occur to people, occasioning a number of disputes'. Some say 'in the

---

[20] *Panarion* 70; Greek text: Karl Holl (ed.), *Panarion, GCS*; ET: Philip R. Amidon, SJ, *The Panarion of St. Epiphanius. Bishop of Salamis.* Selected passages. (Oxford University Press, 1990.)

[21] Theodoret, *Church History* IV.9.

image' applies to the soul; others that it applies neither to the soul nor to the body, but means virtue. Others suggest it means baptism and the gifts conferred in baptism, quoting 1 Corinthians 15.49, 'As we have the image of the earthly, we shall also bear the image of the heavenly.' Others prefer to say that the image of God was in Adam until he fell, ate of the tree and was expelled; but from then he lost the image. Epiphanius reckons none of these accounts should be given attention; rather, one must believe that the image of God is in human being, and in the whole human being, not just one part. The image of God has not been lost, Epiphanius asserts, quoting Genesis 9.3–6: 'Do you not see that God's image is said to be in humankind ten generations after the creation of Adam?' Further quotes from the Psalms and the New Testament make the same point.

Working through the options one by one, Epiphanius first considers the arguments of people who say that God and the soul are invisible movers, active, intelligent, rational – so the soul is 'in the image', mimicking God as it does by moving, acting and doing all that man does rationally. Epiphanius will have none of it: God is more than ten thousand times more incomprehensible and inconceivable than the soul, and knows all things, himself containing all things without being contained; but the soul is contained in a body and has limited knowledge, and whereas God is indivisible, the soul has divisions, a point proved by quoting Hebrews 4.12–13. Next he challenges those who say that the body is in God's image: how can the visible be like the invisible, the corporeal like the incorporeal, or the tangible like the ungraspable? Everything made is inferior to the glory of the incomprehensible Trinity. Likewise the argument about virtue fails, because of different kinds of virtue and the human failings of even the most virtuous. As for baptism, what about Abraham, Isaac, Jacob, Elijah, Moses, Noah, Enoch or the prophets?

Epiphanius now turns to arguments that Theodoret's account of the heresy would have prioritized, and dismisses appeal to texts referring to the Lord's ears, eyes or hands to suggest that the body is in the image of God: of course, the Lord in his kindness appeared as he chose, but the Gospel says 'No one has seen God at any time.'[22] So the Audians are confuted by the truth: God is incomprehensible.

With this account of the Audians Epiphanius is already addressing a central issue of the Origenist controversy. He himself began a campaign against Origen in Palestine, annoying the bishop by his meddling and setting the Latin monasteries of Rufinus and Jerome against each other. But his arguments against the Audians show that Epiphanius shared Origen's perspectives on the utter transcendence of the divine nature and that he could not himself be described as 'anthropomorphite'.

1.4 The Anthropomorphites

The wider Origenist controversy was precipitated by Theophilus, bishop of Alexandria; his paschal letter announcing the date of Easter in 399 denounced those who attributed a human form to God, infuriating many ascetics. Sozomen[23] suggests that the issue had already been agitating the desert monasteries, where some simply read the scriptures without questioning and others searched for hidden meanings. Faced with a storm of protest and demonstrations led by the desert monks, Theophilus publicly declared, 'In seeing you, I behold the face of God.' So the crowd demanded that he anathematize Origen's books, which he was willing to do, despite earlier favouring the position of Origenist monks. The historian Socrates[24] suggests an unprincipled *volte face.*

What lay behind Theophilus' change of mind may be understood better by turning to the coptic life of Abba Apphou.[25] On receipt of

[22] John 1.18.   [23] Sozomen, *Church History* VIII.11.
[24] Socrates, *Church History* VI.7.
[25] Etienne Drioton, 'La Discussion d'un moine anthropomorphite Audien avec le patriarche Théophile d'Alexandrie en l'année 399', *Revue de l'Orient Chrétien* 20 (1915–17), 92–100, 113–28. I am grateful to my former student Duncan Raynor for drawing attention to this material.

the encyclical Apphou was sent by an angel to Alexandria to question an expression not in accord with holy scripture, that expression being, 'It is not the image of God we bear.' Having obtained an interview with Theophilus, he asks for the letter to be read. The offending phrase is reached and Apphou interrupts, saying, 'Like that, this sentence is not correct.' His explanation is an appeal to Genesis 1.26–7. Theophilus suggests only Adam was created in the image and likeness; whereupon Apphou draws attention to Genesis 9.6, which refers to humankind being made in God's image at the time of Noah. Theophilus insists that God is impassible and self-sufficient, reducing the idea of God having human form to absurdity by asking how anyone can think an ailing man squatting to perform his necessities is in God's image. Apphou appeals to the ordinariness of eucharistic bread, yet it is the body of Christ. Theophilus replies that it only becomes Christ's body in the context of the liturgy. Apphou suggests that, as it takes faith to accept that, so it does to accept that humankind was created in God's image and likeness. He appeals to the analogy of the emperor's image: everyone will accept it is the king's image, but at the same time they know it is wood and paints – it cannot lift its head or speak or do any number of other things; but no one remembers these weaknesses out of respect for the king who proclaimed, 'This is my image' – indeed, to deny it would lead to execution for slighting the king. How much more if you slight humankind, in whom abides the breath or spirit of God, and who is therefore alive and honoured above all creatures on earth! All weaknesses are subject to salvation and healing, and one should not slight the glory God has given us.

Scriptural exegesis clearly lay at the heart of this controversy, not some kind of crypto-pagan or simple-minded anthropomorphism. Apphou exploits the point that an image is a representation *in another medium.* Against the affirmation of the soul as God's image, there was pressure to acknowledge the whole human being, including the physical reality of the body, as in some sense representing God. The Cappadocian Gregories had already affirmed the importance of

God's image in the physically distorted bodies of lepers[26] – the ailing man squatting to do his necessities was indeed still a human being made in the image of God. This emerging theme challenged the elitist assumptions of the whole Origenist approach, raising questions about the nature of God as well as the nature of humanity. Deep in the tradition, however, there was another way of addressing the issue.

II Christ as the image of God

The homily outlined in 1.1 failed to pick up a distinction fundamental to Origen's treatment, namely, that the one true image of God is Christ, *according to* which humankind is made.[27] The Christological reading goes back to Irenaeus, but what he and Origen have in common betrays a fundamental difference: Irenaeus attributes the image to the incarnate Christ while Origen applies it to the divine Son of God or Logos.

II.1 Irenaeus

Only in one place does Irenaeus explicitly call the Son the 'image of God'. Quoting Genesis 9.6, he continues:

> the image of God is the Son, according to whose image was man made; and for this reason He appeared at the last times, to render the image like himself.[28]

That one explicit statement, however, illuminates several passages in *Against the Heresies.*

---

[26] Cf. Chapter 1.

[27] A point derivable from the LXX version of Genesis 1.26–7, not the original Hebrew.

[28] *Apostolic Preaching* 22; ET: John Behr, *St Irenaeus of Lyons: On the Apostolic Preaching* (Crestwood, NY: St Vladimir's Seminary Press, 1997).

Arguing against his opponents' assumption that God could not be directly involved in creating the material universe, Irenaeus made it clear:[29]

- that the Word (= the Son) and Wisdom (= the Holy Spirit) of God were those addressed when God said, 'Let us make'
- that creation was God's own handiwork, for it was 'by the Father's hands, that is by the Son and the Holy Spirit' that 'the human being . . . was made in God's likeness'
- that the whole human being, not just part, was made in God's image and likeness, the soul or spirit being only a part of the human being, not the human being itself.

Thus Word and Spirit are involved in making the whole human being according to God's image and likeness.

This whole human being is subsequently[30] taken to be modelled on the Son: 'God shall be glorified in his handiwork, fitting it so as to be conformed to and modelled after his own Son.' The Word 'from the beginning even to the end, forms us, prepares us for life, is present with his handiwork, and perfects it after the image and likeness of God'. This Word was:

> manifested when the Word of God was made human, assimilating himself to humankind and humankind to himself, so that by means of resemblance to the Son, humanity might become precious to the Father.

The image was truly demonstrated, then, in the incarnation, since:

> he himself became that which bore his image and re-established the likeness . . . assimilating humanity to the invisible Father by means of the visible Word.

It was *said* in times past that humanity was created after God's image, he suggests, but it was not actually *demonstrated*; for the Word after

[29] *Against Heresies* IV.20.1.   [30] *Ibid.* V.6.1, 16.1–2.

whose image humankind was created was not yet visible. Now that the Word has become flesh, the fact that humanity was modelled on this image of God has become evident, and the restoration of humankind to its lost 'likeness' has been made possible. So the incarnate Word is the image of God, the model after which humankind is fashioned. If it is the *incarnate* Christ that is the visible image of the invisible God, then that is indeed a representation of God in a different medium.

It is often assumed that Irenaeus made the same kind of distinction between 'image' and 'likeness' which Origen and Basil made, associating 'image' with creation and 'likeness' with eschatology, but reading back this distinction into Irenaeus' work has been challenged.[31] In the first four books of *Against the Heresies* this distinction is nowhere made, and in Book v Irenaeus clearly implies that 'both the image and likeness are related to man's initial creation, and the goal is that *both* are to be confirmed'. Humanity had to be created first, then to receive growth, then to be strengthened and abound, then to be restored, then to be glorified and finally to see the Lord, a vision that would produce immortality. Irenaeus seems to assume a progressive realization of both image and likeness.

So what Irenaeus envisages is creation according to the image and likeness of God in Christ, and failure to realize this fully until the incarnation. The key to his approach is this identification of *the incarnate Christ* as the true image and likeness of God, according to which the human being in its wholeness was created and destined to reach its full maturity. Despite some apparent similarities, Origen's overall understanding was profoundly different, precisely because for him God's true image is not the incarnate Christ but *the transcendent*

---

[31] John Kaufman, 'Becoming Divine, Becoming Human: Deification Themes in Irenaeus of Lyons' (Dissertation for the Degree of PhD, MF Norwegian School of Theology, Oslo, 2009), pp. 196–8.

Logos, and human beings are created according to that image in that they are *logikoi* (rational beings).[32]

II.2 Origen

For Origen, God's image is rationality, which endures despite distortion by sin, while likeness to God is the ultimate goal which may be reached by using rationality appropriately. In this Origen was anticipated by Clement – both, like Philo, correlate the Genesis text with Platonic ideals of assimilation to the divine, but they provide a Christian dress to this spiritual progress by seeing baptism and anointing of the Spirit as the means of grace by which likeness to God is effected. Likeness to God is reached by imitating the Word, who is the true image of God. Strictly speaking, only Christ, as God's Son, can be called the image of God; humanity is 'according to' the image, or 'an image of an image'. The term 'image' is sometimes applied to an object painted or carved on some material, such as wood or stone; that applies to the creature made 'in the image and likeness of God'.[33] Sometimes, however, a child is said to be the image of its parent, when the likeness of the parent's features is in every aspect faithfully reproduced in the child; this applies to the Son of God, who is the 'invisible image of the invisible God'.

Those analogies highlight a distinction as fundamental to Origen's outlook as his resistance to the image having anything to do with corporeality. He would have included Irenaeus among those he criticizes for supposing that the body was in any sense involved in the creation of humanity 'according to the image'. To Celsus, a pagan critic of Christianity, he insists[34] that no Christian holds the view that 'the part of man in the image of God is located in the inferior

---

[32] See Henri Crouzel, *Théologie de l'image de dieu chez Origène* (Paris: Aubier, 1955); his findings are summarized in *Origen* (ET: A. S. Worrall, Edinburgh: T & T Clark, 1989).

[33] *First Principals* I.2.6.

[34] *Against Celsus* VI.63; Greek text: P. Koetschau *et al.* (eds.), *Origenes Werke, GCS*; ET: Henry Chadwick, *Contra Celsum* (Cambridge University Press, 1965).

part of the composite man, I mean, the body'; nor would anyone apply the words 'in the image of God' to both together, as that would make God himself composite.

> That which is made in the image of God is to be understood as the inward man, as we call it, which is renewed and has the power to be formed in the image of the Creator, when a man becomes perfect as his heavenly Father is perfect . . . and assumes into his own virtuous soul the characteristics of God.

Then the body becomes a temple for the soul which is according to God's image and likeness.

Origen has a dynamic concept of progressive assimilation to the divine likeness, a likeness that coincides with knowledge of Christ face to face. Being created 'according to the image' is the starting-point, the freedom that allows one to choose to become 'imitators of God'. The Word forms itself in the Christian by the practice of virtues and by contemplation. Participation in Christ creates 'christs', adopted sons of God, by a process of divinization in which the likeness will be restored eschatologically.[35] 'The highest good, towards which all rational nature is progressing . . . is to become as far as possible like God', he says; recognizing that many philosophers agree, he suggests they got it from Moses, quoting Genesis 1.26–7. All this rests on his fundamental perspective that it is not the incarnate Christ but the transcendent Logos who is God's true image.

11.3 *Fourth-century debates*

The implications of Origen's view eventually came into dispute. The niceties involved are only now being uncovered as scholars realize that an account of the fourth century in terms of a binary opposition between Arian and orthodox is entirely inadequate, the divergences often crossing party lines. All parties accepted that the

---

[35] *First Principles* III. vi.1.

pre-existent Logos was God's image, except, it seems, Marcellus of Ancyra, who confined the image to Christ's body on the grounds that an image is something other than its archetype. Debate centred on how the Logos or Son of God imaged God the Father, the ambiguity of the word 'image' allowing some to underline identity, others to emphasize difference.

At the heart of the theology of Eusebius of Caesarea lay the notion of Christ as God's image. He speaks of a 'Beginning', next to the being of God (who is without beginning), begotten from no other source than the Father, first-born and perfectly likened to the Father, thus known as the image of God, the power of God, the wisdom of God and the word of God.[36] God makes his offspring the foundation of all that is to be, the 'perfect creation of a perfect Creator', 'alone bearing in himself the image of the Godhead' which 'cannot be explained in word or conceived in thought', and he is called God through this image and because of this primary likeness. The Son is the image of the Father by intention and deliberate choice. The generation of the Son did not happen by separation or division, but before time and inconceivably: 'Who shall describe his generation?'[37] Clearly Eusebius wants the 'image' terminology to capture the closeness and similarity of Father and Son. But it also implies difference – non-identity. The Son is:

> the image of God, in a way ineffable and incalculable in our terms, the living image of the living God, *existing in its own right immaterially and incorporeally* . . . but not an image like that which exists among us which is different in its form, but rather himself being the whole identical form, and assimilated to the Father *in his own self-existence.*[38]

---

[36] *Preparation* VII. xv.1, 2; Greek text: K. Mras (ed.), *Die Praeparatio evangelica: Eusebius Werke* VII, *GCS*; ET: E. H. Gifford, *Eusebii Pamphili Evangelicae Praeparationis Libri* xv (Oxford University Press, 1903).

[37] *Demonstration* IV.2.3, quoting Isaiah 53.8; Greek text: I. A. Heikel (ed.), *Die Demonstratio evangelica: Eusebius Werke* VII, *GCS*; ET: W. J. Ferrar, *The Proof of the Gospel,* 2 vols. (London: SPCK, 1920).

[38] *Ibid.* V.1.21.

This is subsequently clarified[39] by an analogy we have met before: Eusebius talks about the way the image of a king is honoured for the sake of the one whose likeness it bears: 'there are not two kings', the true one plus the one represented by the image. The Only-Begotten Son, as the only image of the unseen God, is worthy of receiving the Father's name, but 'as one who receives it and does not possess it in his own right'. He is to be thought of as 'secondary, and as holding a divinity received from the Father as an image of God'. God being 'seen through the Son as by a mirror and image'. So for Eusebius, God's image subsists as another being which nevertheless truly images God and is therefore co-honoured with God's name and worship – even a 'true image' must be different from the thing imaged.

This kind of 'image' theology reached its highpoint at the dedication synod in Antioch in 341, which asserted that the Son of God is the 'unchanging and unaltering, exact image of the Godhead and the substance and will and power and glory of the Father'.[40] The difference gives sense to the imaging. So this council, along with Eusebius himself, has been regarded as Arian. Indeed, Marcellus of Ancyra associated Eusebius with the Arian Asterius, one of whose fragments reads:

> The Father is other, who begot from himself the only-begotten Logos and first-born of all creation . . . God (begetting) God, the exact image of his substance and will and glory and power.[41]

Marcellus also quotes Eusebius as saying:

> Of course, the image and that whose image it is are not conceived as one and the same, but as two essences and two objects and two powers, just as they have two designations.

[39] *Ibid.* v.4.
[40] R. P. C. Hanson, *The Search for the Christian Doctrine of God* (Edinburgh: T & T Clark, 1988), p. 286.
[41] Fragment 21; ET: Hanson, *Search*, p. 36.

Marcellus agreed with Eusebius that an image is always other than that of which it is the image. Fragment 54 reads:

> Images of these things of which they are images are indicative of things not there so that the things not there seem to be manifested through them.

What Marcellus rejected was the notion that the *pre-incarnate Logos* was an 'unchanging image' of the Father's Godhead, substance, will, power and glory. He strongly objected to the notion of two pre-incarnate substances (*ousiai*);[42] so he asserted that image should only be applied to the body of the incarnate Word.[43] The humanity of Christ was a visible pointer to the invisible nature.[44] So the Nicene, Marcellus, and his opponents (Eusebius and the members of the dedication council) used the notion of God's image to establish difference, but with utterly different intentions.

This is just the first indication that different understandings of the 'image of God' crossed party lines. It has been suggested[45] that there were two main approaches:

(1) Arius and Asterius advocated a 'participative' understanding of the Son as the image of God – he is a distinct being who participates in divine attributes by grace and by adoption. In other words, there is no essential difference between the way the

---

[42] J. T. Lienhard, *Contra Marcellum: Marcellus of Ancyra and Fourth-Century Theology* (Washington, DC: Catholic University of America Press, 1999), pp. 75 6.

[43] Kelley McCarthy Spoerl, 'The Schism at Antioch since Cavellera' in Michel R. Barnes and Daniel H. Williams (eds.), *Arianism after Arius: Essays on the Development of the Fourth-Century Trinitarian Conflicts* (Edinburgh: T & T Clark, 1993), p. 117, following Lienhard, 'Acacius of Caesarea: *Contra Marcellum*' in *Cristianesimo nella storia* 10 (1989), 1–21.

[44] J. M. Robertson, *Christ as Mediator: A Study of the Theologies of Eusebius of Caesarea, Marcellus of Ancyra, and Athanasius of Alexandria* (Oxford University Press, 2007), p. 132.

[45] Mark Delcogliano, 'Eusebian Theologies of the Son as the Image of God before 341', *JECS* 14 (2006), 459–84.

Son is God's image and the way any other creature might come to be God-like.

(2) Eusebius and others took a 'constitutive' approach to how the Son was the image of God. Eusebius, for example, quotes texts such as Colossians 1.15 'image of the invisible God', Philippians 2.6 'the form of God' and Hebrews 1.3 'the radiance of the glory and the character of the *hypostasis* of God' as revealing his relationship to the Father's divinity, a relationship which is his alone, and because of which the one God is made known through the Son as through an image. So, for Eusebius, the Son is also God, because he 'bears the utmost accuracy of likeness to the Father in his own essence' rather than by participation through grace.

In rejecting participation, Eusebius was more like Athanasius than the Arians, while Athanasius did not share Marcellus' position. One might conclude that the notion of 'God's image', though scriptural, did little in the end to resolve the issues around the relationship of Father and Son, because of the inherent ambiguities around the relation of image and archetype. However, what did make a difference was the theological insight that the way the Son imaged the Father was a subject which could not be divorced from that other biblical claim – the imaging of God in humankind.

III Incarnation and *theōsis*

III.1 *Athanasius*

'He became a human being that we might become divine.'[46] This was the basis of Athanasius' argument that the Logos incarnate in Christ must be fully divine, *homoousios* with the Father. He is the true Son of God through whom we become adopted sons. He is the

---

[46] *On the Incarnation* 54; Greek text edited and translated by R. W. Thomson, *Athanasius: Contra Gentes and De Incarnatione*, OECT.

archetypal Image of God through whom we come to be in God's image and likeness. What Athanasius did was to hold together the various biblical statements about God's image.

In his two-volume work, *Against the Gentiles–On the Incarnation*, Athanasius reveals how his thinking about God's image is integrated into a coherent vision of God's relations with humanity. The soul should have been able to perceive in itself God's Logos, 'in whose form it had been created'; but once perverted by bodily pleasures, it turned outside itself and made imaginary gods – fleshly desires obscured 'the mirror it had within itself through which alone it was able to see the image of the Father'. This 'mirror' of God's own Logos made humanity rational through its likeness to the divine, and human beings should have conversed happily with God if that grace had been retained.[47] Idolatry, the worship of man-made gods fashioned out of 'gold and silver and bronze and iron and stone and wood' – an utterly irrational practice condemned by scripture[48] – is the principal symptom of the soul's loss of purity. But, with purification of soul, people:

> may be able to contemplate therewith the Word of the Father, in whose image they were made in the beginning ... So when the soul ... keeps pure what is in the image, then ... it can truly contemplate as in a mirror the Word, the image of the Father, and in him meditate on the Father, of whom the Saviour is the image.[49]

This presumes that the true image is the pre-existent Logos of God, and that humankind was created according to his own image by that Logos – in other words, as an image of God's image. The Logos, being the 'good offspring of a good Father and true Son' is 'the power of the Father and his wisdom and Word', not by participation, but:

---

[47] *Against the Nations* 2, 8.   [48] *Ibid.* 12, 13–14.   [49] *Ibid.* 34.

absolute wisdom [*autosophia*], very Word [*autologos*], and himself the Father's own power [*autodynamis*], absolute light [*autophōs*], absolute truth [*autoalētheia*], absolute justice [*autodikaiosynē*], absolute virtue [*autoaretē*] and indeed stamp, effulgence and image.[50]

In other words, being God's image is constitutive of his being, but creatures may participate in this 'absolute' by grace, imaging the perfect image. To enable this participation:

> he became man that we might become divine; and he revealed himself through a body that we might receive an idea of the invisible Father.[51]

Athanasius constructed an overarching plot centred on the incarnation.[52] Human beings, created alongside everything else out of nothing, had the extra grace of being made in God's own image. This gave them a share in the power of the Logos – his life and rationality; but this was lost as a consequence of the perversion which clouded the 'mirror' which potentially gave access to communion with God; so humankind was sinking back into the nothingness from which it had been called into life:

> man who was rational and who had been made in the image was being obliterated; and the work created by God was perishing.[53]

God's solution was the incarnation:

> The Word of God came in his own person, in order that in it death could be destroyed and men might again be renewed in the image.[54]

Athanasius now calls in the familiar parable of the literal image or portrait. Painted on wood and spoiled by dirt, it needs the original sitter to come so that it can be renewed in the same medium: 'even so the all-holy Son of the Father, who is the image of the Father, came

---

[50] *Ibid.* 46.   [51] *On the Incarnation* 54.   [52] *Ibid.* 3–21.   [53] *Ibid.* 6.   [54] *Ibid.* 13.

to our realms to renew man who had been made in his likeness'.
Unlike Origen, Athanasius makes no distinction between image and
likeness, both words referring to what was obscured by 'idolatry and
impiety'. Because this damage involved the loss of the Logos, only
the Logos could rectify it:

> no one else could bring what was corrupted to incorruptibility, except
> the Saviour himself, who also created the universe in the beginning
> from nothing; nor could any other re-create men in the image, save
> the image of the Father; nor could another raise up what was mortal
> as immortal, save our Lord Jesus Christ, who is life itself; nor could
> another teach about the Father and overthrow the cult of idols, save
> the Word who orders the universe, and who alone is the true only-
> begotten son of the Father.[55]

That renewal included the body, which 'because of the Word who
was dwelling in it, became immune from corruption'. Athanasius
is confident that 'corruption has ceased and been destroyed by the
grace of the resurrection', because he 'sanctified the body' and gave
life to the body.[56] The pre-existent Logos is the true image, but the
incarnate Logos is the revelation of this image:

> For because they are men, they would be able to know his Father
> more quickly and more closely through the body corresponding to
> theirs and the divine works effected through it.

The most potent evidence for this is the despoiling of the idols,
false images of the divine.[57] The true, invisible God is made visible
through the incarnation and the restoration in human nature of the
image of God's true image.

In Athanasius, then, three strands in the biblical material concerned with God's image are integrated: the commandment to make
no images, the affirmation that human beings were created in God's

---

[55] *Ibid.* 20.   [56] *Ibid.* 43–4.   [57] *Ibid.* 55.

image and the confession of Christ as the true image have been brought into a creative, systematic relationship.

III.2 Cyril of Jerusalem

That something like this was presupposed in the tradition is suggested both by the way in which Irenaeus anticipates the key elements in Athanasius' overarching schema and also by the *Catechetical Homilies* of Cyril of Jerusalem. Cyril lived through the disputes of the fourth century. Suffering exile more than once and labelled 'semi-Arian', he nevertheless seems a good representative of a traditional Christianity that sought to avoid extremism, and somehow instinctively understood how things hang together. Cyril is clear that God is beyond all images.[58] In all God's good creation, only humankind was made an image of God; and given that a wooden image of an earthly king is held in honour, how much more a rational image of God?[59] The self-governing soul is in the image of the Creator. The body is an instrument, a garment and robe of the soul; it is not the source of sin – it can only act or react when animated by the soul; but it may become a temple of the Holy Spirit, and is to be kept pure for the resurrection.[60] Cyril associates 'image' with the humanity of Christ; he explains[61] that humanity had forsaken God and made carved images of human beings. So since a human image was falsely worshipped as God, God became truly a human being so that the falsehood be done away with. The Lord took our likeness from us to save us, so that sinful humanity might become partaker of God.

So all three biblical strands are found in Cyril in some form and in some degree of relationship. The end of idolatry is explicitly related to the imaging of God in the incarnation; and elsewhere the imaging of God in humanity is related to God's Image in Christ.

[58] Cyril of Jerusalem, *Catechetical Homilies* IV.4–6: Greek text: Migne, *PG* 33; ET: *FC*; selections in Edward Yarnold, SJ, *Cyril of Jerusalem* (London: Routledge, 2000).
[59] *Ibid.* XII.5.   [60] *Ibid.* IV.18, 23, 26, 30.   [61] *Ibid.* XII.15.

But the whole picture is not explicitly highlighted or drawn out in a single exposition; it emerges in a collage.[62] Implicit is the notion of participation in God or *theopoiēsis*.

III.3 *Gregory of Nyssa*

Gregory of Nyssa, in his treatment of God's image in *The Making of Humankind*,[63] emphasizes the human power of self-determination: freewill, as well as rationality, are capacities that imitate the divine. The image finds its resemblance to the Archetype in being filled with all good, he suggests. So:

> there is in us the principle of all excellence, all virtue and wisdom, and every higher thing we can conceive; but pre-eminent among all is the fact that we are free from necessity ... [and] have decision in our power as we please, for virtue is a voluntary thing, subject to no dominion: that which is the result of compulsion and force cannot be virtue.[64]

But there are two other important characteristics of Gregory's thought which take things further:

* Gregory has a strong sense of human solidarity.[65] In Genesis 1.26 the whole corporate human nature is to be made according to its prototype, there being in Christ Jesus neither male nor female. 'In the divine foreknowledge and power all humanity is included in the first creation ... as it were in one body'; for 'the image is not in part of our nature, nor is the grace in any one of the things found in that nature, but this power extends equally to all the race'. 'The whole race was spoken of as one man,' and 'our whole nature ... extending from the first to the last, is, so to say,

[62] Cf. M. C. Steenberg, *Of God and Man: Theology as Anthropology from Irenaeus to Athanasius* (London: T & T Clark, 2009), for his integrated picture of Cyril's theology.
[63] Cf. Chapter 3.   [64] *On the Making* XVI.11.   [65] Cf. Chapter 1.

one image of Him who is'.[66] Thus the church, the body of Christ, becomes potentially the 'truth' of the image in Gregory's thought, as von Balthasar makes clear, quoting words which suggest that 'contemplating the Church' is a way of seeing 'the Invisible One in a more penetrating way'.[67]

- Gregory develops the notion of 'mirror', already noticed in Athanasius. The mind, being in the image of what is the most beautiful and supreme good, 'remains in beauty and goodness so long as it partakes as far as possible in its likeness to the archetype . . . being formed as though it were a mirror'.[68] In his classic study of Gregory, von Balthasar notes that it is characteristic of Gregory that when he speaks of 'image', he immediately substitutes 'mirror', the soul contemplating the archetype in her own beauty as in a mirror and an image.[69] The theme becomes particularly prominent in the *Homilies on the Beatitudes*:

> If a person's heart has been purified . . . he will see the image of the divine nature in his own beauty . . . When [the inner man] has scraped off the rustlike dirt which dank decay has caused to appear on his form, he will once more recover the likeness of the archetype . . . thus he becomes blessed, because when he looks at his own purity, he sees the archetype in the image.[70]

The archetype is, as von Balthasar notes, the perfect eschatological Image that is the total Christ, which is reached by 'the elevation of

---

[66] David Bentley Hart, 'The Mirror of the Infinite: Gregory of Nyssa on the *Vestigia Trinitatis*' in Sarah Coakley (ed.), *Re-Thinking Gregory of Nyssa* (Oxford: Blackwell, 2003), pp. 118–19. See further J. Zachhuber, *Human Nature in Gregory of Nyssa: Philosophical Background and Theological Significance* (Leiden: Brill, 2000).

[67] Hans Urs von Balthasar, *Presence and Thought: An Essay on the Religious Philosophy of Gregory of Nyssa*, ET: Mark Sebanc (San Francisco: Ignatius Press, 1995; French original 1988), p. 152, quoting *On the Song of Songs* 8.

[68] *On the Making* xii.9.

[69] *Presence and Thought*, pp. 115, 121–2, quoting e.g. *On the Song of Songs, On the Soul and the Resurrection, Homilies on the Beatitudes*.

[70] *Homily 6*.

the created image to the plane of the uncreated Image and its integration into it . . . But what integrates us into this Image is love.'[71]
David Bentley Hart,[72] creating a collage of passages, shows how mirroring and light-reflection implicitly hold those same three strands
together in Gregory's thought: the Son is the eternal image in which
the Father contemplates and loves his essence – the hidden Father
made luminously manifest in the infinite icon of his beauty. Human
nature is a mirror, a 'uniquely privileged surface in which the beauty
of the divine archetype is reflected'; when our nature draws near to
Christ, it becomes beautiful with the reflection of his beauty. This
radiance is exactly what was missing when we languished in the chill
of idolatry – we assumed the lifeless coldness of what we worshipped.

III.4 *The emergence of an integrated model*

What emerges is a comprehensive model with the potential to resolve
those tensions noted at the start. Only gradually was it fully articulated. Athanasius and the Cappadocians, those who fashioned the
notion of *theopoiēsis/theōsis* and recognized that it implied Nicene
orthodoxy, were those who had a sense of the interrelationship of
differing aspects of God's image as presented in different parts of
scripture. This doctrinal 'ecology', by which key components mutually sustain one another, was rooted in traditional Christian thinking
as found in Irenaeus and Cyril's *Catechetical Homilies*. The so-called
Arian and Origenist controversies thus present themselves as different stages in a single debate, with similar issues at stake: a tendency
to devalue the physical creation and human embodiment, and to
find mediation through a hierarchical understanding of how God
relates to the creation. In the Nicenes, *theologia* is rooted in God's
oikonomia;[73] the body is potentially the temple of God and the human
person is God's image on earth, while the whole is held together in

---

[71] Von Balthasar, *Presence and Thought*, pp. 168–9.
[72] Hart, 'The Mirror of the Infinite', pp. 117–20.   [73] See Chapter 8.

a Christology which sees Christ as intrinsically God's Image, both as Son of God and also as the new Adam, humanity as it was meant to be.

This integrated model put the incarnation at the centre, and enabled human beings to be incorporated in the body of Christ so as to be recreated in God's image and likeness, the true Son of God ensuring that the archetypal Image of God is imaged in images of the Image, so enabling humanity to be adopted as God's son and heir through participation in him. Embodiment and solidarity were affirmed as the medium in which God is imaged. Gregory Nazianzen's affirmation of the lepers[74] made this crystal clear; the poor are 'essentially "deserving" of assistance ... because intrinsically, even though paradoxically, they represent the presence of God within a fragile world'.[75]

That was a profoundly paradoxical claim, given assumptions about the nature of God. Persistent was focus on the intellect, the potential seat of contemplation and knowledge of God, as the element in human being understood to image God and be the 'divine sense'.[76] Deeply engrained was the notion that regaining God-likeness meant withdrawal from the physical realities of life and the eradication of the passions – the homily outlined in 1.1 above included exhortation to rule over one's irrational passions, the beasts within. Monks and holy men imaged God, the ascetic ideal being *apatheia* (passionlessness), for this, they supposed, characterized the divine. The incarnation, however, along with specific Gospel teachings, provoked quite other perceptions of the divine nature. Gregory Nazianzen's appeal on behalf of lepers was grounded in the view that God is love, and the realization of that image was to be found by imitating God who sends rain on just and unjust alike, while Christ is the model.

[74] See Chapter 1, quoting *Oration* 14.14.
[75] John A. McGuckin, *St Gregory of Nazianzus: An Intellectual Biography* (Crestwood, NY: St Vladimir's Seminary Press, 2001), p. 150, n. 234.
[76] A. N. Williams, *The Divine Sense: The Intellect in Patristic Theology* (Cambridge University Press, 2007).

So God's image in humankind is divine gift rather than inherent property, and communion with one another, with Christ, and ultimately with the Triune God, is found in reciprocal mirroring of the glory of the divine Image.

IV Towards appropriation and extension

In *Eccentric Existence* Kelsey draws attention to the theocentric nature of pre-modern theology,[77] making the point that theological anthropology as a separate discipline scarcely existed before the challenge of the Enlightenment stimulated its development. Others agree: it was 'bound up with the "turn to the subject", commonly associated with the philosophical method of Descartes'.[78] This enhanced focus on individual autonomy, on the nature of the self or human person, hardly encourages the idea that the patristic material has any pertinence. Yet the *Imago Dei* has been the coping-stone of theological anthropology;[79] so current themes are anticipated in patristic material, if in a different key. My argument will be that the integrated position implied in the thinking of the Nicenes is worth appropriating and extending in relation to, and sometimes in critique of, contemporary assumptions.

IV.1 *God's image and human rights*

In popular parlance, being made in God's image is a slogan providing Christian colouring for a modern human rights perspective: every individual, whether male or female, black or white, rich or poor, disabled or able-bodied, is to be treated with the respect and dignity

---

[77] Kelsey, *Eccentric Existence*, p. 29.

[78] Colin Crowder, 'Humanity' in Adrian Hastings, Alistair Mason and Hugh Pyper (eds.), *The Oxford Companion to Christian Thought* (Oxford University Press, 2000), pp. 311–14.

[79] It is interesting that Kelsey, *Eccentric Existence*, treats this in Codas, offering it as the climax of his massive work.

that come from being made in God's image. God's image is treated as something inherent in each individual, rather than as divine gift.[80] Such usage is in line with the way some of the fathers used the idea to attribute dignity to every particular human being, even those marginalized from society as lepers and outcasts, but in their case this rested on explicit appeal to human solidarity, and to Christ as the 'image' through which the dignity of each is imparted. This put claims about human being in a very different framework from post-Enlightenment and post-modern individualism. That theological framework needs reclaiming.

IV.1.1 Solidarity

The inherent dignity of each discrete individual is problematic. Individualism is shown up as wide of the mark by those, like Arthur, whose dependency is such that their very survival is owed to others. Each particular person is not autonomous in practice; only in community and through a sense of human solidarity can all receive dignity and personhood.

Some contemporary theologians have regarded communion and relationships as constitutive of what it means to be human. For Zizioulas:[81]

> being a person is fundamentally different from being an individual or a "personality", for a person cannot be imagined in himself but only within his relationships.

'The mystery of being a person', he writes, 'lies in the fact that here otherness and communion are not in contradiction but coincide'; indeed, this 'does not lead to the dissolving of the diversity of beings

---

[80] The notion that God's image is something inherent in, or 'possessed' by, humankind is criticized by Alistair I. McFadyen, *The Call to Personhood: A Christian Theory of the Individual in Social Relationships* (Cambridge University Press, 1990).

[81] John D. Zizioulas, *Being as Communion* (London: DLT, 1985); quotations are from pp. 105, 106, 102, 115 and 122.

in one vast ocean of being, but to the affirmation of otherness in and through love'. He even identified the fall as 'the refusal to make being dependent on communion'.

> The Word of God does not dwell in the human mind as rational knowledge or in the human soul as a mystical inner experience, but as communion within a community.

The eucharist 'gives [the church] the taste of eternal life as love and communion, as the image of the being of God'.[82]

The general point that humanity should be conceived as fundamentally constituted for relationship is not his alone. McFadyen[83] argues on biblical and theological grounds that 'an orthodox understanding of humanity created in the image of the Triune God and redeemed through God's address in Christ seems to require a relational understanding of human being'. His book explores the social formation of persons. 'There is no "self" in itself, but only as it is with and for others':

- identities are to be construed in terms of response to God and others
- individual identity denotes the way one is for others, and is derived from one's previous relations
- a person . . . is a subject of communication, an 'I' before the 'I' of others, and personhood is fostered through being addressed, intended and expected as a person by others: that is, through relations which take dialogical form.

Thus personal integrity is profoundly related to the mutuality involved in communication, trust and commitment.

---

[82] Zizioulas' position is grounded in Cappadocian theology, but his understanding is contested; see Lucian Turcescu, 'Modern Misreadings of Gregory of Nyssa' in Coakley (ed.), *Re-Thinking Gregory of Nyssa*, pp. 97–109.

[83] McFadyen, *The Call to Personhood*; quotations from pp. 65 and 154.

Such reclamation of the centrality of relationship, both with God and with one another, is embodied in a particular way in the lived reality of the L'Arche communities. Communion within a community enables not merely the imparting of dignity to those who are scarcely dignified, but also a sense of sacramental presence, perceived in a particular person, or experienced in mutual relationship with that person. This appropriates the patristic sense of human solidarity, and extends it beyond the 'top-down' tendency to patronize the poor and marginalized through 'charity' – the fathers' idea that those receiving alms reciprocate by praying for the giver and becoming the giver's means of salvation is now perceived as tainted by power relations. The creation of communities where 'assistants', often themselves young and vulnerable, receive love and affirmation from those they assist puts solidarity into a different register, that of mutuality. But the fundamental point is the challenge to individualism. In response to ideologies of individual rights and autonomy, public policy seeks to offer persons with disabilities independence and choice, but in subtle ways this can actually undermine the quality of life of those with learning disabilities. Often they cannot take the initiative, even to choose to have a birthday party, let alone organize it! Without incorporation into community, they are like disconnected limbs, supported as necessary but scarcely living. They reveal what is in fact the same for everyone: relationships are fundamental. This challenge to individualism is profoundly important. The fathers were almost certainly right that the statement in Genesis 1.26–7 referred to the corporate whole of the human race, not to each discrete particular person.

Yet the 'contrast between individualistic and relational concepts of human being as though they are mutually exclusive' is hardly sustainable;[84] relations between concrete individuals imply 'unsubstitutable personal identities'. Arthur is Arthur and no other, a particular person to whom respect and dignity is accorded within

[84] Kelsey, *Eccentric Existence*, p. 399.

the supportive and responsive networks of others who are in relationship with him.[85] So what does it mean to be a person? In post-
Enlightenment culture a person is defined as:

> a morally perfectible, autonomous centre of self-aware conscious-
> ness, in contradistinction to non-self-aware, nonconscious "things"
> that are subject to physical determinism. A person is a "subject" in
> contrast to an "object".[86]

Kelsey acknowledges the power of this modern concept, which, coupled with the self-expression of romanticism, shapes our experience
of the self and subjectivity;[87] but he counters it by stating that we are
constituted persons by God relating to us rather than by any set of
capacities. God addresses us, so offering us personal status as 'living
human bodies'.[88] This is absolutely vital if Arthur and others like him
are not to be implicitly excluded from personhood. Furthermore, it
is realized only in the solidarity of community.

IV.1.2 Dignity in Christ

Genesis underpins the popular use of the *Imago Dei* to affirm that all
are made in God's image. The fathers, however, read Genesis in the
light of the New Testament, which identifies Christ as the true image
of God. Kelsey[89] makes the same move. The incarnation offers an
important corrective to the idea that the 'image of God' in humanity
is meant to signify the rights of an autonomous individual, inherent
in each human creature. It is 'in Christ' that human beings are found
to be in God's image.

---

[85] For the importance of dignity not being inherent but accorded by others, see David A.
Pailin, *A Gentle Touch: From a Theology of Handicap to a Theology of Human Being*
(London: SPCK, 1992).

[86] Kelsey, *Eccentric Existence*, p. 360. Cf. Chapter 3.

[87] *Ibid.*, pp. 363–78.   [88] *Ibid.*, pp. 274–83. Cf. Pailin, *A Gentle Touch*.

[89] *Ibid.*, pp. 901 ff, 938, 1002.

The principal New Testament passage is Colossians 1.15–20: the Son is the 'image of the invisible God, the first-born of all creation', in whom everything was created. Not only is he the one through whom and for whom all things were created, and in whom 'all things hold together', but 'he is the head of the body, the church'. It was, and perhaps remains, unclear whether the principal focus is on the pre-existent Christ or the incarnate Christ; yet the sense of the passage as a whole is that Christ, as God's image, incorporates all that he has created, and in him it is possible for human creatures to be transformed, reconciled and raised from the dead.

This theme of human transformation in Christ provides the context of nearly all the New Testament passages that use the language of 'image' or 'likeness'. In 1 Corinthians 15.49, a contrast is drawn between 'the image of the man of dust' and 'the image of the man from heaven'; those to be changed by resurrection are to be in the image of the one already raised, namely Christ. In 2 Corinthians 4.4, we read of 'the light of the gospel of the glory of Christ, who is the image of God', which provides the framework for understanding 2 Corinthians 3.18: 'And all of us, with unveiled faces, seeing the glory of the Lord as though reflected in a mirror, are being transformed into the same image from one degree of glory to another.' As Kelsey puts it:

> As *Imago Dei* Christ mirrors the glory of God in such a way that those who "gaze" on that mirror undergo a transformative "seeing".[90]

Again, in Romans 8.29, those whom God foreknew he also predestined to be conformed to the image of his Son, in order that he might be the firstborn within a large family. All these texts associate the image of Christ with human transformation or renewal.

[90] *Ibid.*, p. 1000.

The approach to 'God's image' through the New Testament gives content to the God-likeness given in principle at creation and to be realized in Christ. It directs attention to concrete human living and relationships in the everyday such as are captured in stories of Jesus' life, not to mention the 'mind of Christ' displayed in his *kenōsis* and journey to the cross. Such embodiment of the character of the God who sends rain on just and unjust alike, who lovingly 'lets go' of what has been brought into being out of nothing, allowing it the freedom to become itself, both endorses and challenges the moral autonomy which human individuals have claimed. For, on the one hand, it confirms the idea that the gift of the image involves freedom and potential to make moral choices; on the other hand, it offers an ethical model which cannot be realized through autonomy, but only through self-submission to the good of others and the formation of a habitude of God-like loving in the context of everyday human existence. It also takes account of the limits of autonomy, allowing for the incorporation even of those with profound disabilities who lack capacity for moral responsibility.

As long as we work with an individualistic approach, the grounds for ascribing dignity, or indeed rights, to those whose freedom is curtailed and responsibility compromised seem shaky. But if God's image has something to do with human solidarity, then, even if Arthur is never able to make his own moral choices, he belongs to what might be called a moral community, implicated as he is in the relationships he has with those around him. Together, through communion in community, the gift of God's image and likeness is received and developed; how much more is this so if the model of God's image is the incarnate Christ, and the body of Christ is where God's image is realized in human solidarity.

A Christian approach to God's image in humanity must surely have such a Christological dimension. God's image is not something inherent, nor is it similar to 'human rights', but rather a gift of grace. It points away from discrete, supposedly autonomous, individuals to the solidarity of incorporation into the humanity of Christ, who is truly 'the image of the invisible God'.

IV.2 Towards a positive theological anthropology

In Western Christianity there is a deep strain of pessimism about human nature. The doctrine of 'original sin', Augustine's principal legacy, encourages people to regard themselves as 'miserable sinners', while the evangelical Gospel, calling on individuals to turn from sin and receive Christ as their personal Saviour and Lord, easily slips into reinforcement of personal guilt, with resultant self-deprecation masquerading as humility. Secularized culture has internalized this tradition as an excuse for moral failure: 'We're only human'; while popularized science has made us apes not angels. The notion of being made in God's image fails to act as a corrective to this endemic pessimism. Perceptively, Nonna Verna Harrison[91] draws on patristic material to challenge this pervasive outlook; she dedicates her book to 'all those people whom other people have thrown away', affirming that God does not do that.

Her greater optimism comes from the traditions of Eastern Christianity – not that a sense of sinfulness or the need for salvation is absent from any Christian tradition,[92] but tendencies in Eastern theology offer greater affirmation of human potential: (i) the emphasis on synergism – the capacity of human persons to respond to the workings of the Spirit and form themselves in virtue; (ii) the focus on incarnation rather than atonement; (iii) the idea of theōsis – that the goal of human existence is to realize the gift of God's image and likeness. Harrison writes: 'as human beings we are called to an unending process of becoming more and more like God, especially by sharing God's character and love'.

---

[91] Nonna Verna Harrison, *God's Many-Splendored Image: Theological Anthropology for Christian Formation* (Grand Rapids, MI: Baker Books, 2010). Quotations are largely from pp. 186–90.

[92] See Chapter 5.

Her chapters explore various facets of God's image and like-ness: freedom and responsibility; Christ incarnate as model; human capacity for spiritual perception, which allows for knowledge and love of God; moral excellence, virtue and humility; royal dignity within creation, with consequent responsibility for the planet and its ecosystems; and so on. Her purpose is to show that 'we are invited to work with God to co-create our future identity in a way that is more and more Christ-like', and that 'authentic spiritual perception' brings 'practical wisdom', enabling 'deeply loving service to neigh-bours and to God's creation even in the face of seemingly insur-mountable obstacles'. 'In principle all are called to be saints'; 'we are invited by grace to participate in God's virtues, such as justice, wisdom, humility, compassion, and above all love'. This involves a 'long growth process'; yet the image is a gift to every human being, including men and women, rich and poor, social outcasts such as slaves and the homeless disabled; and everyone as embodied beings may be filled with the divine life, and respond to the call to a royal priesthood – offering to God 'the praise and thankfulness of all cre-ation' and bringing 'God's blessing to all creation'. Human reason, creativity and culture, including science and the arts, manifest God's image, as does human community, which reflects community in the Trinity. Earthed in the theological spirituality of the fathers, this account acknowledges human failings and distortions while cele-brating for the contemporary world the high dignity of God's gift and call through the theme of 'God's many-splendored image'.

Paradoxically perhaps, this high optimism yet deep realism about human nature is best exemplified within contexts such as the L'Arche communities. The essays in *Encounter with Mystery* show time and again how persons with disabilities and their assistants reveal to each other their God-likeness. The way in which together they reflect God's glory is embodied in communities of love and communion. A contemplative ability to discern God's presence is evident – a waiting on God and each other in patience, alongside loving ser-vice and growth in 'God's virtues'. Growth in those supposedly without impairments is generated through identification with those who embody humanity's creatureliness, frailty and vulnerability, those who are utterly dependent on others and yet in their weakness have profound strengths which nourish the gifts of the Spirit: love, joy, peace, patience, kindness, generosity, faithfulness, gentleness and self-control.[93] The gift of God's image can be discerned if we have eyes to see, ears to hear, and the kind of humility that is not self-deprecation but openness to others. This is the dimension caught at L'Arche in the aphorisms: 'Christian faith is not problem-solving but mystery-encountering'; and 'mystery is communicated by participation'.[94]

Reappraisal of the pessimism endemic in Western theological perspectives is enabled by Kathryn Tanner.[95] She asks 'what light might be thrown on the well-worn idea that humans are created in the image of God, if Christ were the key to understanding it'. Developing patristic insights, she contrasts a weaker way of resemblance to God shared by all with a 'much stronger way of being an image through participation in what one is not'. Creatures:

> would image God . . . in virtue of the gift to them of what remains alien to them, the very perfection of the divine image that they are not, now having become their own.

Christ she offers as 'the paradigm of this strong sort of imaging through participation'. The 'perfect hypostatic unity' of incarnation 'makes for perfect imaging', and:

> Ordinary human beings would be the image of God in the strongest sense too . . . not when trying to image the divine image in a created fashion all by themselves, but instead, when drawing near to the divine image, so near as to become one with it.

---

[93] Galatians 5.22–3.   [94] See my *Encounter with Mystery*, pp. x–xi.
[95] Kathryn Tanner, *Christ the Key* (Cambridge University Press, 2010). Quotations are from pp. 1, 12–14, 22, 37, 44, 53, 58.

Jesus Christ is 'more than a paradigm'; 'he has become for us the very means'. Indeed, 'the Word's presence to us seems necessary . . . simply for us to be the sort of creatures God intends us to be'. So 'human nature must be characterized by an expansive openness that allows for the presence of God within it'. Echoing Gregory of Nyssa she writes:

> Humans are unusually impressionable in a way that the language of image often unpacks in a quite concrete, albeit metaphorical, way: they are like soft wax that a vast variety of seals might indent to their image; they are the mirror of whatever it is upon which they gaze.

There is something 'unbounded' about human nature; and thus 'humans imitate God's incomprehensibility', though God's 'unbounded fullness' contrasts with 'an emptiness in our own nature that opens us up to everything intelligible and good'. This sets off discussion of the nature of grace, allowing Tanner to argue that this 'strong sense . . . in which we participate or share in what we are not' is an understanding of grace which should bridge 'the usual theological divides between Protestants and Catholics'.

Kelsey's book offers a similar picture of human existence 'as eccentric, centered outside itself in the Triune God in regard to its being, value, destiny, identity, and proper existential orientations to its ultimate and proximate contexts'.[96] 'Jesus Christ in his humanity' is presented as the 'decisive image of God', which both 'defines how God is most aptly characterized', and also affirms the actual and particular bodily life of each finite human creature, which has 'an unsubstitutable personal identity' and 'concrete ways of interrelating with others'. The 'basic identity' of human beings 'is defined by the direct gift of God of being finite creatures empowered by God to be and to act, to give and receive', by God's 'drawing them to

---

[96] Kelsey, *Eccentric Existence*, p. 893. Further quotations are from pp. 915, 1022, 1042–3, 1050.

eschatological consummation', through a process of judgement and transformation, as well as by being reconciled despite estrangement.

> Jesus is paradigmatic of who all actual living human personal bodies are . . . inasmuch as they are images of the imager of God . . . they, too, are finite mysteries, imaging the image of the triune infinite mystery.

These proposals from recent Western theologians counter that self-understanding as 'miserable sinner', rooting self-affirmation in being the image of the Image of God. Preoccupation with sin fails to transform; affirmation which can transfigure comes from the discernment of God's image in ordinary human beings in everyday relationship with God and others. Optimism about human nature is engendered by attention to others, by empathy with others – human characteristics which evolutionists have struggled to explain, but which Christians have long seen exemplified in those saints who reflect God's image by living Christ-like lives. Even for Augustine, 'the constant identification and owning of sin' meant humility:

> 'purity' is not to be defined in the language of achievement or avoidance but of single-minded self-exposure to God's pure truth . . . The holiness of the indwelling Spirit who causes Christ to be alive in us comes into us through a radical putting aside of self-reliance.[97]

Holiness is not one's own accomplishment, but an emptiness within which it is possible to receive, an emptiness God will fill, but requiring self-abandonment, and a way of turning the desire for perfection into a pure and simple wish for God. Indeed, Augustine himself famously said, 'You have made us for yourself, and our heart is restless until it rests in you.'[98]

[97] Rowan Williams, *Why Study the Past?* (London: DLT, 2005), p. 49.
[98] *Confessions* I.i.(1).

IV.3 *Embodied rationality: wisdom and God's image*

In the Western world, secularism has provoked a divorce between rationality and religion. Aggressive atheists argue that religion is irrational, while many church people affirm faith against reason, and decry the 'cerebral' nature of Protestant Word-centred Christianity, preferring the heart over the head. The notion that God's image is in the rationality with which humans are endowed would hardly seem likely to command positive response in this climate, especially as it has inbuilt elitist overtones which appear to exclude persons with brain damage, such as Arthur. Besides, the patristic warnings against identifying God's image with a particular aspect or part of human nature, such as the soul or mind, are to be taken seriously. Still, the fathers do present a challenge to the split between head and heart, and the somewhat parallel gulf between spirituality and theology. Patristic theology involved the intellect in prayer and contemplation, and for them Christ was the embodiment of God's Wisdom and Word, the latter encompassing Reason or Mind as well as language.

> The emphasis on intellect as a divine attribute, a definitive human faculty, and a basis for human sanctification allows the theologians of the early church to write theology in a way scarcely envisageable today, in which both strictly academic or technical questions can be pursued alongside spiritual ones.[99]

We need to regain such an integrative understanding.

IV.3.1 Integrating head and heart

Reintegration means challenging the post-Enlightenment narrowing of rationality whereby what is subjective rather than objective is bracketed out, while rational knowledge is separated off from the embodied reality of wise, everyday living. The necessary challenge

[99] Williams, *Divine Sense*, p. 2; cf. p. 238.

is offered by Iain McGilchrist in *The Master and his Emissary: The Divided Brain and the Making of the Western World*, an illuminating treatment of the nature of intelligence and cultural history. His sophisticated discussion, informed by current neuroscience, offers pointers to the nature of embodied human wisdom.

It has long been recognized that the brain is asymmetric, that each hemisphere has 'sensory and motor responsibility for, and control of, the opposite (or "contralateral") side of the body', and language is 'the defining difference, the main specific task of the left hemisphere'.[100] But there is a problem:

> attempts to decide which set of functions are segregated in which hemisphere have mainly been discarded, piece after piece of evidence suggesting that every identifiable human activity is actually served at some level by both hemispheres.

Indeed, 'it is no longer respectable for a neuroscientist to hypothesize on the subject'. So McGilchrist rejects popular ideas about the left hemisphere being 'rational, realistic and dull', 'hard-nosed and logical', and therefore 'male', while the right hemisphere is 'airy-fairy and impressionistic', 'creative and exciting', 'dreamy and sensitive', and so 'female'.[101] However, he does insist that the asymmetric nature of the brain is not 'random', and there is 'something profound here that requires explanation'. So he explores the different 'worlds' of the two hemispheres, and the importance of their proper integration for a truly healthy personality and a wise culture.

The fundamental difference, he suggests, lies in the way in which each hemisphere attends to the world. The brains of animals and birds are also divided: 'chicks prioritize local information with the right eye (left hemisphere), and global information with the left eye

---

[100] Quotations in this paragraph are from McGilchrist, *Master and Emissary*, pp. 1–2.

[101] I myself expressed scepticism about this exploitation of the divided brain in my paper, 'From Analysis to Overlay: A Sacramental Approach to Christology' in David Brown and Ann Loades (eds.), *Christ: The Sacramental Word: Incarnation, Sacrament and Poetry* (London: SPCK, 1996), pp. 40–56.

(right hemisphere)'[102] – which means they can successfully peck at individual grains of corn while looking out for predators. Such differences are consistent and may 'foreshadow differences in humans'.

> It might then be that the division of the human brain is also the result of the need to bring to bear two incompatible types of attention on the world at the same time, one narrow, focused, and directed by our needs, and the other broad, open, and directed towards whatever else is going on in the world apart from ourselves.

Developing this basic perception, McGilchrist notes that the two hemispheres contribute different things to language; the right hemisphere takes in the whole context and has facility in using and understanding metaphor and humour, while the left hemisphere is literalizing and limited to the immediate logic of the situation, even if this is against what experience and common sense would suggest. The left hemisphere deals with abstraction and categorization, while the right hemisphere is concerned with relations between particulars. The left is concerned with utility, tools, mechanisms, things devised by human beings, the right with living things, things that have meaning and value for us as human beings, and in particular the recognition of faces. The right mediates 'empathetic identification' and allows one to put oneself in someone else's shoes and surmise what another might be thinking; the right has 'the preponderance of emotional understanding' and is 'the mediator of social behaviour', playing 'a vital role in emotional expression', apart from anger: for 'competition, rivalry and individual self-belief, positive or negative, would be preferentially treated by the left hemisphere'.

So McGilchrist suggests that 'linear, sequential argument is clearly better executed by the left hemisphere', but other types of reasoning, 'including deduction, and some types of mathematical reasoning, are

---

[102] Quotations in this paragraph are from McGilchrist, *Master and Emissary*, pp. 26–7, 49–52, 55–8, 61.

mainly dependent on the right hemisphere'.[103] Insight, or 'the sort of problem-solving that happens when we are, precisely, not concentrating on it, is associated with activities of the right hemisphere'. The right hemisphere specializes in non-verbal communication, and deals with whatever is implicit, whereas the left hemisphere is tied to 'more explicit and more conscious processing'. Subtle unconscious perceptions, such as the reading of facial expressions, are picked up by the right hemisphere. The right can cope with depth, with the unknown, the infinite and uncertain, with what is 'other', whereas the left needs certainty and needs to be right. So the 'sense of self' is 'grounded in the right hemisphere, because the self originates in the interaction with "the Other"'. Indeed, the right:

> matures earlier than the left, and is more involved than the left in almost every aspect of the development of mental functioning in childhood, and of the self as a social empathic being. Social development in the infant takes place independently of language development, another pointer to its right-hemisphere origins.

The human quality of a pre-linguistic person such as Arthur is excitingly illuminated by this observation, and is reinforced by his response to music, also a right-hemisphere function and possibly the 'ancestor of language'.

> The attunement of emotionally expressive facial expressions between mother and baby in the child's early maturing right hemisphere means that, long before the infant either comprehends or speaks a single word, it possesses a repertoire of signals to communicate its internal state.

McGilchrist concludes that the left deals with the kind of knowledge and rationality which is dominant in our culture – repeatable

---

[103] Quotations in this paragraph are from *ibid.*, pp. 65, 71, 82–3, 88, 103–5.

knowledge, "pieces" of information, 'general, impersonal, fixed, certain and disengaged'. But:

> [m]ost forms of imagination, for example, or of innovation, intuitive problem-solving, spiritual thinking or artistic creativity require us to transcend language, at least language in the accepted sense of a referential code. Most thinking, like most communication, goes on without language.[104]

Words 'come into their own' for 'transmitting information, specifically about something that is not present to us'; and they make concepts 'more subtle and available to memory'. But body language, body movement in dance to music, singing – embodied expression which appears useless in evolutionary terms – these are right-hemisphere functions, and they are what creates social cohesion and community, transcending utility and forming civilization. Indeed:

> [m]ost of the remarkable things about human beings, the things that differentiate us from animals, depend to a large extent on the right hemisphere.

These he instances as 'imagination, creativity, the capacity for religious awe, music, dance, poetry, art, love of nature, a moral sense, a sense of humour and the ability to change their minds', and suggests that:

> [i]t is the task of the right hemisphere to carry the left beyond, to something new, something 'other' than itself.

Much else in McGilchrist's argument is of fascination and relevance, but for our purposes the most significant points concern:

---

[104] Quotations in this paragraph are from *ibid.*, pp. 92, 96, 107, 108, 114, 127, 164.

- the way in which the distinguishable characteristics of the two halves of the brain actually work together, indeed the overdevelopment of one in relation to the other seems to lie at the root of some disabilities, autism being a classic of left-brain dominance
- the way in which mind is embodied in physical expressions of community such as singing and dancing – human language and intellect not being just about the manipulation of information, the communication of data or the mounting of logical argument, but also about the arts, literature, music, these being as important as science in expressing truth
- the way in which consciousness and mind are rooted in brain and body – mind is 'a process more than a thing – a becoming, a way of being, more than an entity'; it is 'the brain's experience of itself'.[105] McGilchrist is thoroughly opposed to reductive, mechanistic models: rather, accepting the 'incarnation' of mind and self in the physical brain, while also insisting on the complexity and importance of thinking, planning, creating, feeling and interacting with others, he emphasizes the aspects of human reason which transcend utility, foster relations with others, and facilitate the emergence of both culture and a sense of self
- the way in which the two clusters of functions overlap with the popular distinction between head and heart, so carrying the implication that true rationality requires the embrace of left-brain rationalistic argument within the wider world of right-brain wisdom – in other words, the mutual interaction of the critic's analytical precision and the visionary's holistic perspective.[106]

All these features point to the integration we seek, challenging the logocentric narrowness of scientific materialism, and the atheism

---

[105] *Ibid.*, p. 20. Cf. Chapter 3.
[106] For my earlier treatment of this subject, see 'The Critic and the Visionary', Inaugural lecture, University of Birmingham, 1987, part of which was reproduced in *SJT* 41 (1988) 297–312.

now so aggressively associated with it, by taking up critical reason into intuitive insight and wider wisdom.

IV.3.2 The true theologian

Word and Wisdom are significant concepts in theology. In McGilchrist's terms, religious fundamentalisms, with their literalism and dogma, together with a good deal of academic theology, with its emphasis on critical analysis, are dominated by the left-brain, words without wisdom. Spirituality, on the other hand, with its affective, imaginative and relational leanings, often lacks the wisdom to appreciate the contribution made by left-brain rationalism. The point is we need both perspectives. In Christian theology the Word of God and the Wisdom of God are together incarnated in Jesus Christ. The Word may represent language, propositional reasoning, certainties, purposive action, order (the left-brain's contribution), Wisdom open-ended possibilities, insight and intuition, metaphorical suggestiveness, loving commitment to the other (the right-brain's perspective). The true theologian will image Christ in holding these together.

The fathers anticipate this integration.[107] Gregory Nazianzen puts it in his own terms in his *First Theological Oration*.[108] The 'best theologian', he suggests, is not the one who can give a complete logical account of his subject – for if God is beyond the grasp of human comprehension, then the normal processes of human logic are

---

[107] This is further developed in 'The Critic and the Visionary' and 'The God of the Greeks and the Nature of Religious Language' in W. R. Schoedel and Robert Wilken (eds.), *Early Christian Literature and the Greek Intellectual Tradition*, Festschrift for R. M. Grant, Théologie Historique 53 (Paris: Éditions Beauchesne, 1979). Cf. Williams, *Divine Sense*.

[108] Gregory of Nazianzus, *Theological Orations*: Greek text: P. Gallay and M. Jourjon, *Saint Grégoire de Nazianze: Discours théologiques (27–31)*, *SC*; ET: F. W. Norris, with F. Williams and L. Wickham, *Faith Gives Fullness to Reasoning: The Five Theological Orations of St. Gregory Nazianzen*, Supplement to *VC*.

inapplicable. Rather, the true theologian is one who 'assembles more of Truth's image or shadow'. Heretics he accuses of the clever tricks of logicians who perform acrobats with words, twisting absurdity into apparently reasonable syllogisms and quibbling sophistries – in McGilchrist's terms, the left-brain over-dominant. The true theologian must qualify by meditation, by purification of soul and body, and by genuine commitment to the subject – in other words, by a holistic recognition of the transcendence of the subject-matter, and the significance of embodiment – a right-brain outlook. Religious language is necessarily metaphorical and symbolic, but this does not mean it is irrational. Gregory works within a tradition which recognizes that language has to be 'stretched' so as to point beyond itself. Knowledge of God comes partly through a balance between the analysis of apophaticism and the suggestiveness of analogy and synthesis, by which an overall viewpoint is taken of the way things are and how things point beyond themselves, but ultimately from that kinship to the divine implied by creation according to God's Image, the Word and Wisdom incarnated in Christ.

V Conclusion

Necessarily this discussion has been inchoate, in that hardly any attempt has been made to discuss the nature of the God imaged in human being – that will be the task of the final chapter. Christological material has figured because it has implications for a specifically Christian anthropology, but also because it highlights two significant points for doing theology in dialogue with the fathers: (i) it illustrates the process of theological argument whereby the implications of Christian confessions were articulated, thus implicitly providing a critique of the doctrinal development approach; and (ii) it alerts us to the ways in which different doctrines are deeply integrated with one another. In particular, it is impossible to divorce Christian understanding of the divine gift of God's image from the 'grand narrative' of fall and redemption, which implies the gift's loss or marring. To that we turn in the next chapter.

* * *

Reflections in a mirror

The preacher begins the sermon for the feast of transfiguration:

> What we now see is like a dim image in the mirror; then we shall see face-to-face.[109]

In the ancient world, most mirrors would have been pretty dim – the best technology was polished metal. A clear image would perhaps appear in a still pool, and, like Narcissus, you'd be entranced by the clarity of your own reflection, but generally you'd only see yourself as a dim image in a mirror. Paul goes on:

> what I know now is only partial; then it will be complete – as complete as God's knowledge of me.

So was he talking about knowledge of God or self-knowledge? Maybe we see God dimly by dim reflections of divine glory in our own faces.

In a long and complex passage elsewhere,[110] Paul ponders the story of Moses receiving the law on Mount Sinai. Such divine glory was reflected in Moses' face that he had to put a veil over it, which he only removed when he turned to the Lord. Paul suggests the veil was to conceal how temporary the old covenant was, and the veil is removed when a person turns to Christ. This was a novel way of reading the text to show how, in Christ, the new covenant in the spirit is fulfilled. The climax is this:

---

[109] 1 Corinthians 13.12.   [110] 2 Corinthians 3.

All of us, with unveiled faces, seeing the glory of the Lord as though reflected in a mirror, are being transformed into the same image from one degree of glory to another.

Yes – God's image and glory are to be seen in our faces as we are transformed into the true image, which is Christ. And that must surely mean we are gradually drawn into the transfiguration.

Let me share an illuminating night. I was with a group doing a sponsored trek up Mount Sinai for a disability charity. We were staying at a Bedouin eco-lodge in the midst of the desert. Darkness fell before 6pm, and in the blackness and clarity of the desert, the night sky was a sight beyond anything seen before, pinpoints of light everywhere, with the Milky Way streaking with stunning brilliance across the heavens. Early to bed, I lay awake, unable to sleep. A three-hour meditation moved from scenes of the 'great and terrible wilderness' we'd traversed on foot that day, with its dry wadis and amazing rock formations, to the prospect of the next day's trek up Mount Sinai.

There God spoke with Moses face to face, as a man speaks to his friend; yet when Moses asked God to show him his glory, the response was:

I will make all my goodness pass before you . . . but you cannot see my face; for no one shall see me and live. See, there is a place by me where you shall stand on the rock; and while my glory passes by I will put you in a cleft of the rock, and I will cover you with my hand until I have passed by; then I will take away my hand, and you shall see my back; but my face shall not be seen.[111]

From Moses, thoughts turned to Elijah, the prophet who ran away to the same mountain to escape opposition, and found God not in storm, earthquake or fire, but in that 'still small voice', probably better translated 'a sound of sheer silence'.[112] Next day I would discover

---

[111] Exodus 33.11, 19–23.   [112] 1 Kings 19.11–12.

'Elijah's basin' part way up the mountain, but that night my mind slipped from 'no one can see me and live' to the moment when the disciples discerned the glory of the Lord as Jesus was transfigured on a mountain and was joined by Moses and Elijah.

Emerging from the pitch-black of the stone sleeping-hut, I found the desert transfigured by the silvery light of the moon. Then, in the morning, before our ascent of the mountain, I found myself in the church of St Catherine's monastery at the foot of Mount Sinai and there glimpsed in the apse the famous early mosaic of Christ's transfiguration to which the church is dedicated. The icon showed Christ bathed in light against the dark-blue depths of God's eternal infinity.

No one can see God and live, and God's presence is in a still small voice. It's hard to hear, and we see only God's back. Yet God's glory is seen in the face of Christ, and insofar as we are in Christ, we may reflect that glory, even if only dimly. And sometimes we catch a glimpse in another's face, in an everyday saint who somehow embodies the love of Christ, or in someone who needs us to show the love of Christ – one of those whom neither the sheep nor the goats recognized:[113] someone hungry, or thirsty, a stranger, someone with no adequate clothing, sick or in prison.

It's even possible for a face-to-face meeting to put us in both places at once – meeting each other's mutual neediness. Many years ago I was visiting the original l'Arche community in Trosly-Breuil, and spending the evening at one of the foyers. A man with Down's syndrome settled on the floor at my feet, placed his arms round my knees and stared into my face with love and concentration. Our mutual gaze became deeply significant, as I began to sense that he was offering me the wordless response of love which, at the time, I scarcely received from my own severely disabled son. His name was Christophe – Christ bearer.

<hr/>

[113] Matthew 25.31–45.

What we now see is like a dim image in a mirror, then we shall see face to face. Amen.

* * *

Postlude

Elusive Likeness

A glimpse of an image is caught
in an almost ginger moustache
and a certain look round the eyes.
With its littleness and loss
of brain development
the grandson's likeness belies
the grandfather's dignity
and impressive intellect –
an offence one might surmise.
Yet the glint of a loving smile
encaptures its genesis
in shy, suggestive guise.

So the human likeness to God:
a gargoyle one might surmise,
a mirror-image that lies,
its hazy reflections reversed –
huge hints, yet hard to trace,
that veil their archetype,
yet focussed face to face
reveal what love implies.
So too God's image in Christ:
God's likeness in human guise –
an unlike likeness formed
from utter otherness
in close proximity;

transcendent holiness
in physicality;
in littleness and loss
an outline sketch that tries
to capture its genesis
in that look about the eyes;
intangible, infinite grace
extended in tender touch
and shining from the face –
invisible visage caught
in expressions loving and wise.

Perception[114]

Imagine a life with sound but no word –
A life full of music and buzzing and shouts
But no structure or form. Could meaning be there
At all, or would everything be absurd?

Imagine a life with sight but no sense –
A life full of colour and movement and shapes
But no objects or space. Wouldn't it seem
A random muddle, a jumble immense?

But patterns are there, and proportion discerned
In the slatted light of Venetian blinds,
In the fractals of trees or the web of a grill:
So some sense of beauty is learned.
Yet much blindness remains, and still there's a kind
Of incomprehension that shuts off the mind.

And expressions are there, and moods conveyed
In the tone of voices, in laughter, in tears:

---

[114] An earlier version of this was published in *Face to Face* (revised and enlarged, Edinburgh: T & T Clark, 1990).

In music's dynamics, its beat and its flow –
So some connection is made.
Yet much deafness remains, and still there's a kind
Of incomprehension that shuts off the mind.

Perception has limits. Our brain-damaged son
Lives a life full of colour and music and light,
A life full of loving and sharing and fun,
But really perception has only begun.
He has such limitations – yet still there's a kind
Of mysterious awareness enlarging the mind.

Perception has limits – our vision's too small.
As for loving and sharing, our failures appal.
We have such limitations – but still there's a kind
Of mysterious transcendence enlarging the mind.

Other Observations

Admiration gazes in a pool,
At nature's water-colour portraiture.
A ripple-raising touch spells caricature!
Self-images tend to distort. Only the fool
Refuses to learn self-knowledge in laughter's school.
Reflection writes the unwritten literature
That details character in miniature,
Disclosing truths by likeness, often cruel.
But feeling a fool's not being a fool. The way
To reflect the image of God is to turn the face
Away from self to catch the glancing ray
Disturbing the waters, laughing the laugh of grace.
Bent in the pool is the crutch of vanity.
The sanity of fools is sanctity.

In the Hermitage

Rembrandt's *Prodigal Son* and an icon of the crucifixion

Contemplation gazes at the feet.
All down at heel and travel-worn, the shoes
Gave no protection: shame let stones abuse
His soles, and urged him on through dirt and heat.
Crushed in the crowds all one could see was the feet,
The prodigal's status summed up in that image of strife
With gravelly ground, the humiliations of life.
But somewhere up there his father ran to greet.
Embodied, with feet of clay, another threads
His way by just such pebbly paths. He treads,
His feet in touch with earth and pierced with nails,
Deepening the crippling wounds that hurt entails.
The icon seen from below, those nailed feet raise
The eyes, somewhere up there, to meet love's gaze.

5 | From Adam and Eve to Mary and Christ: sin, redemption, atonement

Prelude

The historian documents the atrocities of the twentieth century; the concert audience inwardly echoes the screaming sounds and relentless rhythms of Shostakovich's 'dark epic', his Eighth Symphony, as it 'continues to ring out as the voice of an individual sensibility speaking for the millions whose lives have been shattered by totalitarianism, militarism and cruelty'.[1]

The abused child is damaged for life. The battered wife, the abandoned husband, each refuses to forgive, while jealous siblings engage in malicious bullying.

The businessman fiddles the books; the financier avoids tax. The official indulges in petty tyranny, and the yob bullies the vulnerable.

The poor are always with us: lack of opportunity, bad luck, exploitation, slavery, the legacies of colonialism or people-trafficking.

The Psalmist asks, 'Why do the wicked prosper?' and the student tentatively enquires whether Job was blaspheming.

The evangelist thunders out the Gospel: Christ died for our sins, paid the penalty on our behalf, made the ultimate sacrifice for us and our salvation; some respond to the altar call, tears streaming, and commit themselves to Christ as their personal Lord and Saviour.

---

[1] Andrew Huth, programme note for the City of Birmingham Symphony Orchestra performance on 22 September 2010.

The Catholic faithful quietly queue to venerate the cross as the recorded voice of Paul Robeson sings, 'Were you there when they crucified my Lord?'

The Serbian Orthodox priest shakes his head and gently observes, 'I really don't know about this atonement . . . '

The massed chorus sings, 'Praise to the Holiest in the Height . . . O living wisdom of our God! When all was sin and shame, A second Adam to the fight, And to the rescue came.'

The mother weeps. A sword has pierced her heart. She's in Lourdes, on pilgrimage with Faith and Light.[2] Someone gently told a man with Down's syndrome, who'd been giving testimony at length, to wind it up. He had one final word – thanks to his wonderful mum. The mother, full of grief and guilt for failing her own severely disabled son, is comforted by a companion with epilepsy and learning disabilities; together they go to the grotto, together they wash each other's hands and face in the holy water.

The woman looks into the face of the 'Walking Madonna', that more-than-life-size figure of Mary in Salisbury Cathedral close, and, making eye-contact with that strong, yet aged and haggard visage, each seems to know the places of grief, loss and peace where the other has been.

* * *

In Adam the image was marred; in Christ humanity was redeemed and the image restored. Fall and redemption have always been at the core of the Christian claim, distinctive from other monotheisms. It arises from a particular reading of scripture as a whole. Emerging to some extent in reaction to gnostic versions of fall and return, it proved both receptive to and critical of Platonist influences, while

[2] Foi et Lumière, or Faith and Light, is a sister organization to L'Arche, also founded by Jean Vanier with Marie-Hélène Matthieu. It began with a Lourdes pilgrimage for families with children with learning disabilities in 1971. Like L'Arche it rapidly spread throughout the world and became ecumenical. This paragraph refers to the 1991 twentieth anniversary pilgrimage.

never being formulated into a doctrine of atonement as such. Salvation was a key factor, along with the doctrine of creation, in driving arguments about Christology and the nature of God; yet the redemption the fathers proclaimed was expressed in a welter of symbols and metaphors, and no systematic theory displaced what we would dub 'myth'. So it might seem implausible that the work of the fathers has much to contribute to current theological reflection on sin and redemption, especially given post-Darwinian scepticism about the historicity of Adam and Eve. I hope again to prove that an over-hasty conclusion.[3]

I Adam and Christ, Eve and Mary

1.1 Irenaeus

1.1.1 *The Demonstration of the Apostolic Preaching*

Irenaeus here summarizes the faith received from the apostles.

Beginning with creation, the making of Adam, his placing in paradise, the forming of Eve, he then describes Adam and Eve as innocent, naked yet unashamed, 'kissing and embracing each other in holiness as children'.[4] The command not to eat of the tree of knowledge of good and evil was a precaution against Adam 'entertaining thoughts of grandeur . . . because of the authority given to him', or because of the privilege of open communication (*parrhēsia*) with God – he might sin by 'passing beyond his own measure' and 'adopt an attitude of self-conceited arrogance against God'. The man

---

[3] This chapter incorporates material from two previously published articles of mine, where fuller references and discussion may be found: '*Theotokos*: Mary and the Pattern of Fall and Redemption in the Theology of Cyril of Alexandria' in Thomas G. Weinandy and Daniel A. Keating (eds.), *The Theology of St Cyril of Alexandria: A Critical Appreciation* (London: T & T Clark, 2003), pp. 55–74; 'Allegory and Atonement' in the *Australian Biblical Review* 35 (1987), Special Issue in Honour of Professor Eric Osborn, 107–14.

[4] *Apostolic Preaching* 14: ET: Behr, *Irenaeus: On the Apostolic Preaching*.

failed to keep this one commandment, misled by the jealous angel hiding in the serpent, who both 'ruined himself and made the man a sinner'.[5] The resultant curse and blessing passed from generation to generation – Cain and Abel; Noah's generation; Ham, Shem and Japheth; the tower of Babel. The stories of Abraham and Moses are sketched, the giving of the law, the arrival in the promised land. The climax comes with the prophets 'sent from God', who by the Holy Spirit 'admonished the people and returned [them] to the God of the patriarchs', and who 'were made heralds of the revelation of our Lord Jesus Christ, the Son of God', the one 'at first with the Father, born before all creation', then 'revealed to all the world at the close of the age as man, "recapitulating all things" in himself, the Word of God, "things in heaven and things on earth"'.[6] Irenaeus explains that:

> because all are implicated in the first formation of Adam, we were bound to die through disobedience, [so] it was fitting by means of the obedience of the One who on our account became man, to be loosed <from> death.[7]

He draws a parallel between the virgin earth from which Adam was formed and the virgin from whom the Lord was born, 'recapitulating this man', so as to 'demonstrate the likeness of embodiment [*sarkōsis*] to Adam' and 'become the man, written in the beginning, "according to the image and likeness of God"'.[8] Just as a disobedient virgin brought death, so life came through a virgin who obeyed the Word of God. Irenaeus insists that Christ was formed exactly as Adam, for:

> it was necessary for Adam to be recapitulated in Christ, that 'mortality might be swallowed up in immortality'; and Eve in Mary, that a virgin, become an advocate for a virgin, might undo and destroy the virginal disobedience by virginal obedience.[9]

---

[5] *Ibid.* 16.   [6] *Ibid.* 30, quoting Ephesians 1.10.   [7] *Ibid.* 31.
[8] *Ibid.* 32, quoting Genesis 1.26.
[9] *Ibid.* 33, referencing 2 Corinthians 5.4; 1 Corinthians 15.54.

Thus 'the transgression which occurred through the tree was undone by the obedience of the tree'.

1.1.2 *Against the Heresies*

The significance of this reading of scripture was doubtless underlined for Irenaeus by the alternative reading offered by followers of 'knowledge falsely so-called', known to us by the label gnostics. Recapitulation is deeply embedded in this work.

In Book I, Irenaeus notes that the Ophites thought *Nous* (Mind) was contorted into the form of a serpent; and *Sophia* (Wisdom) cunningly devised a scheme to seduce Adam and Eve, who by eating of the tree 'attained to the knowledge of that power which is above all'. The god they disobeyed was the fallen Demiurge, Ialdabaoth, who proceeded to cast them into the material world. The serpent brings the spiritual knowledge needed to return to the heavens. Irenaeus called the heretics 'patrons of the serpent'.[10] Some of the gnostic texts recovered in the last century confirm this reading of Genesis.

In Book III Irenaeus sets out the right reading of the scriptures, upturning the story so that the Creator is the one God, to whom Adam is disobedient, while Christ became incarnate to restore what had been lost in Adam. God's Word became flesh so as to 'recapitulate in himself the ancient creation of humankind', in order to 'slay sin, remove death's sting and restore man to life'.[11] Quoting Romans 5.19, Irenaeus explains that:

> As the protoplast Adam had his substance of the virgin earth . . . so the Word himself, recapitulating Adam in himself, duly received from Mary, still a virgin, the birth of that nature in which Adam was recapitulated.[12]

He emphasizes the taking of real flesh from Mary so that 'the very same creation might be recapitulated, the likeness being retained

---

[10] *Against Heresies* I.30.   [11] *Ibid.* III.18.7.   [12] *Ibid.* III.21.10. Cf. Chapter 7.

throughout'. He also recalls Mary's willing and obedient response, 'Behold the handmaid of the Lord', bringing salvation to the whole of humankind, by contrast with Eve's disobedience; but he treats Adam and Eve as 'innocent' and childlike.[13]

Indeed, in Book IV, he asserts that God's creature was at first infantile and could not receive perfection, given its weakness, just as a babe cannot receive stronger nourishment than milk – of course, God could have conferred the perfect gift from the beginning, but humanity was unable to receive it. That was why 'the Lord, recapitulating all things in himself, came to us in the last times, not as he could manifest himself, but as we could see him'. We could never have borne it if he had come in his indescribable glory. God knew in advance human weakness and its consequences, and out of sheer benevolence arranged for the mortal and corruptible to be overcome, even after humanity had received knowledge of good and evil – indeed, Irenaeus recognizes the benefits of that knowledge.[14] He also recognized that there were extenuating circumstances in the case of Adam and Eve: they were deceived by the devil in the form of a serpent and were like captives taken over by hostile forces. Besides, God is long-suffering and unwilling to see his handiwork destroyed. So, exploiting details in the Genesis story, he suggests Adam's repentance and God's compassion: God pitied Adam, and interposed death so that humankind could die to sin and receive new life.

Against the gnostics, then, Irenaeus tells the story not as utterly tragic loss, but as part of a process of maturation: the image and likeness of God is Christ, the form of which Adam and Eve receive proleptically but into which they will grow. Only the incarnation makes sense of it all.[15] But given the gnostic tendency to deny the reality of the crucifixion, he also shows how the passion is an essential aspect of this: he did away with humankind's disobedience with regard to a tree by 'becoming obedient unto death, even death on

---

[13] *Ibid.* III.22.   [14] *Ibid.* IV.38–9.   [15] *Ibid.* V.1.1, 16.1. Cf. Chapter 4.

the cross', in other words by obedience shown on a tree.[16] He healed
human nature through the forgiveness of sins, fastening our debt
to the cross,[17] that 'as we were debtors to God by a tree, by a tree
we might receive the remission of our debt'.[18] This recapitulation of
Adam, Eve and tree is effected through cross, Mary and Christ, and
the cunning of the serpent is conquered by the harmlessness of the
dove. Failure to discern this overall dispensation blinds heretics to
the truth and distorts the story.[19]

1.1.3 A common tradition?

This typological understanding of Adam and Christ, Eve and Mary
is widespread in patristic material. Yet the extent of Irenaeus' direct
influence is contested. Often regarded as the 'first Christian theologian', his importance perhaps lies in voicing the common tradition.
Study of the fathers often projects back modern interest in originality
and creativity onto those who themselves were primarily interested
in faithfully passing on what they had received, even if the exigencies
of their own time meant new emphases and perspectives – as may
have been the case with Irenaeus' resistance to the gnostic reading of
scripture.

 Irenaeus claimed to represent what true Christians universally
affirmed throughout the world, and there were some outline precedents for Irenaeus' reading. Paul set up a typology between Adam
and Christ on two occasions: Romans 5.12–17 and 1 Corinthians
15.45–9; the word 'recapitulation' itself appears in the Pauline corpus
at Ephesians 1.10: according to God's will and pleasure, everything
on earth and in heaven was to be 'recapitulated' in Christ. Paul's
hints had already been picked up by Justin Martyr; when Irenaeus
quotes Justin's lost work against Marcion,[20] the words 'summing up
(or recapitulating) his own handiwork in himself' are likely to be

[16] *Ibid.* v.16.3, quoting Philippians 2.8.   [17] Colossians 2.14.
[18] *Against Heresies* v.17.3.   [19] *Ibid.* v.19.   [20] *Ibid.* iv.6.2.

part of the quotation rather than Irenaeus' comment. We also find in Justin's *Dialogue with Trypho*:

> Christ became man by the Virgin in order that the disobedience which proceeded from the serpent might receive its destruction in the same manner in which it derived its origin. For Eve, who was a virgin and undefiled, having conceived the word of the serpent, brought forth disobedience and death. But the Virgin Mary received faith and joy, when the angel Gabriel announced the good tidings to her that the Spirit of the Lord would come upon her, and the power of the Highest would overshadow her . . . and she replied: 'Be it unto me according to thy word.'[21]

Irenaeus testifies to the emergence of a scriptural canon consisting of the books of the old covenant together with a collection of documents bearing witness to the new covenant, and allows us to see how that scriptural canon came to be read as a single over-arching narrative of fall and redemption, represented by Adam and Christ.

1.2 *Ephrem Syrus*

At the opposite end of the Roman empire some two centuries later we find this theme in the work of Ephrem the Syrian.

In his *Commentary on Genesis*, Ephrem offers a slightly different re-telling of the Genesis story, insisting that Adam and Eve were not children, but fully mature,[22] and that the tempter could not have succeeded had it not been for their own avarice.[23] They would eventually have eaten of both the tree of knowledge and the tree of life – indeed, the serpent by promising divinity actually prevented them getting it;[24] they were created neither mortal nor immortal – that

---

[21] *Dialogue* 100; Greek text: M. Markovich (ed.), *Dialogus cum Tryphone, PTS*; ET: *FC*.

[22] *Commentary on Genesis* II.14; Syriac text: *CSCO*; ET: *FC* and Section II in Sebastian Brock, *Saint Ephrem: Hymns on Paradise* (Crestwood, NY: St Vladimir's Seminary Press, 1990).

[23] *Ibid.* II.16–7.   [24] *Ibid.* II.23.

depended on their choice. Their disobedience was compounded by failure to repent;[25] and their expulsion from paradise was an act of God's mercy – to prevent them from eating from the tree of life and ending up with eternal lives of trial, sweat and pain.[26] So, what was lost in Adam is not merely restored through Christ but surpassed – for the return to paradise means eating of both trees and receiving transformation for eternal life.

The typological parallels appear in Ephrem's poetry, often with intriguing additions:

> Just as from the small womb of Eve's ear
> Death entered in and was poured out,
> So through a new ear, that was Mary's,
> Life entered and was poured out.[27]

> Eve in her virginity put on leaves of shame,
> but your mother, Lord, in her virginity
> has put on a robe of glory
> that encompasses all people,
> while to Him who covers all
> she gives a body as a tiny garment.[28]

> In the month of Nisan our Lord repaid
> the debts of that first Adam:
> He gave his sweat in Nisan in exchange for Adam's sweat,
> the Cross, in exchange for Adam's Tree.[29]

> He gave his hands to be pierced by the nails
> in place of the hand that had plucked the fruit;
> He was struck on the cheek in the judgement hall
> in return for that mouth that had devoured in Eden.

---

[25] *Ibid.* 11.23–9. [26] *Ibid.* 11.35.
[27] *Church* 49.7, quoted in Brock, *The Luminous Eye*, p. 33.
[28] *Nativity* 17.4, in Brock, *The Luminous Eye*, p. 90.
[29] *Church* 51.8, in Brock, *The Luminous Eye*, p. 33.

Because Adam had let slip his foot
they pierced his feet.
Our Lord was stripped naked so that we might be clothed in
modesty;
with gall and vinegar he made sweet
that bitter venom that the serpent had poured into humankind.[30]

Ephrem makes it clear that the parallels embrace all humanity, and in the *Hymns on Paradise* we find biblical stories fused so as to constitute the story of 'everyman':

The king of Babylon resembled
    Adam king of the universe:
Both rose up against the one Lord
    And were brought low.[31]

So did king David, who wept for Adam and his fall; but 'In that king / Did God depict Adam.'[32] The following verse declares that, 'because it was not easy for us to see our fallen state', he depicted it in that king, 'portraying our fall in his fall, and portraying our return in his repentant return'.[33] The hymn draws similar points from Samson, Jonah and Joseph. Thus time and persons are fused into exemplars of a single human narrative of fall and redemption.

Through Mary and Christ restoration to paradise has in principle been effected, and the church is a foretaste of that.

The assembly of saints
    bears resemblance to Paradise:
in it each day is plucked
    the fruit of Him who gives life to all . . .
The serpent is crippled and bound
    By the curse . . .
Among the saints none is naked,

---

[30] *Nisibis* 36.1, in Brock, *The Luminous Eye*, p. 20.
[31] *Paradise* XIII.4.   [32] *Ibid.* XIII.6.   [33] *Ibid.* XIII.7.

for they have put on glory . . .
  for they have found, through our Lord,
    the robe that belongs to Adam and Eve.[34]

For Ephrem, Adam and Christ, Eve and Mary, are universal types, representing two kinds of truth about humanity; each human being may be drawn into this over-encompassing narrative and find themselves reflected in it.

1.3 Cyril of Alexandria

This pattern of fall and redemption, exemplified in the Adam–Christ typology, lay at the root of the theology of Cyril of Alexandria and would drive his defence of the title *Theotokos* for Mary in the Nestorian controversy.

1.3.1 Fall and redemption

Cyril's exegetical writings prior to the controversy demonstrate how significant this tradition was for him. A good example is his massive treatment of the pentateuch known under the title *On Worship in Spirit and in Truth*.[35] The initial question is this: how is the statement in Matthew, that not a jot or tittle of the law will pass away, to be reconciled with that in John, that the Father will not be worshipped in Jerusalem but in spirit and in truth? This conundrum provides the occasion for working through the law to show that it is a 'type', a foreshadowing of proper devotion to God: the beauty of truth is hidden within it. The law is a pedagogue – leading infants to maturity, delivering truth through metaphors and types, stories and pictures.[36] So Cyril will turn Leviticus into spiritual sacrifices and passages on priesthood into types of Christ and the church, with

---

[34] *Ibid.* vi.8, 9.
[35] Greek text: Migne, *PG* 68; no published ET, quotations in author's translation.
[36] Migne, *PG* 68.137–40.

the bloodless sacrifice of the eucharist and the roles of bishops and presbyters prefigured in the law. But first the movement from fall into sin, then through repentance to renewal through God's grace, becomes a universal paradigm, traced out in one narrative after another and applied to 'us'. For each is an instance of the universal story of the human race: it is not hard to see that what happened to Adam happens to each of us.[37]

Abraham is the first exemplar. Caught in Egypt by Pharaoh, Abraham's story is a paradigm of spiritual enslavement, Pharaoh representing the father of sin, who treats us well as long as he can distract us with pleasure. Only God and divine grace could rescue Abraham.[38] Driven by famine, those with Jacob likewise went to Egypt and suffered God's anger through the yoke of slavery – they were tempted by worldly food when they should have been hungry for God's word.[39] All through there is a profound inter-textuality with allusions and quotations from across the prophets and the New Testament.

For Cyril, we, like Abraham, are called to follow God, to leave behind everything in which we take pleasure – homeland, kindred: after all, Jesus spoke of leaving father and mother to follow him. As Abraham leaves what is worldly to build an altar in the promised land,[40] so we receive no grace so long as we are wedded to the world, but, if obedient, we shall journey to the high country, to knowledge of God, and shall stand before God as a living sacrifice well-pleasing to God. The story of Sodom and Lot demonstrates the problem for us all of falling from this state of grace.[41] With immense detail Cyril traces the symbols which point to the progress of the soul and its gradual ascent back to where it had been. Abraham escapes Egypt to build an altar and call on the name of the Lord.[42] Enigmatically his journey shows the importance of changing wholeheartedly, of loving the desert, that is, the purity of mind and heart which humanity enjoyed in the beginning.

---

[37] *Ibid.* 148.   [38] *Ibid.* 152 f.   [39] *Ibid.* 160 f.
[40] *Ibid.* 168.   [41] *Ibid.* 169 f.   [42] *Ibid.* 184–5.

The same basic idea is traced in the story of the Exodus. Both descents into Egypt are seen as resulting from free choice, but the consequent enslavement is oppression from Pharoah, who stands for the devil. Human souls are oppressed and put to hard and useless labours, just like the Israelites. But God took pity on those harassed by Egyptian excesses and lavishes grace on those dragged into sin. For the Israelites God appointed Moses and now writes the law on the heart through the mediator who brings free life to us.[43] God is liberator and saviour, but we need to go out into the desert to prepare a holy feast for God apart from the Egyptians, removed from worldly darkness.[44]

> We are all called to freedom through faith in Christ and ransomed from the tyranny of the devil...this being prefigured in those of old, especially Moses and Aaron, so that by reason of God's gracious arrangement [*oikonomikōs*] you may discern that Emmanuel is, in similar fashion, lawgiver, high priest and apostle.[45]

Thus not a jot or tittle of the law is taken away, but the whole matter concerns worship in spirit and in truth. God's intentions are graciously set out in scripture if we only read the scriptures aright, that is, according to the universal paradigm of fall and redemption.

One particular passage[46] not only shows how Cyril plays with symbolic connections, but hints at the potentially ambivalent significance of snakes.[47] In Exodus 4, Moses is afraid that the Israelites will not believe him. He's told to throw his staff to the ground; it becomes a snake, and he runs from it. God tells him to catch it by its tail, and it reverts to a stick. Cyril comments: God provides a 'wonder' to counter disbelief; the form of the 'wonder' is a figure of salvation in Christ. The staff/sceptre symbolizes kingship: Adam was to rule the earth, but through the snake he was deprived of kingly glory, falling from paradise. The staff fell from the hand of

---

[43] *Ibid.* 188. [44] *Ibid.* 192. [45] *Ibid.* 200. [46] *Ibid.* 240–5.
[47] See further below, *The Serpent-Christ.*, pp. 250–6.

Moses – this signifies that in the beginning there was in the hand of
the Creator a twig from paradise, made in God's image, in the glory
of kingship, but he fell to the ground and in the eyes of God was
like a snake. Moses' flight from the snake is explained by Wisdom
1.5, 'the Holy Spirit of wisdom will flee from deceit and back off
from foolish thoughts' – it indicates how holiness and impurity,
light and darkness, righteousness and unrighteousness are incompatible. But the result of Moses catching him by the tail was reversion
into a sceptre, a twig of paradise. So when God was pleased to recapitulate everything in Christ, creating anew what was made in the
beginning, he sent us the Only Begotten, his right-hand, the Creator
and Saviour of all. He took our humanity, transformed our wildness, our sin, and through sanctification brought us to royal honour
and the tameness that leads to virtue. With many other intertextual
references Cyril expands the theme, his focus resting on the transformation through grace of the whole human race, including the head,
Adam.

1.3.2 Adam and Christ

The *Glaphyra*, Cyril's *Elegant Comments* on Genesis,[48] has more
explicit treatment of the Adam story. The Pauline basis of Cyril's
reading of Genesis is striking: Ephesians 1.10 provides the word 'recapitulation'; 2 Corinthians 5.17 points to renewal; Galatians 5.24 says
the flesh is crucified with Christ, so indicating how the old is done
away. For Cyril re-creation in Christ is the thrust of Paul's message,
but also the meaning of the Genesis narrative. A lengthy exposition
of Adam's story, beginning with the loss of 'singleness' at the creation
of woman from his side, continues with the devil's temptation and
his expulsion from paradise. But then Cyril is back to Paul, quoting
long passages to show that the grace of salvation was given before

---

[48] Migne, *PG* 69.16–32; ET of selections: Norman Russell, *Cyril of Alexandria* (London:
Routledge, 2000).

the ages began,[49] and everything was preordained so that all things work together for good.[50] God foreknew the manner of the Son's incarnation. Redemption would come through recapitulation.

In elucidating that recapitulation, Cyril again exploits Paul. 1 Corinthians 15 is key, with cross-reference to Galatians 3.13 and Romans 5. Christ is the last Adam, recapitulating and reversing the fall of the first. By being a 'type' of Christ, Adam is prophetic of the mystery of the incarnation, of Emmanuel, God with us. The first Adam brought us death, the curse and judgement; the second, life, blessing and righteousness. Adam brought the woman to himself so as to become one flesh and was destroyed through her; but Christ saves, drawing the church to himself through the Spirit. Here is an oblique hint that Eve and Mary will become vital to the fall and redemption pattern in Cyril's theology.

Cyril's *Commentary on John*[51] is saturated with allusions to Christ as the second Adam, even though the Gospel itself has no reference to Adam at all:[52]

> The common element of humanity is summed up in [Christ's] person, which is also why he was called the last Adam: he enriched our common nature with everything conducive to joy and glory, just as the first Adam impoverished it with everything bringing gloom and corruption.[53]

Here the Virgin comes into play: 'he dwelt in flesh, using as his own particular body the temple which is from the Holy Virgin'. In the *Commentary on Isaiah*, Cyril insists, against Jewish exegetes, that

[49] 2 Timothy 1.8–10.   [50] Romans 8.28–30.

[51] *Commentary on John* 1.9 (on 1.12); Greek text: P. E. Pusey (ed.) (Oxford: Clarendon Press, 1872); ET of selections: Russell, *Cyril of Alexandria*.

[52] Robert Wilken, *Judaism and the Early Christian Mind: A Study of Cyril of Alexandria's Exegesis and Theology* (New Haven: Yale University Press, 1971); Lars Koen, *The Saving Passion: Incarnational and Soteriological Thought in Cyril of Alexandria's Commentary on the Gospel according to St John* (Uppsala University, 1991).

[53] *Commentary on John* 1.9 (on 1.14).

7.14–16 does not refer to the birth of Hezekiah, but is a prophecy of
the Holy Virgin:

> For he who is from above, and is by nature the only begotten Son
> of God the Father, emptied himself and was brought forth from
> a virginal womb according to the flesh... you will call his name
> Emmanuel... For it was when the only begotten Word of God
> appeared like us that he became 'God with us'.[54]

This voluntary self-emptying is emphasized again when Cyril discusses the prophecies of Messiah in Isaiah 11.[55] Thus, prior to the
controversy, the *kenōsis* involved in birth from a Virgin already had
a vital role in the overall narrative that was foundational for Cyril's
reading of scripture.

1.3.3 *Kenōsis*

The reading of scripture just outlined generated the principal features
of Cyril's theology in the conflict with Nestorius. *Kenōsis* was key.

The motif of descent and ascent arguably mirrors the pattern of fall
and restoration. In the *Commentary on John*, Cyril indicates that the
ascent of redeemed humanity depends upon the descent, the emptying, of the one who is full of grace and truth.[56] Cyril hastens to say
that this self-emptying is not sufficient to overwhelm his divinity –
indeed it was self-chosen out of love for us. We might almost speak
of a chosen 'fall' to our level. Cyril himself dares to describe him as
'appearing to fall short of God's majesty by becoming a fully human
being', while insisting that the Godhead is in no way diminished by
this chosen path of humiliation. Such thoughts are also expressed in
the *Commentary on Isaiah*.[57] It was necessary that:

---

[54] *Commentary on Isaiah* 1.4 (on 7.14–16); Greek text: Migne, *PG* 70; ET of selections:
Russell, *Cyril of Alexandria*.
[55] *Ibid.* 2.4 (on 11.1–3).   [56] *Commentary on John* 1.9 (on 1.14).
[57] *Commentary on Isaiah* 2.4 (on 11.1–3).

the only begotten Word of God who brought himself down to the level of self-emptying should not repudiate the low estate arising from that self-emptying, but should accept what is full by nature on account of the humanity, not for his own sake but for ours, who lack every good thing.

Full of the Spirit by nature, the Word had to empty himself in order to receive the Spirit for our sake – redemption was a re-rooting of the Spirit in the human race.[58] 'Since he was not consumed by sin even though he became as we are, the Holy Spirit rested once again on human nature.' Cyril insists that it is the 'Lord of all' who was born of the Virgin when he 'made the limitations of humanity his own'.

So the pattern of fall and redemption is mirrored in Christ's descent and ascent. Self-indulgence is reversed through self-humiliation. For Cyril this narrative movement is fundamental, and he will defend it through thick and thin against the apparently fragmenting analysis of a Nestorius. Willing submission to God is the converse of that *hybris* which brought about the fall and is supremely played out in the *kenōsis* whereby the Word was made human that we might be made divine.

Now if obedience and humility provide the key to our redemption, the receptivity of Mary as she becomes *Theotokos* is crucial. She is the one through whom God is formed within humanity. She is the 'type' of the church, of the humanity which is God-receptive and therefore in process of being redeemed. Of course, the Word pre-existed the birth from Mary – this was not, as Cyril put it, 'the beginning of his being';[59] but if he is Emmanuel, God with us, then Mary must properly be called *Theotokos*. Mary is the vehicle of the new creation. Cyril's concern to defend the title *Theotokos* for the holy Virgin Mary is founded on her role in the story of fall and redemption.

---

[58] Cf. Koen, *The Saving Passion*; and Daniel A. Keating, *The Appropriation of Divine Life in Cyril of Alexandria* (Oxford University Press, 2004).

[59] *Explanation of the 12 Chapters* 7; ET: Russell, *Cyril of Alexandria*.

1.3.4 *Theotokos*

The homily on *Theotokos* that Cyril is purported to have preached at Ephesus[60] Quasten called 'the most famous Marian sermon of antiquity'.[61] It consists largely of an incantation of honorific epithets: Mary is:

the sacred treasury of all the world
the unquenchable light
the garland of virginity
the mirror of orthodoxy
the indestructable temple
the container of the uncontainable
mother and virgin.

Moreover, she is the one:

through whom the Trinity is sanctified
through whom the cross is called precious and is venerated
    throughout the world . . .
through whom the tempting devil falls from heaven
through whom the fallen creature is received into the heavens
through whom all creation, held back from idolmania, comes to
    knowledge of truth
through whom holy baptism came for those who believe . . .
through whom churches were founded in all the world
through whom the Gentiles came to repentance
through whom the only begotten Son of God gave light to those in
    darkness . . .
through whom the prophets prophesied
through whom the apostles preached salvation to the Gentiles
through whom the dead are raised . . .
The Virgin Mother – O marvel!

---

[60] *Homily 4*, Migne, *PG* 77; author's ET.
[61] J. Quasten, *Patrology* (Utrecht and Antwerp: Spectrum Publishers, 1963), vol. III, p. 131.

One might be forgiven for imagining that this is a baptized version of some ancient hymn to Diana of the Ephesians as, in Ephesus, the holy Virgin replaces the worship of Artemis.[62] But to set this homily in the context of Cyril's theology is to find the matter more complex. It is unlikely that Cyril had much truck with idolatry, given his track record of opposition to paganism in Alexandria and his great apologetic work *Against Julian*. His veneration of Mary has deeper theological roots.

Again, one might be tempted to think that Mary has usurped the functions of Christ: through her, demons are cast out and the devil falls from heaven; through her, 'the fallen creature is received into the heavens' and through her, 'the dead are raised'; she is the one 'through whom holy baptism came for those who believe', the one 'through whom churches were founded in all the world'. But such an assessment would be untrue to the overall theological position just traced.

Mary is essentially 'the temple' which permits the presence of God the Word to dwell within creation, the essential medium of the Word's *kenōsis*. Where Eve facilitated the entry of sin into the world, Mary allowed herself to be the 'container of the Uncontained' and so the one 'through whom the only begotten Son of God gave light to those in darkness'. What is necessary for salvation is the birth of Christ within humanity. So Mary becomes the unique medium of salvation and the 'type' of the church. Through her, then, 'the Trinity is sanctified' and 'the cross called precious and worshipped throughout the world'. Inseparable from her son, she is the 'mirror of orthodoxy': if her right to be venerated as *Theotokos* is challenged, due honour cannot possibly be given to Christ. The crucial thing for Cyril is that the Word dwelt in flesh, 'using as his own particular body the temple that is from the holy Virgin'.[63]

[62] See Chapter 7.   [63] *Commentary on John* 1.9 (on 1.14).

1.3.5 Redemption and the flesh

The flesh is vital as the medium of eternal life, and Mary *Theotokos* is essential as the vehicle of the Word's enfleshment. Like Athanasius before him, Cyril believed that the incarnation effected the restoration of divine life to humanity, but its appropriation by particular human beings was made possible through the sacraments.[64] Cyril's commentary on John 6 speaks of 'the eucharistic reception of the holy flesh and blood which restores man wholly to incorruption'. The holy body of Christ is life-giving when 'mingled with our bodies' because it is united with the Word that is from God, and so with 'the body of him who is life by nature' and 'filled with his energy'.[65] 'When we taste of it we have life within ourselves, since we too are united with the flesh of the Saviour in the same way as that flesh is united with the Word that dwells within it.' The eucharist 'will certainly transform those who partake of it and endow them with its own proper good, that is, immortality'. The eucharist dispels both death and the diseases that are in us, for Christ comes as a doctor to tend us, his patients.

> It is as if one took a glowing ember and thrust it into a large pile of straw in order to preserve the vital nucleus of the fire. In the same way our Lord Jesus Christ hides away life within us by means of his own flesh, and inserts immortality into us, like some vital nucleus that destroys every trace of corruption in us.[66]

The sheer physicality of this focus on the sacrament is striking. Reminiscent of Ignatius' early description of it as the 'medicine of

---

[64] Henry Chadwick, 'Eucharist and Christology in the Nestorian Controversy', *JTS* NS 2 (1951), 145–64; Ezra Gebremedhin, *Life-Giving Blessing: An Inquiry into the Eucharistic Doctrine of Cyril of Alexandria* (Uppsala: Borgstroms, 1977); Keating, *The Appropriation of Divine Life*.

[65] *Commentary on John* 3.6 (on 6.35).   [66] *Ibid.* 4.2 (on 6.54).

immortality', it demonstrates that incarnation, eucharist and physical resurrection are correlative in this understanding of redemption. The Adam–Christ/Eve–Mary typology structures a whole ecology of inter-related elements in this overall theological schema.

1.4 Appropriation?

What are we to make of all this? It seems to demand that Adam and Eve are genuinely historical figures, a supposition that hardly survives scrutiny in the light of evolutionary theory. Besides, critique both of original sin and of the dire implications for women of their association with Eve would seem to challenge any attempt at appropriation. Yet the over-arching narrative of fall and redemption represents something so fundamental to the Christian claim that one could say that Christian theology stands or falls on whether it is defensible. Ranged against such a position are both the more optimistic views of human nature found in Judaism, Islam and humanism, and the more naturalistic explanations of human evil and aggression offered by the natural and social sciences. How can the story survive if Adam and Eve are treated as 'myth', and damaging myth at that? And what are we to make of original sin?

1.4.1 Myth and reality

It might seem that the mythological status of the one story, that of Adam and Eve, would turn the other, that of Mary and Christ, into 'mere myth', so that redemption in Christ ceases to have a purchase on history. Is it true that the story of fall and restoration is a coherent whole and can retain its meaning only as such?

Well, this is part universal story, part particular story: on the one hand, Jesus Christ focusses the story, deepens it and sharpens it, but on the other, it is the story of 'everyman', and a story that rings true to life. So it is both 'myth' in the technical sense of a transcendent, symbolic, unverifiable story that gives meaning to existence, and history in the sense that the 'myth' has intersected with the actual existence of a certain person on this earth at a particular time in a particular place. The New Testament texts, I suggest, in reflecting on the significance of Christ, stimulated a deeper discernment of the human predicament and so produced a new reading of the Hebrew scriptures, generating the characteristic 'fall and redemption'. In other words, the move was from solution to plight,[67] the experience of salvation in Christ provoking interest in the Adam story as an account of why we need salvation.

The passion-story is a drama exposing the deep 'flaw' in human being. The hero, presented to us as one who challenged the vested interests and uneasy *status quo* of his time, while releasing ordinary people from sorrows, sins and sufferings and offering a single-minded lifestyle based on love of God and neighbour – this innocent 'prophet' is judicially disposed of by the structures and powers of the day. People flock after him, then turn against him. He is roughed up by soldiers guarding him, and the authorities wash their hands of responsibility. He is progressively isolated – the disciples sleep in the garden, the betraying friend kisses him, the right-hand man denies him, the crowds desert him and finally he cries out, 'My God, my God, why have you forsaken me?'[68] The details are particular, but the components of this tragedy are perennial.

So the death of Jesus Christ is a paradigm story, exposing and judging the sinfulness in which all are implicated. As we look back on the last century, with memories haunted by Holocaust and Hiroshima, or indeed consider daily news reports of violence, torture, hostilities, miscarriages of justice, genocide, bullying and scapegoating, how is it possible to retain illusions about the inherent decency of humanity? Besides, what have we done with our much-vaunted autonomy? Group dynamics ensure that individuals easily get caught up in things way beyond their will or imagining.

---

[67] E. P. Sanders, *Paul and Palestinian Judaism* (London: SCM Press, 1977).
[68] Mark 15.34.

The underlying notion that humankind is 'fallen' rings true to reality. Ideology oppresses and power corrupts. Attempts to build a better world turn sour, religion itself conspires with power and sectional interests. Morality becomes self-righteousness, charity patronizing do-goodery. Nuclear armaments, the ecological crisis and global warming confirm the suspicion that human knowledge, so-called wisdom and technological achievement carry with them the serpent's sting, delivering unanticipated dire outcomes. Even apparently benign advances in medical science, prolonging life, compound over-population and condemn many to being officiously kept alive beyond what may be natural or desirable. Maybe we should finally lose faith in progress. Sin is not just individual misdeeds, the little things that shame us into the guilt that hides or confesses, but massive corporate failure on the part of the whole human race, falling short of God's glory, distorting God's image.

But this tragic story, typified in the reality of a particular life actually lived on earth in the time of Pontius Pilate, is not simply a paradigm of the universal tragedy of human existence; it is also a sign of hope. For our anticipated transformation also rings true in remarkable incidents of grace, saintly lives, communities in which love transcends the boundaries of fear and discrimination which we erect for our own protection. The most wonderful paradox is that it is the weak and foolish, even those, like Arthur, with profound learning disabilities, who in their helplessness, suffering and love mirror Christ for us and evoke in us the fruits of the Spirit: love, joy, peace, patience, goodness, faithfulness, gentleness and self-control.[69] The trouble is that in the world of the everyday, 'living and partly living' as T. S. Eliot described it,[70] we are usually blind to the depths, whether of horror and evil, or of love and joy. Hence our failure to discern the relevance and truthfulness of the Christian story. Its mere 'factuality' is not what makes it true; nor is it relevant

---

[69] Galatians 5.22.
[70] *Murder in the Cathedral* (London: Faber and Faber, 1935; 1982 reprint), e.g. p. 19.

because it provides a political programme or a blueprint for utopia. What makes it real is its significance in exposing the depth of our predicament and the promise of transformation.

The story points beyond itself. For it reveals the transforming presence of God at the very point where God is 'absent' in the forsakenness of Jesus, and demonstrates in a particular life that God accommodates the divine self to the limitations of human existence. So it generates that over-arching story. For the reality that everything owes its existence to an eternal love beyond time and, despite fallenness, will find fulfilment in that same love is narrated within time in the form of a story stretching from the beginning of all things to the end. That narrative is universal and symbolic, a story in which we find ourselves and our salvation; for it shows up our need and offers the possibility and hope of transformation both in our present temporal existence and in God's eternity.

Furthermore, through this universal story we discern that transformation is what the New Testament, at its deepest level, is all about. 'All of us are being transformed', wrote Paul,[71] using the same word as the Gospel-writers use for the transfiguration of Jesus (*metamorphoumetha / metamorphōthē*). For 'those whom he foreknew he also predestined to be conformed (*symmorphous*) to the image of his Son',[72] and 'just as we have borne the image of the man of dust, we will also bear the image of the man of heaven'.[73] What Christ initiated is the renewal and re-creation of humanity according to God's original plan. In Christ there is new creation.[74]

1.4.2 Original sin

Since Augustine, Western Christianity has treated sin and guilt as inherited from Adam and passed on through the sexual act.[75] This was a determining factor in the development of the doctrine of Mary's immaculate conception: if from conception every human being is

---

[71] 2 Corinthians 3.18.   [72] Romans 8.29.   [73] 1 Corinthians 15.49.
[74] 2 Corinthians 5.17.   [75] See Chapter 4.

tainted, the line needed breaking if Christ was to be without sin. Such a profoundly negative view of humanity, the so-called doctrine of original sin, is deeply offensive to contemporary susceptibilities, shaped as they are by the optimism and individualism of post-Enlightenment humanism.

A significant argument for original sin came from the practice of infant baptism: babies hardly needed the remission of sins already committed. Rather, all of humanity sinned in Adam, a point reinforced by the Latin translation of Romans 5.12: Adam, *in quo* (in whom) all sinned. Besides undermining individual responsibility, this conclusion has other problematic legacies: the word 'sin' is identified in the popular mind with sexual acts of unconventional, exploitative or sadistic kinds, with other lusts such as greed and covetousness condoned; while hatred, violence and murder lead to the vilification of the perpetrators as incarnations of evil rather than mere sinners like the rest of us. Alongside such confusion about sin and evil, there persists the commonsense view that moral goodness is attainable – most people would be astonished to hear that the doctrine of original sin is one of the most convincing arguments for the truth of Christianity; yet I've heard it described as the only empirically verifiable Christian doctrine.[76]

On 16, October 2010, Ian Birrell, the father of a child with profound learning difficulties, published a column in the *Guardian* newspaper. The occasion was the conviction of a gang of 18-year-olds for torturing a younger autistic boy for three days:

> they kicked him, stamped on his head, scraped his skin with sandpaper, pelted him with dog-shit, forced him to drink alcohol until he passed out and stuck tape to his genitals. The thugs laughed as they filmed themselves abusing their terrified victim.

The reader was reminded that 'three years ago there was outrage after the death of Fiona Pilkington, who killed herself and her disabled

---

[76] Cf. Terry Eagleton, *On Evil* (New Haven: Yale University Press, 2010).

daughter after years of abuse'. Nine out of ten people with learning difficulties have suffered bullying or harassment, said the article – indeed 'a recent report found evidence of 68 violent deaths of disabled people and more than 500 potential disability hate crimes over the past three years'.

> We need to wake up to this whirlwind of hate, driven by fear of difference and symptom of a society that fails to embrace those with disabilities.
>
> We recognise the need to confront racist and homophobic abuse, but tolerate it against people with disabilities.[77]

Ironically, people were often freer and safer in the old campus hospitals than they are in these days of so-called 'community care'; yet those institutions were frequently the scene of serious, hidden abuse. Furthermore, they arose from policies informed by the eugenics movement. Social Darwinism has roots deeper than Darwin: eight years before *The Origin of Species*, Herbert Spencer, who coined the phrase 'the survival of the fittest', had suggested that, however hard it might seem that the unskilled worker suffer hunger, or the sick labourer be unable to compete, or widows and orphans be left to struggle:

> nevertheless, when regarded not separately, but in connection with the interests of universal humanity, these harsh fatalities are seen to be full of the highest beneficence – the same beneficence which brings to early graves the children of diseased parents, and singles out the low-spirited, the intemperate, and the debilitated as the victims of an epidemic.[78]

---

[77] Cf. Katharine Quarmby, *Scapegoat: Why we are Failing Disabled People* (London: Portobello Books, 2011).

[78] Dennis Sewell, *The Political Gene: How Darwin's Ideas Changed Politics* (London: Picador, 2009), p. 33, quoting Herbert Spencer.

By the turn of the century, such considerations led logically towards advocating sterilization for inadequates, and in an address to the Eugenics Society in 1910, George Bernard Shaw even stated:

> A part of eugenic politics would finally lead us in an extensive use of the lethal chamber. A great many people would have to be put out of existence simply because it wastes other people's time to look after them.[79]

'The Mental Deficiency Act of 1913 ... established colonies for the unfit, classifying them under four headings: *idiots, imbeciles, the feeble-minded* and *moral defectives*';[80] and this system remained in place until 1957, less than ten years before the birth of Arthur. I once met an old man who had spent his entire life since childhood in such an institution, having been placed there simply because he failed to learn to read. In the United States similar sentiments fed into parallel policies,[81] while in Germany, eugenic courts operated from 1934, and medical professionals had to report 'details of any children under three years of age exhibiting Down's syndrome, spina bifida, missing or malformed limbs, spasticism and a range of similar conditions'. The first gas chambers were at mental hospitals and clinics dealing with defectives.[82]

There's been strong reaction against this kind of legalized elimination or segregation. Yet most people approve of abortion as a way of preventing birth-defects, and 'community care' frequently fails to protect because society finds the existence of persons with disabilities disturbing. Indeed, that incident reported in October 2010 suggests an ever-present danger of reverting to the situation where people who are different are treated as 'freaks'[83] and so 'fair game' for the bully. This case of 'man's inhumanity to man' is offered rather than such

[79] *Ibid.*, quoting Shaw, p. 51.   [80] *Ibid.*, p. 65, italics original.
[81] *Ibid.*, chapter 4 *passim*; cf. Amos Yong, *Theology and Down Syndrome: Re-imagining Disability in Late Modernity* (Waco, TX: Baylor University Press, 2007), chapter 3.
[82] Sewell, *The Political Gene*, pp. 138–9.
[83] Yong, *Theology and Down Syndrome*, pp. 82 ff.

classics as the Jewish Holocaust, the Gulag, Pol Pot, ethnic cleansing or genocide, not just because learning disability has been our persistent case-study but because we somehow imagine that Western liberal democracies are more enlightened than the societies which included persons with disabilities among those to be eliminated in the search for the master race or produced the notorious orphanages of Romania. Everywhere persecution of those who are different goes on. Such maliciousness defies explanation – those youths simply said they were bored.

All this suggests something twisted in human nature, often exacerbated by group dynamics which carry individuals into doing things they wouldn't do if left to themselves. *Prima facie* humanistic optimism is constantly tested. Christianity's emphasis on sin as more than individual misdeeds seems to provide a more realistic analysis.

Nevertheless, Christianity retains elements of optimism. The Western doctrine of original sin has not been the only way in which the Adam–Christ typology has been understood. Patristic material suggests that a more pragmatic approach recognized that 'all fall short of the glory of God' without denying freedom of choice, suggesting rather that Adam is a representative figure in whom we may identify our own tendency to give way to temptation. If the fathers de-mythologized the talking serpent by identifying it as the devil in disguise, nowadays the devil tends to be de-mythologized out of existence as a mere personification of evil, the presence of which in humanity is then explained by evolutionary or social theory. Yet we still wrestle with ambiguities over responsibility: to what extent did those youths who bullied the autistic boy have responsibility diminished by their own experience of abuse or social deprivation? The actual choices made and excuses resorted to, as both Adam and Eve shifted responsibility onto one another rather than repenting, may stand for the most common reaction to our own wrong-doing – self-justification with recrimination. The story has symbolic power which touches on human realities as we know them.

Modern theologians have tended to interpret original sin in terms of the social context within which every human being develops, an environment which is not only conducive to temptation and moral failure but also traps individuals in a solidarity in sin which is passed from generation to generation, so that even as people struggle to create a better world, the best intentions become distorted. The doctrine thus represents the corporateness of human sin, indeed, the heredity and environment which weights our free choice towards failure to reach goodness. Such accounts, however, fail to challenge the profound moralism endemic in the understanding of sin. Sins are identified as immoral acts, deeds perpetrated as a result of deliberate choices; and then guilt seems resolvable by acts of reparation or atonement, repentance and forgiveness. This approach, though dominant in Western Christianity, overlooks the fact that shame is often attached to things done unintentionally or said inadvertently, and, in fact, atonement in the biblical material deals with involuntary sins. Shame can become a kind of existential condition, a chronic sense of being ashamed, induced by being shamed or abused by others.[84] This *state* of shame can be exacerbated by the kind of moralism that demands perfection, so that one feels all the time that one falls short, and loses every shred of self-esteem. Shamed persons feel naked and want to hide, as Adam and Eve did. There is nothing they can do to help themselves – they feel sinners but are more sinned against. In fact a better way of putting it is that they feel polluted and unclean, stigmatized and excluded. Only a sense of the social dimensions of sin can give an adequate account of this damaging aspect of human experience, too little articulated in most theology. God's merciful provision of covering for their shame would have done more for Adam and Eve than any theory of atonement.

---

[84] Stephen Pattison, *Shame: Theory, Therapy, Theology* (Cambridge University Press, 2000); and Jennifer Erin Beste, *God and the Victim: Traumatic Intrusions on Grace and Freedom* (Oxford University Press, 2007).

Maybe we should think of sins as not so much consciously chosen deeds as distortions,[85] a point well-captured in the old Latin tag, *corruptio optimi pessima* (the corruption of the best is the worst). Goodness, even faith itself, can be distorted into sin – charity may be twisted into patronizing and self-serving do-goodery, love can become a possessiveness which cannot let go of the one loved. A person's faults are often the obverse of their best qualities; other people are more likely to perceive such distortions – few have the requisite self-knowledge. Indeed, people whom others would characterize as bullies justify their actions as virtuous, while racists think they are right: in *The Perfect Nazi*, Martin Davidson[86] set out to uncover his 'SS Grandfather's secret past and how Hitler seduced a generation', and what he found was that his grandfather adored being a Nazi and relished every part of it, that he felt no post-war repentance – he had nothing to answer for. Because it goes beyond analysis in terms of an individual person's conscious choice or deliberate decision, the doctrine of original sin enables a more profound grasp of these deep distortions that make people do the kind of things they do.

A further dimension of the Adam–Christ typology lies in the fact that it shifts the issues away from virtue or vice to relationship with God. Like Greek tragedy, the Bible understands the deepest temptation as the desire to be like God: that is what the serpent suggested to Eve, it is implicit in the parallel story of the tower of Babel, and it is the ambition of the king of Babylon, according to Isaiah 14. For Adam and Eve, the issue is a matter of disobedience or obedience, of a specific response to God's address, and so of the fundamental orientation of self towards God. This may at first sight seem a negative point: modernity rejects submission to divine *diktat* and proclaims human freedom of conscience and autonomy; God is not a necessary sanction for upholding morality, people say. Even theologically there are difficult issues here: God's purpose was hardly to

---

[85] Kelsey, *Eccentric Existence.*
[86] Martin Davidson, *The Perfect Nazi* (London: Penguin, 2010).

create robotically obedient machines – theologians agree that freedom is a fundamental value. Yet human beings need discipline and
structure in their lives, otherwise they go to pieces. Free response to
God clearly involves adopting the values enshrined in the paradoxical commandments to love God and neighbour. For God's creatures
not to seek to live that way implies a turning away, a rejection which
might well be described as 'disobedience'. Relationship with God lies
at the heart of the matter.

So 'obedience' may be a way of describing free response to God.
But to be free to respond requires the ability to step outside that
heredity and environment, the corporate, structural power of sin.
Indeed, Augustine moved from the usual understanding of freewill
as open-ended choice to recognition that freedom is only possible
when released from the bondage of sin through Christ. Even faith,
hope and love may become distorted: Kelsey[87] explores a whole range
of such distortions, demonstrating how sin twists awry even the best
of human responses to God.

There are reasons, then, for a critique of the doctrine of original
sin as it has been passed down to us; but at the same time the deep
symbols captured in the Adam–Christ typology may be grasped as
pointing to quite fundamental aspects of the human condition. It
potentially provides an account which implicates the whole human
race.

1.4.3 Eve, Mary and feminism

The account of sin just given has not privileged pride, the sin
which feminists dismiss as irrelevant to women. However, feminist
objections to the exploitation of Eve and Mary to oppress women
do present another serious challenge to appropriation of the Eve–
Mary typology, not to mention feminist rejection of the fathers as

---

[87] *Eccentric Existence.*

misogynists.[88] It is time to declare my position as a patristic scholar who happens to be a woman.

Growing up in a family committed to academic achievement, with girls as much under pressure as boys, my sense of inferiority came not from my female gender but from not being clever enough. I had a positive role model in my mother, a lay preacher in the Methodist Church, and I was never confronted by questions concerning women's place in society or church until, as a student in the late 1950s, I asked one of Methodism's elder statesmen what place there was for a woman theologian in Methodism; the reply was 'None'. Soon afterwards I felt a call to ordination, then an impossibility for a woman. So ordination was what brought women's issues into focus,[89] years before feminist theology was even dreamed of.

Meanwhile, having grown up in a Protestant environment in which the mother of Jesus was only remembered at Christmas, I discovered a significant identification with Mary – indeed, a kind of Mary-typology – as she played a crucial role in enabling me to accept my own brokenness as a mother.[90] She became deeply associated with Christ's entry into all the 'gone-wrongness' of things, suffering with her son as Pietà, making her own sacrifice as he offered himself for the sins of the whole world. On holiday in Brittany I was captured by the great carved Calvaries depicting Mary with the women at the deposition of Christ's body. I was intrigued by Simeon's words to Mary in the Temple: 'Behold this child is set for the fall and rising of many in Israel, and for a sign that is spoken against (and a sword will

---

[88] Rosemary Radford Ruether, 'Misogynism and Virginal Feminism in the Fathers of the Church' in Ruether (ed.), *Religion and Sexism: Images of Woman in the Jewish and Christian Traditions* (New York: Simon and Schuster, 1974).

[89] See Chapter 7.

[90] This personal statement has been articulated in earlier publications of mine, e.g. *Face to Face*; '*Theotokos*: Mary and the Pattern of Fall and Redemption' in William McLoughlin and Jill Pinnock (eds.), *Mary for Earth and Heaven: Essays on Mary and Ecumenism* (Leominster: Gracewing, 2002), pp. 340–54; 'The Church and Mary', *Ecclesiology* 5 (2009), 272–98.

pierce your own soul also).'[91] Mary's pierced heart was implicated in the passion, and the Pietà became a healing presence, as exemplar, as image and 'type' of the suffering of women down the centuries – for women have so often suffered through their attachment to sons and husbands, brothers and fathers, who've been maimed or lost in violence or war, at sea or down mines. If one were to generalize women's experience over many eras and cultures, tragic suffering through their men-folk must be more nearly universal than almost anything else.

How far is it possible to generalize about women's experience? The experiences that have driven feminism's aggressiveness towards Eve and Mary have not been mine; I have not been on the receiving end of either the impossible ideal of mother and virgin, or the curse of Eve – though shocked to discover that some women have. Nor have I found feminist rejection of the fathers satisfactory, for several reasons:

- Attitudes to women in the patristic material are profoundly ambivalent, even contradictory. Some much-quoted statements reveal a profound misogyny, but that is not the whole story.[92]
- A serious historian knows the inappropriateness of judging the past in terms of the raised awareness of the present; 'the past is another country'. One may question the legacy of the past; but the past may also provide models that challenge present assumptions.
- What the fathers have to say about the human condition contributes to the Christian articulation of the truth of the Gospel of salvation; any tendency to shift blame from Adam to Eve, though regrettable, should not prejudice serious attention to the fundamental symbolism of this recapitulative typology.

---

[91] Luke 2.34.
[92] See Elizabeth A. Clark (ed.), *Women in the Early Church* (Wilmington, DE: Michael Glazier, 1983).

So as a theologian who happens to be a woman I affirm the importance of attending to the typology of Eve and Mary alongside that of Adam and Christ. The Christian Gospel stands or falls on the story of fall and redemption; men and women are together implicated in a 'gone-wrong' world. From the beginning, women have been baptized alongside men, have suffered martyrdom and become saints alongside men, and the redemption of women alongside men has been symbolized for centuries in the version of the *Anastasis* icon which depicts Christ breaking out of the tomb holding hands with Eve as well as Adam. Nor is it without significance that Mary, the *Theotokos*, symbolically anticipates the redeemed destiny of all humanity in her assumption. Cyril's defence of *Theotokos*, grounded as it is in the over-arching story of redemption, and enhanced as it is by a sense of Mary's vital necessity for humanity's appropriation of the divine life through Christ, might prove the starting-point for a better appraisal of Mary as a positive feminist symbol.[93]

II Atonement through metaphors, images, types and allegory

For the fathers, atonement is but one aspect of the story of fall and restoration. To do justice to their approach, the focus needs to shift from tracing precursors of later atonement theories to an appreciation of a kind of prismatic scriptural imagination.[94] There was no accepted or consistent 'doctrine' or 'theory' in patristic times; indeed, the patristic sense of atonement was 'hydra-headed', exploiting a range of allegory, myth and parable. So to grasp what the fathers have to say about atonement, you need awareness of the multi-faceted unity of imagery and allusion, and its scriptural sources. Some of the fathers developed underlying systems, though these were rarely explicit; nor were they theories of atonement as such. Furthermore,

---

[93] See Chapter 7.
[94] Cf. John Coulson, *Religion and Imagination: In Aid of a Grammar of Assent* (Oxford University Press, 1981).

the adequacy of each system depends on its capacity to embrace the richness of typology and allegory in a synthesis – to turn a single image into a system was to produce an inadequate theory.

II.1 The richness of typology and allegory

My erstwhile colleague, Neville Birdsall, stimulated these thoughts by sharing his translation of the exposition of the name of Jesus found in a sermonic address in *The Martyrdom of St Abo of Tiflis*, a Georgian work of the eighth century.[95] The names of Jesus are Door, Way, Lamb, Shepherd, Stone, Pearl, Flower, Angel, Man, God, Light, Earth, Salt, Worm, Mustard-seed, Sun of Righteousness, Son of the Eternal Father and One God. The exposition of each name is sometimes confined to quoting the single obvious scripture passage from Old or New Testament, but often involves imaginative development by drawing on other scriptures, as a few examples show:

> He is called Shepherd because he said, "I am the Good Shepherd". Truly he has turned us wandering sheep back, and has killed our enemy the lion with the rod of the cross and has brought to life again by the power of the Godhead the corpse of the first-formed destroyed by that lion, and has healed by his wound the bite of the venomous wolf and has dissipated the deadly venom by the medicine of his Godhead and has fulfilled the word spoken through the prophet, namely, "He was wounded because of our sins and by his wounds we are healed".

> He is called Salt because he has drawn near to our body corrupted by sin and has removed from us the stench of idol-worship and has

---

[95] J. Neville Birdsall, 'Diatessaric Readings in the *Martyrdom of St Abo of Tiflis*?' in E. J. Epp and G. D. Fee (eds.), *New Testament Textual Criticism*, Essays in Honour of Bruce M. Metzger (Oxford University Press 1981), pp. 313–24.

prepared our souls with sweet savour by the faith of the worship of God.

He is called Flower because as a flower he has sprung from the root of Jesse for the Church from the holy virgin Mary in bodily form, and has spread over us the spirit of grace through the sweet smell of Godhead.

He is called Worm because he said, "I am a worm and not a man". By the brightness of the Godhead, as a hook in a worm, thus he hid his own Godhead in his body and cast it into the nether-regions of the world and drew it up like a good fisherman; about whom he says, "He took the dragon with a hook and put a bridle in his mouth and a spike through his nose", that is the devil he took and whose wiles he broke, about whom the Psalmist David bears witness, "Thou hast broken the heads of the dragon".

The author attributes all this to the witness of the prophetic books, the preaching of the apostles, what is written in the holy Gospels and the faith established by the holy fathers, the teachers. The fish-hook image of atonement is notoriously found in Gregory of Nyssa's *Great Catechism*, while in general the material is traceable back to Amphilochius of Iconium, also of fourth-century Cappadocia; some parallels are already found in Justin Martyr, and there are overlapping lists in the *Acts of Peter* and the *Acts of John*.[96] Despite the document's late date, then, the material is far from untypical. It works by inter-weaving texts, parables and images into allegories of Christ and his saving work. Any attempt to spell out those allegories as if they were 'theories' is doomed. The total effect defies rational analysis, though clearly creates an imaginative whole with considerable persuasive power.

---

[96] Birdsall, 'Diatessaric Readings'.

11.2 Examples of underlying 'systems'

Such reflections could be synthesized into implicit systems or theories. I offer three examples:

11.2.1 Origen

In the course of expounding the meaning of *logos* (word) at the beginning of his *Commentary on John*, Origen treats the name of Christ by offering a list of titles, including Wisdom, Word, Life, Truth, Son of God, Righteousness, Saviour, Propitiation, Light of the World, First-Born of the Dead, the (Good) Shepherd, Physician, Healer, Redemption, Resurrection and Life, Way, Truth and Life, Door, Messiah, Christ, Lord, King, Vine, Bread of Life, First, Last, the Living One, Alpha and Omega – First and Last, Beginning and End, Lion of Judah, Jacob/Israel, Shepherd, Rod, Flower, Stone, a Chosen Shaft, Sword, Servant of God, Lamb, Light of the Gentiles, Lamb of God, Paraclete, Power of God, Sanctification, High-Priest. Clearly the source is scripture; Old and New Testaments provide material, though Johannine titles have a certain pre-dominance.

Many titles overlap with that eighth-century text, but most are developed more elaborately: for example, on Light, the later text simply quotes 'That was the true light which lights every man who comes into the world', whereas Origen catalogues scripture parallels, distinguishes between the 'earthly light' of sun, moon and stars, and the 'spiritual light' with which the Saviour shines, and offers an analogy whereby the moon and stars borrow light from the sun while the apostles and disciples borrow light from the Saviour – nor is this the end of his enquiry into the 'metaphorical sense' by means of the 'mystical and allegorical method'. The detailed development is different, then, but the cast of mind is the same – a kind of free imaginative play with the images of scripture.

For Origen, the plurality of titles is important because the one Christ is a 'multitude of goods'. They are all taken 'for our sakes':

you cannot say that the Saviour is metaphorically a Stone and literally Word – for none expresses the 'essence' of the Saviour's nature. Yet they are not mere metaphor: Christ is Logos because he drives away the irrational; the incarnation was a kind of concentration of rationality in humanity where before it had been imperfect and defective. Origen's fundamental perception is that the Saviour unites in himself the multiplicity of the creation and the unity of God.

In the end that 'linkage', a concept which has its background in the long discussion about the One and the Many in Greek philosophy, is what expresses Origen's idea of atonement: the transcendent God and his marred creation re-married by means of their mutual consummation in the mediating 'second God'. Although this vision of re-integration in Christ would break down in subsequent controversy,[97] it was large enough to embrace the wealth of imaginative perception to which I've drawn attention. It is impossible to say whether Origen's approach to atonement is purely revelatory and educational, or whether it is about overcoming mortality, or conquering the devil, or offering a full, perfect and sufficient sacrifice for the sins of the whole world. All these elements contribute to his vision of how the opposition to re-integration is overcome, how the mystical re-union anticipated in the present is realized in the *eschaton*. The richness of language, symbol, metaphor, analogy, parable, allegory was essential to the vision: Christ is a 'multitude of goods'.

11.1.2 Athanasius

The thinking of Athanasius was very different from that of Origen. No 'second God' or mediating divine being was possible for Athanasius. His fundamental theological outlook could not permit a blurring of the distinction between Creator and creation. Hence his

---

[97] See Chapters 4 and 8.

battle with those he dubbed 'Arians', and the demise of the Origenist approach through the fourth century.

Yet an examination of *Against the Gentiles–On the Incarnation* shows that Athanasius too had a composite vision, a multi-faceted set of images which provided a rich imaginative language in which to sketch his sense of salvation. Much he shares with both Origen and that later homiletic material. It is equally difficult to specify what 'theory' Athanasius espoused, as is clear if we return to a passage partially quoted in the last chapter:

> His holy disciples teach that everything was created through him and for him, and being the good offspring of a good Father and true Son, he is the Power of the Father and his Wisdom and Word, not by participation . . . but he is absolute Wisdom, very Word, and himself the Father's own Power, absolute Light, absolute Truth, absolute Justice, absolute Virtue, and indeed stamp, effulgence and image . . . At the same time [he] condescends to created beings to give them knowledge and an idea of the Father, he is absolute Holiness and absolute Life, he is Door, Shepherd and Way, King, Guide and Saviour for all, Life-giver and Light and universal Providence.[98]

The climax is a list similar to lists already examined. The basis is another philosophical theory: because he is the true Son, embodying absolute life and absolute holiness, particulars can participate in that holiness and life, and be adopted into that sonship.

Athanasius thinks that creatures have certain qualities because they participate in the absolute form of that quality. The 'absolute' is not just another instance of the quality; it is essentially different, being the principle which makes possible the participation of other entities in it. The Logos is Saviour because he is not a creature who merely participates in divinity or sonship, not 'another instance' of qualities which creatures may share in; rather, he is the very

---

[98] *Against the Nations* 46–7.

principle of Sonship or divinity which provides the possibility of participation. He must therefore be fully divine, in order to be this absolute, the source of these 'virtues' or qualities. *Theopoiēsis* and *huiopoiēsis* (being made 'god' or 'son') are ways of speaking of this participation, which for Athanasius is salvation.

So creation being taken up into God through participation is his understanding of atonement, and this can only be effected through the fully divine Logos. We become 'sons of God' by adoption and participation, because he is 'the Son of God' in reality and truth:

> We will begin, then, with the creation of the world and with God its Maker, for the first fact that you must grasp is this: the renewal of creation has been wrought by the Self-same Word who made it in the beginning.[99]

He became human (Man), that we might become divine (God).[100]

Such is Athanasius' total vision; in *Against the Gentiles–On the Incarnation* many other ways of speaking about salvation are integrated with this. In the Longer Recension of the second volume, the problem of dealing with the devil is faced, and used as a justification for the particular mode of Christ's death on the cross; but conquest of the devil is not the essence of Athanasius' understanding of atonement (*pace* Aulen). It's said that Athanasius is more concerned about death than sin, and the restoration of life to creatures that were sinking back to nothingness is paramount in his exposition of salvation; but death is the wages of sin, and the loss of the Logos also meant the loss of rationality. So illumination and purification, sanctification and propitiation are likewise essential aspects of the saving process, as Athanasius describes it. The vision is as multi-faceted as that of Origen, or the popular preaching tradition, and ultimately derives from the same biblical sources.

---

[99] *On the Incarnation* 1.   [100] *Ibid.* 54.

II.1.3 Irenaeus

In some of his statements Irenaeus anticipated Athanasius:

> The Logos became Man, that Man united with Logos and receiving his adoption might become the Son of God.[101]

> Because of his measureless love, he became what we are in order to enable us to become what he is.[102]

Like Athanasius, he envisaged many different processes embraced in this:

> The Lord through his passion destroyed death, brought error to an end, abolished corruption, banished ignorance, manifested life, declared truth, and bestowed incorruption.[103]

But Irenaeus understood all this in terms of 'recapitulation':

> . . . the sin of the first-created was amended by the chastisement of the first-begotten . . . Therefore he renews all things in himself, uniting Man with the Spirit.[104]

Adam was created in God's image and likeness, but the similarity was lost and marred. The renewal of God's image and likeness, and the fulfilment of God's real intention in creation is Irenaeus' fundamental thought. So the context of his statements is not quite the same as the context of Athanasius' similar language. He does not envisage *theopoiēsis* but rather new creation.

II.1.4 The common thread

Reviewing these three underlying systems, each capable of holding together a whole range of different images of salvation, we might notice that, though diverse, they have a family likeness, namely a

---

[101] *Against Heresies* III.19. [102] *Ibid.* v. Praef. [103] *Ibid.* v.20.2.
[104] *Ibid.* v.19–21.

comprehensive sense of the reintegration of a shattered order, of return to a unity disrupted (at-one-ment), or the incorporation of creation's diversity into the simplicity of the divine. All alike refuse both an ultimate dualism and an undifferentiated monism, and, though differing in detail, each is itself comprehensive enough to permit a wealth of imagery, symbol, myth, parable and typology, the imaginative vehicles of the Gospel's communication.

11.2 Appropriation?

In the West there has long been tension over the doctrine of atonement, tension which cuts across historical denominational boundaries. On one side are 'conservative evangelicals', along with some Pentecostals and Catholics, who believe that the Gospel stands or falls on the penal substitution theory; on the other side are so-called 'liberals' who have difficulty with that view of atonement, both on moral and theological grounds. Theologians largely seem to pass this by, focussing on other doctrines, such as the Trinity, or other issues, such as feminism, or attending to apparent alternatives, such as liberation theology.[105] But this is an area where passions and hurts recur from one generation to another. The controversy is closely tied up with rival readings of scripture and differing attitudes to biblical authority; so it seems hardly likely to be resolved by appeal to the church fathers. Yet maybe the pluralist and imaginative approach of the fathers fits a post-modern setting. The two rival theories of atonement are usually traced to Anselm and Abelard, but it is not my purpose here to rehearse again the history and the old arguments; nor do I propose to give another account of the important work of Gustav Aulen in rehabilitating the 'classic' view of atonement.[106]

[105] Witness the dearth of reference to atonement in David Ford (ed.), *The Modern Theologians: An Introduction to Christian Theology in the Twentieth Century* (Oxford: Blackwell, 1997).
[106] See my book *Can These Dry Bones Live?* (London: SCM Press, 1982).

Rather I set all three in broader perspective, implying that each has a significant contribution to make, but each is problematic principally because it claims a comprehensiveness which it cannot in principle have on its own.

'Salvation' is fundamentally an everyday word. When someone cries out to be saved, what they need depends on what their predicament is – a hand if they have slipped in the mud, a lifebelt if they have fallen into a canal. Julian of Norwich offers a parable from just such a situation:[107] she saw a lord and his servant, the servant standing ready to do the lord's will, the lord looking at the servant with rare love and tenderness. Sent off to do something for his lord, the servant:

> starts off at once, running with all speed, in his love to do what his master wanted. And without warning he falls headlong into a deep ditch and injures himself very badly. And though he moans and groans and cries and struggles he is quite unable to get up or help himself in any way.

Julian 'sought to find some fault in him, and to know if his lord regarded him as blameworthy', but found neither. Basically it was his own good will and great longing that had caused his fall. Then Julian began to see how the lord was planning some well-earned rest and great honour for this loyal servant who had suffered hurt and discomfort only for love of him. So she began to see that it is only pain that blames and punishes, but that our gracious Lord comforts and sympathizes. In other words, humanity fell over, but it was a slip rather than a devastating fault.

The servant did need forgiveness. Christians speak a lot about God's offer of forgiveness and the demand that we forgive others even as we pray, 'Forgive our trespasses as we forgive those who trespass against us.' What we rarely articulate is the difficulty of

---

[107] Julian of Norwich, *Revelations of Divine Love* 51; ET: Clifton Wolters (Harmondsworth: Penguin, 1966).

receiving forgiveness. People usually want to save face, they find excuses, explanations, justifications for what they have done. As long as we defend ourselves against acknowledging responsibility, avoid climbing down and recognizing our fault, and indulge in self-justification or self-pity, there can be no forgiveness for us – we have to accept our need for it first. And then the sense of guilt needs resolution.

The appeal of a theory that suggests that Christ made up to God for our wrong-doing lies precisely there. Another parable may help: an 8-year-old boy comes home from school with a friend and they disappear down the back garden. Some time later Mum discovers to her horror that they've been throwing stones and have broken the window of a derelict-looking stable across the neighbour's fence. An old couple have a flat in that loft. To resolve the situation several things are needed:

- The boy needs to appreciate the wrong he's done – those stones were bouncing over the couple's living-room carpet.
- The boy needs to apologize in person.
- The parent needs to make restitution by replacing the broken window on his behalf.
- Together they need to offer a gift – say a box of chocolates or a bunch of flowers – to restore relations.

In other words wrong-doing has to be acknowledged and confessed, and reparation has to be made, even if the perpetrator cannot do it for himself but needs someone to do it for him. So Christ died for our sins, making atonement on our behalf.

Wrong-doing needs exposure, but evangelism in the West has too often stirred up guilt in order to preach resolution. The problem may be shame rather than guilt; often shame arises from being shamed or abused by others.[108] The consequent absence of self-worth is compounded by an evangelism that creates the shame of inadequacy

---

[108] Pattison, *Shame.*

and a manufactured guilt. Reparation is wide of the mark. The person feels polluted, dirty, unworthy; purification is required, deep cleansing. Rituals and sacrifices once offered such possibilities, but psychologically resolution is most likely to come through what others do – offering signs of affirmation and respect, dignity and love. Slowly this may bring a self-acceptance that can break through self-enclosure and isolation. This is the salvation required for some, a salvation coming through the Gospel of God's unconditional love in Christ, who suffered and died to reveal the lengths to which God goes to demonstrate the worth, value and dignity of each person.

Maybe this enables us to answer the question what salvation would be for someone like Arthur. Given his pre-linguistic consciousness, neither guilt nor shame would appear to have much relevance. On the few occasions when he contrives to do something 'naughty', such as throwing a plate of food off the table, his response to being reprimanded is to grin, chuckle or even laugh. Some might suggest that, for him, salvation would be healing,[109] but such a hope is problematic – even if his brain were to be made whole, he would have missed out on years of learning experience, and if that could be remedied, his identity would surely be different.[110] Salvation for Arthur is welcoming acceptance into a loving and supportive community which fully affirms him as essential to its being, in other words, incorporation into the body of Christ in such a way as to fulfil Paul's vision in I Corinthians 12, whereby honour is accorded even to parts of the body which might for shame be hidden away. Salvation is the offer of unconditional love rather than neglect, abuse or stigmatization, overt demonstration of his worth, value and dignity by those who attend to him, fulfilment in being fully part of the redeemed community, receiving and reciprocating the love of others and of God, a reality potentially anticipated on earth but consummated in resurrection life. This possibility is evidenced in the l'Arche

---

[109] See Yong, *Theology and Down Syndrome*, chapter 8, for fuller discussion of this issue.
[110] See Chapter 3.

communities. Such an account of salvation, evoked by Arthur's particular circumstances, may provide insight into what we all fundamentally need, the 'system' of 'at-one-ment' which encompasses every way of expressing what God has done to rescue the human race. 'Salvation is the transformative work of the Spirit of God that converts human hearts from lives of sin, estrangement, and inauthenticity to lives of peace, wholeness and reconciliation between human beings and God.'[111]

But then there are those who need salvation from a sense that the world is 'gone-wrong'. Oppressed by disasters, by life's unfairness, by evil, violence and war, people used to look on God as the one to save them from the powers of evil, personified in the devil, but now they are more likely to challenge or abandon the idea of a good God. The modern world's demand for a theodicy receives no satisfactory philosophical answer, only a few palliatives. Ransom from the clutches of evil powers and victory over death constituted the 'classic' way of understanding the cross, as Aulen argued, but with evil de-mythologized and theodicy the prime question, this approach meets the case only in some cultural contexts. Insofar as human beings are calling God to account, God needs to make reparation for creating a world like this, otherwise there can be no atonement. Some might think that way of putting it blasphemous. Yet surely the greater blasphemy is not to be honest before God, to suppress doubts and complaints, offer an artificial face of piety and not take God seriously. That is what Job refused to do in the face of his so-called 'comforters'. Human beings are reconciled to God by God taking responsibility for all the 'gone-wrongness', entering into the depths of our darkness and transforming it from within.

For John's Gospel the cross is the 'hour of glory'.[112] It was in Lourdes on Good Friday 1991 that this was dramatically played out for me as I followed the life-size tableaux of the Stations of the

---

[111] Yong, *Theology and Down Syndrome*, p. 229.   [112] See Chapter 1.

Cross up the hill behind the grotto. As I met Mary, the mother of a suffering son, the tears began to flow, and they continued as I joined the women of Jerusalem, inwardly bringing my child with theirs for a blessing from Jesus as he went on the way to the cross. When I got to the upper reaches of the hill, the low afternoon sun was dazzling, and I could hardly open my tear-filled eyes; but then the cross was a dark silhouette surrounded by glorious light. So I knew at a more profound level than before that all the 'gone-wrongness', including that experienced personally through Arthur's profound impairments, would not be resolved by magic or miraculous healing, yet everything was capable of transformation simply because of the cross: God reconciling the world to God's self by taking responsibility, by entering and redeeming all the darkness, all the 'gone-wrongness', turning darkness into light from within.

So all three prevailing theories of atonement have some purchase on aspects of the human predicament. For diverse persons and multiple cultures the pluralism of image and symbol, parable and metaphor found in the fathers is precisely what is needed in our postmodern, multi-cultural context. Our 'felt needs' differ and demand different solutions; and so do our hidden, unconscious, unhealed wounds. The approach of F. W. Dillistone in his book, *The Christian Understanding of Atonement*, was perhaps ahead of its time, but might now be welcomed as anticipatory of the pluralist perspectives we need. Published in 1968, the book built on the conviction that:

> the New Testament contains a richly comprehensive interpretation of the death and resurrection of Christ and that we cannot afford to neglect any facets of this interpretation in any age. Yet it is altogether likely that the sociological and psychological needs of a particular era will manifest themselves in such a way that a particular theory or explanation will commend itself as most relevant and meaningful at that particular time ... To say this is not to adopt a light-hearted relativism ... But it does mean that no *absolute* sanction can be

accorded to any human formulation and that every Christian theologian must be constantly seeking to relate himself imaginatively to the particular needs of his own age.[113]

The result is a wide-ranging exploration of the scriptures, ancient mythologies, historical cultures, family dynamics, drama, literature, liturgy, etc., showing how these resonate with the Gospel.

As in the fathers so in Dillistone one can trace an underlying commitment to the reintegration of a shattered order, and a refusal to reduce things to an ultimate dualism or an undifferentiated monism. We are offered a 'density of metaphor' which admits of no 'reduction' – in other words, a wealth of imagery, symbol, myth, parable, typology, etc., which can become the vehicle of the Gospel's communication. Religious language was described by Coleridge as consisting of:

> words that convey all their separate meanings at once, no matter how incomprehensible or absurd their collective meaning may be.

> To be wise I must know all things as one; to be knowing I must perceive the absolutely indivisible as infinitely distinguishable.[114]

Instinctively the fathers knew this: somehow Christ is paradoxically both Shepherd and Lamb, Priest and Victim. Only those conceptions of atonement which can embrace this richness of metaphor are truly successful. Simple transactional theories, whether involving the appeasement of God or the conquest of the devil, and doctrines which focus exclusively on either the objective or subjective aspect of atonement, just cannot be found in the patristic literature. The underlying images of such theories and doctrines are there, but to

---

[113] F. W. Dillistone, *The Christian Understanding of Atonement* (Welwyn: Nisbet, 1968), p. 26.
[114] Cf. Coulson, *Religion and Imagination*, chapter 1, the source of the citations from Coleridge.

elevate any of them into an exclusive, objective account is quite simply destructive of the integrity of the patristic purchase on our condition and its resolution.

Surely we need to reclaim this approach. The trouble with allegory is that it can be as flat and uninspired as an explained joke, but the glory of allegory, and especially typology, is the possibility of a poetic integration expressible in imaginative language. Christian art depended on such symbolism, and iconography is far from idolatry simply because its non-literal reference has been explicit. Could we reclaim such imaginative integration? We would need criteria for testing the insights of imaginative intuition, but vision is in danger of getting lost through fear of fantasy. Maybe we will never appreciate what atonement is until we dare imagine the marriage of heaven and hell.

* * *

The Serpent-Christ

The preacher ponders a striking crucifix she'd seen in an old tumble-down church in a French village – a modern art-work, just two planes of wood stuck together, one dark, one light, one in the shape of the cross, the other an outline figure remarkable in its curvacious, almost coil-like shape – the serpent-Christ. On the bike a few days later she'd almost ridden over a snake basking in the sun on the heated tarmac. These happenings triggered insight into a whole series of biblical associations, somewhat in the manner of the fathers' collages of texts producing *theōria*. Now as the preacher prepares to address a university congregation it all came together – the tensions between human wisdom and divine.

Where should she begin? The tension is clearest in Paul's first letter to the Corinthians. But the train of thought started with John 3.14–15: 'Just as Moses lifted up the serpent in the wilderness, so must the Son of Man be lifted up, that whoever believes in him may have eternal life.' Christ lifted up on the cross brought life, as

Moses' bronze serpent saved those bitten by snakes in the desert. Turning to Numbers 21.4–9 that strange story took on new meaning. The Israelites, impatient with their wanderings around the desert, started to long for Egypt and its decent meat.

> The people spoke against God and against Moses, 'Why have you brought us up out of Egypt to die in the wilderness? For there is no food and no water, and we detest this miserable food.'

This 'miserable food' was nothing other than God's gift of manna. Then we're told, 'the Lord sent poisonous serpents among the people, and they bit the people, so that many Israelites died'. So the people come to their senses, confess their sin and ask Moses to plead with the Lord to rid them of the snakes. Moses intercedes and is told to make a serpent and set it up on a pole so that anyone who'd been bitten could look on it and be healed. The bronze serpent is the antidote to the snakebites.

In the ancient Egyptian *Book of the Dead*, snakes appear in positive as well as negative guises – as hostile beings to be repulsed with spells, but also with magical powers for renewal of life.[115] Generally in antiquity, the serpent was a symbol of wisdom. Statuettes of the Cretan goddess of wisdom show her with snakes in her hands. The healing wisdom of the god Asclepius was symbolized by the snake. Jesus is reported to have said, 'Be wise as serpents.' The name, Naasenes or Ophites, was given to certain gnostic heretics of the early Christian centuries; clearly they were snake-worshippers (*naas* = snake in Hebrew; *ophis* = snake in Greek), the snake symbolizing the knowledge or wisdom which brought salvation. In Genesis the snake tempts Adam and Eve with the promise of knowledge, and some rediscovered gnostic texts depict the serpent as the 'goody' in the Genesis story, offering the knowledge needed to escape from

---

[115] *The Ancient Egyptian Book of the Dead*, British Museum Exhibition, November 2010–March 2011. See John H. Taylor, *Spells for Eternity: The Ancient Egyptian Book of the Dead* (London: British Museum Press, 2010), p. 65.

the clutches of the 'baddy' Creator-God. From the point of view of mainstream Jewish and Christian traditions they read Genesis upside-down; but what was there to stop them? The serpent was a symbol of wisdom.

So the symbolism of the biblical story suddenly came alive: the snake-bite from which the Israelites were suffering was an attack of worldly wisdom. After all, with all that hardship in the desert, who wouldn't want to return to the fleshpots of Egypt? When you're dying of hunger and thirst, and heat and cold, and not getting anywhere, what's the commonsense thing to do? Go back, of course, where at least you won't starve and there's some semblance of security! Why face the wilderness for an entirely unknown future? The antidote to bites from the snakes of worldly wisdom was the bronze serpent raised on a pole – the true wisdom that comes from God.

So arises the Gospel insight that the wisdom of God was embodied in Jesus, the Son of Man, lifted up on the cross as the antidote to the serpent's curse. The preacher's mind reverts to Paul:

> For it is written, 'I will destroy the wisdom of the wise . . . ' Where is the one who is wise? . . . Has not God made foolish the wisdom of the world? . . . For the Jews demand signs and Greeks desire wisdom, but we proclaim Christ crucified, a stumbling-block to Jews and foolishness to Gentiles, but to those who are called, both Jews and Greeks, Christ the power of God and the wisdom of God. For God's foolishness is wiser than human wisdom, and God's weakness is stronger than human strength.[116]

Before that university congregation, the preacher would face a challenge. For, reinforced by verses 26–9 (there are not many wise, but God chose the foolish things of the world to shame the wise), this passage has generated many an anti-intellectual sermon. But actually Paul was indulging in double-think, or at least a game of rhetoric,

[116] 1 Corinthians 1.18–25.

for he soon asserts that he does speak wisdom. His contrast is not between faith and reason, not between heart and head, but between the wisdom of the world and the wisdom of God. Christ crucified, he says, is the wisdom of God; and that challenges the wisdom of the world.

The rhetorical thrust of Paul's argument was probably best appreciated by one who was himself a rhetorician, the most famous preacher of antiquity, John Chrysostom (the Golden-mouth). For him it was all about *kenodoxia* (vainglory), about the passion with which people pursue success, reputation, the empty glory which is the goal of worldly wisdom – in our terms, becoming a celebrity, achieving prowess in sport, academia or business, getting on in the world, earning a top salary, enjoying authority, influence, power. The wisdom of the world encourages anything and everything people boast about. By contrast the wisdom of God is found in Christ crucified. The fear of the Lord, which is the beginning of wisdom, requires an all-round self-emptying that imitates the emptying of Christ on the cross. So the key to wisdom and understanding is humility.

Intellectual humility was cherished among early Christian theologians. Heretics were too clever by half, thinking they could know God precisely so as to define the divine Being in all exactitude.[117] For Chrysostom and his contemporaries, to receive knowledge of God required the humbling experience of having all categories of thought exploded, because the divine is infinite, invisible, immortal, incomprehensible beyond speech or thought, beyond human language or conception. Understanding was only possible because God had accommodated the divine self to the human level – in the incarnation, in the language of scripture. The fourth-century Syrian poet and theologian, Ephrem, has a lovely picture of someone teaching a parrot to speak by holding up a mirror in front of his face so that the parrot would imagine it was communicating with one of its own

---

[117] See Chapters 4 and 8, particularly on Eunomius.

kind: God had to do something like that in order that human and divine could stumblingly find a common language. The wisdom of God transcends the wisdom of the world. Yet the Gospel is about knowledge and wisdom; for the wisdom of God is found in Christ Jesus. That wisdom, for Chrysostom, was humility, a challenge to pride and worldly wisdom.

Chrysostom read Paul in the light of his own concerns; but still there are ways in which his reading alerts us to the thrust of Paul's rhetoric. The rhetorical opposition turns out to be somewhat similar to the way in which Chrysostom's near contemporary, Augustine, in his classic work on the *City of God*, plays off against each other the two loves which produce the two cities that constantly struggle with each other in human history and in human lives – namely, the love of God and the love of self.

And that makes the preacher wonder whether Paul's rhetoric doesn't strike nearer the bone than Chrysostom's intellectual humility. Paul surely hints at the necessity of redemption from a wisdom that is motivated by self-aggrandisement. The rulers of the world wouldn't have crucified Christ if they'd known what they were doing, he suggests. They were blinded by the demands of common sense:

- to appease the occupying power by getting rid of the trouble-maker
- to avoid facing the challenges he presented to the establishment and to social order
- to hold on to their positions of power.

Paul has discerned the potential corruption of human wisdom. For it is so easy for human cleverness to over-reach itself, to build a tower of Babel or an atom bomb – indeed, to challenge God, to become something demonic.

For the over-arching story of the Christian Gospel – the story of fall and redemption – rings true to our world: the worst thing is the corruption of the best. This applies to the intellectual life as to any other aspect of human life. Christianity is not anti-intellectual, but it does challenge an intellectual life geared merely towards utilitarian ends, it does challenge the success-values of our culture, it does suggest that curiosity and wonder should motivate research, and even that worship is at the heart of it all, for true wisdom is fear of the Lord.

* * *

Postlude

The Serpent-Christ[118]

Deep, deep in the veins is the poison lodged.
The mind is crippled: no antidote
For wisdom's sting, while the serpent sleeps
In the noon-day sun, warm on the tarmac,
                  beautiful.

Weak, weak is the heart by venom infected –
Yet seemingly strong: for the serpent-coils,
Tensed like a spring, speak power to leap
To the heavens, up the heated stones of Babel,
                  masterful.

Strong, strong is the fiery flow of the tide:
No eel-like twist of the soul up the fall
Can bring Christ down. It beats its wings
On the cloud of unknowing, heavy with blessings,
                  impenetrable.

Beaten, beaten down like wheat in a storm
Are dreams of good: no peace but a sword
While the wound festers. The serpent sleeps

---

[118] Biblical references: Genesis 3.1–7, 11.1–9; Romans 10.6; Numbers 21.4–9; John 3.14–15; Luke 10.18–19; Isaiah 40.31.

In the noon-day sun, warm on the tarmac,
                  beautiful.

High, lifted on high, is the antidote:
For life is hid with the serpent-Christ
Who bears the serpent's curse, and refines
Knowledge of good and evil – now
                  inseparable.

Deep, deep in the veins is the needle plunged.
The self is at-one-d, by the serpent-Christ
Who treads on the serpent's head as Satan falls
Like lightning from heaven, and the coil springs,
                  powerful.

Joy, joy in the heavens: the Pentecost
Volcano erupts, and the cloud breaks.
They that wait on the Lord shall rise,
Rise up on wings like soaring eagles,
                  Spiritful.

Pietà[119]

Mary, my child's lovely.
Is yours lovely too?
Little hands, little feet,
Curly hair, smiles sweet.

Mary, my child's broken.
Is yours broken too?
Crushed by affliction,
Hurt by rejection,

---

[119] Previously published in *Face to Face*.

Disfigured, stricken,
Silent submission.

Mary, my heart's bursting.
Is yours bursting too?
Bursting with labour, travail and pain.
Bursting with agony, ecstasy, gain.
Bursting with sympathy, anger, compassion.
Bursting with praising Love's transfiguration.

Mary, my heart's joyful.
Is yours joyful too?

Breakthrough

The womb of the earth is as good as dead
    like the barren womb of Sarah
    and the barren womb of Hannah
        and Elizabeth's aged womb.
Each one stretched forth her hand
    to touch the hem of his garment
    like the one with the flow of blood:
        and each one laughed or sang
        at birth in the realm of death:
            'The Lord kills and brings to life
            He brings low, he also exalts.'

The womb of the earth is flowing with blood;
the womb of the earth is as good as dead;
    the earth is on the waiting-list
        for a hysterectomy.
    No garment to touch,
        no laugh, no song,
        as the cruel raping goes on

and the womb of the earth is ripped out
and death mocks the source of life:
'The Lord makes poor, the Lord makes rich,
He brings low, he also exalts.'

The womb of the virgin conceives life.
Instead of an ancient barren womb,
instead of the bleeding womb of the earth,
He chooses a sprig of freshness and youth,
a girl who's known no blood.
Instead of birth from the bowels of death,
instead of renewing, instead of healing,
He starts afresh
with a germ of new vitality,
a young untouched creation,
as the Spirit overshadows
the womb of the virgin earth:
'He who is mighty has done great things
And holy is his name.'

Now the womb of the heart receives the Spirit.
The chaste womb of the mind laughs,
and then breaks forth in song:
'Glory to God in the Highest.
Peace on earth, goodwill to men.'

Another observation

Imagination gazes at the trees,
At Nature's outlines etching stained-glass panes,
Depicting mystery-stories in their frames,
Encapsulating truth in moving frieze
Of still snap-shots, for people on their knees:
Pietà, blessed in her laboured pains,
Successful traitor, reckoning up his gains,

Frozen militia, daring not to seize.
From tree of knowledge on to tree of life,
From Eden's apple on to Calvary,
The sheltering cedars cover human strife,
And in their veins secrete typology,
While over-arching like a mighty nave,
The wood for cross and manger gladly gave.

6 | From inspiration to sanctification: discerning the work of the Holy Spirit

Prelude

The wind stirs the trees, it spirits waves on the waters and jinns in the desert sand, coming from nowhere, a hidden force of inspiration.

The kids, full of high spirits, set off on their hiking expedition; while the football coach struggles to instil spirit into the team; and the barmaid releases strong spirits from the optic into the glass for the customer.

The ancient Egyptian traced the outline of a mummy on the papyrus and then the bird-shaped *ka*-spirit of the dead person hovering over it.

The dictionary lists apparently disconnected meanings: vital principle: the principle of thought: the soul: a disembodied soul: a ghost: an incorporeal being: enthusiasm: actuating emotion, disposition, frame of mind: a leading independent, or lively person: animation: verve: courage: mettle: real meaning: essence, chief quality: a breath of wind: a breathing: a distilled liquid...

The teacher notes that in Hebrew, Aramaic and Syriac, the word for spirit is feminine, in Greek neuter, and in Latin masculine, all basically meaning 'wind' or 'breath', acquiring less material meanings through metaphor which then becomes so dead that the dictionary entry reverses the order!

The biblical scholar finds in the analogy with wind the Spirit's power and freedom, along with its deep unpredictability:

- The Spirit of God moving on the face of the waters[1] is like a whirlwind.
- Saul meets a band of ecstatic prophets and falls into inspired frenzy.[2]
- Jesus says[3] that the wind/spirit blows where it chooses, and you hear the sound of it, but you do not know where it comes from or where it goes – so it is with everyone born of the Spirit.

Then she discerns deep ambivalence between the Spirit of God and the human spirit:

- Job complains that the arrows of the Almighty are in him, and his spirit drinks their poison;[4] but also speaks of the spirit of God being in his nostrils as his breath is in him.[5]
- Paul states unambiguously that he too has the Spirit of God,[6] while the arrival of Stephanas and others refreshed his spirit;[7] yet ambiguity reigns when he uses the adjective 'spiritual'.

* * *

In a typical history of doctrine the major question would be, 'Is the Spirit fully divine, or some kind of power or mediating angel?' Here,[8]

---

[1] Genesis 1.2.   [2] 1 Samuel 10.10.   [3] John 3.8.   [4] Job 6.4.
[5] *Ibid.* 27.3.   [6] 1 Corinthians 7.40.   [7] *Ibid.* 16.17–18.
[8] This chapter incorporates material from previous publications of mine, where fuller references and discussion may be found: selections from *Biblical Exegesis* and *From Nicaea to Chalcedon: A Guide to the Literature and its Background* (London: SCM Press, 2010); 'Christian Scripture and the "Other"' in Michael Ipgrave (ed.), *Scriptures in Dialogue: Christians and Muslims Studying the Bible and the Qur'an Together*, a record of the seminar "Building Bridges" held at Doha, Qatar, 7–9 April 2003 (London: Church House Publishing, 2004); 'Inner Struggle: Some Parallels between the Spirituality of John Wesley and the Greek Fathers' in S. T. Kimbrough, Jr (ed.), *Orthodox and Wesleyan Spirituality* (Crestwood, NY: St Vladimir's Seminary Press, 2002); 'Songs without Words: Incorporating the Linguistically Marginalized' in Stephen Burns, Nicola Slee and Michael N. Jagessar (eds.), *The Edge of God: New Liturgical Texts and Contexts in Conversation* (London: Epworth Press, 2008); 'University Sermon for the Tercentenary of the Birth of John Wesley', *Epworth Review* 31 (2004), 44–51.

however, we shall focus on the fathers' understanding of the presence and activity of the divine Spirit within the created order, in people's lives and in the church, from prophetic inspiration to the holiness imparted to saints by the indwelling Spirit. Inspiration and the hope of sanctification have repeatedly generated an 'enthusiasm' hard to contain in the life of the church: examples ancient and modern will be assessed.

I Inspiration – the Holy Spirit and prophecy

1.1 The prophetic scriptures

1.1.1 The spirit of prophecy: Justin Martyr

From the beginning, Christians assumed that Old Testament prophecies were inspired by the Holy Spirit and fulfilled in Christ and the church. The work of Justin Martyr was to articulate this belief in detail.

Justin was addressing a culture steeped in oracles and accustomed to unpacking riddles and metaphors to discern predictions – emperors even decided whether to go to war on the basis of books of Sibylline Oracles. So the biblical prophecies provided a key plank in his apologetic enterprise. Responding to the charge that Christ appeared to be Son of God by performing mighty works through magic, he shifts the argument to the proof from prophecy. For him 'the strongest and truest evidence' lies in the precise way in which events already predicted actually occurred. There were 'among the Jews prophets of God through whom the prophetic Spirit made known beforehand things that were to come to pass'; these prophecies were collected in books in the original Hebrew, then Ptolemy heard of them and, endeavouring to create a comprehensive collection in his library, obtained these books from Herod and had them translated. Justin suggests that even though Jews all over the world have these books, they do not really understand them and are hostile to Christians. Yet in these books of the prophets:

we found Jesus our Christ foretold as coming, born of a virgin, growing up to adulthood, and healing every disease and every sickness, and raising the dead, and being hated, and unrecognized, and crucified, and dying and rising again, and ascending to heaven, and being called, Son of God.[9]

Justin proceeds[10] to quote Genesis 49.10–12, showing how it applies to Christ. The fact that 'the sceptre shall not depart from Israel . . . until . . . the obedience of the Gentiles is his' is fulfilled by the fact that the Jews had kings until Christ appeared but not subsequently, while some in every nation now look for him to return; 'binding his foal to the vine' and washing 'his garments in wine and his robe in the blood of grapes' refer to the triumphal entry and the passion. This introduces a collection of prophetic texts through which the Gospel story is told, including Isaiah 7.14 (birth from a virgin) and Micah 5.2 (birth at Bethlehem), through Isaiah 9.6 (unto us a child is born), Psalm 22 (the passion) and Zechariah 9.9 (the king riding on a donkey). Justin faces the objection that such prediction implies fate or necessity,[11] his response turning to the prophets themselves – they quite clearly indicate punishment and reward on the basis of merit, which implies free choice and accountability. The foretelling of future events does not imply fate but God's foreknowledge.

Commonly designated a Logos-theologian, Justin's attention to the Spirit is often overlooked; but evidently Justin does relate inspired prophecy to the Spirit. In a sense the argument sketched in *I Apology* provides the project for his *Dialogue with Trypho*. The opening narrative of how he worked through various philosophies, never quite satisfied, until he met the old man by the sea, finds its climax in a shift to acknowledging the prophets, inspired by the Holy Spirit, as alone those who can assist the mind to see God.[12] In subsequent

---

[9] *1 Apology* 30–1; Greek text: M. Markovich (ed.), *Iustini martyris apologiae pro Christianos, PTS*; ET: *ACW*.
[10] *Ibid.* 32 ff.   [11] *Ibid.* 43–4.   [12] *Dialogue* 4 and 7.

discussion with Trypho, the Holy Spirit of prophecy is invoked as pointing to Christ,[13] in Psalms as well as prophets, often announcing events by parables and similitudes,[14] so interpretation is needed to spot the reference. Often the point is that believers in Christ from all nations have replaced Israel as God's chosen under a new covenant; for numerous prophecies point to Jesus, even predicting his crucifixion, and indicate that Christians now constitute Israel.[15] Leah and Rachel are types of the synagogue and the church. There are two houses of Jacob, one begotten by blood and flesh, the other by faith and the Spirit.[16] Justin admits that Jews are not now in the habit of sacrificing to Baal, 'as were your fathers', but 'you have not accepted God's Christ'. So through inspired prophecies he shifts to the supersessionist claim that prophecy has ceased among Jews, the Spirit transferring to Christians.

1.1.2 Appropriation?

Several issues immediately arise:

- The common sense of our culture, as distinct from that of the ancient world, is sceptical about the proof from prophecy.
- Justin's response to the charge that prophetic fulfilment implies fate hardly seems adequate.
- After the Holocaust, the supersessionist logic of this approach to scripture has become deeply offensive.
- Modernity would characterize the unpacking of riddling oracles as allegorical eisegesis of the most implausible kind, and attribute its practice, in the Dead Sea Scrolls as well as the New Testament and elsewhere, to the cultural presuppositions of the Roman world.

[13] E.g. *Ibid.* 32, 34, 36.   [14] *Ibid.* 77.
[15] *Ibid.* 123.   [16] *Ibid.* 134–5.

Appropriation, then, seems neither attractive nor convincing. Yet this is to cut ourselves off from traditions still enacted in performances of Handel's *Messiah* and Services of Nine Lessons and Carols, not to mention the programme of mosaic decorations or stained-glass windows in historic chapels and churches, from Ravenna to Oxford's Lincoln College. Can we obviate this impoverishment? Perhaps some of the hermeneutical ideas sketched in Chapter 1 could suggest perspectives for dealing with this dilemma.

My first suggestion comes from the observation that texts have a future and may acquire fresh meaning and significance from hindsight. Doubtless the historical Isaiah was investing hope in a birth expected in his own day when he spoke the words, 'A young woman shall conceive and bear a son';[17] but the words gain heightened significance in the light of Christian belief that Jesus was indeed 'Emmanuel' – God with us. The possibility of texts taking on new associations is the greater when metaphorical and therefore potentially ambiguous or open-ended. So my second suggestion is that poetic expressions may appear so directly apposite as to be read as prophecy – Justin's treatment of Genesis 49.10–11 might be a case in point, layers of potential meaning only being exposed by seeing a text in the light of later events. My third suggestion takes up the notion of interpretative communities. The *Dialogue with Trypho* is a classic example of conflicting interpretations arising from dialogue partners belonging to different reading traditions. Texts which Justin treats as prophetic of Christ Trypho refers to Hezekiah; or, if he admits they're messianic, assumes the Messiah is still to come. Justin's identification of certain texts as prophetic riddles is part of a larger enterprise whereby Christ becomes the key to what scripture is all about. Fulfilled prophecies belong in the same file, as it were, as the Christian re-reading of Genesis in the light of Christ's redemption.

---

[17] Isaiah 7.14.

However resistant we are to the notion that the meaning of a prophetic oracle is found in the claimed fulfilment, we may still want to take seriously the tradition of a christocentric reading of the Christian canon. That, however, seems to assume a providential plan; Justin's freewill defence leaves philosophical problems that elude final solution, and even if his general point is granted, a providential view of the created order runs up against the problem of evil and suffering.[18] However, if the point here is fulfilment of prophecy in Christ – not general providence, but rather God foreseeing the fall and making provision for redemption – then the importance of hindsight comes into play: the dénouement makes sense of the whole. Indeed, this may sometimes seem true of that strange sense of destiny, call or guidance claimed by individuals or groups, both in scripture and in the history of the church. On any reading, scripture seems to demand God's involvement in history, working out the divine purposes. Here these challenging questions will be registered but not resolved; God's activity in the world is a topic for Chapter 8.

So to the third issue: christocentric reading of the Bible co-opts the Hebrew scriptures into the supersessionist perspective. In an age of enhanced sensitivity to the horrific history of anti-semitism, such that the text of the Oberammergau passion-play has been modified to avoid its anti-Jewish slant, the question is how far this is essential to Christian self-understanding. Christianity defined itself, on the one hand, against polytheistic idolatry and, on the other, against Judaism, claiming that the new covenant in Jesus Christ rendered the old obsolete. Such self-definition seems intrinsic to Christian identity. Yet:

(1) it's a mistake simply to characterize early Christian exegesis as Christological and anti-Jewish. II *Clement*, an early Christian homily, contrasts sharply with anti-Jewish interpretation of prophecy; prophetic texts are referred to the 'brethren' – so

---

[18] Cf. Chapter 2.

they should beware lest they deserve the words of Isaiah 29.13: 'this people honours me with their lips, but their heart is far from me'.[19] It is of those who have not kept the seal of baptism that Isaiah said, 'Their worm shall not die, and their fire shall not be quenched, and they shall be a spectacle for all flesh.'[20] Previously Hebrews 3.7 – 4.13 warned its readers not to be like the generation in the wilderness, quoting Psalm 95. Nowhere is there a hint that these old warnings might apply to contemporary Jews or indeed to Jews who rejected Christ; rather, they are potentially warnings for Christians who run the risk of unfaithfulness.

> The Lord says, 'Continually my name is blasphemed among the nations' . . . Wherein is it blasphemed? In that you do not do what I desire.[21]

This is how I remember the Old Testament applied as I grew up in the Methodist Church. I never remember blame accorded to contemporary Jews on the basis of scriptural passages from either Testament; when I subsequently became aware of Christian anti-semitism, I was shocked. The scriptures speak of judgement, most often God's judgement on God's own people – judgement is the obverse of love.[22] Paul in Romans 9–11 sees both covenant communities as in the same case – utterly dependent on God's mercy; and Jesus said, 'Judge not, that you be not judged.'[23]

(2) supersessionist traditions contributed not just to centuries of tension, suspicion and violence between Christians and Jews, but also with that other monotheism, Islam, which in its turn claimed to have the final revelation. Competing truth claims have made these closely related faiths particularly prone to foster hostilities, and, in the perspective of that history, the

[19] *11 Clement* 2.1, 3.5, Greek text: Kirsopp Lake (ed.), *The Apostolic Fathers*, 2 vols., *LCL*; ET: Maxwell Staniforth and Andrew Louth (eds.), *Early Christian Writings*, London: Penguin, 1987.
[20] *Ibid.* 7.6.   [21] *Ibid.* 13.2–3.
[22] See my reflections on this in *Face to Face*.   [23] Matthew 7.1.

popular perception that religion is a cause of conflict and war is not wide of the mark. The irony is that all three faiths confess the one transcendent God, Creator of all that is, and in the scriptures of all three are theological perspectives that challenge their tendency to exclusivity. Indeed, there is another side to history – their mutual influences and their peaceful sharing of saints and shrines in the Middle East, at least under the Ottoman Empire.[24] Yet monotheism has a curious tendency to slip into henotheism – the one universal God becoming exclusively the God of a particular 'tribe'.

In the Christian Bible, particularity and universalism are in tension. The 'Old Testament' is specific to a particular nation; God is described as 'the God of Abraham, Isaac and Jacob', who entered into a covenant with their descendents: 'If you obey my voice and keep my covenant, you shall be my treasured possession out of all the peoples.'[25] But this very text also insists that God is the God of all the earth: 'Indeed the whole earth is mine, but you shall be for me a priestly kingdom and a holy nation.' This tension may point to a challenging theological possibility, namely, that it is through particularities that the universal Creator God chooses to engage with the creation.

The New Testament inherits such exclusiveness, yet breaks across boundaries. One of the most contested issues in early Christianity was whether Jesus was a Jewish prophet, sent only to the lost sheep of the house of Israel,[26] or brought revelation to non-Jewish peoples (the Gentiles). For the Pauline tradition, a new humanity had been forged in Christ in which the old divisions between Jews and Gentiles had been healed and transformed. Yet a strong differentiation between those who accepted the Gospel and those who did not, together with new identity markers, rapidly undermined that implicit universalism.

---

[24] William Dalrymple, *From the Holy Mountain* (London: HarperCollins, 1997).
[25] Exodus 19.5.   [26] Matthew 15.24.

Chapter 1 argued that scripture is to be read in the light of reason, universal moral values and contemporary experience, under the guidance of the Holy Spirit and in prayerful commitment to find the way of Jesus for today. These principles mean repenting of Christianity's superiority, its exclusivism, as well as its supersessionism. The three great monotheisms have a sibling relationship, captured in the Sufi parable of different groups making their way up the mountain and seeing different views: in terms of that parable Christians may acknowledge with humility that others genuinely respond to God in their own diverse ways, while holding dear their own tradition that God actually came down the mountain to meet them in Jesus Christ.

1.2 Prophecy alive in the church?

In the last days, according to Joel's prophecy, the Spirit would be poured out on all humankind, 'your sons and daughters shall prophesy, your young men see visions and your old men dream dreams'.[27] At Pentecost, according to the book of Acts, this was fulfilled. There is considerable evidence of 'live' prophecy in the texts of early Christianity.

Reaction set in with the fresh outpouring of the Spirit in second-century Phrygia known as the 'New Prophecy', or Montanism, a reaction which provoked its marginalization as heretical, though precisely on what grounds is unclear. A generation later, the first theologian to write in Latin, Tertullian, joined the movement, though whether that meant he left the 'catholic' church for what was a distinct sect is less clear than is usually assumed[28] – there may be analogies with the twentieth century-charismatic movement, in that the church at large was both influenced by and divided by the claims

---

[27] Joel 2.28–32, quoted in full in Acts 2.17–21.
[28] Christine Trevett, *Montanism: Gender, Authority and the New Prophecy* (Cambridge University Press, 1996), p. 73.

of those who supported the 'New Prophecy'.[29] Indeed, analogies there are with later movements, the fundamental issue being on-going manifestations of the Spirit in church life. Here I attempt to identify perennial issues, while keeping an eye on potentially false parallels, though ascertaining the particular character of the Montanist movement is not easy. Fragmentary sources preserved largely in hostile literature make it difficult to follow the custom adopted so far of reviewing particular texts; instead, a series of subsidiary questions shapes the discussion.

1.2.1 What made this prophecy 'new'?

The charge of novelty has been brought against many movements in church history, from Symeon the New Theologian, through Pietism and John Wesley to Azusa Street and Pentecostalism. How the church accommodates novelty is one perennial issue. The dangers arising from self-deluded prophets is the other side of the coin – the church seems justified in looking for criteria to distinguish between false and true prophets, while at the same time challenged not to quench the Spirit by relying on rule-bound precedent. The New Testament encourages the expectation of newness, while warning of the need for discernment. Charismatic gifts constitute the prime issue, but similar problems about accommodating novelty arise with respect to the ordination of women. Indeed, the issue of women's place in the church was itself raised in relation to Montanism: the women prophets, Priscilla and Maximilla, were as significant to the movement as Montanus himself, and were followed by others – later sources accused Montanists of ordaining women. Immediate anxieties, however, focussed on the legitimacy of their prophetic inspiration, alongside the fact of novelty.

---

[29] The classic work of R. A. Knox, *Enthusiasm* (Oxford University Press 1950) associates together various movements in church history; Trevett, *Montanism*, p. 15, judiciously cautions against 'such comparisons with later phenomena'.

True, some scholars have treated Montanists as in continuity with earlier Christian prophets, both men and women, the real issue arising from increasing institutionalization which took charisms as threats to the authority of established clergy. Certainly one response on the part of the 'catholics' was to consign prophecy to the time of the apostles, but there is surely a danger of anachronistic reading of the situation in light of later conditions when movements of renewal did indeed challenge a formalized and authoritative hierarchy.[30] Montanism arose when the church was still a persecuted minority and, if the satire of Lucian is anything to go by, with a liability to respond with over-enthusiasm to travelling charismatics. Reaction against institutionalization is unlikely to be the primary cause – indeed, increasing regularization of the Spirit's presence in sacraments and established authorities may rather have been a significant outcome.

More plausible as precipitating cause is the impact of contemporary crises: there was serious plague in the 160s, not to mention earthquakes, wars on more than one frontier, heavy taxation, revolts and persecution of Christians.[31] These were 'signs of the times'; Montanism was probably a call to greater rigorism in preparation for the coming of the End. There was, perhaps, expectation that the new Jerusalem would appear from heaven at Pepuza, though the material suggesting this might be understood in terms of attempts to create in 'holy' Pepuza the pure 'Jerusalem' community awaiting Christ's return. Either way, apocalyptic hopes are a plausible explanation, comparable to other outbreaks of millennarianism over the centuries.

What was recognizably new and disturbingly distinctive was a more exacting call to holiness as preparation for the expected dénouement. The authority of the Spirit was claimed for new demands for purity.[32] This, surely, was what attracted Tertullian

---

[30] Knox, *Enthusiasm*, sees this as a perennial aspect of renewal movements.
[31] Trevett, *Montanism*, pp. 42–5.   [32] So *ibid.*

a generation later in the West. It would also have been a challenge to traditional practice, and so to the authority of the bishops. The 'New Prophecy' made new demands.

1.2.2 What about holiness?

Renewal movements and outbreaks of prophecy often focus on short-comings in the church, calling people to renewed commitment to holiness and sanctification. John Wesley wrote:

> A few worshipped him in spirit and in truth . . . Nay, I have doubted whether that Arch-heretic Montanus, was not one of the holiest men in the Second Century.[33]

No surprise should be occasioned by the fact that Montanus was particularly concerned with sin and holiness: it was exactly the business of a prophet. In the *Shepherd* of Hermas, themes of warning and judgement predominate: a series of visions oscillate between critique of sin and failure, and promises for those who keep the commandments. The object was to produce repentance – one advance made by this work of prophecy was to allow for second repentance after baptism. Its core subject is the way to live the Christian life: how fasting is to be practised, the virtue of 'single-mindedness', the appropriate place of chastity or 'virginity'. The demand for holiness was the classic point of prophecy.

Montanists prolonged traditional fasts, tightened discipline by making them obligatory and even instituted new, occasional fasts in response to prophecies. As for sexual continence, there's little evidence that dedicated virginity was required, though Montanus was accused of allowing annulment of marriages and his associate prophetesses of abandoning their husbands, while second marriages were certainly outlawed. No sinner could be re-embraced

---

[33] Quoted *ibid.*, p. 233, n. 3.

by the holy community – Montanists certainly wouldn't countenance second repentance. Tertullian thought that the Paraclete
came to perfect discipline in the mature church, and this meant
firmer rules were to be applied than in earlier days;[34] God's will
is our sanctification – God's image is to be holy as God is holy.[35]
Christian perfectionism was given a significant boost by this 'New
Prophecy', which gave tightening of the rules the authority of spiritual
revelations.

Such 'holier-than-thou' attitudes provoke divisiveness. Analogies
abound in the course of church history. The failure of the Anglican
Church to contain Wesley and his followers is explained by the facts
that Wesley felt called to spread 'scriptural holiness' throughout the
land, that 'entire sanctification' became a watchword of the evangelical revival and that the doctrine of Christian perfection is one
of the distinctive features of Methodism. The promises found in the
New Testament were to be realized in Christian life here and now. Of
course, claims to holiness carry within them awful temptations to
self-promotion: as Bishop Butler said to Wesley, 'Sir, the pretending
to extraordinary revelations and gifts of the Holy Ghost is a horrid
thing, a very horrid thing.' Wesley was himself alive to this and careful to criticize claimants to perfection, while limiting the perfections
promised. More recently, demonstrable sanctification is expected in
Pentecostal circles, while Seventh Day Adventists rigorously apply
texts enjoining purity, refusing not just alcohol but coffee in their
endeavours to keep the body holy for the resurrection. The crucial
theological issue here concerns the nature of the transformation
effected by the Spirit within the present realities of this life – are
not these eschatological gifts eschatological, and what constitutes
holiness anyway?

---

[34] See e.g. Tertullian, *On Monogamy* 1–2, *On Fasting* 1, 11, *On the Veiling of Virgins* 1. For
fuller discussion see Trevett, *Montanism*.
[35] Tertullian, *On Chastity* 1.

1.2.3 Does new revelation challenge scripture?

'New' revelations have the potential to challenge the Bible. Hippolytus stated that 'they allege that they have learned something more through these than from the law and prophets and the Gospels'.[36] That their revelations were attributed to the Paraclete is well documented.[37] Some, then, identify as a significant issue the collection of new books of oracles to form a kind of 'third testament'. But this seems as anachronistic as reaction against institutionalization. The 'New Prophecy' arose before the scriptural canon was determined – indeed may have contributed to pressures that caused its definition. It also appeared before the language of testament/covenant was associated with collections of books. Furthermore, it appears that the visions and prophecies actually functioned as interpretations of texts treated as sacred.[38] Proof-texts from the Gospels and Acts were used to defend the 'New Prophecy' alongside texts from Jewish scriptures, while Paul, Hebrews and Revelation were exploited to support their claims.[39] In modern Pentecostalism, the outbreak of prophecy is seen likewise, as a fulfilment of scripture rather than a challenge to it. Indeed, 'charismatic Christianity tends overwhelmingly to see the testimonies of the Spirit and of the Word not to be in conflict'.[40] Montanism provides some parallel with the co-existence in Pentecostalism of a literalizing approach to scripture and new prophetic manifestations; prophecy actually involves the

---

[36] J. Stevenson (ed.), *A New Eusebius: Documents Illustrative of the History of the Church to AD 337* (London: SPCK, 1957), p. 112, quoting Hippolytus, *Refutation of all heresies* VIII.19.1–3.

[37] Montanus is reported to have said, 'I am the Father, the Word and the Paraclete' (*A New Eusebius*, p. 113). Cf. Tertullian's famous protest that Praxeas 'crucified the Father and put the Paraclete to flight' (*Against Praxeas* 1).

[38] Trevett, *Montanism*, p. 133.   [39] *Ibid.*, pp. 130–1.

[40] Simeon Zahl, *Pneumatology and Theology of the Cross in the Preaching of Christoph Friedrich Blumhardt: The Holy Spirit between Wittenberg and Azusa Street* (London: T&T Clark, 2010), p. 3.

application of inspired scripture to the present, and indeed reading the 'signs of the times'.

1.2.4 Inspiration – of what kind?

The fundamental issue was whether these new revelations were authentically from God's Spirit or deceptions of the devil – indeed, this would appear to be the ground on which battle was actually fought.

Already in second-century literature, warnings abound about false prophets. Hermas is a case in point, and the *Shepherd* provides some criteria.[41] The false prophet is open for business – responding to enquiries like a pagan soothsayer, telling people what they want to hear and charging for it. The true prophet speaks 'as the Lord wills', never receiving remuneration and humbly living a good and simple life. The one who only seems to have the Spirit exalts himself, wants the first seat, is bold and talkative, lives among luxury and delusions, and only prophesies for reward. Such were the charges brought against Montanus, Priscilla and Maximilla.[42]

One of our earliest sources, however, suggests that it was the nature of the inspiration itself which was contested.[43]

A little while ago I visited Ancyra in Galatia and found the local church deafened with the noise of this new craze – not prophecy, as they call it, but pseudo-prophecy, as I shall shortly prove.

It is said that a recent convert named Montanus . . . was filled with spiritual excitement and suddenly fell into a kind of trance and unnatural ecstasy. He raved, and began to chatter and talk nonsense, prophesying in a way that conflicted with the practice of the Church handed down generation by generation from the beginning. Of those

---

[41] Hermas, *Shepherd, Mandate* 11.   [42] Apollonius in Eusebius, *Church History* v.18.
[43] The 'Anonymous' quoted by Eusebius, *ibid.,* v.16–17.

who listened some . . . regarded him as possessed, a demoniac in the grip of a spirit of error . . . They . . . tried to stop his chatter, remembering the distinction drawn by the Lord, and his warning to guard vigilantly against the coming of false prophets. Others were elated as if by the Holy Spirit or a prophetic gift . . . and forgot the Lord's distinction. They welcomed a spirit that injured and deluded the mind and led the people astray.

This hostile report implies possession – no longer being in control of oneself but taken over by some supernatural power: 'the pseudo-prophet speaks in a state of unnatural ecstasy', says our source, adding that this is not the kind of prophecy found in scripture or indeed in Christian tradition – alluding to Acts, he mentions Agabus, Judas, Silas and Philip's daughters. That opponents called this sect 'Phrygians' or 'Cataphrygians' suggests that they were associated with group frenzies such as those found in Dionysiac religion. Some scholars have suggested pagan influence, noting the implication of calling Montanus a recent convert. One of Montanus' oracles might appear to confirm that this kind of ecstatic take-over was precisely what was involved:

> Behold a man is as a lyre, and I fly over it like a plectrum. The man sleeps, and I remain awake. Behold it is the Lord that stirs the hearts of men, and gives men hearts.[44]

Origen makes similar claims, distinguishing between the prophecy of 'the Pythian priestess, who is out of her senses and has not control of her faculties when she prophesies' and 'the prophets among the Jews, illuminated by the divine Spirit':

> because of the touch, so to speak, of what is called the Holy Spirit upon their soul they possessed clear mental vision and became more radiant in their soul.

---

[44] *A New Eusebius*, p. 113.

What possesses the Pythia must be a 'daemon' like those which Christians exorcise, whereas the Jewish prophets were wise and 'chosen by providence to be entrusted with the divine Spirit and with the utterances that He inspired on account of the quality of their lives'.[45]

LXX usage may have encouraged the view that the prophets were wise messengers rather than ecstatics: the Hebrew *nabi* was rendered by the Greek *prophētēs*, 'spokesperson'. However, according to the apologist, Athenagoras, the prophets:

> in the ecstasy of their thoughts, as the divine Spirit moved them, uttered what they were inspired to say, the Spirit making use of them as a flautist might blow into a flute.[46]

This image, found in Philo as well as Plutarch, was standard. One suspects that Montanus picked up something acceptable in Christian circles until his movement provoked the differentiation. What our source describes in terms of 'chattering' and 'talking nonsense' is plausibly identified as the phenomenon of 'speaking in tongues'. Or is it?

In *Prophecy and Inspired Speech in Early Christianity and its Hellenistic Environment*, Christopher Forbes maintains the charge that Montanism arose from pagan influence while resisting the attribution of the Corinthian glossolalia to that context.[47] He argues that Paul and his converts believed they spoke unknown languages miraculously, as had happened at Pentecost and as some modern Pentecostal anecdotes also suggest: Hollenweger[48] reports the story of a Rabbi who heard someone address him with a personal message in perfect Hebrew while ignorant of the language and of the fact

---

[45] *Against Celsus* VII.4–7.   [46] *Embassy* 9.

[47] Christopher Forbes, *Prophecy and Inspired Speech in Early Christianity and its Hellenistic Environment* (Peabody, MA: Hendriksen, 1997).

[48] Walter J. Hollenweger, *The Pentecostals* (London: SCM Press, 1972), pp. 3–4; cf. pp. 330–44.

that he had spoken it. John Chrysostom[49] used the Acts account and its reversal of Babel to exegete 1 Corinthians 14. Irenaeus and Novatian suggest that glossolalia continued in the churches beyond the apostolic age; Tertullian challenged Marcion to produce, as gifts of his god, 'a psalm, a vision, a prayer' given 'in a rapture, whenever an interpretation of tongues has occurred to him', claiming that 'all these signs are forthcoming from his side without any difficulty'.[50] The patristic references, Forbes suggests, imply the belief that it was foreign languages that were being spoken miraculously, whereas Montanists produced ecstatic utterance of a pagan kind.

The upshot of Forbes' distinctions is that the glossolalia found in the New Testament was not indebted to paganism, whereas the supposedly inspired speech of the Montanists was, so it was not glossolalia. But can these distinctions be sustained when prophecy, tongue-speaking, trances, visions, exorcism and miraculous signs, especially healings, are commonly found associated together in both ancient and modern contexts, in both Catholic and sectarian groups, not to mention religious practices reported by anthropologists from non-Christian contexts around the globe – indeed the charismatic phenomena have been described as 'natural religion'? Those questions I cannot resolve here, but debate about Montanist inspiration may occasion theological assessment of such outbreaks of strange 'spiritual' phenomena in the life of the church.

I first consider critical reactions and then offer some appreciation:

Critical reactions

- Rationalist critics, ancient and modern, believers or not, seek natural explanations in hallucination, hypnosis, etc.[51] Psychological

---

[49] John Chrysostom, *Homilies on 1 Corinthians* xxxv.1: Greek text: Migne, *PG* 61; ET: *NPNF.*

[50] Tertullian, *Against Marcion* v.8: Latin text and ET: E. Evans, *Adversus Marscionem, OECT.*

[51] See e.g. Hollenweger, *Pentecostals*, pp. 343–4; cf. the appendix to David Middlemiss, *Interpreting Charismatic Experience* (London: SCM Press, 1986).

accounts of 'shamanism', comparisons with the effects of drugs, not to mention 'brain-washing', are all part of the armoury. In the late 1950s Methodist students were challenged by the book *Battle for the Mind*,[52] which drew attention to parallels between the kind of religious conversion-experiences typical of the evangelical revival, political indoctrination techniques and the behaviour of Pavlov's dogs. Similar critiques are easily applied to late twentieth-century charismatic phenomena, such as the 'Toronto blessing'. Excessive emotionalism is the charge; as Ronald Knox put it in his 1950s classic, *Enthusiasm*, 'good Christian people who do not relish an eccentric spirituality find themselves in unwelcome alliance with worldlings who do not relish any spirituality at all'.[53]

- Suspicions are compounded as those 'carried away' by these phenomena adopt an anti-intellectualist stance, appealing to feelings and experience as a way of knowing without doubt, and not entertaining the possibility of self-deception.[54] The 'signs' of the Spirit are for them incontestable, despite the facts that Jesus resisted the demand for a sign and, as the early Christians realized, the same phenomena may be a sign of 'demonic possession'.

- Charismatic churches often have highly authoritarian personalities as leaders who exploit biblical authority and the power of the Spirit to impose extreme ethics and extract full tithes – so resembling the Montanists in the demand for higher levels of commitment and purity, as well as those prophets who prophesied for monetary reward. Such characteristics offend ecclesial tradition, offer a kind of consumerist religion with a dubious sales-pitch, encourage self-promotion and provoke the suspicion that such congregations are brain-washing 'sects'.

[52] William Sargant, *Battle for the Mind* (London: Doubleday, 1957).
[53] Knox, *Enthusiasm*, p. 1.
[54] Zahl, *Pneumatology*, e.g. p. 6 ff; cf. Middlemiss, *Interpreting Charismatic Experience*.

- The stand-off within Christianity between those maintaining a sceptical stance and those claiming charismatic experience is deeply divisive, often splitting church communities, as happened with the Montanist movement. Charismatics tend to be elitist, treating others as not fully Christian – 'psychics' rather than spiritual, as Tertullian would have put it, 'almost Christians', as John Wesley would have said. There is a converse elitism among so-called liberals, who tend to denigrate extremists, enthusiasts and fundamentalists. Neither does much to foster respect and communion.

- 'Signs and wonders', claims to miraculous healings, often accompany the 'miracle' of glossolalia. Miracles apparently continued in the life of the early church,[55] but they've become a notorious problem in the post-Enlightenment context. Does God ever override the fundamental constitution of things? There are no records of persons with learning disabilities such as Down's syndrome being miraculously healed,[56] nor are severed limbs made to grow again. People with disabilities experience damaging pressures from those suggesting they don't have enough faith. Many affirm that the promise of miracle is a fundamental threat to their identity: 'the complaints about Pentecostal-charismatic healing revivals are legion in the disability literature', writes the Pentecostal theologian Amos Yong. He and I have reached similar conclusions: astonishing miracles may occur, but they do not necessarily 'break the laws of nature', and there can be deep healing without physical cure.[57]

- Belief in miracles encourages a theology of success. This is to bypass the significance in Christian theology of Christ's suffering on the cross and of what has been called our 'negative experience'.[58] It has been suggested that the personality of Jeremiah:

[55] E.g. Irenaeus, *Against Heresies* II.32.4.
[56] Middlemiss, *Interpreting Charismatic Experience*, pp. 163–4.
[57] See Chapter 5; and Yong, *Theology and Down Syndrome*, pp. 242 ff.
[58] Zahl, *Pneumatology*.

would be unacceptable in many current charismatic churches. An attempt would probably be made to cast out his demons...[and] to criticize his lack of faith, as he has not healed himself, and is not living in material or emotional prosperity.[59]

- Pentecostal traditions have spawned new religious movements, such as the Zionists in South Africa or the Kimbanguists of Central Africa, which are often treated as syncretistic: the assimilation of features from tribal traditional religion has triggered charges of heresy, resembling the way in which the Montanists were accused of being influenced by Phrygian paganism.
- As Origen realized, there is a significant difference between those who see inspiration enhancing natural gifts of wisdom, and those who assume that human mental capacities are submerged by divine 'take-over'. This is now paralleled in different approaches to the inspiration of scripture: is scripture the outcome of direct 'dictation' through the Spirit's inspiration, the human instrument being simply a kind of automatic amanuensis, and the divinely sourced words being therefore 'infallible'? What kind of a God is implied by this view? Is it the Christian God?

Appreciation and responses to the critique

- Worship in Black Pentecostal churches is characterized by prolonged singing, clapping, dancing and the release that accompanies this whole-person involvement. To dismiss this as 'emotionalism' is to fail to appreciate its sheer physicality, and so miss its coherence with the significance of our bodily nature.[60] This is not to explain away the spiritual dimension: given the transcendent otherness of God, God's activity in the world is bound to be mediated through what's natural – of course it is impossible objectively

[59] Middlemiss, *Interpreting Charismatic Experience*, pp. 167–8.
[60] Cf. Chapters 3 and 4.

or experimentally to distinguish Christian charismatic experience from other phenomena arising from unusual brain states. The significant thing is experience of 'ecstasy' or 'enthusiasm' in the ancient sense of being caught up in something bigger than oneself or filled with the divine – in other words, the discovery of self-transcendence through participation in worship which lifts the spirit, and allows the Spirit to help our weakness.[61] For some people, silent meditation, traditional hymns, cathedral anthems or even secular classical music played live in the concert hall produce more culturally congenial routes to self-transcendence, but whatever form the uplift takes, it engages more than the left-brain, logocentric intellect – it is being 'taken over' and feeling physical responses, a pounding heart, shivers down the spine, as the physiology of conversion-experiences is liturgically re-played, cementing commitment. One charismatic chorus goes, 'I keep falling in love with him, over and over, and over and over again'; while for centuries Christian mysticism has experienced devotion through identifying with the lovers in the Song of Songs.

- Such physical engagement enables congregational participation. In recent decades mainstream churches have striven to get people to participate in worship by playing an active part, reading lessons, offering intercessions. Does this really mean greater participation? Participation in a concert or in a theatre production is not a matter of going on stage oneself, but of so responding as to be caught up into the action or the music. Arthur's presence in worship reinforces this point. How does he participate? Mainly by silence and the rapture on his face when the singing is lifting his spirit, sometimes by echoing the intonation of the preacher's voice, or shouting his own name, often by vigorous hand-clapping. Such is his response at his own level, and for the rest of us too it is response that matters. Great music lifts the spirit to inner realms of wordless worship, even more effectively than singing

[61] Romans 8.26, 15–16.

oneself – though hymn-singing is mostly the way of actual participation. Great preaching, like great acting, claims attention and moves people to respond, to see things differently, to change their attitudes, to live in a different imaginative world which provides a larger perspective within which to discover meaning and live out their day-to-day lives. The aim of worship surely is to create the kind of participation which takes people out of themselves so that they become more truly themselves in the larger whole.

- What this generates is not sheer emotionalism. Charismatic worship at its best involves not just feeling but body and mind, putting our minds into our hearts. Fruitful outcomes guarantee the depth of worship; for, as the early church recognized, 'by their fruits you shall know them'.[62] Black Pentecostal churches show the fruits of the Spirit – love, joy, peace, patience, kindness, generosity, faithfulness, gentleness, self-control[63] – as they create community, providing one another with mutual support and affirmation in an often racist environment. Some of us find similar fruits elsewhere, such as living in relationship with persons with profound learning disabilities, the kind of communion and mutual dependence that happens in the L'Arche communities. Characteristic of both kinds of community is their infectious welcome, and their grounding in faith, hope and love sustained against the odds.

- That 'against the odds' is a counter to the suggestion that there is insufficient attention given to the cross. There is sometimes over-emphasis on promises of health, wealth and prosperity – a Gospel of success eclipsing other aspects of the Christian tradition – but to generalize this is untrue to the realities. Montanism sustained martyrs through their ordeals; and engagement with the reality of congenital disability contributed to a kenotic and cross-centred perspective in the theology of the Pentecostal theologian Amos Yong.[64]

[62] Matthew 7.20.   [63] Galatians 5.22–3.
[64] E.g. Yong, *Theology and Down Syndrome*, pp. 176 ff; cf. pp. 254 ff.

- As for speaking in tongues, some would describe it as primarily the gift of a language in which to offer prayer and praise.[65] After all, worship goes beyond comprehensible words. Twentieth-century liturgical revisions, along with multiple updated translations of the Bible, seem to imply that we should understand. But if we imagine we can comprehend God, then God is reduced to the size of our own minds, a point made repeatedly by the fathers.[66] Liturgy is always more than words – the words both point beyond themselves and are performative – liturgy is an *act* of worship. Arthur, along with those who speak in tongues, reminds us that we are caught up in something bigger than ourselves – bigger than our words and bigger than our understanding. Speaking in tongues in public worship has been described as producing a 'cathedral of sound';[67] indeed, the sense of sacred place, atmosphere and music may be more important than words for creating worship.
- Another gift received from Black Pentecostal churches is the need to listen respectfully to scripture as addressing us now – it becomes the Word of God for those who have ears to ear. Some may espouse unsatisfactory theories of inspiration, being entirely innocent of the fallible human and historical processes that produced the King James Version, yet through inspired insight this Word of God speaks directly in the now of 'to-day',[68] to expose our lives, to offer judgement and mercy, to call us to new action in church or world.
- The greatest debt I owe to Black Pentecostal worship is a lively sense of God's presence. The Spirit is expected, and this enables

[65] E.g. David Ford, in an unpublished paper entitled 'Divining Tongues: Glossolalia as a Twenty-First Century Symbol' (April 2010): 'Paul sees tongues as one of the gifts of the Spirit in the church; tongues is primarily addressed to God . . . is about praying, praising God, singing, blessing and thanking with the Spirit/spirit rather than with the mind.'

[66] Cf. Chapter 8.

[67] Daniel W. Hardy and David F. Ford, *Jubilate: Theology in Praise* (London: DLT, 1984), p. 19.

[68] Hebrews 3.15–4 *passim*.

liturgy to become not idle repetition, but the potential vehicle of deeply moving, fresh performance of utterly familiar material, evoking memories while facilitating a unique, unrepeatable, particular moment of encounter with the otherness of the Holy. Being in worship with Arthur, too, helps us to recognize that what we do or feel matters less than being bathed, like him, in the music of voices and the smiles of presences, in a sense of abandonment to the sensations of sounds and sight, even bodily movement, as we receive grace through familiar liturgical actions and one another. Indeed, Arthur confirms the power of memory and familiarity: one evening there were carols on the television, 'Away in a Manger' provoking immediate recognition, and by the end tears were running down his cheeks – this inarticulate adult physically moved, responding from somewhere deep within, remembering his Granny singing it to him as a lullaby when a child. He reminds us that often we receive grace without being aware of the fact, and there is more to receive than we can know. Someone once said to me, 'Arthur's presence in church is Gospel.' Surely persons with even the most profound limitations have a vocation; they are a 'sign' in the biblical sense, pointing beyond themselves. That surely is the kind of sign found in charismatic gifts of the Spirit, if received in humility and respected by the congregation, even those who do not have the gift.

1.2.5 Live inspiration: concluding remarks

All this bears on my own Methodist tradition, which figures large in Knox's classic work on 'enthusiasm'. I grew up expecting to find God and as a teenager responded with feeling to the occasional altar call, only to become suspicious of the seemingly artificial generation of guilt and emotion, and of the highly self-oriented spirituality implied – indeed, of the likelihood of self-delusion. But now I affirm moments of revelatory inspiration, as well as the significance of the powerful stirring of memory and feeling that is evoked by familiar

Wesley hymns. At the same time, ecumenical experience has enabled a taste of being caught up by other powerful devotional cultures, the Pentecostal legacy of Wesleyan holiness movements, the musical purity of the Anglican cathedral tradition, the mystical up-lift of Eastern Orthodox liturgical singing. The Spirit is found in the deep breathing of singing and physiological responses to music's beat and harmony, in a kind of whole person self-transcendence.

In the biblical languages, as in English, there is a deep ambiguity in the word 'spirit': it expresses the core of a personality, or passing moods, or group dynamics – we speak of a spirit of mischief, of despair or joy, or of Christmas or springtime, or team spirit. And inspiration is not confined to sacred worship in community. Not for nothing did the ancients regard poets as inspired, and the notion that great art, literature and music somehow come from beyond its author lives on in our culture. Writing, especially writing poetry, is not experienced as simply the formulation of one's own ideas, or even as feelings recollected in tranquillity, for there is a surprising 'givenness' about the initial idea, which is then enriched in further surprising ways, often through struggling with constraints of form or rhyme. The strange depth and creativity of the human spirit emerges in inspiration which points beyond itself to hidden winds of the divine Spirit. So God surprises me – in ordinary moments made extraordinary, in new responses to old, familiar texts, especially in the search for next Sunday's sermon. Of course, one must test the spirits to see whether they be of God. The ultimate question must always be whether the spirit at work is holy or unclean, self-oriented or humbly consistent with the spirit evident in the Jesus we know from the Gospels. Wisdom in this emerges from the community of the faithful.

It was Easter communion in an inner-city Methodist church. For the first time ever, I placed communion in all kinds of different hands – black hands and white hands, old hands and young hands, the smooth hands of office-workers and the rough hands of labourers. Someone had taken the initiative to push the wheelchair to the front so that Arthur was included. All of a sudden it seemed as though I saw the Lord, high and lifted up in the Temple . . . The early church sensed it was caught up to heaven in worship – the use of Isaiah's vision is already present in the book of Revelation, and the Sanctus lives on in the liturgy: 'Holy, holy, holy Lord, heaven and earth are full of your glory.'

II Sanctification – the Holy Spirit and holiness

> Holiness was your intent as you stretched out your hands to Almighty God, . . . praying that God would be merciful if you had inadvertently sinned.[69]

> If you are slow to anger and steady, the Holy Spirit which dwells within you will be unalloyed, and . . . will rejoice and be glad, along with the body which is its dwelling-place, and so from its inner well-being will worship God with great joy.[70]

In the *Apostolic Fathers* the Spirit is associated with the pure and holy lives characteristic of the baptized, as it is when Paul addresses his letters to the 'saints' (*hagioi* – holy ones). Through the early centuries martyrs were assured of sainthood, having been baptized not only in water, but in blood. After Constantine, it would be monks who inherited the martyrs' mantle. That the on-going battle with the world, the flesh and the devil should be concentrated in the solitude of caves might appear implausible, yet the resultant contemplative tradition has continued to echo down the centuries, to be embodied for the twentieth century in a figure such as Thomas Merton. Other legacies of the ascetic tradition, however, are particularly alien to our culture and undermine positive evaluation of holiness as an ideal. This issue will be addressed first; then one example of ascetic literature will be used to set out more sympathetically the way of holiness in the monastic tradition.

[69] *1 Clement* 2.1–3.   [70] Hermas, *The Shepherd*, *Mandate* 5.1–2.

11.1 Ascetic ideals: 'virginity' and apatheia

Lives dedicated to chastity were a feature of Christianity from its earliest days. The Apologist, Justin, 'presented Christianity...as a religion distinguished from all others by the stringency of the sexual codes observed by its married believers'.[71] In the second century, the medical writer Galen commented:

> Their contempt for death is patent to us every day, and likewise their restraint from intercourse. For they include not only men but also women who refrain from intercourse all through their lives.

The *Acts of Paul*, an apocryphal work rejected by Tertullian as the work of a deposed presbyter, includes a section known as the *Acts of Paul and Thekla*. Popular over a long period, it survives in Greek, Syriac, Coptic, Slavic, Arabic and four independent Latin versions; by the fourth century we know of several churches and a monastery dedicated to Thekla.[72] In this influential text Paul's teaching is reported as follows:

> Blessed are the pure in heart, for they shall see God.
>
> Blessed are they who have kept the flesh pure, for they shall become a Temple of God.
>
> Blessed are the continent, for to them God will speak...
>
> Blessed are they who have wives as if they had them not, for they shall inherit God...

---

[71] Peter Brown, *The Body and Society: Men, Women and Sexual Renunciation in Early Christianity* (London: Faber and Faber, 1989); quotations, including that from Galen, from pp. 33–4.

[72] Egeria visited one such church; Gregory Nazianzen retreated to Thekla's 'Parthenona', presumably a monastery: see McGuckin, *Gregory of Nazianzus*, pp. 229–30.

> Blessed are the bodies of the virgins, for they shall be well-pleasing to God, and shall not lose the reward of their purity.[73]

Thekla overheard this, abandoned her arranged betrothal and went off to follow Paul. Tertullian contested the view that Thekla's example supported the right of women to teach and baptize, but undoubtedly she provided an example for would-be virgins, both female and male. So the fourth-century monastic movement[74] was not entirely novel in its asceticism. In Egypt the novelty lay in withdrawal to the desert; elsewhere, city-based monasteries developed, while pilgrims flocked to 'holy men' living on the margins, in caves or tombs, or on pillars, acting as prophets and charismatic healers for a society being Christianized. The church accommodated or excluded extremists, occasionally managing both at the same time as, despite their condemnation, writings emanating from Origenist and Messalian sources were reattributed and adopted into mainstream monastic literature.

Ascetic extremes were controversial. We find persistent criticism of gnostics for their renunciation of the world, given that it is God's good creation. Why then did sexual renunciation become so characteristic of Christianity? The cultural background provides only partial explanation – Jews and pagans would renounce sex for short periods for religious reasons, while, for both, prophecy and continence were linked. Brown's classic study[75] focussed on several factors: the drive for purity of heart, understood as single-mindedness; the need to specify a purity code once Torah was not required of Gentile converts; the ideal of becoming a temple of the Holy Spirit and a new creation; the symbolism whereby continence restored paradise, undid the power of death and made one equal to the angels who

---

[73] Quoted from E. Hennecke, *New Testament Apocrypha*, vol. II (W. Schneemelcher (ed.), ET: R. McL. Wilson, London: Lutterworth, 1965), p. 354.

[74] See further *From Nicaea to Chalcedon*, chapter 3.

[75] Brown, *Body and Society*, chapters 2–3.

neither marry nor are given in marriage.[76] Apocalyptic visions and hopes for resurrection challenged 'this-worldly' desires and encouraged anxieties about keeping the body pure, so affecting both intake into the body and bodily emissions.

Stress on virginity, or celibacy, is particularly alien to our culture, and in today's world this ancient tradition poses problems. For a few celibacy may be chosen, but emerging scandals indicate the difficulties for those of whom it is expected, while sexuality is a dividing issue in church life. For many people a loving and supportive relationship is the temple-like place within which the presence and love of God are mediated, and the sexual act a sacrament – a material sign of a spiritual reality. The fathers understood this at least spiritually, through the image of Christ as bridegroom and the church as bride, metaphors reinforced by their exegesis of the Song of Songs. But ancient society, being hierarchical and patriarchal, had little conception of mutual attraction between notional equals except between male friends. So the fathers were unable to take their affirmation of the body, or indeed of marriage, far enough to find holiness outside renunciation. Distractions, emotions and sexual acts remained problematic. We need critical appraisal of this.

The ideal of *apatheia* (passionlessness) comes in for particular criticism. Originally Stoic, this informed the interior motivation for external ascetic practice, defining what 'purity of heart' might be. The Origenist monk Evagrius is especially associated with suppression of the 'passions' and analysis of those inner 'demons' that threaten the ascetic's contemplation and peace of mind. Jerome accused him of teaching 'insensibility, like that of a stone', but Evagrius himself wrote, 'Love is the offspring of impassibility, and impassibility is the blossom of the practical life' – by 'practical life' he meant the cultivation of detachment by challenging the desires of body and

---

[76] Matthew 22.30.

soul, but love was its aim.[77] This challenges our assumptions, and invites us to probe more deeply into the meaning of *apatheia*.

Much is clarified by Sorabji's book, *Emotion and Peace of Mind*. Two points deserve comment: the first concerns *propatheia*, the term for 'first impulses' or 'immediate reactions' which only become *pathē* when one gives in to them; as Sorabji puts it, 'emotions are due not to nature, but to our own judgement, which on the Stoic view involves voluntary assent' – they 'can be inhibited or self-induced'.[78] In the Origenist tradition, these *propatheia* became bad thoughts or temptations to be resisted, Didymus even stating that Jesus himself was subject to such *propatheia*, though he never gave way to them,[79] while Evagrius, anticipating the medieval seven deadly sins, catalogued eight 'thoughts' or 'demons' to be resisted by the ascetic seeking *apatheia*.[80] The second point concerns *eupatheia*. A string of feelings we'd regard as emotions were not included by Stoics among the *pathē*: goodwill, kindness, love; gladness, delight, cheerfulness; modesty, piety.[81] So love is not incompatible with *apatheia* in Christian writings.

Christian thinkers like Evagrius were eclectic. Accepting the Platonic tripartite soul, he understood the practical life as the harnessing of the driving energies of the soul, the emotional horses being reined in or directed by the charioteer, the mind. The desirous element (*epithumia*) is meant to long for virtue, and the irascible (*thumos*) to struggle for that goal; so these 'two major energy sources in the

---

[77] *From Nicaea to Chalcedon*, p. 107, quoting Jerome, *Epistle* 133; Evagrius, *Praktikos* 81, 84: Greek text: A. and C. Guillaumont, *Évagre le pontique: Traité pratique ou le moine I & II, SC*; ET: Robert E. Sinkewicz, *Evagrius of Pontus: The Greek Ascetic Corpus* (Oxford Early Christian Studies, Oxford University Press, 2003).

[78] Richard Sorabji, *Emotion and Peace of Mind: From Stoic Agitation to Christian Temptation* (Oxford University Press, 2000), pp. 45–6.

[79] *Ibid.*, pp. 346, 351; cf. *From Nicaea to Chalcedon*, pp. 99–100.

[80] *Ibid.*, chapter 23; cf. *From Nicaea to Chalcedon*, pp. 101–16; Angela Tilby, *The Seven Deadly Sins: Their Origin in the Spiritual Teaching of Evagrius the Hermit* (London: SPCK, 2009).

[81] Sorabji, *Emotion and peace of Mind*, pp. 47 ff.

human personality'[82] may have, as their pathology, lust and anger, but as their health, love of God and resistance to sin. *Apatheia*, which Evagrius believes is never actually attained in this life, should be understood as 'emotional integration', or that detachment which is essential to true love. It is nearer than appears at first sight to cultivating a well-balanced personality. It means never acting against one's better judgement, or giving way to fears, anxieties, depression, desires or bad temper. In the thinking of antiquity, *katharsis* or purification involved not just the use of emetics, but resistance to bad humours; for contemporary medical theory tended to provide physiological explanations for the desires and tempers that distracted the soul from contemplation. In the Christian tradition, this interiority was reinforced. After all, as Jesus said, it is not what goes into a person that defiles – for it does not go into the heart but into the stomach and then straight through and out of the body; it is what is inside, what is in a person's heart, that pollutes: the evil thoughts that produce fornication, theft, murder, adultery, avarice, pride, folly.[83] Besides, since God was beyond body, parts and passions, to become like God meant seeking *apatheia*.[84]

Appreciation of the cultural context may help us to understand better the emphasis on *apatheia*, but it hardly makes it easier to accept it as wisdom worth appropriating. Modern psychology takes a very different stance, suggesting that considerable dangers arise from suppressing emotion or attempting to sublimate sexual desire. Yet perhaps we should hesitate to dismiss patristic ideals too hastily. Emotions such as anger and envy remain potentially destructive, while others are easily corrupted – love itself can become damaging possessiveness and jealousy. Sometimes what passes for love is really self-centred anxiety, as I have realized when time and again distressed by Arthur's distress, finding it hard to cope when he is unsettled,

---

[82] Columba Stewart, Introduction to Harriet A. Luchman and Linda Kulzer (eds.), *Purity of Heart in Early Ascetic and Monastic Literature* (Collegeville, MN: Liturgical Press, 1999), p. 13.

[83] Mark 7.18–22.   [84] See Chapter 8.

unwell, or in pain, cannot express what is wrong, and the more we try to sort the problem the more frantic and furious he gets, hating to be handled, not understanding that we're trying to deal with his discomfort. Frustration mounts, creating its own distress and anger, which hardly helps his – in fact compounds it. Too easily inner demons of self-pity, a sense of failure, inadequacy and helplessness take over. So I recognize that I really need *apatheia* in order to love properly. Love requires a degree of detachment, an ability to let the other person be, to be 'other', to be what they are rather than what you want them to be.

The first time a group of theologians met at the original L'Arche community in Trosly-Breuil, a little paper was offered by a Lebanese Roman Catholic priest, Father Youakim Moubarac; it spoke deeply to my heart. Engaging with the extremes of early Syrian monasticism, he drew attention to 'extreme states in modern existence', and particularly to L'Arche, as 'a privileged place for meeting God' such as ascetics had in the desert. I quote:

> In as far as I understand Jean Vanier, daily dealings with people who have handicaps makes those involved face their own violence. Confronted by the irreducibility of the other, the one whom they mean to serve but whose condition they cannot ameliorate, they discover with horror that they are capable of striking them, or even wanting to do away with them. It is this, then, that I call a privileged desert place. The anchorites took themselves off to the desert, they said, to fight with Satan on his own territory. We know now that it is enough to pay attention to the most defenceless people among us to find ourselves given up to our interior demons. But if only we force ourselves not to lose heart, if only grace comes to the aid of our weakness, we apprehend that to spend time with the poorest of all is not to do them charity, but to allow ourselves to be transformed by them and to apprehend God as gentleness.[85]

---

[85] Y. Moubarac, 'Alongside L'Arche' in my *Encounter with Mystery*, pp. 89–93.

11.2 The 'Macarian' Homilies and Scriptural Holiness

11.2.1 The Homilies: origins and legacy

The *Spiritual Homilies of Macarius*[86] have an interesting ecumenical afterlife. Their influence across the Byzantine world is patent: several different collections are to be found in the manuscript traditions, as well as versions in Syriac, Arabic, Georgian, Latin and Slavonic. But they also influenced Protestant Pietism, were published in an English translation in 1721, and in 1750 John Wesley included selections in the first volume of his *Christian Library*, a compendium for the education of his preachers. Their influence on John Wesley is evident: his diary entry for 30 July, 1736 indicates that travelling by boat in Georgia, with the wind set fair, and later in the rain, he read Macarius and sang. Even when 'not a little affrighted by the falling of the mast . . . he again read Macarius and sang'.

Wesley believed that these homilies were written by the 'great Macarius of Egypt' and, in the preface written for the *Christian Library*, offers an exemplary sketch of Macarius' life, suggesting that:

> what he continually labours to cultivate in himself and others is, the real life of God in heart and soul, that kingdom of God, which consists in righteousness, and peace, and joy in the Holy Ghost.

He affirms that Macarius was educated in the holy scriptures, and his knowledge of them was 'not merely literal or speculative', but 'true and practical', 'able to save his soul'. Using phrases which indicate his perception of congruence between Macarius' thought and his own, he writes:

> He is ever quickening and stirring up his audience, endeavouring to kindle in them a steady zeal, an earnest desire, and inflamed ambition, to recover that Divine image we were made in; to be made

---

[86] Greek text: H. Berthold (ed.), *Makarios/Symeon: Reden und Briefe* (2 vols.) in *GCS*; ET: G. A. Maloney, SJ, *Pseudo-Macarius: The Fifty Spiritual Homilies and the Great Letter*, in *CWS*.

conformable to Christ our Head; to be daily sensible more and more of our living union with him as such; and discovering it, as occasion requires, in all the genuine fruits of an holy life and conversation, in such a victorious faith as overcomes the world, and working by love, is ever fulfilling the whole law of God.

Wesley and Macarius had a common practical theology, a common drive towards perfection as the goal of the Christian life, a common emphasis on the incarnation and the Holy Spirit as the generators of perfection, a common stress on the love of God. Indeed, what Wesley did could be described as a 'democratizing' of the old monastic ideal of holiness.

However, these texts were not actually from Macarius of Egypt. Twentieth-century scholarship[87] has confirmed earlier hunches that their teaching is close to Messalianism, a movement which suffered hostility from the church, as did Wesley himself in another age – Knox would have placed the Messalians in the same 'enthusiasm' camp. They were accused of being possessed, and calling their dreams and fantasies prophecies; they were said to reject the sacraments and the efficacy of ecclesiastical liturgies and authorities, while denying that such charges applied to them. We need not pursue the complex critical questions surrounding these homilies; even if they did emerge from this dubious background, they became important for the monastic tradition when passed off as the work of Macarius; and in fact, recent work has stressed the range of different influences on the 'Macarian' material, creating a 'rich synthesis' of Syrian themes, Hellenistic philosophy, Origen's theology, Egyptian monasticism, Alexandrian Christology and Cappadocian thought.[88] They

[87] See Columba Stewart, in *'Working the Earth of the Heart': The Messalian Controversy in History, Texts, and Language to AD 431* (Oxford: Clarendon Press, 1991).

[88] Stewart reviewing Marcus Plested, *The Macarian Legacy: The Place of Macarius–Symeon in the Eastern Christian Tradition* (Oxford Theological Monographs, Oxford University Press, 2004) in *JEH* 59 (2008) 528.

function as representative texts for pursuing the nature of the monastic goal of holiness.

II.2.2 Scriptural holiness

These texts treat at length the spiritual struggle for perfection and the work of the Holy Spirit in the heart. They are riddled with scriptural quotation:

> We have not yet been immersed in the leaven of sincerity (I Cor. 5.8), but we are still in the leaven of evil... "We have not yet put on the new man who has been created after God in holiness" (Eph. 4.24), because we have not yet put off "the old man that is corrupt according to the sinful lusts" (Eph. 4.22). We have not yet "given birth to the image of the heavenly" (I Cor. 15.49) nor have we been made "conformed to his glory" (Phil. 3.21)... We have not yet been "transformed by a renewal of the mind", since we are still "conformed to this world" (Rom. 12.2) "in the vanity of the mind" (Eph. 4.17). We are not yet "glorified with Christ" because we have not yet "suffered with him" (Rom. 8.17).[89]

Another habit is citing biblical models: 'We have offered these examples from Holy Scripture to show that the power of divine grace is in man and the gift of the Holy Spirit which is given to the faithful soul comes forth with much contention, with much endurance, patience, trials and testings.'[90] The basis of 'Macarian' teaching is scripture, read so as to discern what is true for the heart on its spiritual journey to union with God.

Pervasive interiority is characteristic. The focus is on experience, assurance, sensation, communion, found in prayer:

> One kneels down in prayer and at once his heart is filled with the power of God. And his soul exults in the Lord as a bride with

[89] Collection II.xxv.3–5.   [90] *Ibid.* ix.2–7.

the bridegroom... The interior man is caught up in prayer and plunged into the infinite depths of that other world with great sweetness...

At times the fire flares out and burns with more vehement flames. At other times it burns more gently and slowly... It is always burning and giving off light, but when it is especially trimmed, it burns more brilliantly, as though intoxicated by the love of God.[91]

'Macarius' admits that this intensity is not permanent: 'there are times when grace burns more brightly, consoles and refurbishes more completely. Then at other times the grace subsides and is clouded over.' One reason for this is that if a person stays on the top step of grace, the highest level of perfection, he could not bear to take any interest in anything else, but would simply 'sit in a corner lifted up and intoxicated'. Macarius has 'not yet seen any perfect Christian'. Those who claim to be perfect are deceived by lack of experience. No matter how much a person is 'at rest in grace', 'experiencing mysteries, revelations, and the immense consolation of grace', 'sin still abides in him'.

The model of perfection is Christ, whose most important designations are 'light' and 'image', since transformation or transfiguration is the ultimate goal of the ascetic's life. 'Macarius' describes Christ as a portrait-painter, endeavouring to reproduce his own image in the believer. The soul needs to have Christ stamped on it if it is to be coin in the treasuries of the kingdom.[92] The bodies of the saints are like lamps lit from the fire of Christ:

For as the body of the Lord was glorified when he climbed the mount and was transfigured into the divine glory and into infinite light, so also the bodies of the saints are glorified and shine like lightning.[93]

---

[91] *Ibid.* viii.1, 2.   [92] *Ibid.* xxx.4–5.   [93] *Ibid.* xv.38.

Their transfiguration takes place by 'putting on Christ', the 'garment of salvation', the 'ineffable light'. Christ thus lies at the core of this transformative reading of the Bible; Christians become his friends, his brothers, his fellow-heirs, participators of the divine nature, conformed to his glory.[94]

One fascinating passage is a reflection on Ezekiel's vision of the chariot-throne of God.[95] For 'Macarius', Ezekiel's vision is all about the 'mystery of the human soul that would receive its Lord and would become his throne of glory'. The soul is covered 'with the beauty of the ineffable glory of the light of Christ, who mounts and rides upon the soul'. It is 'Christ who drives, guides, carries and supports the soul about and adorns and decorates the soul with his spiritual beauty'. The animals that bore the chariot represent the will, the conscience, the mind and the power of loving. The rider – Christ, the authentic charioteer – is mounted on the soul and guides it with the reins of the Spirit. What we seem to have here is an astonishing adaptation of the Platonic notion of reason controlling the soul's passions. Christ takes control and knows the way – elsewhere 'Macarius' speaks of Christ as pilot of the soul. With Christ in the driving seat, the whole soul becomes eye, totally light – 'all light, all face, all eye', 'all glory, all spirit'. This happens while in the body, and anticipates the resurrection; it is no longer necessary to go up to heaven, as in apocalyptic visions, to see God on the glorious throne. The ascetic teaching is an interiorization of the cosmic struggle of apocalyptic, and the soul becomes the locus of theophany – the pure in heart shall see God.[96]

---

[94] E.g. *ibid.* xxv.4–5, quoting New Testament texts; cf. many other examples, e.g. xxvii.1; xlviii.2.
[95] *Ibid.* i.1–3.
[96] A. Golitzin, 'A Testimony to Christianity as Transfiguration: The Macarian Homilies and Orthodox Spirituality' in Kimbrough, (ed.), *Orthodox and Wesleyan Spirituality*, pp. 129–56; and 'Temple and Throne of the Divine Glory: "Pseudo-Macarius" and Purity of Heart, Together with Some Remarks on the Limitations and Usefulness of Scholarship' in Luchman and Kulzer, *Purity of Heart*, pp. 107–12.

Seeing with the mind the desirable and only ineffable beauty, such a person is pierced with divine passionate love and is directed in the way of all virtues by the Spirit.[97]

The ascetic endeavour makes a person 'salt without savour' unless he 'feel in his soul...the pleasure of the Spirit', unless he be 'clothed...with the clothing of the light of the Godhead', unless he 'know with assurance the satisfaction of the communion of the heavenly bridegroom in his soul' and 'the joy of the Spirit interiorly', unless he 'receive the heavenly consolation of grace and a divine filling in the soul in the appearance to him of the glory of the Lord'.[98] Reading scripture profits nothing if a person does not receive the gift of life. The human body is a temple of God, and the human heart is an altar of the Holy Spirit.

So 'Macarius' emerges as theologian of the Holy Spirit and of transformation. 'If anyone is in Christ, he is a new creature',[99] he says, 'for our Lord Jesus Christ came for this reason, to change and transform and renew human nature, and to recreate this soul that had been overturned by passions through transgression.' Christ came to 'mingle human nature with his own Spirit of the Godhead', to effect in those who believe 'a new mind and a new soul and new eyes, a new spiritual tongue, and, in a word, new humans', to 'pour into them new wine which is his Spirit'.[100] The Spirit is 'the Lord himself shining in their hearts', and those who possess the Spirit fulfil 'all the commands justly and practise all the virtues without blame, purely without forcing and with a certain ease'.[101] To reach this state, hearers should meanwhile force themselves to observe the commandments, begging God to grant the gift of 'the heavenly grace of the Spirit'.[102]

Striving for perfection in Christ is what it is all about. Frequent are references to 'a "mixing" of the Holy Spirit with the human soul', 'to becoming "one spirit" with the Lord, to being changed into a

[97] Collection II.xxviii.5.   [98] *Ibid.* xlix.1.   [99] 2 Corinthians 5.17.
[100] Collection II.xliv.1.   [101] *Ibid.* xviii.1–2.   [102] *Ibid.* xix.7.

"divine nature"'. God comes to dwell in the soul, and then obedience to the commandments becomes 'natural and easy'. 'The "mature" Christian is the one who has grown up through the ascetical struggle, and been "completed" by the gift of the Spirit.'[103] Many passages speak of advancing 'to maturity, to the measure of the full stature of Christ',[104] or progressing from children's milk to the solid food of the mature.[105] There is a profound oscillation between the need for constant struggle and the promise of reaching the goal, which is a return to paradise and restoration of the image of God. Renewal goes even further, however: 'by the power of the Spirit and the spiritual regeneration', one 'not only comes to the measure of the first Adam, but also reaches a greater state than he possessed. For man is divinised.'[106]

Meanwhile, however, the soul engages in a 'war' in its 'inner thoughts' against 'arrogance, presumption, unbelief, hatred, envy, deceit, hypocrisy'. This interior struggle can only be concluded through God's grace and power, though in practice a synergism of divine grace and human will is recognized. The battle is with one's own nature, with its old habits, with the customs with which one grew up:

> for a certain hidden and subtle power of darkness is revealed that has been entrenched in the heart. And the Lord . . . puts in you secret, heavenly thoughts and he begins interiorly to give you rest. But he allows you to be disciplined, and grace directs you in these very afflictions.[107]

Someone who really strives, battling, longing, diligently seeking, should be able to attain to holiness and perfection, because they receive the love of Christ and the Holy Spirit. Someone overwhelmed by temptations ought not to lose hope. For evil diminishes and dries

---

[103] Quotations from Stewart, *Working the Earth of the Heart*, pp. 78–82.
[104] Ephesians 4.13. Cf. Colossians 1.28.   [105] Hebrews 5.12–14.
[106] Collection II.xxvi.2.   [107] *Ibid.* xxxii.10.

up in a person who constantly puts their hope in God. Sin and grace are at war within us: heaven is anticipated among those who are born of God, but this is 'purchased only with labour, and pains, and trials, and many conflicts'; and is always vulnerable. Ultimately it is entirely dependent upon God's grace.

The 'difference between true Christians and the rest of human beings is that the mind and intellect of Christians are always centred on heavenly thoughts', because 'they participate in the Holy Spirit', 'have been born above from God and are children of God in truth and power', and 'have arrived, through many labours and sweat', at a 'state of equilibrium, tranquillity and peace, freed from further sifting'. The language of grace, of renewal and of new creation is used; 'they have received in the inner person another Spirit'. Nevertheless, few successfully complete the race; it takes complete self-denial.[108] Renunciation and fulfilment are two sides of the same coin in the search for holiness.

11.2.3 Wesley's appropriation of 'Macarius'

Wesley's doctrine of Christian perfection was derived from the same reading of scripture as that found in the 'Macarian' Homilies. It is built up out of the scriptural promises; so those who could not accept it did not trust God to fulfil those promises. Faced with misunderstanding by opponents and over-enthusiasm among supporters, Wesley tried to spell out what was and was not meant by Christian perfection. Defined as 'perfect love', it was seen as something dynamic – not a state attained, nor something absolute, but something always improvable: indeed, 'one perfected in love may grow in grace far swifter than he did before'. Like 'Macarius' Wesley stressed that security was never possible in this life.[109]

---

[108] *Ibid.* v.1–6.
[109] For *A Plain Account of Christian Perfection*, see Frank Whaling (ed.), *John and Charles Wesley: Selected Writings and Hymns*, CWS, pp. 299–377.

Perfection is not something of which anyone can boast, nor does it eliminate the possibility of struggle or future fall. Wesley affirms that none are ever wholly free from temptation,[110] despite suggesting that if the Spirit has purified the heart, evil thoughts cannot spring up any more:

> Tho' numberless temptations fly about them, yet they trouble them not. At all times their soul is even and calm, their heart is steadfast and unmovable.[111]

Temptation remains the environment in which the perfected one must exist. Sanctification does not come immediately; according to a sermon on the fullness of faith, it begins at the moment of justification, but soon 'temptations return and sin revives; showing it was but stunned before, not dead'.[112] The experience of converts is that two principles are at war within them, the flesh lusting against the Spirit, nature opposing grace. They may have the power to believe in Christ and to love God, yet feel in themselves something of pride or self-will, sometimes anger or unbelief. Wesley quotes 'Macarius', suggesting that while the inexperienced may imagine they have no more sin, the more mature recognize that even those who have the grace of God may be molested again. We have the first-fruits of God's Spirit; but the harvest is not yet. Christians are open to attack precisely where their strength lies: by concentrating on their guilt and sinfulness rather than the hope of the gospel; by letting their confidence in God's salvation wane. This is perhaps Wesley's version of the sin of *akedia*.

The parallels between Wesley and 'Macarius' are striking, not least in the choice of Pauline texts referring to adoption and new birth. Couched in positive terms as potentially realizable in the holy life of

[110] *Ibid.*, p. 307.   [111] *Ibid.*, p. 311.
[112] Albert C. Outler (ed.), *John Wesley* (Oxford University Press, 1964), p. 274.

the Christian, the collage with which our discussion of 'Macarian' thought began could well have been Wesley's.

11.2.4 Appropriation now?

Wesley appropriated 'Macarius'; but we do not live in the eighteenth century any more than the fourth. So the question of appropriation remains. The kind of 'liberal' Methodism which is my heritage has largely de-mythologized the struggle with temptation that was so vibrant for 'Macarius' and the eighteenth-century evangelicals. Yet many of us, I suspect, have struggled with the legacy of perfectionism, with that sense of always falling short. Too often the Gospel of grace is drowned out by self-recrimination, shame, a sense of inferiority and embarrassment at less than perfect reactions or responses in everyday encounters. Re-reading the evangelical revival through 'Macarius' might encourage self-acceptance as flawed yet perfectible (or to put it in Luther's terms, *simul iustus et peccator*), but perfectible through the sanctification of the Holy Spirit, not through our own efforts. John Wesley had a lively sense of the doctrine of justification by faith, not least through his Moravian contacts. The experience of trusting in God alone for salvation lay at the heart of his so-called conversion-experience, and those of his followers. Experience of profound release, when the burdened heart is suddenly touched by the gracious acceptance of God, can recur in private prayer or communal worship. Such experience, the source of deepest thanksgiving, informs theology, particularly for those of us privileged to be among 'the people called Methodists'.

As for 'heart' religion – it would seem to be the only kind to hold people these days; no one feels obliged to remain committed for social reasons, and the intellectual scepticism of our culture provides no incentive to identify with a faith stance. 'Macarius' and Wesley warn us that we need more than emotionalism; as whole persons we are to be caught up in the way of love. For Wesley that meant engaging in social action. Faith must issue in works, and works are the product of a deep synergism, the co-operation of the inner self with the Holy Spirit within.

According to both Wesley and 'Macarius', the promises of the New Testament are effective here and now, yet always elusive. Theological reflection on the eschatological tensions of the New Testament, the 'now and the not yet', reached a new level of sophistication in twentieth-century theology, and may permit a more realistic appraisal of what the promises of God and the gifts of the Spirit might mean ahead of the *eschaton*, as we make our pilgrim way through this present evil age. We also need a greater sense of the church, a body that transcends the individual and provides the 'means of grace' through which sanctification is realized; 'enthusiastic' movements generally tend to have implicit rather than explicit ecclesiologies. To that the next chapter will turn, but meanwhile we observe that Wesley provides more leads than 'Macarius', with his emphasis on the sacrament of communion, on meeting in groups for fellowship and mutual support, and the kind of ecumenical openness found in his sermon, 'On the Catholic Spirit'.

* * *

Celebrating the legacy of 'enthusiasm'

The preacher begins:

With the benefit of hindsight, we can see that Wesley was a bag of contradictions. He was an eighteenth-century rationalist, yet anticipated the Romantic reaction to the Enlightenment, appealing to the heart, not just the head. He was a high Tory, yet gave hope, education and aspiration to the masses. He was profoundly self-absorbed, yet revealed his inner life, not for self-glorification but for the sake of saving the souls of others, as testimony to the work of God's Spirit within him. He struggled with temptations and believed he could overcome them in the power of the Spirit, yet misled more women than his hagiographers have felt comfortable with. Like the apostle Paul, whose words he read and re-read, quoted and quoted again, he was a figure that divided, repelling some, attracting others, a person impossible to live with, yet filled with something that captured and motivated people towards a better life. And his legacy is similarly paradoxical – his influence both in Britain and in the US surely contributed to the introspection, self-consciousness and individualism of modernity, yet he also offers profound challenges to these developments. His heritage may be worth reclaiming simply for its potential to give people something to live for beyond the allures of immediate gratification in a world of consumerism, choice and transient commitment.

Religion has itself become a matter of choice, and the evangelical transformation of Christianity bears some responsibility for this. If Christianity is a personal decision for Christ, if traditional ritual and nominal adherence is not enough for salvation but 'conversion' must be experienced to precipitate that decision, then it is a short step to faith becoming a private matter. The whole onus is on the individual whether they can buy all the stuff in the creed or the Bible; and fewer and fewer find they can sign up to it all, understood as it is in an impoverished, literalizing way. So religion is marginalized, and instead of contributing to a general sense of meaning and truth, it becomes the preserve of a defensive minority competing with other minorities for attention.

The corrosive effect of individualism cannot simply be laid at Wesley's door. Romanticism and the development of the novel reflect an increasing cultural focus on the self, while individual freedom is enhanced by inclusive democracy. Besides, Wesley belongs to a succession of influential figures in Western Christianity who moulded what has been called the 'introspective conscience of the West'. Through their personal journeys Augustine and Luther forged a reading of Paul whereby the Gospel became salvation of the individual through the grace of God justifying each in Christ, removing their guilt and sanctifying them with the Spirit. They'd become models of Christian conversion. So, at a quarter to nine on 24 May 1738, when someone was reading from Luther's Preface to Paul's epistle to the Romans, Wesley felt his heart strangely warmed, felt he did trust in Christ, Christ alone for salvation, and an assurance was given 'that he had taken away *my* sins, even *mine*, and saved *me* from the law of sin and death'. In publishing this account in his *Journal* Wesley reinforced an existing paradigm.

The fact is that this provided people with a story to tell which gave meaning to their lives and a sense of being part of something bigger than themselves. It's easy to criticize, even mock, the Methodist tradition of testimony – the endless narratives of conversion following the same pattern. Someone once gave me a bound collection of Primitive Methodist magazines, and what immediately struck me were the obituaries. If ever form-criticism could demonstrate its basis, it was here – the same pattern of godly life celebrated according to convention and stereotype, a set form into which each life was moulded. And yet each is a particular story of a particular adopted son of God. And isn't that the point? Each was made up of layers shaped by membership of an intense religious community, yet each self was able to mature and develop, feel remorse and gratitude, because held in fellowship with those who dared to confront one another with their faults, support one another in their tribulations, pray with one another on a pilgrimage through the ups and downs of life. Introspection was shared, triumphs over temptation celebrated. There was accountability to one another and to God. You cannot pray to a God 'to whom all hearts are open, all desires known, and from whom no secrets are hid' and then try to get away with it! If Methodism fostered individualism, it also provided a context in which that was tempered and shaped for the good of others.

For Wesley's legacy, taken as a whole, draws on a broader Christian tradition than is represented by the introspective conscience of the

West. We taste this by considering three key themes of his preaching – the spirit of adoption, the spirit of holiness and the catholic spirit.

- One of Wesley's favourite texts was Romans 8.15: 'Ye have not received the spirit of bondage again unto fear; but ye have received the **Spirit of Adoption**, whereby we cry, Abba, Father.' He saw himself as once serving God out of fear, like a slave or a servant, and never quite being able to do it – always struggling against the same temptations, never sure he was pleasing God, so always anxious, embodying the spirit of bondage, since fear of judgement was the sole motivation of his religious life. We might say he had a poor self-image, was entirely wrapt up in self-concern, and the driving forces of his life were guilt and duty. But then he was granted the spirit of adoption – he was drawn into a different kind of relationship with God as the Spirit bore witness with his spirit that he was a child of God, that God loved him and Christ gave himself for him out of sheer love. So his obedience now arose out of the joy of a son who knew he was loved – his heart was engaged and his life filled with a different kind of spirit. But this salvation meant not just that *I'm* OK, but that the human race, whose members generally followed too much the devices and desires of their own hearts, or struggled out of conscience to do their duty – a classic recipe for hypocrisy – this *fallen* human race could learn to *love* in return for the gracious love of God who first loved us, and so could obey the double command to love God and love our neighbours. We can all receive the spirit of adoption whereby we cry 'Abba, Father' and know we are God's children, and the Spirit of God can then transform our lives. Because 'those who do not love a brother or sister whom they have seen, cannot love God whom they have not seen',[113] the spirit of adoption challenges all

---

[113]   1 John 4.20.

individuals who appeal to personal conversion-experiences to live differently in society.

- Which naturally leads on to the **Spirit of Holiness**. It's said that John Wesley was raised up by God to spread scriptural holiness throughout the land. But what is it to be holy? Holiness belongs to God, and at its core is a sense of God's separateness, transcendence, aweful purity. In the Bible, God calls a people to be holy and separate – 'You shall be holy, for I am holy.' In the history of Judaism and Christianity many groups have sought separation from the world – Pharisees and Essenes, monks and Puritans. But separateness has devalued the word, making us fearful of being 'holier than thou', fostering self-righteousness and hypocrisy. John Wesley, knowing early Christian writings which interpreted the scriptures in terms of total dedication to God, so that God's holiness and perfection were embodied in the believer, found there his doctrine of Christian perfection, a process whereby, through Christ, believers are indwelt by the Spirit of holiness, and so reach perfect love – love of God, love of neighbour, love even of enemies. Defending his controversial doctrine, he asserted that unless being a Christian means being conformed to the image of Christ and transformed into the self-same image through the work of the Spirit of holiness, God's promises are rendered empty and void. 'Be perfect as your Father in heaven is perfect', Jesus said, pointing to the mercy and generosity of a God who makes his sun rise on evil and good alike, and sends rain on the righteous and on the unrighteous. Holiness, then, is not separation, but a new quality of being, of openness like that of God, of generosity and mercy in relation to the whole world.

- And that introduces the third theme – **the Catholic Spirit** – 'catholic', of course, in the sense of universal. John Wesley was a great controversialist. He knew his own mind and resisted vigorously what he saw as distortions of scriptural teaching – like predestination, or the idea that since we are justified by faith we should sit quiet letting God do everything. No! The sheer grace and love of God should so turn us inside out that we love with God's love – not just neighbours but enemies. Actually in Wesley's view the most problematic was to love fellow-Christians. He knew all about people so concerned with right doctrine that their hearts were hard. He also knew of simple people with saintly hearts whose doctrines were quite muddled. So in a famous sermon on the catholic spirit he typically went to the heart of the matter, spelling out what were for him the essentials and suggesting that all those who know God's love and show it in their lives should shake hands, love one another, pray for one another, support one another – even if they belong to different churches. For John Wesley the work of God in people's hearts means that saints are recognizable across boundaries and divides. I guess John Wesley would be delighted to find that in the present context his followers are engaged in the ecumenical movement and in multi-faith dialogue.

Yes – there are truths here which might speak to our culture, if only there were ears to hear, and we can find the right language – truths about the human condition, about the need for the self to mature in relationship with those who are different, by telling constantly developing narratives that express identity, while respectfully attending to the stories that others tell, so as to negotiate difference.

To God be the glory, Amen.

* * *

Postlude

Recluse

Yes – it's pitch-black, warm and fecund,
This cave, which now I embrace as my choice –
Not as constriction, not as a trap,

But a wrestling ring for trial of the self,
For true discernment of inner demons,
As the soul's pierced with the sword of the Spirit
In the long dark hours of the night-watch;
A solitude filled with the sound of silence,
The gift of a voice in the echoing vault,
A presence sensed in the luminous darkness;
An inner desert to be peopled through prayer,
A walled garden where seeds of wisdom
Are carried beyond containment, beyond
The bounds, on the wind of the Spirit of Jesus;
A womb where the fungus of life might mushroom –
For the soil is pitch-black, warm and fecund
Like the Black Virgin, the dark icon
Of birth and re-birth through pain and death.

Alleluia, Amen.

Renewal

Well of water deep
Source of joy untapped
Dry anxiety
Energy all sapped.

River running full
Overflow of love
Flood of power and peace
Pouring from above.

Fountain welling up
Melody within
Spring of life and hope
Flushing out our sin.

Water of the Spirit
Baptism of fire
Swelling seas uprise
Praises to inspire.

Pool reflecting light
Image of God's face
Well of water deep
Source of joy and grace.

More observations

A breeze stirs, the fog lifts; and now
Discernment opens up, horizons break
Through murky mist, the light begins to make
Things clear. That secret stirring shows just how
The Spirit lifts the spirits from the slough
Of dark despond, and never does forsake
The lost and weary, till their hearts can take
Their heavy burdens t'wards the promised brow.
Once there the gentle winter sunshine lights
The billowing tops of mist that fill the dips
And sheltered hollows down below. The heights
Expose the way ahead. The wind whips;
Its chill, with purifying piercing, bites,
While burning coals of fire touch the lips.

The music moves my heart-strings. Sheer its sound
Stimulates the ear, and beauty fills
My resonating being. Nothing stills
The deep yearning melody that's bound
To conjure vision of the panting hart
Thirsting for water-brooks, unsatisfied.

And yet a yearning want that's not supplied
A thirst for self-transcendence can impart.
The Spirit prays with my spirit, its ways
Beyond the telling; yet, with love's release,
Embodied exultation may amaze
Into forgetfulness, and passions cease.
Communion cradles me in wordless praise,
Apostles me to preach the word of peace.

7 | From the church to Mary: towards a critical ecumenism

Prelude

The ecumenical gathering in the annual Week of Prayer for Christian Unity hears the epistle: 'For as in one body we have many members, and not all the members have the same function, so we, who are many, are one body in Christ, and individually we are members of one another';[1] then comes the Gospel, Jesus praying to the Father, 'that they may all be one'.[2]

The Eastern Orthodox bishop, sitting next to the Western Protestant pastor at a Faith and Light international gathering, comments, 'We've been apart for 1,000 years; it'll take another 1,000 years to get us back together.'

The representative from the united Church of North India shares two disappointments: the lengthy and on-going legal battles, particularly over property, and the loss experienced in no longer belonging to global denominational networks. The Orthodox protest against the ordained woman doing critical Bible studies in the context of daily prayers.[3]

The organist berates the preacher for omitting to announce the anthem, while the music group complains about the old-fashioned music. The simple faithful, the doubter and the devout, the anxious and the anguished, the bigoted and the bored, the self-righteous and the sinner, the radical and the conservative, the traditionalist and the campaigner, the fundamentalist and the theological enquirer – how could they ever agree?

---

[1] Romans 12.4–5.   [2] John 17.20, 23.
[3] Snapshots from the World Faith and Order Conference in 1993.

313

The communicant sips from the chalice; a fire of intercession flows through her body as she receives for others – persons with disabilities, the prisoner of conscience with whom she corresponds, family members who do not share her faith . . .

The woman is stopped at the traffic lights. Suddenly, 'You should get ordained,' says the voice in her head. She drives home on automatic pilot, her whole life passing before her and inexorably leading to this conclusion. Against the odds, including her own reluctance, the call is fulfilled, and tongue in cheek she occasionally refers to her 'Damascus Road experience'.

The Roman Catholic priest, arriving at eucharist in an ecumenical theological college, unexpectedly found that a woman would preside; he didn't know what to do, but stayed, and by the end knew that, even though he had theological difficulties, he had no prejudice.

A man with Down's syndrome, miming the part of Jesus, goes to tell Mary, a woman with learning disabilities, to fetch his brothers and sisters and tell them to love one another. The cardinal, the archbishop, the Anglican bishop and the Protestant woman minister embrace one another, then together bless the crowd.[4]

* * *

Sacramentalism

The preacher begins:[5]

You know, Christianity is fundamentally materialist. We imagine religion is spiritual, and over the centuries spiritualisation has repeatedly obscured how physical Christianity is; but it keeps on resurfacing.

Of course, it's the incarnation that drives this. Christians affirm that: ' . . . what we have heard, what we have seen with our eyes,

---

[4] Snapshot from the Faith and Light Lourdes pilgrimage, Easter 1991.
[5] Anticipated in the sermon ('The Materialism of the Christian Tradition') preached for the seventy-fifth anniversary of the Methodist Sacramental Fellowship and published in their *Bulletin* No. 138 (Epiphany 2011), 4–10.

what we have looked at and touched with our hands, concerning the word of life – . . . we have seen it and testify to it . . . '[6] Yes, *touched* – physically touched! When Helena, the mother of the emperor Constantine, made her pilgrimage to the Holy Land, she took a load of soil back to Rome to be spread on the floor of her private chapel so that she could pray on ground on which the feet of the Saviour had trod.

The notion that matter might be sacred was alien to the religious philosophy of the ancient world: the soul was prized over the body, deplored was the corruption of spiritual realities by the grossness of matter, and of rationality by coarse emotions. And yes – Christianity was and is profoundly influenced by these attitudes.

The struggle began already in New Testament times, but came to a head in the second century. So-called 'gnostic' sects proclaimed salvation *from* this material universe, in which spiritual beings had been trapped by the Demiurge or fallen creator God. This is perhaps not all that far removed from otherworldly versions of the evangelical Gospel which proclaim escape from the world, the flesh and the Devil, and eternal life in heaven as salvation for the soul – pie-in-the-sky-when-you-die! What the struggle with the gnostics did was to ensure that Christians would affirm that the utterly transcendent God, containing all things yet not contained, was not ashamed to get the divine hands dirty creating the material world – which meant that what was created was not dirty at all but sacred; it was declared good by the Creator, and the hands that made it were God's own Word and Spirit. Not for nothing were the eucharistic elements described as fruits of the earth, offered in thanksgiving to the Creator of all. This ordinary stuff of the earth was sacred.

What those early interpreters of the Bible recognised was that creation and resurrection are acts of a kind, that the body, as well as the soul, would receive the necessary changes for resurrection to eternal life. Which means that the image of God is expressed in the physical medium of human flesh and blood, that the material is

[6] 1 John 1.1–2.

the vehicle of the spiritual.[7] For it is in seeing the glorious autumn colours, hearing the physical sounds of music, touching the hand of the one we love, smelling the scent of flowers, and tasting the bread of life that we have tactile contact with the hidden presence of the divine. And we find that presence above all in providing concrete material assistance to those in need, in everyday bodily caring for our Lazaruses, giving and receiving from them physical signs of mutual regard. Someone increasingly disabled by a degenerative disease once said, 'I need to be loved by someone with skin on.'

Ordinary, everyday material things constitute precisely what is holy.

This is expressed particularly in a concrete church community of embodied persons in liturgy. The eucharistic thanksgiving is doxology for our physical existence, its redemption in Christ and its restoration at the resurrection. The *anamnēsis* is a commemorative representation of the actual physical dying of Christ on the cross. The communion is the means whereby the participants assimilate the body of Christ, and so the divine life: as an early bishop put it, the 'holy flesh and blood' is 'mingled with our bodies' so that we are 'filled with his energy'.[8] That spiritual meaning requires the physical act of eating and drinking actual material things. To spiritualise this away by reducing the eucharist to mere symbol or mere memorial of the one and only sacrifice offered for the salvation of the world is to abstract it from this utterly concrete materiality, and to do less than justice to the fact that through this sacrament we are in touch with the incarnate Christ.

Jesus said to them, Very truly I tell you, unless you eat the flesh of the Son of Man and drink his blood, you have no life in you. Whoever eats my flesh and drinks my blood has eternal life, and I will raise them up at the last day. For my flesh is real food and my blood is real drink. Whoever eats my flesh and drinks my blood remains in me, and I in them.

Thanks be to God. Amen.

---

[7] See Chapters 3 and 4.   [8] See Chapter 5.

* * *

The sacraments of the church are 'the means of grace' by which members receive the sanctification of the Spirit; indeed, they are the means whereby the new creation is effected in those who belong to Christ. The presence of the Spirit in the church is the foretaste of the eschatological promises, and a crucial argument for the true divinity of the Spirit.[9] The corporate nature of the Body of Christ is a corrective to that individualism which can be the outcome of 'enthusiasm' and its claim to be led by the Spirit. Yet the history of the church is one of factionalism and division, exclusiveness and self-righteousness, and apparent failure to embody the spirit of Jesus, a condition which still holds as new church-dividing issues emerge, and institutionally the churches find it hard to respond to the (post-)modern world. Ecumenism struggles, its achievements in breaking down prejudices, fostering cross-denominational friendships and reaching shared understandings of historic differences[10] constantly threatened by fresh causes of suspicion. *Prima facie* the patristic legacy compounds the problems as appeals are made to tradition and to the supposedly united church of that era.

The subject of the church, then, is potentially vast. Here much will be taken for granted. Crucial contemporary issues will generate exploration of how appeal has been made to the fathers, beginning with debate about the ordination of women, then taking up a matter arising, namely the ecumenically contested figure of Mary. From these discussions will emerge the need to move towards new and creative conclusions beyond anything the fathers could themselves have imagined; yet in the final section we'll discover in

---

[9]   Cf. Basil of Caesarea, *On the Holy Spirit*: Greek text: B. Pruche (ed.), *SC*; ET: *NPNF* and David Anderson, *St Basil the Great: On the Holy Spirit* (Crestwood, NY: St Vladimir's Seminary Press, 1980).

[10] E.g. the agreed statement on *Baptism, Eucharist and Ministry* (Faith and Order Paper no. 111, the 'Lima Text', Geneva: WCC, 1982).

their thinking perspectives which could both challenge their own ideology of the church and stimulate a new approach to our ecumenical goals.[11]

I The ordination of women

In controversy about the ordination of women both sides appeal to precedent as if that settled the issue; but in the matter of historical reconstruction neither side is convincing. So how are scripture and tradition to be interpreted? How can novel developments be justified in the continuing life of a body that seeks to be faithful both to its tradition and to its foundation documents?

1.1 Appealing to the past

Conservatives unite in appealing to historical arguments – scripture having primacy for Protestant, tradition for Catholic or Orthodox, especially the tradition of the fathers. A section of the Anglican report on *Women Bishops in the Church of England?*[12] is taken as representative of appeal to the past.

The report speaks of 'the ancient threefold order of ministry consisting of bishops, priests and deacons', which 'emerged in the first centuries of the church's existence'. It acknowledges a variety of patterns in the New Testament, but then appeals to various scholars in support of a claimed ecumenical consensus. Certain fathers of

---

[11] This chapter incorporates material from three previously published articles of mine, where fuller references and discussion may be found: 'Hermeneutical Questions: The Ordination of Women in the Light of Biblical and Patristic Typology' in Ian Jones, Janet Wootton and Kirsty Thorpe (eds.), *Women and Ordination in the Christian Churches: International Perspectives* (London: T&T Clark, 2008); 'The Church and Mary'; 'The "Penultimate" Nature of the Church – the *Eschaton* Is Not Yet!' in S. T. Kimbrough Jr (ed.), *Orthodox and Wesleyan Ecclesiology* (Crestwood, NY: St Vladimir's Seminary Press, 2002), pp. 199–211.

[12] *Women Bishops in the Church of England? A Report of the House of Bishops Working Party on Women in the Episcopate* (London: Church House Publishing, 2004).

the church (Ambrosiaster, Jerome, John Chrysostom, Theodore of Mopsuestia) are quoted to show that, though they saw no great difference between the office of bishop and presbyter in the beginning, they upheld the threefold order, accepting that a clear distinction soon emerged – indeed, a fourth-century writer who argued there was no distinction was condemned as a heretic. Despite the hypothetical nature of the evidence, the claim is made that the origin of the episcopate belongs to the first century and is associated with St John. So the threefold order is apostolic.

The subsequent historical outline emphasizes that the bishop was originally the chief minister of the local church, with pastoral and priestly responsibilities, that the mon-episcopate emerged to ensure unity in the church, that the bishop was the guardian of the apostolic tradition and the minister of ordination, and that leadership in mission was a key role. Gradually the bishop came to exercise oversight over more than one congregation in a particular locality, and presbyters became the local ministers of word and sacrament as delegates of the bishop. The historical survey comes to a climax with an account of ministry in pre- and post-Reformation England. Then a convergence is claimed between the bishop's role in the Church of England today and that of a patristic bishop, insisting this is not accidental but the fruit of a commitment to maintain historical continuity with the early church, despite changes as the office adapted to changing circumstance. The question is then posed, whether the ordination of women as bishops:

> would simply be a further adaptation of the episcopal office to meet the circumstances of our time and our changed theological understanding of the relationship between men and women in the Church, or whether it would represent a fundamental break with the historic continuity of the episcopate which the Church of England has hitherto sought to maintain.[13]

[13] *Ibid.*, pp. 64–5.

Appeal to precedent constitutes the nub of this argument. But historical accounts are reconstructions on the basis of evidence which requires interpretation, and interpretation is contestable. In this case the following points pose problems:

1 Sources show that in the early period tithes and offerings supported bishops, presbyters, deacons, sub-deacons, readers, singers, door-keepers, deaconesses, widows, virgins and orphans.[14] Were three orders clearly differentiated from other roles?
2 Research suggests that the mon-episcopate was still contested in the third century, particularly in Rome![15] Earlier texts quoted are not necessarily evidence for an existing norm: why did Ignatius protest so much about the importance of being in communion with the bishop? Probably because in the early second century he saw it as a potential solution to damaging disunity. A century later the struggles of Cyprian's episcopate suggest he was trying to establish the bishop's authority among competing charisms.

So interpreting the evidence is problematic; and it is even trickier when terminology fossilizes while reality changes. The language may suggest continuity, but the medieval prince-bishop surely had precious little in common with the *episcopos* occasionally referred to in the New Testament. The terminology of *episcopos* and *diakonoi* comes from the ancient household,[16] comprising the extended family of several generations, servants with their overseer or head steward, clients and tenants – perhaps fifty people all told. The early church met in houses, hosted by a patron, and familial language was adopted for the Christian family whose *pater familias* was God – they addressed each other as brother and sister, and the pastoral leader

[14] E.g. *Apostolic Constitutions* II.25.
[15] Peter Lampe, *From Paul to Valentinus: Christians at Rome in the First Two Centuries* (ET: Michael Steinhauser, ed. Marshall D. Johnson, London: Continuum 2003).
[16] For detailed references see my article, 'On Episkopos and Presbyteros', *JTS* NS 45 (1994), 142–8; and *The Theology of the Pastoral Letters* (Cambridge University Press, 1994).

would soon be addressed as 'father' (that is, *papa* or pope). The organizer was the 'overseer', God's steward, assisted by menservants and maidservants – hence the *episcopos* and the *diakonoi*. The elders in the family (*presbyteroi*) would have authority, as older people did in traditional societies – they would carry the communal memory; but they also needed material support because of their age, as did the older women, widows and orphans. In other words, it is quite possible to read I Timothy as a kind of 'household code' for the church.

This sketch suggests that, despite a century of scholarly consensus, presbyters were probably not identical with bishops in the early period. It's perhaps confirmed by later texts which reveal that the presbyters both appointed the bishop and form his advisory council. Papias' well-known comments about preferring the living and abiding voice to things written in books and so consulting presbyters, who apparently belong to both the apostolic and the second generation of Christians, would appear to bear out the fact that these presbyters were the wise, elderly 'guardians of the tradition'. Furthermore, as early as Ignatius, the presbyters are said to be in place of the *synedrion* (= sanhedrin or council) of the apostles, while the bishop presides in the place of God (just as a head secretary would act for his master in his absence), while *diakonoi* are entrusted with Christ's service; and, incidentally, some later texts add that deaconesses are to be honoured as in the place of the Holy Spirit. Apostolicity is connected with the presbyters, not the bishop; and the deacon rather than the priest is a type of Christ. The classic account of the origins and significance of the threefold order of ministry cannot be regarded as securely based.

The household model lent itself to developments parallel with state organization. The phrase 'Caesar's household' was used for the civil service; implicit in that was the ancient cliché that the head of state was analogous to a *pater familias* writ large. Ideally, the ruler was a beneficent and wise philosopher who sought the good of the domain over which he ruled. Such ideals were transferred to sketches of the good bishop. The very word 'diocese' is a word from Roman imperial governance; by the fourth century, ecclesiastical boundaries followed imperial subdivisions, and metropolitans emerged analogous to provincial governors. Thus ministry in the early church reflected its societal locus, a point further demonstrated by parallels with municipal government: the emerging distinction between clergy and laity reflects that between officials and plebs. History, far from supporting an unchanging structure, poses the question whether the church should really maintain in a post-modern democratic society the sort of governance that emerged in societies that were monarchical, hierarchical and feudal.

This account is offered, not as definitive history, but to illustrate the precariousness of appeal to precedent when debatable interpretations and reconstructions are inevitable. The same applies when the promoters of women's ordination offer their own claimed precedents:

> Understanding why and how women, once leaders in the Jesus movement and in the early church, were marginalized and scapegoated as Christianity became the state religion is crucial if women are to reclaim their rightful, equal place in the church today. Jesus' message and practice were radically egalitarian in their day and constituted a social revolution that likely provoked his crucifixion. It is high time that the church, which claims to embody his good news to the world, stop betraying its own essential heritage of absolute equality.[17]

So Karen Jo Torjesen. But such claims are more difficult to substantiate than the presumed consensus about the threefold ministry.

Torjesen does take seriously the social context of the early church and makes significant historical observations, such as the effect of the church's move from the quasi-private sphere of the house-church to the public world of the city and empire. It would indeed have been easier for women to have influence in the private sphere, and women

---

[17] Karen Jo Torjesen, *When Women were Priests* (San Francisco: HarperCollins 1993), p. 7.

householders did act as patrons of Christian communities – tellingly, Torjesen documents the gap between the patriarchal theories of society and the practical realities of women running households and even businesses. Evidence for women's leadership in Jewish synagogues of the Diaspora is rehearsed; the many hints, in Paul's letters and other early Christian material, that women played leadership roles in the mission of the church and were active as prophets and deacons are also rehearsed. That women's leadership was contested is acknowledged – yet that is itself evidence that women were leaders. The distinction between clergy and laity starts to matter in the third century, she suggests, as the church begins to emerge from the private sphere and ministry shifts into governance, modelling its offices on that of the municipality. The move from house to basilica in the fourth century was the final nail in the coffin of women's ministry, for the church accepted society's perception that a woman's prominence in the public sphere was a scandal.

But can an argument for women's leadership, which itself suggests that the emergence of distinct clerical orders excluded women, establish a precedent for women's ordination to the differentiated clergy that eventually emerged? With some justification defenders of women's ordination appeal to texts which show there were deaconesses in the early church.[18] With less plausibility they suggest that widows constituted a ministerial order.[19] But in each case the argument is subject to the similar objections. Deaconesses almost certainly had different roles from deacons, just as menservants and maidservants in pre-modern societies did different jobs in the household; widows probably did constitute some kind of order, though largely as the beneficiaries of charity. None of this justifies the ordination of women as priests since it doesn't constitute a

---

[18] E.g. John Wijngaards, *The Ordination of Women in the Catholic Church: Unmasking a Cuckoo's Egg Tradition* (London: DLT, 2001).

[19] Bonnie Bowman Thurston, *The Widows: A Women's Ministry in the Early Church* (Minneapolis: Fortress Press, 1989).

genuine precedent. Women clearly were patrons of house-churches, but simply to put it in those deeply unfamiliar terms demonstrates the difficulty of reading the organization of the early church in ways that we recognize.

The argument from precedent, whether made for or against the ordination of women, is deeply problematic from the point of view of serious historical enquiry.

1.2 Interpreting scripture and tradition

The best advocates for women's ordination have not resorted to precedent, but have sought to discern the thrust of the biblical material or the living dynamic of the tradition. Such argument, we might observe, proceeds in the same way as the patristic authority, Athanasius: faced with the challenge of Arius, he produced novel and original ideas – indeed, was accused of doing so by opponents; however, this he justified on the grounds that it represented the 'mind' of scripture better than the text-slinging or verbal conservatism of the opposition.[20] In a similar way, the debate about women's ordination has provoked serious consideration of what is really at the heart of scripture and tradition. Two examples, from Ruth Edwards and Elisabeth Behr-Sigel are worth considering, to which we now turn.

1.2.1 Ruth Edwards' case for women's ordination

Ruth Edwards' book[21] distinguishes between general scriptural principles and more detailed culture-related prescriptions. The ideals of ministry in the New Testament suggest inclusion: spiritual gifts are given to all, irrespective of gender, ministry is corporate, and Paul's fellow-labourers are both male and female; the model for men

[20] See further my *Biblical Exegesis*, chapter 2.
[21] *The Case for Women's Ordination* (London: SPCK, 1989).

and women is Christ. This brief summary belies Edwards' careful exegesis of texts and sensible acceptance of historical realities – of course, given the social context, the apostles were all men! What informs her discussion overall is a search for the implications of scripture. So too with respect to tradition: examining key themes – God, Creation, 'Man', Sexuality, Priesthood – she shows that the implications do not lie in ideas such as only a man can represent God, or novelty is impossible:

> Women's ministry should . . . be seen as a natural consequence of the Gospel message, comparable to the admission of uncircumcised Gentiles to table-fellowship, carried out despite Jesus' original command not to go to the Gentiles.[22]

Here we have the distillation of principles from the 'hermeneutical interaction' of scripture, tradition, reason and experience, allowing for the creation of new insight out of the very fabric of what is received; thus continuity is ensured, along with faithfulness to the tradition and its foundation documents, without excluding change and development.

1.2.2 Elisabeth Behr-Sigel and the Orthodox tradition

Associated with the great twentieth-century thinkers of the Orthodox diaspora in the West, people like Meyendorff, Bulgakov, and Endokimov, Elisabeth Behr-Sigel confessed that, on the matter of women's ordination to the priesthood, she'd moved further than most Orthodox could; constructively critical of the Western feminist movement, she insisted that the Orthodox church must come to terms with modernity. In her essays she too sought to tease out the implications of the tradition.

With some passion she insisted that tradition should be 'living'. She worried about 'the argument from Tradition' being 'brandished

---

[22] *Ibid.*, p. 182.

about without discernment' in a way 'offensive to the Church and the Spirit that is at work in her':

> The whole history of the Church reveals... that even though the life of the Church is continuity, it is also dynamism and creativity. Authentic faithfulness to Tradition is creative and requires each generation to respond to new needs and challenges according to the dynamic of Tradition. Faithfulness to Tradition is the work of the Spirit in the Church.[23]

So, acknowledging that much in the past has been coloured by archaic taboos, she looked for new possibilities within tradition.

The fathers she saw in a very different light from that common among Western feminists. She documented how they affirmed the common vocation of all the baptized, women and men:

> All through the centuries, Christian women have been baptized, chrismated and invested with the fullness of the royal priesthood; they have confessed their faith in Christ, endured martyrdom, evangelized, prophesied and attained the heights of holiness in the life of consecrated virginity as well as in married life.[24]

She stressed the priesthood of the whole people of God: together men and women 'have the vocation of being the kings and priests of the creation, of being the celebrants of the cosmic liturgy'.[25] Orthodox women are conscious of participating in this royal priesthood of the laity, knowing they are called to holiness, to deification not only in the life of the world to come, but also here and now. For Orthodoxy, Christ alone is the High Priest, and all priesthood derives from him; as members of the Body of Christ all participate in the priestly offering of worship.[26] Thus Behr-Sigel

---

[23] Elisabeth Behr-Sigel, *The Ministry of Women in the Church* (ET: Stephen Bigham, Crestwood, NY: St Vladimir's Seminary Press 1999), pp. 18–19.

[24] *Ibid.*, pp. 116–17.   [25] *Ibid.*, p. 42.   [26] *Ibid.*, p. 140.

distilled the essence of the tradition, backing it up with patristic quotations.

1.2.3 Typology and priesthood

No argument reviewed thus far establishes specific grounds for ordination of women to the particular priesthood held dear in Orthodox and Catholic traditions. Insistence on the priesthood of all believers as a scriptural doctrine enabled post-Reformation churches to ordain women, ministers having a functional role, representative of the priesthood of the community and proper to the ordering of the church, but not ontologically different from any other believer. The distinct connotations of priesthood came into the Catholic/Orthodox tradition through typology.

Typology is many-faceted.[27] For early Christianity, past narratives foreshadowed, or prefigured, future events, but it was not just events that became 'figures' – the association of presbyters and deacons with priests and Levites is already found in I *Clement*. The key moment for church order comes in the third century with Cyprian, who developed the tradition that persons of the Old Testament were prophetic prefigurations of Christ, while persons in the church may become 'postfigurations'.[28]

In *Epistle* 63 Cyprian speaks of Christ being prefigured in the priest Melchisedek: so, in Genesis, 'the image of sacrifice clearly constituted in bread and wine is already present proleptically. Fulfilling and

---

[27] See my article 'Typology' in Stanley E. Porter, Paul Joyce and David E. Orton (eds.), *Crossing the Boundaries*, Essays in Biblical Interpretation in Honour of Michael D. Goulder (Leiden: Brill, 1994), pp. 29–48; and *Biblical Exegesis*.

[28] The following argument, which I made first in 'Presbyteral Ministry in the Catholic Tradition or Why Shouldn't Women be Priests?' (London: The Methodist Sacramental Fellowship, 1994), owes much to John D. Laurance, *'Priest' as Type of Christ, the Leader of the Eucharist in Salvation History according to Cyprian of Carthage* (New York: Peter Lang, 1984), pp. 29–48, though he should not be held responsible for my conclusions.

completing this reality, the Lord offered bread and the cup mixed with wine.' As Melchisedek prefigures, so the eucharistic president postfigures:

> For if Christ Jesus . . . first offered himself as a sacrifice to the Father, and commanded that this take place in his memory, that priest indeed truly functions in the place of Christ who imitates that which Christ did, and consequently offers a true and complete sacrifice in the Church to God the Father . . . the Lord's passion is the sacrifice we offer.[29]

Once this move was made, almost inevitably typology validated virtually indiscriminate transfer of features from priests of the old covenant to priests of the new. Here lies the origin of so many arguments for women not being admitted to the priesthood; for (i) priestesses were not a feature of 'Old Testament' religion (being associated with those fertility rites from which the prophetic tradition sought to distance Israel), and (ii) scripture excluded from priesthood anyone with a blemish or impurity, archaic taboos putting women into that excluded category.

Typology, then, is the crucial issue. But the claim that no woman can be a type of Christ is an extraordinary misunderstanding of the dynamics of typology. Even Cyprian regarded one who has put on Christ in baptism as a living type of new creation in Christ, humanity re-fashioned in God's image. Above all, martyrs were types of Christ, expressing 'to the fullest the common vocation of all Christians to live typologically the *passio* of Christ'.[30] Women were baptized, and there were in Cyprian's time famous women martyr-saints. So there's nothing to stop a woman being a type of Christ; gender is not the point of comparison. Types of Christ are like ikons – they represent not as literal portraits, but as symbols that bear Christ's presence. The eucharist is not like a passion-play, with the priest acting out the role of Christ at the Last Supper. The Body of Christ is the gathered

---

[29] *Epistle* 63.14, 17.   [30] Laurance, *'Priest' as Type of Christ*, pp. 193–4.

church; and the whole sacrament represents the one perfect and sufficient sacrifice made by the priest, Christ, in offering his own body for the sins of the whole world.

So far my argument challenges the 'literalizing' of typology in terms of gender representing gender. I now offer a positive typological argument for including women among those who may act as priests at the eucharist by building on Behr-Sigel's discussion of the role of the *Theotokos* (Birth-giver of God). Mary's willing consent is a 'type' of every believer responding to God, and so 'brings to God the willing agreement of all humanity'.[31] In her Dormition, 'believers are called upon to contemplate the glorification of all creatures at the end of time when all things will be accomplished', for Mary anticipates the end for which all mankind was created, and 'we participate through faith in this end while still groaning in the labor pains of the new creation's birth'.[32] So Mary is 'the image and personification of the spirit-bearing Church, the womb of the new humanity'.[33] Behr-Sigel concludes that 'in the Orthodox vision Mary is not seen mainly as the model for women or as the archetype of womanhood in the banal or sociological meaning of the term'. Rather, the 'signification of Mary is both unique and universal, both cosmic and eschatological'. 'It is of no small consequence, however, that this new creation, having Mary as its human root, has a woman's face'.[34] Mary, then, is a figure of the church, of the Body of Christ, of which men and women are members. So, Behr-Sigel argues, the priesthood of the church could properly be represented by a man or a woman.

I suspect we could press this argument further. For in Orthodox feasts and in icons there's much that places Mary in a priestly role. Icons show her in the *orans* (praying) position: at the Ascension she is there *orans* at the centre of the group of the apostles; in the *Deesis* she leads the saints of the New Covenant in intercession, as John the

---

[31] Behr-Sigel, *Ministry of Women*, p. 77.   [32] *Ibid.*, p. 198.
[33] *Ibid.*, p. 207.   [34] *Ibid.*, p. 210.

Baptist leads those of the Old Covenant. Leading the church in intercession is surely a priestly role. This priestly role is surely expressed symbolically in the feast and icon of her presentation in the Temple, Mary becoming typologically the archetypal high-priest who enters the Holy of Holies. The hymnography of these feasts celebrates Mary as the Ark of the Covenant, the place of God's presence, the temple of the Holy Spirit and the tabernacle of God's Word. So she mediates God to the world in Christ, as the living temple. She is all-holy, her purity from contamination making possible the incarnation, and so our purification. Again we may speak of a priestly role.

In the preface to Behr-Sigel's book, Anthony Bloom wrote:

> Twice Mary had a properly priestly ministry: once when she carried her son who was destined to be sacrificed to the Lord, and once when, at the foot of the cross, she completed the offering by uniting her will, in heroic abandoning of self, to the will of the heavenly Father and to that of the Son of God who by her had become the Son of Man and the sacrificial Lamb.

The Roman Catholic, John Wijngaards,[35] traces the notion of Mary's priesthood within Western tradition, citing medieval evidence and indicating that recent Roman theology, which contrasts the apostolic-Petrine tradition with the Marian tradition, is responsible for excluding this view. If Mary had a priestly ministry, then through that typology priesthood can surely not be withheld from women, particularly when it is set in the broader context of Mary's role as 'type' of the church.

1.3 Conclusion

What we need, then, is a hermeneutic that eschews the notion of finding precedents, while discovering that living tradition which

---

[35] Wijngaards, *Ordination of Women.*

remains in continuity with the past but ever seeks renewal by following through the logic of its trans-cultural instincts. With respect to the ordination of women, the heart of the tradition points beyond discrimination, while typology, so far from suggesting that only a male priest can represent Christ, in fact points to the Christ-likeness of every saint, woman or man, as well as offering a specific typological model for women in the priesthood of Mary.

II Mary and the church

Ecumenically, however, Mary is a contested figure. For Orthodox as for Protestant, the promulgation of the Marian dogmas in the nineteenth century created difficulties. The Vatican II statement, which places teaching about Mary in the chapter on the church, has gone some way to easing the tensions, though responses to the ARCIC document *Mary: Grace and Hope in Christ* show that difficulties remain. After considering Protestant objections to Mariology, we enquire whether a more positive response isn't required by the deep thrust of Christian theology.

II.1 The Protestant critique

In the critique of Mariology three elements may be distinguished:

- It goes beyond scripture.
- It challenges the centrality of Christ.
- It is a kind of idolatry – replacing as it did the goddesses and myths of ancient paganism.

II.1.1 Beyond scripture

Many aspects of Mariology derive from a second-century apocryphal work, the *Protevangelium of James*, where we find features designed to prove Mary's virginity, and perpetual virginity confirms her purity.

FROM THE CHURCH TO MARY

She has sanctuary at home until the age of 3, then lives in the Temple as a pre-menstrual girl. She enters the Holy of Holies, where she is fed by an angel. She and other virgins spin the veil of the Temple – Orthodox icons and some Western depictions of the Annunciation reflect these narratives. Much of this cannot have any basis in history. Some elements, such as a girl living a dedicated life in the Temple and entering the Holy of Holies, were impossible in a Jewish context. The 'undefiled daughters of the Hebrews' seem suspiciously parallel to the vestal virgins in Rome; while the girls of Athens used to make the new veil or robe for the statue of the virgin Athena.[36] There is biblical precedent in the dedication of the child, Samuel, to the Temple – a special child with a special call, no matter that she's female. Also, her mother, Anna, is modelled on Hannah, and her miraculous birth to a barren couple reads like a typical biblical story. A pastiche of motifs[37] is created, then, to fill in what scripture fails to tell us. This is a development of the Gospels, elaborated by someone confused about Palestinian geography and Jewish customs, but aware of biblical narratives. The natural reaction of most Protestants would be to ask how legitimate it is to base liturgy and theology on non-scriptural texts which cannot be historical. Traditional Mariology goes beyond scripture.

11.1.2 Challenging the centrality of Christ

The second Protestant objection to Mariology, that it challenges the all-sufficiency of Christ, seems reinforced by factors which contributed to the emergence of Marian piety in the fourth or fifth centuries.[38] Up to the time of the Arian controversy, the Logos was conceived as the mediator between the transcendent, unknowable

---

[36] Stephen Benko, *The Virgin Goddess: Studies in the Pagan and Christian Roots of Mariology* (Leiden: Brill, 1993), p. 202.

[37] Marina Warner, *Alone of All her Sex: The Myth and Cult of the Virgin Mary* (London: Weidenfeld and Nicolson, 1985), chapter 2, is good on this!

[38] Cf. Chapter 5 re Cyril's homily, and Chapter 8, section I.1.

God and mere creatures: the visible face of the invisible God. Being God's own Word or Son, while acting as God's instrument in creation and revelation, and, above all, having lived as a human creature in the incarnation, Christ occupied the 'space', as it were, between God and the created order. Arius suggested that the Logos could not really be God's Logos, but must be a creature – admittedly the first and greatest of the creatures, created to be the Creator's instrument of creation and revelation, but still not really God. The argument went on for half a century. Its conclusion crucially shifted perspectives and prepared the way for the Byzantine depiction of Christ as Almighty Lord, King and Judge (*Pantocrator*). Soon Mary's role became prominent as intermediary, closer to human beings in their need, yet exalted enough to be able to intercede on their behalf.[39] The *Deesis* icon would express this graphically. Mary replaces Christ as mediator, to the dismay of Protestants.

11.1.3 A kind of idolatry?

Protestants took seriously the biblical prohibition of images. The ubiquitous images of Mary were a prime target. This Protestant prejudice is reinforced by a 'history of religions' approach: 'In its veneration of the Virgin Mary, not only did Roman Catholic Christianity absorb many elements of the cults of Greek and Roman goddesses, but Mary in effect replaced these deities and continued them in a Christian form.'[40]

The council of Ephesus was a crucial moment for Mariology: afterwards veneration of Mary increased, churches began to be dedicated to her and apocryphal writings about her gained in popularity. In the classic history of Mariology, Hilda Graef noted the potential

---

[39] See Marta Camilla Wright, 'Mary in Contemporary Ethiopian Orthodox Devotion' in R. N. Swanson (ed.), *The Church and Mary* (Studies in Church History vol. xxxix, Woodbridge: Boydell Press, 2004), pp. 368–76.

[40] Benko, *The Virgin Goddess*, p. 2; cf. p. 4: Mariology 'is paganism baptized, pure and simple'. Also others, e.g. Warner, *Alone of All her Sex*.

parallel between the crowds in Acts shouting 'Great is Diana of the Ephesians!' and those chanting 'Praised be the Theotokos!' in 431.[41] To quote a more recent author: 'the fact that Mary was officially declared to be *theotokos* in Ephesus, where "the temple of the great goddess Artemis" stood, must not be set aside as insignificant'.[42] To visit the Ankara museum is to be brought face-to-face with the depth of this ancient mother-goddess worship in Asia Minor. Tiny images of a large, pregnant or nursing mother go back to the sixth millennium BCE; move on through time and you find yourself confronted with the Hittite goddess, Kubaba, who then becomes Cybele. In Ephesus Cybele, the mother-goddess, was assimilated to Artemis, the chaste huntress: so 'Diana of the Ephesians' was both virgin and mother. Cyril's sermon on Mary, preached at the time of the council in Ephesus,[43] takes the form of an incantation modelled on the aretalogies of divine figures customary in various pagan cults. All this suggests that the council was not solely about Christology.[44] Mariology was already an issue.

Indeed, the controversy which occasioned the council erupted in Constantinople, where already Marian sermons had been preached by Proclus. He also eulogized the virgin Pulcheria, who was effectively empress-regent and probably encouraged the cult of Mary as a Christianized civic religion.[45] Twenty years earlier John Chrysostom had already warned against turning Mary into a goddess;

[41] Hilda Graef, *Mary: A History of Doctrine and Devotion* (London: Sheed and Ward, 1963/5, reissued 1985), p. 109.

[42] Benko, *The Virgin Goddess*, p. 256.   [43] Quoted in Chapter 5.

[44] *Pace* Richard Price in Sarah Jane Boss (ed.), *Mary: The Complete Resource* (London: Continuum, 2007), and Swanson, *The Church and Mary*.

[45] Vasiliki Limberis, *Divine Heiress: The Virgin Mary and the Creation of Christian Constantinople* (London: Routledge, 1994) probably overstates her thesis; see in Swanson, *The Church and Mary*, Averil Cameron, 'The Cult of the Virgin in Late Antiquity: Religious Development and Myth-Making' (pp. 1–21); Richard M. Price, 'Marian Piety and the Nestorian Controversy' (pp. 31–8); Kate Cooper, 'Empress and *Theotokos*: Gender and Patronage in the Christological Controversy' (pp. 39–51).

earlier still are the references to Marian heresies in the works of Epiphanius. Behind Ephesus there's a complex interaction between pious practice and doctrinal dispute,[46] Mary's importance already going beyond marginal groups. The significance of Ephesus is probably the formal recognition of that importance by a church council, where earlier there had been reservations.[47] Protestants still worry about those reservations when it comes to honouring Mary.

11.1.4 Another assessment?

But is this Protestant reading the only possibility? An overview of pagan parallels by Stephen Benko suggests that Roman Catholic veneration of Mary is the proper Christianizing of ancient religious instincts.[48] Might not the process of assimilation be a baptizing of the old religion into Christ – enculturation in other words? Were not aspects of paganism *Praeparatio Evangelica*? The continuities and depth of history with which I was confronted in the Ankara museum generated excitement rather than simply confirming Protestant prejudices! Besides, doesn't the charge that Mariology goes beyond scripture apply equally to Christology and the doctrine of Trinity, doctrines which are deductions from the New Testament? Might there not be a 'uniquely Christian dimension to Mariology, stemming from scripture, theology and liturgy'?[49] The inner dynamics of Christian theology may demand of Protestants a reassessment of the deep traditions of Marian veneration in the churches of the East and Roman Catholicism.

---

[46] Antonia Atanassova, 'Theological and Cultic Components of Mariology in the Context of Ephesus', paper given at the Fifteenth International Conference on Patristic Studies in Oxford, 2007.

[47] NB the opposition of Epiphanius, John Chrysostom and Nestorius.

[48] 'Rather than being a "regression" into paganism, Mariology is a progression toward a clearer and better understanding of the feminine aspect of the divine', Benko, *The Virgin Goddess*, p. 5.

[49] Atanassova, 'Theological and Cultic Components'.

11.2 Mary's theological significance

Two aspects of those inner dynamics have already been discussed: Chapter 5 explored the Eve–Mary typology and the essential role of Mary in the story of redemption; this chapter has shown how Mary is the 'type' of every believer, anticipating the end for which humankind was created. Further consideration of this typology is needed, along with Mary's significance for Christology.

11.2.1 Mary as 'type' of the believer

Mary as model has proved problematic: Marina Warner, in her influential book, *Alone of All her Sex*, showed how the veneration of Mary did not liberate women – rather, she was turned into a model of submissiveness, humble acceptance and obedience, so subjecting women to male dominance.

One factor enhancing Mary in the fourth century was her role as model for a life of asceticism and virginity. Preserved in Coptic is a *Letter to Virgins* from Athanasius; he describes Mary as withdrawn from public gaze, spending her time in prayer, supporting the poor, reading the scriptures, eating and drinking just what she needs, with no greed or desire, and remaining a virgin so as to be a pattern for everyone: ' . . . recognise yourselves in her as in a mirror', he writes to the virgins of Alexandria.[50] For Athanasius, the perpetual virginity of the truly human Mary modelled permanent virginity, which came to be regarded as a bridge between humanity's fallen state and its eschatological transformation. But this notion of Mary as model was undercut when Protestantism challenged the ideal of celibacy.

Nevertheless, the notion of Mary being an 'exemplar' of the life all are called to lead, men and women alike, could become

[50] David Brakke, *Athanasius and Asceticism* (Baltimore: Johns Hopkins University Press, 1995), pp. 277 ff.

ecumenically significant. For me,[51] it was through personal and 'typological' identification with Mary that my pilgrimage from Protestant blank to ecumenical richness was initiated. This unexpected journeying with Mary became a literal journey in 1991, when Jean Vanier invited me to join the Faith and Light pilgrimage to Lourdes; I experienced inner healing, purification and reconciliation as I re-trod my own path in Mary's company.

Such ecumenical experiences challenged my Protestant suspicions, and I would now affirm Mary as the pattern for believers, women and men. Different contexts bring out different insights. If in the fourth century Mary was depicted as the model for consecrated virgins, at the Reformation Luther recognized that Mary provided a model of someone receptive of God's grace through no merit of her own. Today Jean Vanier[52] speaks of Mary as the model of all those who live ordinary lives, simple and hidden, fulfilling everyday tasks, in communion with Jesus, as always close to the weakest, the littlest, persons who are sick or have disabilities, as she was close to Christ on the cross. Commenting on Gregory of Nyssa, Verna Harrison wrote:

> Notice that an essential feature of Mary's virginity and also that of the Christian soul is receptivity to God. Her purity and integrity open a place within her where God can enter, where Christ can be formed, and from which he can come forth . . . For Gregory the virginal soul, like Mary, receives the entrance of God and brings forth Christ, though spiritually not physically.[53]

Thus even *Theotokos* turns out to have typological potential in relation to the call of the disciple. This idea is also found in Erasmus at the time of the Reformation:

---

[51] See Chapter 5 and the poem, *Pietà*.
[52] Jean Vanier, *Visages de Marie* (Paris:Nouvelles Éditions Mame, 2001).
[53] Verna Harrison, 'Gender, Generation and Virginity in Cappadocian Theology', *JTS NS* 47 (1996), 56–7.

> O Virgin Mother, may your Son grant us that in imitation of your most holy life we may conceive the Lord Jesus in our innermost soul and once conceived may we never lose him.[54]

Now this may not be simply an interior spiritual conception. What about Mary's espousal of an upside-down world in the Magnificat? From 'the background of an evangelical Protestant upbringing, from experience of living in a Third World country, from her own experience of motherhood', the Roman Catholic convert Tina Beattie writes of *Rediscovering Mary*.[55] In her writing Mary becomes a figure of great courage, providing a liberating vision of a new world, challenging a world of violence and exploitation, teaching her son to be a dangerous subversive. Mary is identified with the poor, the victim and the refugee in the dark process of giving birth in a stable and fleeing to Egypt.

> When God chose Mary, he did not choose her because she was submissive and meek and obedient. He chose her because she was a woman of extraordinary determination and perseverance, a woman of loving resistance and struggle. Her son would learn by her example.

II.2.2 Mary as 'type' of the church

Providing a pattern for believers, being the 'type' of redeemed humanity, Mary is naturally seen as 'type' of the church.

The motif of the church as woman and mother pre-dates Mariology: Cyprian stated that 'he who does not have the church as mother cannot have God as Father', while Clement of Alexandria wrote a striking encomium to the church as virgin mother:

---

[54] Quoted by Leonardo Boff, *Praying with Jesus and Mary* (ET: Maryknoll, NY: Orbis Books, 1983/2005), p. 172.

[55] Beattie, *Rediscovering Mary: Insights from the Gospels* (Tunbridge Wells: Burns and Oates, 1995).

The universal Father is one, and one the universal Word; and the Holy Spirit is one and the same everywhere, and one is the only virgin mother. I love to call her the Church . . . She is at once virgin and mother, pure as a virgin, loving as a mother. And calling her children to her, she nurses them with holy milk, the Word for childhood.[56]

Tertullian says that, just as from the side of Adam Eve was formed, so from the wounded side of Jesus the church, 'the mother of all living', arose. Given the Eve–Mary typology, that comment potentially associates the church with Mary, and indeed Irenaeus had already suggested that Mary was 'prophesying on behalf of the church' when she sang the Magnificat. Mary explicitly becomes 'type' of the church in Ambrose, and in Augustine[57] we find:

Imitate Mary, who gave birth to the Lord . . . If the Church, then, gives birth to the members of Christ, then the Church greatly resembles Mary.

This background explains why Vatican II placed Mariology within the statement on ecclesiology, while for Orthodoxy the connection between Mary and the church is evident in the icons of Pentecost, the Ascension and the *Deesis*. The church's mission is a re-play of Mary's vocation, to bring Christ into the world, giving birth to the redeemed who become members of Christ's body.

This was Mary's fundamental vocation, over-shadowed by the Holy Spirit, to give birth to the new humanity. Paul had associated Adam and Christ,[58] and suggested that in Christ we are a new creation;[59] Eve and Mary were associated with Adam and Christ in the pattern of fall and redemption.[60] Mariology emerges from the logic of incarnation and salvation-history. The humanity of Christ is

---

[56] Clement, *Paedagogos* 1.6; for this and other references see Benko, *The Virgin Goddess*, pp. 229–34.

[57] Augustine quoted by Tina Beattie, 'Mary in Patristic Theology' in Boss, *Mary: The Complete Resource*, p. 94.

[58] Romans 5.12–17; cf. 1 Corinthians 15.45–9.   [59] 2 Corinthians 5.17.   [60] Chapter 5.

a fundamental Christological principle – what is not assumed is not healed; and humanity is Mary's gift to God on behalf of humankind in general, enabling the incarnation.

11.2.3 Mary and the incarnation

Irenaeus was clear that anyone suggesting Christ took nothing from Mary was far astray: for if he did not take the substance of flesh from humanity, he did not become human.[61] Holding Christology and Mariology together precludes interpretation of the biblical stories of the virgin birth as analogous to pagan myths. Christ cannot be conceived as a divine–human hybrid. Luke echoes Genesis when he speaks of the Holy Spirit overshadowing Mary, implicitly suggesting the parallel with the virgin earth; and there are other inner biblical resonances also – the Holy Spirit overshadows the Ark of Covenant and the Holy of Holies, while the burning bush mediates the divine presence as does the mother of Emmanuel, God with us. These reflections appear in story-form in the *Protevangelium*: Mary herself enters the Holy of Holies, while Salome touches the virgin and, as Uzziah when he touched the Ark, pays the penalty. The icons representing these stories convey the specifically Christian sense of Mary's holiness, rather than some kind of pagan mother-goddess or fertility-myth.

In the Eastern tradition we find the Marian icons of lovingkindness (*eleousa*). Jean Vanier speaks of Mary as a woman who has done nothing extraordinary apart from love and desire for communion with him. To enter the world, he writes, the Word of God needed a mother – he needed her to nourish him as an infant and to give him love.[62] This puts prime emphasis on her humanity. The implication could be critique of some Marian developments: she may be confessed as the human mother of God the Son, the human daughter

---

[61] *Apostolic Preaching* 31–3; *Against Heresies* III.22; cf. Chapter 5.
[62] Vanier, *Visages de Marie*, pp. 61, 16.

of God the Father, and the human temple of God the Holy Spirit, but surely we need caution with respect to the 'Queen of heaven'. She may be honoured for her purity and her reception of grace, but the Immaculate Conception idea risks removing her from common humanity, as do notions about painless birth and intact virginity. The humanity of Mary is required for Christology.

Deductions from scripture may validate some ideas found in the apocryphal narratives and the traditions enshrined in Eastern icons. The icon of the Sign, positioned in the iconostasis at the centre as an expression of the Emmanuel prophecy 'God with us', expresses the notion that Mary is the container of the uncontained. Christ is for us in and through Mary, and this was prepared in advance. Like Jeremiah, Mary was 'predestined': 'Before I formed you in the womb I knew you, and before you were born I consecrated you.'[63] Yet nothing was predetermined: she had to accept in order to receive God's grace. She accepted, so enabling the presence and action of God through her, as did the prophets and others responding to God's call. And so she anticipates our eschatological transformation – the icon of the Dormition grasps this better than depictions of her Assumption as Queen of heaven.

Developing traditions about Mary may thus be treated as deductions from scripture. They do not make her more than human, but put her in the same category as prophets or saints, confirming her role as model for the disciple and 'type' of the church.

11.3 Conclusion

Christology is impoverished by the Protestant neglect of Mary,[64] and so is ecclesiology. The Protestant critique is important in re-focussing

---

[63] Jeremiah 1.5.

[64] David Yeago, 'The Presence of Mary in the Mystery of the Church' in Carl E. Braaten and Robert W. Jenson (eds.), *Mary: Mother of God* (Grand Rapids, MI: Eerdmans, 2004), pp. 58–79.

attention on the particular Christian motivations for honouring her, over against assimilation to pagan and idolatrous tendencies, but Mariology persists as a challenge to Protestants. Mary also challenges Orthodox churches and Roman Catholics, particularly about the place of women in the church. The veneration of Mary could point to future possibilities if doors are not closed in advance by inherited prejudices, and we continue to engage in honest ecumenical dialogue.

The logic of Christian reflection:

- preserves Mary's humanity as essential to the humanity of Christ
- recognizes her essential place in the plan of salvation and the providence of God
- honours her call and her response
- acknowledges her holiness, prepared by God's grace, so that the new creation could be effected through her and in her – she is already what we shall be
- offers her as a model for the believer
- accepts that she is 'type' of the church and mother of the saved
- confesses that her intercession sums up and models the priestly ministry of the church.

III Ecclesiology

Ecumenical conversations and doctrinal discussions of the church alike start from the credal affirmation, 'one, holy, catholic and apostolic'. But unlike ecumenists, the fathers presupposed that this ideal was to be realized by exclusion of those with views or practices differing from their own 'orthodoxy'. Given that such exclusive attitudes towards those perceived to be heretics and schismatics were matched by an hierarchical and patriarchal understanding of church order, appropriation of their outlook seems unlikely to prove fruitful. Yet a broader and deeper look at some of their perceptions might provide stimulus to a critique of current ecclesiologies, ecumenical or otherwise, and a more realistic vision for the church on earth.

iii.1 *Extra ecclesiam nulla salus*

Cyprian's treatise on *The Unity of the Catholic Church* is the classic exposition.[65] He was, of course, writing in a situation of division. Attributing the invention of heresies and schisms to the devil, he regarded his opponents as deceived into thinking they were still in the light when they were in darkness – they still called themselves Christian, despite having abandoned the Gospel of Christ. In response, his basic tack was to assert that the mark of the true church is unity with the bishops. He grounds this in Christ's commission to Peter, though there are notoriously two versions of Cyprian's text at this point, only one of which implies that Peter's successor in Rome has primacy; possibly the second version was a modification made after Cyprian found himself at odds with Pope Stephen. His fundamental point is that each bishop is the focus of unity in his own locality, but each church is part of a larger whole.[66]

However far the church spreads and multiplies through fecund growth, it remains one, he affirms – just as the sun's rays are many, yet there is one light, or a tree's branches are many, yet the strength coming from its root is one, or many streams flow from one spring:

> So too the Church glowing with the Lord's light extends her rays over the whole world; but it is one and the same light which is spread everywhere, and the unity of her body suffers no division. She spreads her branches in generous growth over all the earth, she extends her abundant streams ever further; yet one is the head-spring, one the

---

[65] Cyprian, *On the Lapsed* and *On the Unity of the Catholic Church*; Latin text and ET: Maurice Bévenot SJ, *Cyprian: De Lapsis and De Ecclesiae Catholicae Unitate* (Oxford University Press, 1971).

[66] *Unity* 3–4.

source, one the mother who is prolific in her offspring, generation after generation: of her womb we are born, of her milk we are fed, from her Spirit our souls draw their life-breath.[67]

Thus Cyprian slips into the motif of the church as our mother, then immediately assumes she's the spouse of Christ, who cannot be defiled, is inviolate and chaste. Anyone who breaks with the church enters into an adulterous relationship. Implicitly adapting to the church the Old Testament motif of Israel as God's spouse, whose disloyalty and idolatry constitutes adultery, he adds the frequently quoted remark: 'You cannot have God for your Father if you no longer have the Church for your mother.' The holiness and oneness of the church he links together, implying an exclusivity which is expressed by reference to Noah's Ark – 'if there was any escape for anyone outside the Ark, there will be as much for anyone outside the Church'.[68]

In the course of his argument, Cyprian develops other biblical material: the undivided robe of Christ, the one flock and the one Shepherd, the Passover lamb which was to be eaten in a single home, Paul's hymn to love, the dominical commands, and so on. But a recurring theme grounds the peace and harmony of the church in God's unity:

> God is one, and Christ is one; His Church is one and the faith is one; and the cement of fellowship binds all the people together into the body's solid unity. That unity cannot be broken; that one body cannot be divided by any cleavage of its structure, nor cut up in fragments with its vitals torn out.[69]

This creates a theological imperative for his warnings against heresy and schism, his assertion that not even martyrdom outside the church can purge this sin,[70] and his identification of the

---

[67] *Ibid.* 5; ET: Bévenot, *Cyprian*, p. 67.   [68] *Ibid.* 6.   [69] *Ibid.* 23.   [70] *Ibid.* 14.

united church as consisting of those with, and not against, the bishops.[71]

This uncompromising ideology can easily be treated as the general perspective of the fathers: unity was achieved by exclusion. The history of the church through the Middle Ages and the Reformation demonstrates how its legacy lived on. It still has influence: it continues to hold out a particular vision of what the church reunited might be, while new differences lure Christians into treating opposing groups as beyond the pale. But there is in the patristic material another perspective.

III.2 Now and yet not yet

It is customarily said that, as contrasted with that of the West, Eastern teaching about the Church remained immature, not to say archaic, in the post-Nicene period. In the main this is a fair enough verdict, at any rate so far as concerns deliberate statements of ecclesiological theory.[72]

So Kelly. Quoting phrases from Cyril of Jerusalem, he further comments, 'These are time-honoured commonplaces.' But it would be strange if the Greek fathers provided us with no reflection on the church – they do, of course; you simply have to look for it. The search yields dividends, turning up material which reveals a pragmatic sense of the church's penultimate state on earth, despite its ultimately eschatological character.

III.2.1 The Apostolic Constitutions

Texts concerned with canonical rulings are naturally pragmatic, but they also carry a vision of the nature of the church for which

[71] Ibid. 17.
[72] J. N. D. Kelly, Early Christian Doctrines (2nd edn, London: A&C Black, 1960), p. 401.

ordinances are being made. The work known as the *Apostolic Constitutions*, an important text for scholars interested in church order and liturgy, seems to belong to the fourth century but incorporates earlier texts.

Book VIII documents intercession for the church, asking that 'God would preserve and keep it unshaken, and free from the waves of this life, until the end of the world, as founded upon a rock'; after the eucharistic consecration appears further intercession for the church, spread throughout the world and 'purchased with the precious blood of Christ', that God will 'preserve it unshaken and free from disturbance until the end of the world', then for 'this people' that God will make them 'a royal priesthood and a holy nation'. Other prayers ask that God look down on 'this flock' and keep them firm and blameless, 'that they may be holy in body and spirit, not having spot or wrinkle'. God is addressed as 'their protector, helper, provider and guardian, their strong wall of defence, their bulwark and security'.[73] The implication is that, while the church's life is anchored in God and will reach safe harbour in the end, for the moment it needs divine assistance to withstand the storms and temptations of earthly existence, and may potentially fail if not given divine protection.

Based in scripture, the various images of the church found here are anticipated in the earlier books. The picture of the 'flock' with the bishop as 'shepherd' recurs, with warnings that one 'scabbed sheep' may infect the rest, and with long quotations from Ezekiel and elsewhere alerting people to the existence of bad shepherds. Old Testament passages about Israel, whether its sin and sedition or its worship and priesthood, are taken to apply directly to the church. Indeed, the church is a 'holy nation', 'God's people':

> You, therefore, are the holy and sacred church of God, enrolled in heaven, a royal priesthood, a holy nation, a peculiar people, a bride adorned for the Lord God, a great church, a faithful church.

[73] *Apostolic Constitutions* VIII.10–12; Greek text: Marcel Metzger (ed.), *SC*; ET: *NPNF*.

As escapees from the ten plagues, who have received the ten commandments, learned the law, kept the faith and believed in Jesus, they should offer tithes and sacrifices, understood now to be prayers, thanksgivings and eucharistic offerings. Bishops are their high-priests, presbyters their priests, and deacons are instead of Levites. The one above all these is the high-priest, Christ, to whom all the offerings belong.[74] They are a people who were once not a people.[75]

The biblical image of the vineyard also appears, and the catholic church is called 'God's plantation', containing those who are heirs by faith, partakers of the Spirit, free to call God 'Father', enjoying the benefits of the 'sprinkling of the precious blood of Christ' and the promises of God.[76] People are exhorted not to leave for the polluted temple of the heathen or the synagogues of Jews or heretics – how would they answer for it on the day of judgement? The church is:

> the daughter of the Highest, which has been in labour pains for you by the word of grace, and has formed Christ in you, of whom you are made partakers, and thereby become his holy and chosen members, not having spot or wrinkle, or any such thing; but as being holy and unspotted in the faith, you are complete in him, after the image of God that created you.[77]

The bishop is charged with treating those who cause disturbances and division in the church as superfluous members of the body, to be amputated as a surgeon deals with physical excrescences – for the church is a perfect body, with sound members who believe in God, in the fear of the Lord and in love. The bishop is a physician. Implicit all the time is a tension between the church as a 'safe haven of tranquillity' and as a vessel tossed on the storms of sin and heresy.

---

[74] *Ibid.* II.15–25; cf. VI.1–5, 18.   [75] *Ibid.* III.15.   [76] *Ibid.* I.1; cf. II.15.

[77] *Ibid.* II.61, alluding to Ephesians 5.27; cf. II.20, 43 and 57 for the following descriptions.

Indeed, the most striking feature of this compendium of texts is its description of the assembling of the church – for it takes the ship metaphor as its basis. The building is to be long, with its head to the east, so as to be like a ship. The bishop is the commander, so his throne is to be placed in the middle, with the presbytery on each side of him and the deacons standing by – for they are like the mariners and managers of the ship. The laity are all set in their proper places and order, men and women apart, young and old in their special places, while the door-keepers and deaconesses keep watch like sailors over men and women respectively, and the bishop speaks after the presbyters, 'as being the commander'. We may recall the prayers that the church may be 'free from the waves of this life, until the end of the world'.

III.2.2 Basil of Caesarea

Now this focus on the church as a ship is by no means a peculiarity of this text. A trawl through the letters of Basil of Caesarea[78] reveals its persistent use, especially when Basil is appealing for help in the face of heresy and schism. A few examples include these:

- The times are difficult, 'having need of a great helmsman because of the continual storms and floods which rise against the Church'.[79]
- Basil requests prayers 'in order that the holy God may some day grant calm and repose to our concerns here, and may rebuke this wind and sea, so that we can find rest from the tempest-tossing and confusion in which we now find ourselves, ever waiting to be plunged utterly into the deep'.[80]
- 'No-one in his right mind would board a boat without pilot, nor entrust himself to a Church in which those who sit at the helm are themselves causing the billows and the tossing.'[81]

---

[78] Basil, *The Letters*; Greek text and ET: R. Deferrari, *Basil, The Letters*, 4 vols., *LCL*.
[79] *Epistle* LXXXI.   [80] *Ibid.* XCI.   [81] *Ibid.* CCX.

In many other letters we find the metaphors of being 'tossed about', of potential 'shipwreck', of 'continual storms', 'fierce tempests', 'floods', 'torrents' and 'a sea of evils', of the need for someone reliable to hold the tiller – almost to the point of this cluster of expressions becoming dead metaphors. The *eschaton* certainly is not yet!

Letters, it might be said, are bound to reflect a pragmatic viewpoint, especially given Basil's situation as an opponent of the emperor Valens; shouldn't we look elsewhere for Basil's serious understanding of the church? In fact, we find exactly the same metaphor in his work *On the Holy Spirit*, despite its affirmation of church life as the place where the sanctifying work of the Holy Spirit is evident. The present condition of the church is compared to some naval battle, fought by people who cherish a deadly hate against each other, with long experience of naval warfare and eager for the fight:

> See the rival fleets rushing in dread array to the attack. With a burst of uncontrollable fury they engage and fight it out. Imagine the ships driven to and fro by a raging tempest, while thick darkness falls from the clouds and blackens the scene . . . From all sides the winds beat on one point where the fleets are dashed against one another.[82]

Basil speaks of combatants becoming traitors or deserting, sailors split into parties, utter confusion 'from howling winds, crashing vessels, boiling surf, and the yells of the combatants', of inability to hear a word from admiral or pilot. From this rhetorical picture he turns to the unhappy reality of the church's tempest and the shaking of every foundation, wondering who could make a complete list of the wrecks, when we see churches, crews and all, dashed and shattered upon the sunken reefs of heresy.

Basil's letters reveal his use of other common metaphors traced in the *Apostolic Constitutions*, such as the flock and its shepherds.[83] The idea of the body and its members recurs, with the suggestion that the body is sick, or suggesting that 'to unite these parts and

[82] *On the Holy Spirit* xxx.76.   [83] E.g. *Epistle* ccxliii.

bring them together in the harmony of a single body belongs to him alone, who by his ineffable power grants even to dry bones a return once more to flesh and muscles'.[84] The idea of correcting or healing hidden maladies before facing the day of judgement is frequent enough almost to become another dead metaphor, and is a reminder that the eschatological perspective generates a pragmatic realism about the life of the church on earth.[85]

III.2.3 Cyril of Jerusalem, *Catechetical Homilies*

Eschatological tension, then, is present, if not named, in Greek texts of the fourth century. Let's return to the *Catechetical Homilies* of Cyril of Jerusalem, dismissed as merely conventional by Kelly. In the eighteenth homily Cyril reaches the clause 'one holy catholic church'.[86] He says it is called 'catholic' because it extends over all the world, from one end of the earth to the other. But he also gives other reasons: because it teaches universally and completely all the doctrines people need to know about things visible and invisible; because it subjects the whole human race, educated and uneducated, to godliness; because it universally heals all kinds of sins, whether of soul or body; and because it possesses every form of virtue and every kind of spiritual gift. He then discusses the term *ecclesia*, suggesting that it is used because the church calls forth and assembles all humanity, that it is the scriptural word (a point he documents with many texts), but that, since it is a common word used for many other gatherings, some of them dens of wickedness and heresy, the addition of these adjectives is important. The holy church, he says, is the mother of us all and the spouse of our Lord Jesus Christ, the figure and copy of the Jerusalem which is above, in which God has set every kind of wisdom and virtue. In former days she crowned martyrs; now she receives

---

[84] *Ibid.* xxx, lxvi.

[85] E.g. *Ibid.* cxxv; cf. cxiii; other texts of this period confirm these findings: e.g. Gregory of Nazianzus, *Oration 2*; John Chrysostom, *On Priesthood.*

[86] *Catechetical Homilies* 18.22–7.

honours from kings, while she alone transcends the boundaries of earthly kingdoms.

Here Cyril would seem to be making a strong eschatological claim. Particularly interesting is his wide-ranging definition of the word 'catholic'. Yet what he says implies a process of teaching and healing, and elsewhere he affirms that the need for teaching relates to the fact of temptation, suggesting that the church is Christ's school, gathered around the scriptures.[87] Furthermore, the Holy Spirit is the church's helper and teacher, guardian and sanctifier, a mighty champion on our behalf, and pilot of the tempest-tossed, who leads wanderers to the light, presides over combatants and crowns the victors.[88] Cyril warns and encourages his catechumens: the Christian life remains one of struggle as long as one is in the body. However, he is confident that the Holy Spirit keeps the church on track, and the church's teaching enables its members to struggle through to victory.

Much of the imagery and many of the assumptions found in these Greek texts overlap with what we saw in Cyprian, but there is also a sense that this vision of the church will only be realized at the *eschaton*. The eschatological tensions found in the New Testament by twentieth-century scholars are present also in this patristic material: what the church is transcendently is not yet realized on earth. Interestingly enough, the same sense of 'now but not yet' is to be found in Augustine.

III.2.4 Augustine

Augustine upholds the sort of ideology found in Cyprian and yet sets it in an eschatological perspective which makes a substantial difference to its implications. His position has been well expounded

---

[87] *Ibid.* 4.1, 33. For the church as school, see my article '*Paideia* and the Myth of Static Dogma' in Sarah Coakley and David Pailin (eds.), *The Making and Remaking of Chrisian Doctrine*, Essays in Honour of Maurice Wiles (Oxford: Clarendon Press, 1993), pp. 265–83.

[88] *Catechetical Homilies* 16.14, 19; 17.13.

by Robert Markus,[89] who shows how Augustine developed away from a sharp dualism between the church and the world to a much more subtle appreciation of how each was ambiguous: the Roman empire and the empirical church were not to be identified *simpliciter* with 'the two cities'. The Roman empire was 'theologically neutral', neither being the Babylon of apocalyptic nor having 'a sacral significance in terms of the history of salvation', as Origen and Eusebius had suggested;[90] while the church 'could be seen simultaneously as holy and as wicked', and 'whatever the sense in which the church is "holy", this must admit the possibility – the need – for tolerating sinners within it until the end'. Markus argues that Augustine learned this from Tyconius, who 'was the first to have elaborated a theology of the Church's holiness as eschatological'. So, 'as in the case of the "earthly city", we must recognise that the "heavenly city", too, both is and is not identifiable with a particular society'.[91]

Yet the two cases are not quite commensurable. The church is to be regarded as God's holy people, and this holy people is the community gathered around their bishop in sacramental communion, and only here is salvation to be had; so despite the presence of sinners, there is a link with the heavenly city – indeed:

> the Church is the historically visible form of the City of God. Its very substance lies in its continuity with God's eschatological community, into which it is always growing.

> The Church is subject to the permanent tension between what is here and now and the eschatological reality to be disclosed in and through it.[92]

III.3 Developing these pointers

The 1960s generated ecumenical hopes which shaped the commitments of a generation. Vatican II opened up the possibility of

---

[89] R. A. Markus, *Saeculum: History and Society in the Theology of St Augustine* (Cambridge University Press, 1970/88).

[90] *Ibid.*, p. 55.   [91] *Ibid.*, pp. 116–17.   [92] *Ibid.*, pp. 119, 120.

rapprochement with other churches of East and West, now respected as conversation partners, worthy of the designation 'church', ecclesial rather than heretical or schismatic communities.[93] This was a move beyond patristic perspectives, despite the implicit assumption that somehow the church of the early centuries had been providentially led to exclude false belief while the divided churches now are somehow different. Closer to home, actual proposals for the reunion of Methodists and Anglicans were on the table, while united or uniting churches came into being out of disparate Protestant denominations in India, south and north, Australia and Canada. There was a general acceptance of the view that the credal affirmation of the 'one, holy, catholic and apostolic church' should be realized for the sake of mission, and that as long as the church was divided it could hardly bear witness to the reconciling Gospel.

Since then, ecumenical conversations have produced the agreed statement on *Baptism, Eucharist and Ministry* (Lima, Peru, 1982), and many bilateral talks have produced reconciling statements on key dividing issues, such as authority or justification by faith. Theologians from different denominations and across the spectrum of academic disciplines (Bible, patristics, systematics, philosophy of religion, inter-religious dialogue, etc.) now teach and research alongside one another, not just in secular universities, but also in denominational institutions, reading the same literature, meeting in conferences, finding alliances across the historic dividing lines. Denominational differences have begun to be transcended, not just through friendships and personal relations, but in common commitment to scripture and increasingly assimilated liturgies. Yet for all that, there is a widespread sense that ecumenism has run into the sand, that it does not comprehend the full spectrum, given the non-involvement of Pentecostal and evangelical/independent churches, and that current deep controversies are only multiplying causes of

---

93 See Hans Küng, *The Church* (London: Burns and Oates, 1968), p. 283.

division within and among churches, so undermining progress on the old historic issues.

To some extent the distinction between the 'now and the not yet', which first emerged in twentieth-century attempts to expound New Testament eschatology, now found reflected in some patristic material, has modified the tendency to speak of the church as if it already were what ideological doctrines of the church assert. In the wake of Vatican II Hans Küng wrote:

> The Church ... is the pilgrim community of believers, not of those who already see and know. The Church must ever and again wander through the desert, through the darkness of sin and error. For the Church can also err and for this reason must always be prepared to orientate itself anew, to renew itself.[94]

> The historical nature of the Church is revealed by the fact that it remains the pilgrim people of God ... it journeys through history, through a time of complex imperfection, towards the final perfection, the eschatological Kingdom of God, led by God himself. It is essentially an interim Church, a Church in transition, and therefore not a Church of fear but of expectation and hope: a Church which is directed towards the consummation of the world by God.[95]

This parallels the statement on ecclesiology made by the British Methodist Church in 1999 and entitled *Called to Love and Praise*:

- 'The Church has been brought to birth, but has not yet attained its fullness. It comprises a pilgrim people seeking to enter, and to help others enter, the fullness of God's kingdom.'
- '[T]he Church, a pilgrim people journeying towards the End, must testify to, celebrate, and hope in the God who remains active in his creation, working out his purpose for its salvation.'
- So the affirmation of the church as 'one, holy, catholic and apostolic' provokes the observation that 'the Church continually fails.

[94] *Ibid.*, p. xi.   [95] *Ibid.*, p. 131.

Often, these characteristics are barely discernible in the Church's life, and repentance is an ever-present requirement.'

- At the same time, as expressed 'in Charles Wesley's lines, "Fortified by power divine, The Church can never fail." Such belief in the "indefectibility" of the Church does not mean believing that it already has that "perfection without spot and wrinkle" (Eph. 5.27), which belongs only to the end of time. It means believing in a God who perseveres in re-creation, and who provides the essential means of grace in word and sacrament ... The saints on earth remain on pilgrimage, journeying towards and praying for an ever fuller expression of unity, holiness, catholicity and apostolicity.'[96]

It would seem that the patristic tension between the empirical church and the eschatological church is now acknowledged in these and other denominational traditions.

Yet, despite the slogan 'unity not uniformity', when it comes to the goals of the ecumenical movement, the continuation of distinct ecclesial communities never seems to be envisaged, and the ancient Eastern Orthodox and Roman Catholic churches alike refuse eucharistic sharing without unity and full intercommunion; whereas what we need, surely, are ways of offering a eucharistic sign of the eschatological reality of our unity in the body of Christ, while acknowledging the fact that our historically bound institutions are necessarily flawed, and so unlikely to achieve institutional union without imposing compromises unacceptable to some parties, so proving newly divisive. Various experiences have suggested to me that the penultimate reality of the empirical church should be taken more seriously:

- At the World Faith and Order Conference in Santiago di Compostela in 1993, I listened to Spanish Protestants telling how they

[96] *Called to Love and Praise* (Peterborough: The Methodist Church, 1999) 1.4.4; 2.1.11; 2.1.10; 2.4.8, 12, 13.

were not allowed to exist under Franco; this was a salutary reminder of the importance of religious freedom, something for which our predecessors fought and suffered. Then that very evening, the local Franciscans lent their basilica so that those Spanish Protestants could break bread with their brothers and sisters from around the world, surely a sign of a new vision for ecumenism – hospitality offered to those who are different.

- In Russia I have been welcomed by and worshipped with Methodists and Russian Orthodox. But I have also sensed the undercurrents of the ambiguous position both of Methodists and of those Orthodox who are ecumenical, especially Faith and Light groups – Orthodox, but belonging to an organization which originated in the Catholic West, as well as affirming those marginal people who have learning disabilities and so are different from the social norm and 'ought to be' in institutions. Institutional church unity here would surely suppress such minorities and remove expressions of valid aspects of the Christian Gospel.

- Once at an Anglican eucharist I was struck by the sharp cracking sound at the moment of fraction. I began to wonder if it is not necessary for the church to be broken, fractured into diverse pieces so as to be scattered in mission to diverse others; as the *Didache* put it, 'As this broken bread, once dispersed over the hills, was brought together and became one loaf, so may the church be brought together from the ends of the earth into thy kingdom.' The empirical church is the broken body, distributed across the *oikoumenē*, not just geographically but in different cultural manifestations, to be reunited in the *eschaton*.

- Attending mass in the converted barn at Trosly-Breuil, the chapel of the original L'Arche community, I have often felt the sharp pain of exclusion and empathized with the bafflement of people with learning disabilities, who simply cannot understand the canonical rules which keep people who live in community with one another but come from different ecclesial traditions from sharing eucharist with each other. Yet I have also presided at eucharist at the very same altar, offered the open invitation of the Methodist tradition, and observed how some felt able to respond to that invitation while others did not, torn apart by those canonical rules.

- I remember John Wesley's view that the eucharist is a converting ordinance – if adopted more widely, our open invitation to receive communion whoever you are, and so discover Christ and begin to be transformed, might be the route to ecclesial repentance, renewal and a form of union which expresses the 'now' of the eschatological church despite the 'not yet' of the empirical church. And could this not be a greater sign for the world than actual institutional unity, a demonstration that by the grace of God the most fundamental differences between human beings can be transcended and reconciliation effected?

A lifelong ecumenist, shaped by the hopes of the 1960s, I have been enriched by so many ecumenical contacts and deep friendships in Christ across ecclesial divides; but those very experiences have challenged the accepted ecumenical vision. Should we not move on to a critical ecumenism, earthed in realities that are more clearly attested by the Christian understanding of our sinful condition than by ideologies, religious or secular, which preach a utopian unity in the here and now? Our union belongs to the eschatological future – we live in hope; yet constantly we find anticipations of that unity, if we have eyes to see and ears to hear and hearts open to the good things which pass our understanding prepared for us by God.

* * *

Welcoming difference

The preacher is preparing for a chapel service at the local theological college; it is to be at the end of a day focussing on disability, and, contrary to usual practice, the preacher is intending to take Arthur along. When this had been suggested, however, it had been greeted with consternation, expressed in the question, 'Why? Was he to be used as a visual aid?' The preacher had been quite taken aback. But now she is taking the question seriously, examining her motives – there probably is an element of feeling people should confront the reality of what they have been talking about all day! But the more she thinks about it, the more she feels that Arthur's presence is essential to what she wants to say on this occasion. A compromise has been reached: he will be taken out for the sermon, since there remains sensitivity about talking about him in his presence – although the only thing he would pick up would be recognition of his own name, which he would probably then repeat over and over again!

The whole incident, however, has sharpened up what the preacher needs to say. 'There is neither Jew nor Greek, there is neither slave nor free, there is neither male nor female',[97] and these days, she would suggest, we would most of us naturally go on, 'black nor white, rich nor poor, Catholic nor Anglican, Orthodox nor Methodist, for you are all one in Christ Jesus'. But is it so obvious that we would add reference to those with disabilities? She would challenge them with what had happened. She had received the invitation with not only a sense of privilege, but also of joy, because it would provide an occasion when Arthur could join the worship of the community without a feeling of intrusion. This had been shattered, but this very shattering revealed the true meaning of his presence: it was a celebration of our wholeness together, and that celebration was essential to what the preacher had to say. The trouble is that wholeness is associated with perfection – we imagine a state in which all loss and brokenness, all sin and pain and failure are wafted away, and it is that which we think is perfection. Disability seems to undermine that wholeness. But our wholeness in Christ is a wholeness that can absorb and transfigure loss, brokenness, disability, failure, sin, hurt and death – we become whole when we can live with the cross at the centre of the community.

* * *

97 Galatians 3.28.

Postlude

Contemplation in the Night-Time[98]

An extended meditation on the traditional icons of Mary, Mother of
God, and other Marian images.

Proem

Wide-eyed with wonder the little owls embrace.
Wisdom resides in child-like naivety,
Where silence slips between the interstices
Of knowledge, where darkness is luminous and truth
In strange insights one hardly dares to voice
Caught up in a pattern of meaning beyond one's self
By intuition of archetypal fit.
The owls' wisdom is found in receptiveness,
To what is given by grace in beauty and love.

* * *

Orans

The two gazed at the icon: the Mother of God,
Bowed head, hands raised in contemplation and prayer,
Before her Son in glory, Redeemer, Judge.[99]
'That's you!' he said. The woman turned and wept.
Relieved she sat down as the burden rolled from her back.
Awe-struck she inwardly sighed, 'Jesus, Lord,
Have mercy, *Kyrie eleison*.' With deepening dread,

[98] The title of a stained-glass miniature in childish style, depicting two owls embracing, given by the Taizé community to the L'Arche community of Trosly-Breuil, and placed high up in the eaves of their barn-chapel above the altar.

[99] The icon of the *Deesis* shows Christ the Saviour with John the Baptist on the right and Mary on the left, both in the attitude of prayer – the *orans* position.

She barely breathed, 'Not unto us, not
Unto us, not unto us, the glory, Lord!'[100]
She melded with the *Deesis*, accepting this gift –
To pray the church's prayer, to rest in the peace
And confidence that the Spirit prays with our
Spirit, to offer her nothingness to the great
Song of all creation in heaven, on earth.
'Today the Virgin stands in the midst of the church;
With choirs of saints she prays to God for us.
Angels and bishops worship, prophets rejoice
With apostles, since it's for our sake she prays
To the pre-eternal God.'[101] The woman's heart
Leapt, as icon after icon spoke
Of Mary, supreme exemplar of Christian faith
Creating a living sign with many layers,
As lenses were focussed by hindsight to clarify
The delicate web and woof of providence –
The provision of God to fulfil his purpose of love.
Mary, type of the church, stands and prays,
As she stood at the foot of the cross alongside John
The Theologian, partners in destiny;[102]
As she stood with the other disciples on the Mount
Of Ascension, watching him rise up out of sight;[103]
So now, *orans*, hands raised, head bowed, she prays
To the human face of God, *Pantocrator*,[104]
Her son, Jesus, Saviour, Brother, Friend.

---

[100] Psalm 115.1.   [101] From the *kontakion* of the feast of the Virgin's Protection.
[102] The icon of the cross has Mary on the left and John the Apostle (the beloved disciple) on the right.
[103] In the icon of the Ascension Mary dominates the picture, standing in the *orans* position, surrounded by the disciples.
[104] Christ Almighty, enthroned on high, often depicted in the dome above the congregation in a traditional Orthodox church.

She entreats for us the Giver of Mercy she bore,[105]
She offers intercession for all the world,
Taking up into her praying the prayer of those
Who belong to her Son – Lord Jesus Christ,
Have mercy on all. 'Have mercy, Lord, on me,'
The woman softly sighs; then with the church
She sings in praise: 'It's truly right to bless
You, *Theotokos*, ever blessed, most pure,
The Mother of our God. More honourable than
The cherubim, more glorious beyond compare
Than the seraphim, you gave birth
Without corruption to God the Word. True
Theotokos, you we magnify.'[106]

* * *

The Sign

She stands and prays – she fulfils the prophetic sign:[107]
'A Virgin shall conceive and bear a son,
His name "Emmanuel" (that's "God with us").'
And so she embodies the ways of providence,
As God with love incomprehensibly
Prepares ahead the receptacle of the Word –
The Mother predetermined ages before
And preached by prophets.[108] No wonder the church read back
Behind her call to celebrate her birth![109]

[105] From the Canon of the Small Paraklesis, Canticle 7.
[106] From the divine liturgy of St John Chrysostom.
[107] In the icon of our Lady of the Sign, usually placed in the *iconostasis* at the centre of the row of prophets, Emmanuel (Isaiah 7.14) is depicted on Mary's breast.
[108] Phrases gleaned from Leonid Ouspensky and Vladimir Lossky, *The Meaning of Icons* (rev. edn, New York: St Vladimir's Seminary Press, 1982), p. 153.
[109] Cf. the icon of the nativity of the Virgin.

'O Virgin, your nativity has now
Proclaimed joy to the whole universe!
The Sun of Righteousness, the Christ, our God,
Has shone from you, the *Theotokos*. Thus
Annulling the curse, a blessing he bestowed;
Destroying death, he granted eternal life.'[110]
No wonder her icons and feast-days anticipate
Her sacred vocation – her consecration before
Her birth. Prophetic precedents point to this:
Isaiah, Jeremiah, Samuel –
Before I formed you in the womb, before
Your birth, I knew, I consecrated you.[111]
The woman remembers how pregnant, perturbed by war,
Her mother, Mary's namesake, like Hannah had prayed
And dedicated her child ahead of the birth.
Then stillness fills her heart – do the types ring true?
The woman remembers the mother who'd lost a son,
The one who'd instinctively known her first-born child
In danger, and prayerfully held in love the one
Who'd strangely fulfil that lost brother's call:
A priestly vocation – a sign to be spoken against
When the priestly call of women met with denial.
She hardly dares articulate the thought,
The delicate web and woof of providence.
Mary, type of the church, 'a chosen race,
A royal priesthood, a holy nation',[112] leads
Into the temple above the heavens. She is
God's living temple, pure and undefiled,
Filled with the Holy Spirit and heavenly grace.
No wonder her icons and feast-days include the time

[110] *Troparion* for the Feast of the Nativity of the *Theotokos*.
[111] Jeremiah 1.5.   [112] I Peter 2.9.

When the Virgin entered the temple,[113] when she's said
To have passed the priest and proceeded all the way
Into the Holy of Holies and there filled
The sacred space with her grace and loveliness.
Mary, type of the royal priesthood, thus
Reveals the priesthood of men and women, called
To represent God to the world, the world to God.

* * *

Annunciation

Mary, a teenage girl, sits and spins.[114]
The angel touches down and greets her – amazed,
Perplexed, she raises her hand to ward him off.
'Strange are your words to me, hard for my soul';[115]
'How can a child be born of my virginal womb?'[116]
'Childbirth comes from mutual love – but I
Don't know the pleasure of marriage at all. So how?'[117]
'I tell of the birth of God,' the angel said.
'Rejoice, heavenly ladder, by which God
Descended, bridge leading from earth to heaven.'[118]
'The beginning of our salvation is today,
The revealing of eternal mystery.
The Son of God becomes the Virgin's Son,
As Gabriel announces the coming of grace.
To the *Theotokos* let's cry together with him:

---

[113] Cf. the icon for the Feast-day of the Presentation of the *Theotokos* into the Temple.
[114] The icon of the Annunciation may depict or combine three moments – Mary's surprise, her perplexity and resistance, or her consent. The Akathistos Hymn explores the same three moments.
[115] *Kontakion* ii from the Akathistos Hymn.   [116] *Ikos* ii from the Akathistos Hymn.
[117] Liturgy for the Feast of the Annunciation.   [118] *Ikos* ii from the Akathistos Hymn.

Rejoice, full of grace. The Lord's with you.'[119]
She bows her head in consent. Receptive, she feels
Empowered in the depths of her womanhood
As the Spirit overshadows her and new
Creation begins within her. She'll sing with strength,
Firmly convinced of a world put to rights.
Then after the pain of the cross she'll stride forth
To bring the Risen Christ into the world –
The 'Walking Madonna'[120] – woman's free response –
To become again what she was meant to be:
A priestly person, blessed and blessing, a type
Of the church, lifting creation before God's throne.
Reflecting on this, the woman feels empowered.
Amazed she wonders how it is that this
Unique woman could be her archetype.
She knows she is, yet she isn't. Content with the grace
That's given, she honours Mary, Mother of God.

* * *

Nativity

Mary, *Theotokos*, lies at rest.[121]
After the birth she lies and just lets go
Allowing the midwife to bathe her infant son,
Wide, wondering eyes focussed beyond.
Joseph, tossed about in a storm of doubt,[122]
Is greatly troubled and fearful, yet there for her.
The woman sees the type of the faithful spouse,
Type of the loyal agnostic, bound in love,

[119] *Troparion* for the Feast of the Annunciation.
[120] A remarkable statue of the aged Mary in Salisbury Cathedral Close.
[121] Cf. the icon of the Nativity.   [122] *Kontakion* iv from the Akathistos Hymn.

Compassion built on a rock, steadfast and true;
While in the cave beasts bow their heads
At the babe in swaddling grave-clothes lying there;
And gathered around are those with expectancy,
Confronted by angels and strange stars while at work
In the open fields or the astrological lab –
Ordinary people about their business, types
Of humankind, learned, ignorant, rough,
Clever, travelled or local, from different faiths.
Taken up in this moment is all the world;
Present, future, past is contained herein –
In extraordinary ordinariness, touching the heart.
The woman gives thanks, lets go of doubt, finds peace
In the thought of new creation accomplished by grace.

* * *

Intercessor

Mary, type of the church, stands and prays,
Type of each believer, called like her
To bring Christ into the world, to ponder and gaze,
Wide-eyed with wonder, discerning the signs right here
Of Presence within the strangest places of all –
Real Presence in a cattle feeding-trough,
Radiant Presence in the face of a son born bruised
In body, mind and future. At the foot of the cross
She stands, the *Theotokos*, her breast pierced
With a sword, as Simeon had foretold. 'Look,
Mary, my child's lovely,' the woman cried,
'Is yours lovely too? With silky hair
And little hands and tiny feet, and smiles
And shiny eyes that transfigure his face. But see,
My child's broken – is yours broken too?'

Yes – crushed by affliction, rejected and lost,
Disfigured, disabled. Silently stricken with grief,
She stands and prays, taking up in her prayer
The anguish and anger, the labour, the travail and pain
Of every mother and all creation at once.
'My heart's bursting, Mary – is yours too?'
Yes – bursting with joy, ecstasy, pain and praise!
She stands, embodies compassion, her hands raised,
Spreading a veil of protection over the church;[123]
Or, *Eleousa*, embracing her Son in love,
In lovingkindness, cheek to cheek with her babe,[124]
She gazes with pity on suffering humanity:
Mother Mary, our mother, hear our prayer.
'Entreat the Giver of Mercy whom you bore.
Grant me the depths of your compassion: to you
I turn, pure Mother; you bore the compassionate One.'[125]

* * *

Dormition

Mary, type of the Church, lies at rest.
Dormition[126] reflects Nativity – roles reversed,
In swaddling bands her soul is mothered by Christ.
The wisdom and beauty make one gasp with awe –
He was made man, he emptied himself, that we
With her might rise, assumed into divine

---

[123] Cf. the icon of the Protection, where the Mother of God stands, *orans*, her protecting veil overshadowing everyone.
[124] The icon the *Eleousa* or 'merciful and loving', showing Mary cheek to cheek with her Son.
[125] Canticle 4 and Canticle 7, Canon of the Small Paraclesis.
[126] Cf. the icon of the Dormition.

Life, when raised in glory to be with him.
Other companions are there at her final sleep –
Apostles and early bishops stand for the church,
While cherubim and seraphim offer a sign
Of heaven open, receiving us all with her.
The woman remembers her mother, suddenly stricken
When very old, sinking to her last sleep.
'In falling asleep you did not forsake the world.
You were translated to life, O Mother of Life,
And, by your prayers, you deliver our souls from death.'[127]

* * *

Seat of Wisdom

So we rejoice – for the Son of God once dwelt
In you, the *Theotokos*; you became
A holy temple, the house that Wisdom built,
And God's living mercy-seat;[128] the Word
Is enthroned on your lap,[129] and from there blesses the world
With knowledge and life, salvation, truth and light.
Wisdom is seated there in your adult-child –
Wisdom incarnate – the foolishness of God –
Divine Wisdom, deep in the human heart,
In Mary, Mother of God, Wisdom's seat.

* * *

[127] *Troparion* for the Feast of the Dormition.
[128] Thomas Hopko, Introduction to *A Manual of Prayer and Praise to the Theotokos* (rev. edn, Otego, NY: Holy Myrrhbearers Monastery, 2004), p. xii. All above quotations from the liturgy and hymns are taken from this manual.
[129] Cf. the ikon known as Hodigitria.

Coda

A wise old owl would never believe the truth –
That wisdom resides in child-like naivety.
Yet wide-eyed with wonder the little owls embrace.
Divine wisdom is found in receptiveness
To what is given in beauty and grace by love.

8 | From dogma to *theōria*: the Christian God

Prelude

The teenager sits in tears among the sand dunes and watches the sun rise from behind the mountains; sensitized by grief for her younger brother who'd recently died from Hodgkin's disease, she's touched by awareness of God's presence in loss. Another woman reflects, 'I would sit for hours, gazing at the outline of the great Andes mountains, which came into vision and then disappeared as the clouds moved across the sky. I think that these mountains spoke to me even more powerfully of God than does the sea; for their appearance and disappearance mirrored my experience of the felt presence and absence of the Divine.'[1]

The atheist demands evidence of God's existence; the agnostic acknowledges the ambiguity of everything; one believer points to supposed acts of God, while another sees God present in the ordinariness of everything.

Victims of torture describe their darkest moments as being when they felt deeply alone, bereft of even God, despairing because God, whether through powerlessness or implicit permission, allowed the torture to continue; yet many, many times victims, often the very same persons, have spoken of how they knew, deeply knew, that God was with them: an experience of God's absence and presence which mirrors that of Jesus on the cross – 'My God, my God, why hast Thou forsaken me?'; 'Father, into Thy hands I commit my spirit.'[2]

---

[1] Sheila Cassidy, *Confessions of a Lapsed Catholic* (London: DLT, 2010), pp. 113–14.
[2] Adapted from 'Face to Faith', *Guardian*, 12, February 2011, by Shoshana Garfield, a psychologist and therapist who helps torture victims.

The harpist picks out the triad, and sets the instrument resonating with overtones and harmonics – *perichorēsis* in an overflow of grace?

The Black pastor spells out the Oneness Pentecostal understanding of God, basing it on a collection of unambiguous scripture texts: God is Spirit – the one God who is Creator and King of the Universe, Father of all; and this Spirit, which is God, became incarnate in Jesus, and is known in the lives of those who are born again. The listening theologian hears re-played the third-century voice of sincere modalist monarchians – how could one not respect that voice as a valid reading of scripture?

The old man, Gerontius,[3] confesses his faith:

Firmly I believe and truly God is Three and God is One;
And I next acknowledge duly Manhood taken by the Son.

But when he goes before his God, in anguish his heart cries out:

Take me away and in the lowest deep, there let me be.

* * *

Meeting God

The preacher's address followed lections from Genesis 18 and John 4:

Meetings are among the most frequent of life's experiences: casual meetings and arranged meetings, anticipated meetings and unexpected meetings, meetings dreaded and meetings hoped for, meetings symbolic, meetings contrived, meetings to be avoided at all costs, trivial passings in the night and meetings that prove to be deeply significant, sometimes only by hindsight. I suppose it's a bit of a post-modern cliché but it's still true that you discover your own identity through genuinely meeting and attending to the 'other',

---

[3] From John Henry Newman/Elgar, *The Dream of Gerontius.*

the stranger, through crossing boundaries and leaving your comfort zone.

The story we read from the Gospel is doubly a boundary-crossing narrative. It wasn't exactly conventional for a man to accost a woman in a public place as Jesus did, and what's more, Jews and Samaritans were mutually suspicious and, despite their common heritage in the books of Moses, faced each other with certain taboos – refusing to share cups or eat together since they regarded each other as unclean (in other words they were not all that unlike those Christian churches who refuse each other eucharistic hospitality). Yet despite all that, Jesus had asked her for a drink. Doubly boundary-crossing! Boundary-crossing meetings are nerve-racking, but also life-changing. We can only guess how it was for the Samaritan woman after meeting Jesus; yet, with her less than perfect past exposed and against all convention, she rushes off to gather her neighbours, and her testimony led many Samaritans to believe, we're told. Her life can't have stayed the same!

Now, let's go back to the other story we read from the Bible. It's a story of desert hospitality, reflecting custom and practice among nomads in the arid regions of the Middle East. Encamped by the oaks of Mamre, Abraham receives three travellers, hurries out to welcome them, sees their dusty feet washed and food prepared. Hebrews perhaps refers to this story when it urges its readers not to neglect to show hospitality, since by doing this some have entertained angels unawares.[4] Of course, the word 'angel' means 'messenger', and these three strangers had an important message to deliver: they said that when they'd return in a year's time, Abraham and his wife Sarah would have a son. We're told that Sarah overheard this and, being well past child-bearing age, laughed. Then we read, 'The LORD said to Abraham, "Why did Sarah laugh and say, 'Can I really have a child now that I'm so old?'" The message re-confirmed, Sarah's scared; and she lies, claiming she didn't laugh, but he (presumably the Lord) said,

---

[4] Hebrews 13.2.

'Oh yes, you did laugh.' Then the men went on with their journey, and Abraham went with them to set them on their way. So what is the relationship between the three strangers and the LORD? The same strange shift occurred at the beginning: the LORD appeared to Abraham by the oaks of Mamre, it said, and he looked up and saw three men standing by. So the story is about three men, strangers with a message, and yet it's God who is discerned as present in the visit, and God who is addressing Abraham.

The early church interpreted this story as a revelation of the Trinity, a fact captured in Rublev's famous Trinity icon: it's actually a depiction of the three strangers that Abraham entertained, but with this deep ambiguity of reference.

Now this is surely parallel to the story in the Gospel. It's Jesus the Jew who accosts the Samaritan woman, and yet is it just two human beings crossing boundaries? Surely there's more going on here. Explicitly, the person the woman meets is God's Messiah; implicitly, in the Gospel context as a whole, it's God's very own Word who's addressing the woman. Both of these biblical meetings are, on the face of it, with ordinary human beings, and yet there's an extraordinary dimension to each. Should we expect meetings like that? If not, why not? Yet how would we know it? Do we miss it because we don't expect it?

Permit me to end with a personal testimony – I once started a sermon with the words, 'I met God in the Raddlebarn Road.' Yes, putting it like that was meant to startle people. I actually met an old priest who'd obviously had a stroke, limping along with a limp arm on the same side. Reflective hindsight made me put it like that.

For some years I'd been struggling to hang on to faith in God after my first son was born with profound disabilities. I still took my children to church each Sunday, and the disabled one continued in the crèche, since there was no way he could learn anything in Sunday school. I'd just had a visit from the minister who'd tried gently to say that, now he was so big and could be noisy, people thought he shouldn't be there disturbing the babies and toddlers. My head knew this was reasonable; my heart felt the church was rejecting my son. So now I was pushing my son up to the local shops in his buggy and passing the Catholic church when that old priest hobbled up to us, stopped, spoke to my son and then to me. It was a simple act of unconditional acceptance.

I met God in the Raddlebarn Road. Without that meeting, and other significant meetings over the years, I would not be standing here speaking as an ordained minister. As the Bible puts it, let those with ears to hear, hear. Amen.

* * *

As a student, I once heard a fellow student expounding Christian theology from the top down, waxing eloquent about the Trinity as the starting-point. This I found very difficult as a procedure. The fundamental reason was the deep empiricism of the education to which I'd been subjected; historical subjects, under the influence of scientific method, had long since abandoned pure narrative for the investigation of evidence and argumentative reconstruction. For theology, then, it seemed appropriate to start with the evidence, to argue from what is known, from where we are, establishing first what resources might be relevant. The Trinity would be the end-result rather than the starting-point. You might deduce from the order of these chapters that my approach remains empirical, and therefore deeply modernist, and you might be partly right. But now there are other theological grounds for my position, and they are derived not at all from the empiricism of modernity, which notoriously fails to substantiate a theological reading of the universe, but from elsewhere, notably the fathers.

What follows is not an historical or developmental account of patristic theology. The fathers were identifying what was necessary for coherence and responding to their context in the light of tradition and the scriptures, so articulating the characteristic Christian doctrinal discourse. What I present, therefore, is a hermeneutic of their theological drivers. I shall develop certain discrete observations, gradually drawing them into an overall construction[5] which will demonstrate how Christianity radicalized assumptions about the divine, and forged through argument a pattern of insights that remain vital for Christian identity. This claim will be illustrated by drawing out parallels and contrasts with my own progression as a late twentieth-century theologian, moving through modernity to a recapitulation of pre-modern theological perspectives.

I Son of God: Christ in a world of hierarchies

1.1 The hierarchical universe of early Christianity

My first observation draws attention to a couple of theological puzzles seldom faced directly. The first is why Paul and the earliest Christians were apparently unaware that their confessions concerning Christ were a threat to monotheism – this surely demands explanation. The second puzzle is this: why do the various systems of the second to third centuries, whether philosophical, syncretistic, gnostic, Jewish or Christian, bear such a distinct, and perhaps disturbing, family likeness? That question may be unexpected, but to my mind, it is inescapable.

From this distance, it looks as though the structure of the universe underlying the argument between Origen and Celsus is much the same, even though they contest many details. So is the structure

---

[5] The content of this chapter is largely drawn from earlier publications of mine, though forged into a new synthesis and with new material alongside; principal contributions are from 'Christology and Creation: Towards an Hermeneutic of Patristic Christology' in T. Merrigan and J. Haers (eds.), *The Myriad Christ* (Leuven University Press, 2000), pp. 191–205; my essays in John Hick (ed.), *The Myth of God Incarnate* (London: SCM Press, 1977); 'The God of the Greeks'; 'From Analysis to Overlay'; 'Proverbs 8 in Interpretation (2): Wisdom Personified' in David F. Ford and Graham Stanton (eds.), *Reading Texts, Seeking Wisdom* (London: SCM Press, 2003); 'Exegetical Method and Scriptural Proof: The Bible in Doctrinal Debate', *SP* 24 (1989), 291–304; 'The "Mind" of Scripture: Theological Readings of the Bible in the Fathers', *International Journal of Systematic Theology* 7 (2005), 126–41.

of gnostic systems. And, surprising though it may seem, so is the structure of Judaism at that time. All presuppose a hierarchy, with one God at the apex, and a ladder of descending beings, divine, angelic, spiritual, cosmic and earthly. The bones of contention lie around two issues: the proper object of worship and the evaluation of the material or carnal side of existence. Thus, the gnostics would regard themselves as belonging to the transcendent divine world, awaiting redemption *from* material existence; while Irenaeus and Tertullian would affirm the goodness of God's material creation, and Origen would try to have it both ways. As for the object of worship, Celsus, and later a Neoplatonist like Porphyry, would argue that the supreme transcendent God is worshipped indirectly by pursuing the traditional polytheistic rituals, whereas Origen, like the Jews, would argue that only the one true God is to be worshipped, even though there are many angelic beings who are God's servants.

My point is this: though there were areas of contention, they all belonged to a hierarchically conceived universe, and where Christ, or the Logos, was important, he took his place within the hierarchy. Exactly what that place was might be contested, even between different groups claiming to be Christian; but that he had a place in a hierarchy of beings would be simply assumed. So the answer to both our initial questions is the same: there was at this stage a common fuzziness about the distinction between God and everything else. Divinity was not clearly distinct from other orders of being. Gods might emerge through the apotheosis of human heroes and divine rulers – that was the well known Euhemeran theory of religion, and Celsus and Origen threw it at each other, *mutatis mutandis*. Souls were eternal, and in their own way divine. God's immanence, even in Judaism, was mediated through angels who had names deriving from divine attributes, and also through human prophets and righteous men who were God's sons, inspired by God's Word, Wisdom or Spirit; indeed, Enoch was assumed to heaven, like any other 'divine man'. The hierarchical structure of belief meant a common blurring of the line between the one God at the apex and the rest, between the divine and the human; or rather a failure to perceive that such a line might be significant. Only when that line was clarified was there any real Christological problem as such.

In Chapter 4 we explored the Christology of 'image' which was promulgated by Eusebius of Caesarea and others in the fourth century. The very ambiguity of the use of 'image' enabled a kind of hierarchy in which the Logos or Son of God somehow belonged both with the ultimate divine nature and with the creatures which owed their being to the Creator. Behind Eusebius' position lay the Origenist position outlined in Chapter 5, where the many names of Christ associated with the Oneness of the Logos allowed the link between the One God and the multiplicity of creation, thus mirroring the One–Many or the Indefinite Dyad of Middle Platonism. Philosophical though this sounds, the approach was not entirely without scriptural basis. Jesus Christ was the visible form of the invisible God, because he was the incarnation of one who was God's image and Son.

1.2 *The persistence of hierarchical thinking*

At first sight, all this may seem remote from theological concerns today. However, popular understanding of the biblical picture of Jesus persistently reflects the same kind of hierarchical perspective: Jesus is not quite an ordinary human person but someone with exceptional powers because he is Son of God, and, as Son of God, he is not quite God in the same way as the Creator.

In the mid-1970s a young theologian composed a couple of essays which were published in *The Myth of God Incarnate*.[6] At the time they were motivated by the need to affirm the true humanity of Jesus, so often obscured in the unexamined discourse of believers yet fundamental to the quest for the Jesus of history and any approach to 'Christology from below'. Reflection suggests another factor – an

---

[6] 'A Cloud of Witnesses' and 'Two Roots or a Tangled Mass?' in Hick, *The Myth*.

instinctive need to challenge the implicit hierarchical thinking that remains the default position of popular Christianity.

The primary essay attempted to distil the results of the historico-critical approach to the Christology of the New Testament and the fathers. It described the New Testament as the first and greatest 'testimony-meeting', in the sense that here are gathered together a group of documents which testify to the saving effects of the life, death and resurrection of Jesus. It observed how modern discussion had long revolved around the various 'titles' of Jesus, exploring the possible connotations of Messiah, Son of Man, Son of God, Lord, Logos, etc. On the basis of these 'titles' was traced the range of expectations around at the time – political, social, nationalistic, prophetic, religious, various kinds of apocalyptic and supernatural hopes, sometimes overlapping, sometimes distinct, sometimes incompatible, all associated with particular kinds of 'title' and particular ways of interpreting scriptural promises. The New Testament reflects a sort of compulsion to see all such hopes fulfilled in Jesus. Needless to say, this creates a multiplicity of possibilities discernible in the texts of the New Testament, each motif with some kind of soteriological thrust. The way the fathers developed their reflections on the *epinoiai* (names) of Christ,[7] also soteriological in its driving force, was surely an appropriate reception of the New Testament material. Yet common to these different ways of thinking was the sense that Jesus came on God's initiative. By the very fact that Jesus was identified as each of these figures, a figure emerged whose essential characteristic was that he was the embodiment of all God's promises brought to fruition. Such a characterization, I suggested, represents New Testament Christology better than the idea of incarnation, and it was in fact the germ of more and more Christological ideas, as the whole of the Old Testament was seen as fulfilled in Christ: in the patristic writings we find the Christological application of Old Testament texts firmly established.

[7] See Chapter 5.

Christological formulations, then, derived from a sense of having experienced God's promised salvation in and through Jesus Christ. The force of this is to make Jesus the one intermediary through whom God is revealed, and the agent of God sent to effect God's promises. This agent sometimes seems a human person called or even adopted to fulfil God's purposes (adoptionism), sometimes a supernatural agent sent in human guise (e.g. 'angel-Christologies', usually implying docetism). So the material lends itself to hierarchical interpretation, and some 'titles' or 'names' ambiguously represent these intermediary positions: e.g. 'son of God' could refer to the king of Israel or the Messiah, or to any righteous person or to an angelic being. A similar intermediary position is assumed when concepts such as the Logos are employed, or indeed personified Wisdom. Neither the early fathers nor unreflective contemporary believers err in reading the New Testament in this way. New Testament Christology is not the Christology of the Chalcedonian Definition.

Yet, as we shall see, the deep intuition of the doctrinal tradition is that the hierarchical understanding simply is inadequate, as also an approach that endeavours to operate primarily 'from below'.

II The otherness of God

II.1 Hellenization radicalized by scripture

It was once a commonplace that Christianity lost its biblical thrust in the process of Hellenization. The biblical doctrine of resurrection gave way to the Greek idea of the soul's immortality. The dualism of Hellenic anthropology destroyed the biblical sense of a person's psychosomatic unity. God became a philosophical idea rather than the living God of the Bible. Earlier chapters challenged the former points: now I challenge the last, suggesting that the so-called Greek concept of God was itself profoundly radicalized by traditions grounded in key biblical texts combined with the doctrine of *creatio ex nihilo*. Indeed, there was a genuine kinship between Jewish monotheism and the emerging consensus of the philosophers, a kinship which Christian thinkers were able to discern and exploit to good effect.

All through the history of Greek philosophy the gods of literary myths and religious rituals were in the background, if not the foreground, of discussions concerning the divine, and it was by exposing the absurdities of anthropomorphism and idolatry, by anticipating Feuerbach's observation that religion is a human projection, that philosophical monotheism was reached. In their attacks on polytheism and idolatry Christian apologists used criticisms drawn from the philosophers to reinforce motifs borrowed from Judaism. Indeed, it is in the works of Clement of Alexandria that we find fragments from the presocratic philosopher, Xenophanes, showing that humans make gods in their own image:[8]

> Ethiopians make their gods black with turned-up noses, Thracians make them with red hair and blue eyes; mortals think that gods are born and have their own food, voice and shape, but if oxen or lions had hands and could draw or produce images like men, horses would draw the shapes of the gods like horses, oxen like oxen, and they would produce such bodies as the bodily frame they have themselves.

According to Clement, Xenophanes asserted that there must be one God who is quite unlike mortals in form and thought; other reports describe this God as eternal, unoriginated and impassible, as one and everything, as neither finite nor infinite, neither moved nor at rest, but the greatest and best of all things. Late witnesses may have distorted Xenophanes' vocabulary, but they clearly thought that his description anticipated Parmenides' One and the apophatic theology of later Platonism.

Thus, radical critique of anthropomorphism made a significant contribution to the development of the doctrine of a transcendent being with largely negative attributes. It can be argued, however, that included among those negative attributes were neither infinity nor

---

[8] Clement, *Stromateis* v.12.81–2.

incomprehensibility. Infinity was attributed to formless matter, for something without bounds could have no form or beauty, nor could it in principle be known, being necessarily indefinite. Platonism affirmed knowledge of God, grounded in the soul's kinship with the divine and possible when the soul is freed from the distracting chains of the body. So did many of the fathers, notably Clement and Origen.

Meanwhile, the critique of anthropomorphism can be paralleled in Jewish tradition by texts such as the brilliant parody of idolatry found in Isaiah 44:

> The carpenter...cuts down cedars...Half of it, he burns in the fire...He roasts meat...Also he warms himself and says, 'Aha, I am warm, I have seen the fire!' And the rest of it, he makes into his god...and worships it...he prays to it and says, 'Deliver me, for thou art my god!'

The prophets can be read as presenting a God impervious to influence through sacrifices and offerings, an eternal and unchangeable being. Jews never made images of God and never pronounced God's name, while their scriptures asserted that 'no one can see God and live',[9] and that God is beyond compare.[10]

> My thoughts are not your thoughts, neither are my ways your ways, says the Lord. For as the heavens are higher than the earth, so are my ways higher than your ways, and my thoughts higher than your thoughts.[11]

All this contributed to a theology which expressed radical transcendence. Indeed, words emphasizing God's otherness and incomparability were particularly characteristic of Hellenistic Judaism, and so entered Christian tradition: unapproachable, untraceable and inscrutable, incomprehensible. Many of the terms of Hellenistic Judaism and of philosophy overlapped, and in Christian tradition they tended to be amalgamated, as previously in Philo, so as to point

---

[9] E.g. Exodus 33.20.   [10] E.g. Isaiah 40.18, 25.   [11] Isaiah 55.8–9.

to a more ultimate transcendence than the mainstream Platonist tradition suggested. God in God's self came to be regarded as beyond human understanding, as well as beyond human language.

I would argue, then, that the Christian sense of God's otherness, if anything, was more Hebraic in its roots than Hellenic, its genesis arising from the fathers' attempt to make sense of scripture within a particular philosophical context. Repeatedly they referred to the passage where even Moses, the greatest prophet of all, with whom God used to speak face to face as one speaks to a friend,[12] could not see God's glory:

> I will make all my goodness pass before you . . . But you cannot see my face; for no one shall see me and live . . . While my glory passes by, I will put you in a cleft of the rock, and I will cover you with my hand until I have passed by; then I will take away my hand, and you shall see my back; but my face shall not be seen.[13]

It was the congruence of Hellenistic-Jewish with Platonic motifs which contributed to the Christian understanding of God as radically 'Other', a view only reinforced by the arguments which produced the doctrine of creation out of nothing.

11.2 Modern critique of the so-called Greek philosophical concept of God

Modern theologians have criticized the fathers for their adoption of the Greek philosophical notion of God and particularly called in question their commitment to God's impassibility. That young theologian in the 1970s wrote:

> For me, experience of suffering, sin, decay and abnormality as a constituent part of the world, would make belief in God impossible without a Calvary-centred religious myth. It is only because I can see

[12] Exodus 33.11.   [13] Exodus 33.18–23.

God entering the darkness of human suffering and evil in his creation, recognising it for what it really is, meeting it and conquering it, that I can accept a religious view of the world.[14]

In summary: 'God is to be understood as *a suffering God*, at least in the same sense as we can talk of him as loving.'[15] In adopting this position, I was aligned with Moltmann's then recently published book, *The Crucified God*,[16] and in agreement with Brian Hebblethwaite,[17] one of the critics of *The Myth of God Incarnate*: in the face of the world's ills, he said, 'only a suffering God is morally credible'. Indeed, such a position has been widely adopted among theologians and believers.[18]

However, I was brought up short on this issue at the colloquium gathered in the year after the publication of *The Myth of God Incarnate*. Basil Mitchell was the catalyst:

> As Frances Young points out, what we chiefly look for in people who could help us is the kind of sympathy which comes from their having suffered too. But . . . following through Frances Young's human analogy, so far as it can take us, we find that the people who can help us are not those who continue to be overwhelmed by suffering, but those who have in some way overcome it.[19]

---

[14] 'A Cloud of Witnesses' in Hick, *The Myth*, p. 34.

[15] *Ibid.*, p. 36 (italics original).

[16] Jürgen Moltmann, *The Crucified God: The Cross of Christ as the Foundation and Criticism of Christian Theology* (ET: R. A. Wilson and John Bowden, London: SCM Press, 1974).

[17] Brian Hebblethwaite, 'The Moral and Religious Value of the Incarnation' in Michael Goulder (ed.), *Incarnation and Myth: The Debate Continued* (London: SCM Press, 1979), p. 94.

[18] See e.g. Richard E. Creel, *Divine Impassibility* (Cambridge University Press, 1986); Paul S. Fiddes, *The Creative Suffering of God* (Oxford University Press, 1988); Paul Gavrilyuk, *The Suffering of the Impassible God: The Dialectics of Patristic Thought*, Oxford Early Christian Studies (Oxford University Press, 2004).

[19] Basil Mitchell, summing up in Goulder (ed.), *Incarnation and Myth*, p. 240.

The same point is made by Paul Gavrilyuk:

> Many compassionate actions do not require emotional identification with the sufferer. Consider the case of a compassionate doctor who needs to perform a sophisticated surgical procedure that may have fatal consequences for the patient. What is required from such a doctor is his ability to improve the situation of his patient . . . An act of compassion must always go beyond mere emotional reproduction of another's grief.[20]

The truth of this observation has become increasingly evident to me in forty-five years of caring for Arthur.[21] It has taken years to discern the high degree of self-concern endemic in anxiety and distress for another. Compassion requires a love which transcends anxiety, is calm and calming. 'A God who is a mere replica of suffering humanity is incapable of being a Redeemer,' says Gavrilyuk;[22] and to show that 'divine compassion far surpasses human compassion precisely because God is not overpowered by our suffering', he quotes Augustine:

> You, Lord God, lover of souls, show a compassion far purer and freer of mixed motives than ours; for no suffering injures you.

So God's *apatheia* is not necessarily a misconception. Even Moltmann acknowledges that *apatheia* was important in opposing the capriciousness of the gods and establishing God's all-sufficient freedom.[23] 'Apathetic' or 'impassive' was never meant by the word *apathēs*; it was always consonant with affirmation of God's goodness, justice, love and providential care – indeed, guaranteed the constancy of these. As John Chrysostom put it:

> If the wrath of God were a passion, a person might well despair as being unable to quench the flame which he had kindled by so many

---

[20] Gavrilyuk, *Suffering of the Impassible God*, pp. 9–10. This work makes similar arguments to my own for a reappraisal of patristic notions about God's *apatheia*.
[21] Cf. Chapter 6.   [22] *Suffering of the Impassible God*, p. 13.
[23] Moltmann, *The Crucified God*, p. 268.

evil doings; but since the divine nature is passionless, even if He punishes, even if He takes vengeance, He does this not with wrath, but with tender care, and much loving-kindness.[24]

Gavrilyuk demonstrates that divine *apatheia* was simply an 'apophatic qualifier', signifying that 'God is unlike everything else, and therefore acts and suffers action in a manner different from everything else'.

Many modern theologians, assuming that *apatheia* implies insensitivity like a stone,[25] have deduced that the notion prevents genuine relationship. Asserting that with 'the message of the cross of Christ something new and strange has entered the metaphysical world', Moltmann charged the fathers with failing to grasp this because of their attachment to *apatheia*.[26] But, for the fathers, anxieties about Patripassianism were instrumental in argumentation for the very doctrine of the Trinity to which Moltmann later resorts: Tertullian's quip against Praxeas, 'he crucifies the Father and puts the Paraclete to flight', is notorious. As for Christology, the God-forsakenness suffered by Christ on the cross made resort to paradox inevitable – Cyril proclaimed *apathōs epathen* (he suffered unsufferingly). The problem of divine passion was so important to the formation of Christian doctrinal discourse it surely demands our attention.

Moltmann's fire was trained not just on *apatheia*, but embraced the whole 'philosophical concept of God, according to which God's being is incorruptible, unchangeable, indivisible, incapable of suffering and immortal'.[27] This apophatic concept he conflated with theism, charging Western theology with being 'no more than a weakly Christianised monotheism',[28] readily susceptible to critique from protest atheism and in the end the equivalent of idolatry. In my view,

---

[24] Quoted by Gavrilyuk, *Suffering of the Impassible God*, p. 62: Chrysostom, *Ad Theodorum* I.4.

[25] Cf. Jerome on Evagrius: discussion in Chapter 6.

[26] *The Crucified God*, pp. 215, 229.   [27] *Ibid.*, p. 228.   [28] *Ibid.*, p. 236.

too, the theism of Western philosophical theology has tended to produce an idolatrous notion of God, easily caricatured as a 'superman'
projected onto the heavens, omnipotent, omniscient and, of course,
masculine. Yet surely it is precisely the apophatic tradition, fostered
so much better in Eastern theology and liturgy, which provides a
corrective. The sense of God's utter otherness enhances the amazing generosity of the divine grace which, withdrawing in love and
self-emptying in humility, allows things other than the divine self to
exist, and then loves to the end.

Significantly, the sense of God's utter otherness may prove to be
a converting notion. Thomas Merton was a typical young man in
the interwar years, sceptical about religion (especially as he could
discern in it the projection of human anxieties and desires), full of
the joys of life, ambitious, sociable, but also open-minded enough to
read a little mediaeval philosophy.[29] There he discovered the 'aseity'
of God: the fact that God is, as Latin would put it, *a se*, 'of himself',
not dependent on anyone or anything – that God just is, and is the
divine self, not what we project onto him. In other words, God needs
no defender. Merton could not turn his back on such a God. After
years of struggling with the theodicy questions raised by the birth of
Arthur, release came in grasping the same point in a radical way –
God's existence no longer depended on my capacity to believe it! The
moment remains vivid; I remember precisely what chair I was sitting
in, that I was sitting on the edge of it, ready to get up to go and do
something in the kitchen, when a 'loud thought' came into my head:
'It doesn't make any difference to me whether you believe in me or
not.' I had a sense of being stunned, of being put in my place. Nothing
dramatic happened, but since that moment I have not seriously
doubted God's reality. God confronted me as utter otherness. I guess
Job's answer is somewhat similar: Job couldn't let God be God, but
trapped God in his questions, until confronted with the divine reality.

---

[29] Thomas Merton, *Elected Silence: The Autobiography of Thomas Merton* (London:
Hollis and Carter, 1949), p. 139.

III Mediation

III.1 Mediation without hierarchy

In the pre-Nicene period there was little appreciation of the implications of that radicalized apophatic theology, let alone its consequences when brought into relation with the doctrine of creation out of nothing. To take both seriously would mean the dissolution of the hierarchical model, and the recognition of the absolute gulf between the ultimate divine nature and created orders of being, including angels. It would no longer be any good appealing to the kinship of the soul with the divine to guarantee an intuitive grasp of God; only through God's grace, God's initiative, God's will to reveal the divine self, could the gulf be bridged.

These issues would be clarified by the prolonged debates generated by the controversy labelled Arian. Those arguments exposed the hierarchical model's incompatibility with the radicalized otherness of God and the notion of creation out of nothing. The Logos could no longer be treated as an intermediary being, linking in a hierarchy the one God with the many diverse orders of creation: either the Logos was 'the first and greatest of the creatures', as Arius suggested, or he was 'of one substance with the Father' as the Nicene Creed stated – in other words, the underlying issue concerned the question on which side of the gulf the Logos should be situated. This question was not explicitly put by either side – my observation is more systematic than historical; but the underlying issue between Arius and Athanasius was whether the Logos incarnate in Jesus belongs to the divine or created order, a question which was bound to shatter the traditional Logos-theology and create what we know as the Christological problem. The evolutionary model which posits 'development of doctrine' is inadequate, because post-Nicene theology had to be innovative. It was innovative precisely in taking account of the consequences of elements in Christian theology perceived to be key to its structure.

So the questions were posed in a new way, and it was only by embracing novelty that theological thought could do justice to tradition in the new situation. It was surely inconceivable that the Logos of God was created out of nothing, or that the generation of the Logos divided the divine substance, or that Father and Son were simply two faces of the One God. This last issue had already had an outing in the so-called Monarchian controversies, and there was deep suspicion of Sabellianism. It is hardly surprising that for fifty years people struggled to hold on to traditional confessions, but, as we discovered earlier,[30] the focus on ideas such as 'Image', or even 'Son', did little to resolve the problems. It was necessary to resort to non-scriptural terms to safeguard what scripture was about, as Athanasius showed in his defence of the *homoousios*. Hierarchical assumptions could no longer stand. Mediation had to be reconceived. The incarnation somehow had to be the union of two utterly different natures, the fully divine Logos assuming truly human being, so as to mediate across the gulf of otherness. So the classic definition of the person of Christ was arrived at by a process of debate and controversy leading up to the council of Chalcedon in AD 451. The agreed statement affirmed that Jesus Christ was truly God and truly Man. So it was established that this was the true meaning of scripture and creed.

III.2 *Defending the Chalcedonian Definition*

It's been claimed, notably by John Hick, that the Chalcedonian Definition is incoherent, a logical impossibility like the square circle: indeed, he would state that no one has ever satisfactorily given an account of what this statement means in practice.[31] I now hazard an account of Christian claims about Jesus which might go some way to making sense of them, at least for those who take seriously the notion that theology is faith seeking understanding, and that there

---

[30] Chapter 4.   [31] See Hick, *The Myth* and Goulder, *Incarnation and Myth.*

are some givens with which we need to work. The classic definition, in my view, makes the right connections, because what we call
Christology, the doctrine of Christ's person, is inextricably bound
up with all other doctrines, with Christian understanding of human
nature, of creation and redemption, of God's nature, of worship and
spirituality.

The Chalcedonian Definition has an important analytical thrust.
Things or persons are necessarily defined over against other things
or persons. To define is to determine boundaries. Like Adam naming
the animals, a child points and names things in its environment. This
differentiation is the only way to know things; the process of trying
to name different birds or flowers, for example, leads to a much finer
perception of the particular detailed characteristics of each, as well
as enabling recognition.

Ancient philosophy was dominated by the issue: what exactly is
this? Is it to be defined in terms of the matter out of which it is
composed? Or the particular characteristics that make it what it
is and not something else? If the latter, is it the features it has in
common with other examples of the same thing, or those which it
distinctively has itself, in its particularity? Or is it what it is because
of what it will become? This meant the question of a thing's being or
substance was the prime analytical question.

Some have dismissed Chalcedon because it is framed in so-called
outdated substance language, or in static ontological terms. But early
in my theological formation, I learnt from Donald MacKinnon that
that suggestion fails to grasp what 'substance' is about. It's a question
about what exactly a thing is. I suppose we would put the same issues
in terms of identity. It is naive to think that modern believers have
never wondered about the identity of Jesus Christ, or been puzzled
about the claim that he is to be identified as God and as Man. Could
a particular living creature be identified as both gnat and elephant?

The analytical argument reached an apparently impossible paradox. God was not to be confused with any other existent thing. God's
identity and the identity of everything else were each defined by

contrast with one another, by differentiation. In the debates immediately preceding the council more than anything else controversy
was fuelled by concern to preserve the 'Godness' of God, the 'otherness' of the divine. Established as characteristic of Christianity was a
fundamental analytical distinction which required the exclusion of
inadequate accounts of the identity of Jesus Christ as either some
kind of mediating being – neither fish nor fowl, we might say – or as
a confusion between God and humanity. That distinction remains
vital for Christian theology. Also the genuine humanness of Jesus
needs preserving against the persistent tendency of popular Christianity to divinize him in a way analogous to pagan mythology – to
that extent, I couldn't ever go back on what I argued in *The Myth
of God Incarnate*. The analytical process remains essential. To put it
in the language of Chalcedon, there are two distinct natures, divine
and human, which we dare not confuse, and yet we find, perhaps to
our embarrassment, that we have to assert that Jesus Christ has to
be identified as being wholly both.

Yet Chalcedon worked in the end, I suggest, because the differentiation of Creator from creature meant that the divine nature was
conceived, insofar as it was possible to conceive it at all, by contrast
with created beings. So it did not suffer from the same limitations
as created entities. Place and shape, time and structure, and most
certainly gender, were regarded as irrelevant to the totally 'other'
nature of the divine Being; therefore there was no contradiction in
the divine, as it were, occupying the same space as another entity.
Divine Being could be both differentiated from and yet identified
with another being – one on which God had chosen to put the divine
name.[32] God could be envisaged as transcending human nature, but
even so human nature could mirror God, even receive God's impress,
while God could accommodate the divine self to human form, and
express the divine communication in human language. Through
overlaying concepts and images, through the metaphor of the divine

[32] Cf. 1 Kings 14.21.

389

imprint, through a sense of interpenetration, mediation could be understood, not in terms of a 'semi-divine' being, or a 'mixture', but in terms of the whole character of God being 'imaged' in a wholly human medium.

The structure of Christian belief, I suggest, demands such an account of the person of Christ. Christ's uniqueness is constituted by the fact that this overlay of divine and human was not in any sense accidental: here was not the adoption of a good man, or the mere inspiration of a prophet, but God's will to stamp the divine imprint on human nature, to re-create the divine image in humanity. Christ is therefore unique, but not disconnected. The truly divine and archetypal Word and Wisdom, Image and Son was the basis of creaturely participation in God's own Word and Wisdom, Image and Sonship.[33] The ambiguities of 'image' may not have resolved the issues, but once the analysis had been established, it did facilitate synthesis. A kind of overlay of meanings became possible – Jesus Christ as the image of God is a statement about:

(i) the perfect humanity which God intended being realized in Jesus

(ii) the possibility of our humanity being transformed so that it, too, becomes God's image – the 'selfsame image' as Christ[34]

(iii) the immanence of the divine Wisdom in all creation, the presence of God's own glory

(iv) the divine Son being the spitting image of his Father.[35]

The notion of God's image belongs to a synthetic way of thinking. It involves metaphors about mirrors and reflections, about the imprint of seal in wax – for it is by giving us the Spirit of Jesus in our hearts as a first instalment that God has anointed us and sealed us.[36] The Pauline material encouraged the idea that human nature may be

---

[33] Cf. Chapter 4.   [34] 2 Corinthians 3.18.

[35] For patristic discussion of these overlaid themes, see Chapter 4.

[36] 2 Corinthians 1.21–2; cf. Ephesians 1.13.

stamped with the divine imprint, through and in Christ; and the divine imprint is as real as the human wax.

The apparent paradox of two natures which coinhere without confusion, a natural impossibility which, as the fathers kept indicating, cannot be conceived by such analogies as mixing wine and water, or combining sugar and flour, is the only way of expressing the identity and significance of Jesus Christ. In the end the fathers faced at Chalcedon a theological problem very similar to the problems about creation raised earlier. God has to be conceived as in some sense withdrawing, yet supremely present, both in the act of creation, and on the cross. God is not a cause alongside other causes, but a love of such generosity it can abandon and be abandoned. God is both beyond suffering and deeply implicated in it, and, as an aspect of God's otherness, *apatheia* enables passion. The 'two natures' analysis is essential for grasping both the enormity of the incarnation and its very possibility.

IV God-talk: knowing the unknowable as Trinity

IV.1 *The nature of religious language according to the fathers*

The utter otherness of God necessitated reflection on how to articulate the inevitable paradoxes generated – the oddities of simultaneous passibility and impassibility, absence and presence. Religious language became an issue for the fathers. The Cappadocian treatment of this theme is sophisticated, with a double thrust: on the one hand, it is possible to speak of God because God has accommodated the divine self to our level, and, insofar as it may be expressed in human language, what God has articulated cannot be other than true; on the other hand, it is always inadequate. So human language has to be stretched beyond its natural meaning, metaphor and symbol are unavoidable, and, above all, no single statement can capture the reality of God and one statement has to be counter-balanced by another. Thus paradox is as essential to theological discourse as the humility of the theologian explored earlier.[37]

IV.1.1 God's indefinability

It was Eunomius who concentrated minds. Like Arius, Eunomius defined God as *agenētos*, that is, as the one being who had never come into being; then he insisted that therefore the one begotten (*gennētos*) of the Father was other than God. The Cappadocian response was to examine the whole question of definition.

Gregory Nazianzen distinguished between God's existence and God's essence, arguing that while the former is incontestable, the latter is indefinable and incomprehensible. None of the negative terms of apophatic theology, Gregory argues,[38] can tell us what God is in the divine being and *hypostasis*; their opposites – corporeal, mortal, begotten, etc. – may be used of a man, a horse or a cow; we need to know what the subject is in order to present these objects clearly to the mind. Eunomius' claim to know God on the basis of defining God as *agenētos* is therefore false. God's being is beyond our grasp and comprehension: indeed, the mind has no resting place as it seeks to contemplate the depths above, and it is impossible to get to the end of the divine.[39] God's incomprehensibility is no longer attributed to the inadequacies of the imperfect mind, but to the infinite nature of God's very being, a position associated also with Gregory of Nyssa.

Thus the apophatic tradition reached its epitome, and the possibility both of religious language and of religious knowledge was denied. The denial was partly philosophical: there is no logic common to ordinary language and language used of the divine. But it was also religious: a God worthy of worship is beyond comparison with anything derivative from the Creator. Chrysostom, too,

---

[37] Chapter 4.   [38] *Oration* 28.   [39] *Ibid.* 38.

preaching against Eunomius, stressed the religious awe inspired by the one beyond speech or knowledge.[40]

IV.1.2 God-talk and the Trinity

So how is the theologian to speak of God at all? As already observed,[41] Gregory of Nazianzus expected the mind of the theologian to be stripped of pretentiousness, affirming that the nature of the First Being surpasses the power of mind. Yet in the following discourses Gregory is able to discuss many names given to God and give a detailed account of relationships within the Trinity. Does he provide any clue as to how he can use religious language when his previous discussion suggested its impossibility?

The only explicit clue in Gregory's theological orations is his statement that God is known not in his essence but in his attributes or activities (*energeiai*):

> The divine cannot be named . . . For no one has ever breathed the whole air, nor has any mind located, or language contained, the Being of God completely. But sketching God's inward self from outward characteristics, we may assemble an inadequate, weak and partial picture. And the one who makes the best theologian is not the one who knows the whole truth . . . but the one who creates the best picture, who assembles more of truth's image or shadow.[42]

On this basis Gregory proceeds to list significant names of the God-head and of each person within it, distinguishing names which are of God's essence and names which are relative to his creatures.

Gregory of Nyssa grounded his theory of religious language in a general theory of language: all language depends upon created human speech, and the existence of different languages is a clear

---

[40] *On the Incomprehensibility of God*: Greek text: A. M. Malingrey, *Jean Chrysostome: Sur l'incomprehensibilité de Dieu, SC.*
[41] Chapter 4.   [42] *Oration* 30.

indication that God allowed humankind the freedom to invent and develop linguistic expression.[43] So 'whereas no one suitable word has been found to express the divine nature, we address God by many names, each by some distinctive touch adding something fresh to our notions of him'. However, 'we do not say that the nature of things was a human invention, but only their names'. Furthermore, the names of God are more than a figment of the human imagination; though God has to accommodate the divine self to the limitations of human perception, God cannot be a party to deception, so creation and scripture are expressive of God's will and God's truth.

So when scripture honours the only begotten with the same names as the Father, it must imply that he shares the dignity and honour of the Godhead. Besides, if the Word of God names God the Father, God must, eternally and unchangeably, really have been Father, and therefore must have had a Son. However, 'we think of human generation one way; we surmise of the divine generation in another', for in the case of divine generation, the mind has to reject notions of sex and passion, of time and place, and think simply of the Son as being eternally derived from the Father. Indeed, so wide is the gulf between Creator and creature, finite and infinite, that different attributes or names have to be associated together in order to correct one another. This process of counter-balance lies at the heart of Gregory's discussion of religious language: 'because ... there is no appropriate term to be found to mark the subject adequately, we are compelled by many and differing names ... to divulge our surmises ... with regard to the deity'. Yet, even though 'the infinity of God exceeds all the significance and comprehension that names can furnish', if such names are truly predicable of God, they should be understood in their most natural and obvious sense, though with a heightened and more glorious meaning. The names have sufficient

---

[43] The source is Gregory's *Against Eunomius*, principally Book I (Jaeger's enumeration; II in *NPNF*); detailed references may be found in 'The God of the Greeks'.

grounding in reality, then, to form a basis for theological argument. What is needed is a way of reaching beyond the human level; paradox, or the counter-balancing of one notion with its opposite, provides a way of doing that.

Thus the two Gregories adopted into the new Nicene framework Origen's analysis of the many *epinoiai* of Christ,[44] together with his distinction between names attributed absolutely or relatively to the Logos. This enabled them to treat human language as symbolic, but also to draw meaningful conclusions and make significant distinctions: God, for example, is understood to be Father absolutely in relation to the Son, but only relatively in relation to creatures. Theology only produces a partial picture of divine reality, and the meaning of religious language is only made clear by endless qualifications, but, through attributes revealed by God, some grasp is made possible. The biblical narratives, treated imaginatively rather than literally, can become luminous of the divine reality beyond human expression; and the complete incarnation of one who was by nature totally transcendent was the crown of God's loving accommodation to humankind, and the triumph of sheer grace which enabled humanity's assimilation to God. The possibility of religious language was now located not in any natural kinship to the divine, but in God's will to create and redeem; and the symbolic character of religious language was no longer confined to allegorical exegesis, but was fully recognized in formal theology.

IV.1.3 The Trinity and the 'economy'

This discussion of religious language illuminates the distinction found in Gregory Nazianzen between *theologia* and *oikonomia*. This has usually been taken to correspond, roughly speaking, with the distinction in systematic theology between the immanent Trinity and

---

[44] See Chapter 5.

the economic Trinity. But this has been contested by Christopher Beeley,[45] who argues that:

> Through faith, one comes to recognise that Jesus Christ and the Holy Spirit, who have been met in the economy of salvation, share fully in the divinity of God the Father. This act of confessing the divinity of the Father, Son, and Holy Spirit in the economy of salvation Gregory typically calls "theology" (*theologia*). The doctrine of the Trinity builds on the "theology" of the Son and the Spirit, not simply in the obvious sense that it combines Father, Son and Spirit to make a unity of three persons, but in that it expresses the meaning that the divine economy has possessed all along.[46]

Thus, Beeley offers a profound challenge to 'the consensus of Eastern and Western interpreters'. True, 'theology does concern the transcendent life of God . . . but it is always based on God's revelation in the divine economy'. The transcendent God is not to be separated from the God revealed – there is no 'extra-economic theology'.[47]

This reading of Gregory's position is important. It affirms the generous love with which God accommodates the utterly other divine self to the level of its own creatures not only in order to communicate, but also in such a way as to assimilate them to the divine through *theōsis*. Knowledge of the Trinity through God's *energeiai* breaks open the logic of human reason, challenges the notion that God, though simple, is not simply simple, and invites into an unexpected and profoundly humbling relationship of love and communion. The 'sketch' discerned in the *oikonomia* is true to the reality of God in God's own self – the gulf is there, but not unbridged, since God takes the initiative to bridge it. The reality of the divine is truly communicated through scripture, through the incarnation and

---

[45] Christopher Beeley, *Gregory of Nazianzus on the Trinity and the Knowledge of God* (Oxford University Press, 2008).

[46] *Ibid.*, pp. 194–5.   [47] *Ibid.*, pp. 197–200.

through the experience of the Spirit in the life of the church. So it was that in the face of Eunomius' logic the Cappadocians articulated a Trinitarian position which embraced both the otherness and the providential presence of God.

IV.2 *Discerning and speaking of God as Trinity now*

Our theological problem, emerging from earlier chapters, lies exactly there: how is it that God is providentially present within a created order which implies God's absence? Key clues I pick up from the fathers, especially that deep connection between *theologia* and *oikonomia*, a connection grounded in God's primary initiative – to reach across the gulf of otherness, to choose to put God's name on particular things, places or persons, to teach us a language in which to address God through scripture and liturgy, to visit us in person so as to enter into a relationship with us. It is because we are on the receiving end of these acts of grace that we can begin to reflect and connect and contemplate the mysterious reality which gave us our being and encompasses us. We therefore have to begin where we are with the resources we've been given, with pondering scripture and ascertaining the first principles of the theological enterprise, then letting it all be a response of heart and mind to the generous love of God. The outcome for us, as for the fathers, will be an affirmation of God as Trinity.

IV.2.1 Liturgy and the Trinity

Starting from where we are, then, and discerning clues through the *oikonomia*, as Gregory did, we confess the Trinity in accordance with the liturgical life of the church. So we speak first of the Creator, the God who let us be and allowed us to be ourselves, who with a maternal love yearns for us and invites us to respect him as Father. We then speak of one who is truly Son of the Father, enabling us through his incarnation to become adopted sons and heirs (whatever our gender), to be one Body with him, and to participate in his God-likeness. Also we speak of our sanctification through the Spirit in the life of the church, of the recognition of God's approach through the Spirit's inspiration of the scriptures, of our discernment of God's presence through the faces of those in whom the fruits of the Spirit are maturing and in the mutuality of communion with them and with God. Shaped by the tradition of the church, we thus begin with the *energeiai* of God within the *oikonomia*. Yet when we consider the Divine Nature, it is necessarily to stretch human language and comprehension through *theōria* (contemplation, insight, discernment) so as to provide a sketch of what is in principle beyond us; it is to offer *dogma* (teaching), not in the spirit of laying down precisely in propositions exactly what the truth is, but rather in the way of inviting ourselves and others to contemplate the implications of what we have seen of God's *energeiai* in the *oikonomia* – after all the doctrine of the Trinity was actually formulated in reaction against claims to define God with precision.

So Trinitarianism needs to be pragmatic rather than speculative, theoretic rather than dogmatic, yet celebratory and confident because God is to be trusted. It needs to accept the way in which it can never be pinned down and seems always elusive. The Cappadocians suggested that the Christian understanding of God was a 'mean' between monotheism and polytheism; perhaps we need to insist that doctrines of the social Trinity are never adequate without the corrective of monotheism, while the theistic philosophical theology traditional in the West constantly needs as its counterbalance the celebration of the Trinity which pervades the liturgy of the Eastern church. By a multiplicity of pictures and outlines one approach corrects or counter-balances another. By deep contemplation of metaphors and symbols God's character may be discerned in scripture. By participation in worship paradox takes on reality and the Spirit bears witness with our spirit that we are God's children.

IV.2.2 A 'personal' God?

This counter-balancing of statements, so as to sketch a divine reality which is in principle elusive, surely has an important bearing on the use of the language of personhood with reference to God, as well as the claim of some believers to have a personal relationship with God. There are several related questions here:

- If 'personhood' is taken to be a fundamental category for articulating God's nature, how can one avoid anthropomorphism?
- If one denies personhood to God, does one not reduce the divine to an impersonal force with which relationship is impossible?
- How does the claim that God is 'personal' relate to the traditional language about God being 'in Three Persons'? And in any case, isn't the idea of person very different now compared with what was meant in antiquity?

The Cappadocian ways of stretching human language, and of using paradox and a multiplicity of differing images and metaphors to speak of God, bears on these questions in that it highlights the inadequacy of any one definition of the nature of God and implies that personal language is to be constantly balanced by other images, always to be treated as indicative and sketchy, pointing to something beyond what we understand. Thus the unity of the three Persons of the Trinity is not to be understood straightforwardly as three distinct personalities in a close relationship of love – the social Trinity is far too much like tritheism. Yet the notion that God is love may evoke a union in communion of individual beings (*hypostases*) who are not discrete individual persons as we know them, but are constituted as themselves by their very relationship of co-inherence. In Chapter 4, we found Zizioulas distinguishing between being a person and being an individual or personality precisely on the grounds that persons become what they are in relationships: 'the mystery of being a person lies in the fact that here otherness and communion are not in contradiction, but coincide'. If relationship is key to human personhood, how much more key to divine personhood, given the gracious gifts of God's generous love mediated to us! Yet to get an inkling of Trinitarian relationships, our limited experience of finding and losing ourselves in mutual love for an other has to be stretched into the unknown, ungraspable reality of divine unity and simplicity.

V *Oikonomia* – sacramental presence

v.1 *God's 'accommodation' to creatures*

If God's astonishing outreach to the *oikonomia* is fundamental to Trinitarianism, how much more is this the case with respect to Christology? In the Christological controversy between Cyril of Alexandria and the so-called Antiochenes, both sides were advancing critically important elements in the understanding of Christ. The Antiochene tradition has often been characterized in twentieth-century scholarship as upholding the true humanity of Christ, but examination of the texts indicates that they were as concerned, if not more concerned, to defend the 'Godness' of God. The reaffirmation of the Nicene *homoousion* in 381 meant that the Logos had to be conceived of as sharing in the utter otherness and transcendence of God – so the whole process of the incarnate life became highly problematical, especially Christ's suffering and death. How could the changeless change? It was to safeguard the divine nature that the human nature had to be more roundly affirmed. Yet that risked bringing the gulf between Creator and created right into the heart of the Christ. Cyril was not entirely incorrect in his caricatures – in the end there is a sense in which the parameters of the discussion necessitated 'Two Sons'. Cyril himself, however, was justifiably charged with attributing change to the changeless, as he insisted that it was truly the Logos himself who was the subject of the incarnate experiences and actions.

The nub of the issue was how to do justice to the divine initiative in not merely affirming the goodness of the material world, but in actually accommodating the divine self to its limitations, the Son of God taking upon himself the nature of humankind, so that its eschatological destiny might be fulfilled. In some ways, prior to the controversy, the Cappadocians anticipated what was needed, opposing the Apollinarian solution whereby the Logos enfleshed lacked a human mind while resisting the idea of 'Two Sons'. Their Christology is hard to place in the categories of the subsequent controversy; the terms in which the debate was couched, with philosophical language used in different ways by the two sides and all kinds of muddle about different kinds of mixture and combination, obscured rather than clarified what was fundamentally necessary. Somehow the utterly other God remained other – or, to put this in terms used earlier, God's absence or withdrawal was essential to the existence of anything other than God. Yet (whether or not we can find a language or conceptuality adequate to this) a being who remains the utterly other God has also to be affirmed as becoming a particular human creature. Indispensable to the particular narrative found in the scriptures is a way of counter-balancing, on one side, two distinct natures, on the other, the *kenōsis* whereby the Logos becomes the subject of all the incarnate experiences through 'becoming flesh' or 'taking the form of a servant'.

Somehow, then, the interests of both Cyril and his opponents had to be accommodated, and to that extent the Chalcedonian Definition may be treated as a historic compromise. But knowingly or unknowingly, the fathers were doing rather more than meets the eye; they were shaping a statement which ultimately structures Christian theology across a broad range of fronts. Doctrines are not discrete but encapsulated within one another, and Christology becomes the example *par excellence* of the deeply incomprehensible ways in which God relates to the created order. Indeed, within the structure of Christian theology, Christology is the lynchpin. Christ is God, and is other than God. The bread and wine of the eucharist is bread and wine, and yet also the body and blood of Christ. The words of human beings, physically recorded in the scriptures by fallible authors, are not, and yet are, the Word of God. The church is the body of Christ, and yet evidently a flawed human institution. The two natures may never be confused; yet they interpenetrate in ways beyond human analysis, effecting the sacramental presence of God within the very created order whose existence and freedom depends on the divine absence.

So, structurally, patristic Christology is a significant element in the resolution of the question how the Creator relates to the creation. God is and is not present everywhere in the created order. God chooses to put the divine name on, and to be present in, with and through particular things, events and persons, despite the divine otherness, yet in accordance with the possibilities which that otherness allows. The incarnation is and is not the supreme exemplification of God's engagement with the *oikonomia* – it is, because it displays *par excellence* the features of providential provision and fulfilment, vocation and election; it is not, because it is the unique embodiment of God's accommodation by *kenōsis* to the conditions of creatureliness. And those statements reflect the apparently incompatible positions of Cyril and the Antiochenes in proper counter-balance.

v.2 A theology of presence for today

If we begin from where we are, with science and its inductive methods dominant, then providence, miracle, prophecy, special revelation and prayer, along with anything suggesting God's direct intervention in the world, modernity has long since deemed highly problematical. Not only nature's apparently self-determined order, but also the challenge of theodicy, make it implausible to deduce God from the world as it is and possible to explain away claims to exceptional interventions of the divine. God's *energeiai* within the *oikonomia* are hardly identifiable. This is reinforced by the accepted outcomes of biblical criticism and by the application of the historico-critical method to the development of Christian doctrine, with the resultant rehabilitation of heretics and recognition that the creeds were honed through such exercise of power and political manoeuvring as casts doubt on any kind of providential guidance to the truth. Thus doctrinal criticism became a respectable academic project, and there has been open season on rethinking outcomes such as the Chalcedonian Definition. The fathers, though challenged by the notion of the transcendent God directly interacting with the material creation, did not face in the same way the empiricist demand for evidence which trumps all counter-evidence when it comes to claims about God's action in the world.

Symptomatic of the empirically minded tradition of theology in the Anglican-dominated universities of 1980s Britain was the debate in Oxford concerning God's activity in the world. Attempting to forge a philosophical theology from a base that took biblical criticism seriously, David Brown[48] relied on two fundamental positions: (i) that theism, as distinct from deism, requires an intervening God; (ii) that 'core experiences compel an interventionist dialogue model of revelation'. One target of Brown's critique was Maurice Wiles, whose position Brown treated as deistic. Wiles responded with his Bampton Lectures.[49] Both see religious experience as problematic, yet crucial, to the issue whether divine agency can be identified, and both presume that agency implies divine personhood. What drives Wiles' resistance to 'claims about particular, specifiable acts of God' is that such 'traditional understanding of God's providential direction of history' necessarily 'leads us back to the all controlling God who does not respect the freedom of the world he has created'. For both, Christology provides the crucial paradigm test, and both challenge the tendency to isolate incarnation as a 'startling exception to the uniform pattern of God's relation to the world'. Their difference lies in Brown's insistence on a pattern of interventions, over against Wiles' insistence on the single action of God in bringing into being and sustaining a world such as the world is.

---

[48] David Brown, *The Divine Trinity* (London: Duckworth, 1985).
[49] Maurice Wiles, *God's Action in the World* (London: SCM Press, 1986).

Perhaps asking about intervention is the wrong question. For the fathers, God's *energeiai* were constantly engaged, and miracles were not defined as arbitrary acts over-riding natural laws, but were received as amazing clues to the underlying reality of God's loving wisdom in managing the universe, of God's constant holding of all things in being, and continuing gracious involvement in providential and sanctifying activities. If beginning from where we are involves adopting empirical starting-points, then it is remarkably easy to run into difficulties when specifying God's activity: if I can point to good outcomes from the life of Arthur, does that remove God's responsibility for not preventing the tragedy of his malformation in the first place? If, however, we begin, as the fathers did, with the notion of God's utter otherness, then the issue of God's causality in relation to secondary causes is perhaps put on a different footing. Inevitably, all that the empiricist can see is secondary causes. Discernment of anything else relies on God's initiative – the opening of eyes and unblocking of ears, so that *theōria* (a kind of 'seeing through') is made possible, and ordinary things become extraordinary. The human mind generally tends to dissect and analyse – to find clarification through 'either–or'. But the fathers suggest other possibilities, by their resort to counter-balancing or synthesizing things that seem to be opposites, and by their recognition of the inadequacy of all language and conceptuality for God. Maybe both deism and theism should be relativized by a Trinitarianism which acknowledges the need to complexify the notion of God's personhood (as argued earlier), while affirming the generous love and union in communion that lie at the heart of all existence.

My intellectual journey from the empiricist starting-point to such a theological position has been shaped by the coming together of three crucial factors:

- the move from struggling with theodicy to seeing that, through Arthur, I have privileged access to the deepest truths of Christianity

- the discernment of God's reality in the living faith and worship of ordinary people in diverse congregations and communities, in ecumenical communion with those who are 'other', and particular surprise encounters with life-changing implications
- professional engagement with the theology of the fathers.

I am not alone, of course, in engaging in the post-modern project of critical appropriation of pre-modern understanding. But let me reiterate three points which open a path beyond the modernity with which my journey began.

(1) God's essential otherness is precisely what makes the transcendence and immanence of the divine possible. Neither can be fully grasped by our ape-like brains; yet it seems likely that our super-large brains may have developed in order to cope with intimate relationship,[50] which implies the possibility of openness to others and so to an imaginative grasp of a Being with a unique relationship with everything that is.

(2) God's presence and providence are to be seen as themselves aspects of the divine otherness. Neither can be like the presence or purposive action of created beings: God is not an item alongside other items in the universe, nor a cause alongside, prior to, or constitutive of other causes. 'Interventionism' assumes that the self-determined natural order is a closed reality, occasionally disrupted by God poking his finger in, as it were; but the 'clockwork' analogy has long since given way to a recognition of the complexity and plasticity of things, within which the potential influence of the divine Other may not necessarily be ruled out as a hidden factor. It is often by hindsight that the workings of providence are discerned, perhaps precisely because it is found in the enigmatic but consistent way in which God makes provision for the outworking of the divine purposes and seeks to rescue the situation when things go awry. Though with reserve,

---

[50] Dunbar, *How Many Friends?* See Chapter 3.

we may speak of this anthropomorphically, because God is ever accommodating the divine self to our level and our situation, seeking our response to that wise and generous love.

(3) The absence or withdrawal of God, posited in Chapter 2 under the influence of Simone Weil, is not meant to imply deism – with the cosmos wound up and left to get on with it. Rather, it is presented as the prior condition for the existence of beings other than God, and therefore the necessary condition for relationship between 'others', as distinct from the coercive absorption of creatures within the deity. It is perhaps no accident that the freedom, both of God and of God's creatures, has been a major issue in modern theology. 'Letting go' is the prior condition of any relationship of love, and love is free gracious mutual opening up to an 'other'.[51]

Now each of these points to God as other, and so to worship as the essential context within which God is in relationship with people, individually and corporately. The potential openness of this complex and plastic creation to its Creator is paralleled by the deep and mysterious openness of the human being as it prays to one 'unto whom all hearts are open, all desires known, and from whom no secrets hidden'. These things demand intellectual humility. I am struck by the emphasis in the *Apostolic Fathers* on this interior aspect of God's reality, by the implications of Psalm 139, by the development of 'mental prayer' in the tradition of Christian spirituality. I am struck too by the oddity of strange concatenations of thoughts – even of events, which the modernist would dismiss as coincidences – as if there were divine 'nudges'. Even more intriguing is the experience of looking back over a life and discerning how things not only fit into a pattern, but seem strangely to lead up to a vocation, tragedy itself turning into blessing. So I honour my Methodist forebears who sought God's guidance by applying scripture to their circumstances and respect

[51] Cf. Haught, *God after Darwin.*

them for their unconscious continuation of the patristic traditions of
typological reading. The otherness of God means God's absence, the
impossibility of identifying discrete manifestations of God among
the web of physical and mental events which make up our lives.
Yet there are 'means of grace' whereby God's presence and providence may be discerned through the *oikonomia*. Through scripture,
through liturgy, through human relationships in the worshipping
community, God's outreach to us in incarnation and inspiration is
traceable.

VI Word and Wisdom – scripture and doctrine

VI.1 *Doctrine and scripture in the fathers*

So far, then, we have observed that Nicene theology required the
end of hierarchical thinking and recognition of the inadequacy of
creaturely language and conceptuality for expressing the utter otherness of God, with a consequent demand for metaphor and imagery,
for the counter-balancing of apparent opposites, and the deliberate exploitation of paradox. This facilitated the reclaiming of that
vast web of interconnections that had become traditional as earlier theologians created collages from scripture. The over-arching
idea of our *theōsis* through the incarnation of God's image could
then become the schema which united the multiplicity of 'names',
titles and metaphors drawn from scripture.[52] All the 'names' of
Christ were, in a sense, taken 'for our sake', to effect salvation for
humankind; yet at the same time, some of the key 'names' provided,
insofar as it is possible in human language, hints and sketches of the
true nature of the one who became incarnate.

But what is the relationship between this creative use of scriptural
collage and the articulation of dogmatic theology? Patristic reflection
on Proverbs 8 might illuminate this. In Justin's *Dialogue with Trypho*

---

[52] Cf. Chapter 5.

61, Proverbs 8.21–36 is quoted in full, to justify the claim that before all creatures God begat a Beginning, and this is named by the Holy Spirit in scripture, now the Glory of the Lord, now the Son, now Wisdom, now an Angel, then God, and then Lord and Logos. So the Son of God, who is God's Logos, is identified with personified Wisdom. By the time the Proverbs text was catapulted into controversy, this conflation had become an unquestioned assumption: Arius deduced from the words, 'The Lord created me as a beginning of his ways', that this so-called 'Begotten' One was the first and greatest of the creatures. At one level, he was taking the wording of the text literally, but at another he was presuming a particular understanding of the reference agreed by all protagonists in the controversy.

Arius' opponents produced a range of differing responses, using a variety of exegetical ploys. The problem lay in the word *ektisen* (he created). Marcellus and Athanasius claimed that this referred to the incarnation rather than the origin of the Logos, Athanasius cross-referencing other passages, such as Ephesians 2.10, 'We are his workmanship, created in Jesus Christ'. Eventually Athanasius arrived at a classic distinction: God's offspring (*gennēma*) was begotten then made, made flesh for our salvation in the *oikonomia*, whereas creatures (*poiēmata*) were made then begotten through Christ, becoming sons by grace. He is 'the first-born of all creation' as being the origin of the new creation; he could not be first-born of God, since he is only-begotten of God. The basis of this exegesis is the observation that whereas *ektisen* (verse 22) is modified by an expression of purpose, 'for his works', *genna(i)* (verse 25) does not have a similar modifier. So the 'begetting' is stated absolutely, whereas 'created' is relative, relative to the *oikonomia*. This distinction between speaking absolutely of the Son's Being and speaking of him relative to the created order is fundamental to Athanasius' discernment of the 'mind' of scripture.

Athanasius assumed that the meaning of each scriptural text should cohere with the supposed 'mind' of scripture as a whole. This 'mind' of scripture was not to be discerned by pressing the literal sense of proof texts, but rather by making deductions from a collage of disparate texts. You cannot take 'the Lord created me' according to the letter and assume it is a statement about the origin of the Logos when it's clear that the rest of scripture has another sense. In the *De Decretis* Athanasius seeks to answer the charge that the Nicene council had introduced non-scriptural ideas in espousing words like *homoousios*. He insists that the bishops were obliged to collect the 'mind' of scripture and restate it in non-scriptural formulae. Discernment of the mind of scripture meant discovering its unitive testimony to the true Son of God; and that involved both a critical stance towards a literalizing view of religious language and the embracing of that web of interconnections long since held dear in the fathers' reading of Old and New Testaments.

VI.2 *Doctrinal reading today*

This observation concerning the 'mind' of scripture is fundamental to the relationship between doctrine and scripture. Brought up, as it were, when modernism was at its height, this was not a perspective I considered prior to extended work on patristic exegesis and the hermeneutical challenges of post-modernism. I now think that it is an insight not yet taken with sufficient seriousness by theologians.

  Of course, the difficulties of doctrinal reading are immense:

- Historical consciousness has made it impossible to assume a common 'mind' running across documents deriving from many different historical contexts. We think it is inappropriate to interpret John by Paul, and even more inappropriate to interpret Proverbs in the light of Christ. Ironically, now that we have the whole Bible in a single book (as the fathers did not), we see the assumption of the Bible's unity as the construct that it is, and resist the claim that the doctrinal tradition is the principal criterion for biblical interpretation.

- Post-Holocaust embarrassment about supersessionism reinforces the historico-critical rejection of Christological readings of what Christians call the Old Testament.[53] In the post-modern era, we are acutely aware of the social locus of both text and reader.
- The pressures of our culture have reduced our spiritual horizons. The modern 'earth-bound' approach to the texts focusses primarily on the 'letter' or 'wording' and its historical context. Interpreters then divide on the question how far we should still follow ethical injunctions that come from a different 'world', and to what extent we may regard as 'mythological' whatever sits badly with modern (scientific) understanding of the way things are.
- We recognize that it is anachronistic to assume that what are evidently later doctrinal concerns correspond with the intention of the author. We are culturally suspicious of timeless truths.

There is, then, a crucial gap between us and the fathers, a radical disjunction between modern (and post-modern) biblical scholarship and the reading of scripture that produced the doctrinal legacy that systematic theologians attempt to clarify or interpret for the (post-)modern world. Our dilemma is that doctrine emerged out of a patristic reading of scripture which is now regarded as historically anachronistic, and even politically incorrect.

Liturgical renewal and ecumenism have benefited from shared historico-critical approaches to scripture. So has Christian–Jewish dialogue. Systematic theology has attempted to take account of modern historical studies of the Bible and patristics – yet what it actually needs is an acceptable approach to doctrinal reading. It needs to justify the orthodox doctrine which it seeks to interpret as an appropriate reading of scripture within our very different intellectual context. Surely we should at least learn from the fathers that the analysis and historical work of biblical scholarship needs to be balanced by an overall theological framework which sets the parameters for

---

[53] See Chapter 6.

Christian reading. The merit of canon-criticism was that it sought to find unity in scripture, but it set about it without explicit reference to an external framework such as the creed. Without reference to the traditions of how to read the Bible Christianly, we conjure up the same possibilities of twisting it to suit our own ideas as did Arians and others – at least in the eyes of an Athanasius. It's no accident that the *sola scriptura* slogan of the Reformation has produced the fissiparousness of Protestantism. Scripture is part of tradition, and engagement with the doctrinal legacy is important for reading scripture as Christian scripture. To put it controversially, doctrine should have primacy over biblical criticism for Christian theology.

Christianity, as distinct from biblical scholarship, reads the Bible in terms of the over-arching narrative captured in the classic creeds: creation, fall, redemption and consummation – the story of God's constant engagement with the world to redeem, to turn chaos into creation, to bring good out of evil, a divine work supremely effected through the life, death and resurrection of Jesus Christ, but already adumbrated in the story of Israel, and re-played in the lives and history of those who follow Christ and are endowed with the Holy Spirit. This highlights certain features of the biblical narrative as constitutive of its fundamental plot. It can be characterized as a selective reading, indeed as a framework imposed from 'outside' (or rather by the orthodox Christian community), but a doctrinal reading is impossible without it. Surely the function of systematic theology is to keep on critically and constructively engaging with this vital framework within which scripture is read.

The fathers were clear that the 'mind' of scripture was the Word within the words which gave the Bible its unity. Just as the fathers were forced to speak of one Christ in two natures, so we may need to speak of one Bible in two natures: the Word of God and the words of human authors, inseparable and co-inherent, therefore often hard to distinguish. In the period after modernity's historical consciousness, we can take even more seriously than the fathers the divine engagement with, and mediation through, the messiness of human life and history.

With such perspectives, we might recapture something of the extraordinary richness of the imaginative ways in which the fathers detected those interconnections of meaning and metaphor. Ephrem the Syrian[54] spoke of scripture as an inexhaustible fountain:

> For we leave behind in it far more than we take from it, like thirsty people drinking from a fountain . . . God has hidden within His word all sorts of treasures, so that each of us can be enriched by it . . . Anyone who encounters Scripture should not suppose that the single one of its riches that he has found is the only one to exist; rather, he should realize that he himself is only capable of discovering one out of the many riches which exist in it.

Yet this does not mean that it is easy to see how the words point to the Word. The eye of the beholder needs to be clear:

> The Scriptures are placed there like a mirror:
> He whose eye is luminous beholds there the image of reality.

So the reader needs to be inspired, and also informed by the all-encompassing story of God's engagement with creation as fall and redemption are played out time and again. Such a perspective might open up a rich doctrinal reading of scripture. But we shall have to learn not simply to repeat what the fathers did, but to re-forge it for a different world.

VII Faith seeking understanding – towards a conclusion

Theology is an exploratory, rather than an explanatory, discipline, and creeds were meant to be doxological rather than propositional.[55]

---

54 Brock, *The Luminous Eye*, from which are taken these quotations from Ephrem.
55 As argued in my unpublished F. D. Maurice lectures in 1988; cf. also my *The Making of the Creeds* (London: SCM Press, 1991).

These statements need unpacking, but they reflect something profound in the work of the church fathers, and justify my chapter title, 'From dogma to *theoria*'.

There are, of course, explanatory elements in the theological endeavour. Exegesis, whether of scripture or of the work of other theologians, consists largely of explanation, as meanings are teased out by reference to linguistic, historical, sociological and other factors that have contributed to what is written and how it is written. Systematic theology may be explanatory in seeking to show how different doctrines fit together and make a coherent account of the way things are. Yet theology is not a kind of scientific hypothesis to explain the world or anything in it – it is not explanatory as such. Rather theology is in principle exploratory since its subject-matter is essentially a mystery. 'Mystery' is a word I generally eschew. It too easily becomes a lazy excuse for avoiding hard and clear thinking, the last resort against critical challenge. Yet where one is concerned with a subject in principle beyond the capacity of human thought, then the metaphor of exploring the unknown characterizes something essential about the endeavour. What we need to envisage is a given reality, within which we live and move and have our being, through which we journey, constantly discovering more than meets the eye, deepening understanding but also learning to live well.

This is one of the most fundamental things I have learnt from the fathers. Gregory of Nyssa's *Life of Moses* provides a classic example. Gregory intended his exposition of the scriptural story to provide a pattern of life, his theme being perfection and its attainment. Perfection in this world needs 'boundaries' – this was a classical idea: chaos is not beautiful; rather, beauty is found in the perfect shape of a statue or other artifact. So perfection requires defining limits. But, says Gregory, virtue is not like that.[56] Like the nature of the infinite God, perfection is boundless, and there is no stopping-place or final attainment. It is always growth in goodness. Through

<hr>

[56] See *Biblical Exegesis*, pp. 258–62, for detailed references.

contemplation of Moses' life we perceive what the perfect life might be, treating it as a kind of map or guide to the spiritual journey.

For Gregory, spirituality is a constant deepening of theological understanding which shapes the heart of one's life and worship. If at first religious knowledge comes as light, deeper penetration discovers the invisible and the incomprehensible, the darkness in which seeing consists in not seeing, for no one shall see God and live. Moses enters the luminous darkness of the cloud of the presence. Transformed by God's glory so that no one can look at him (he has to veil his face),[57] he speaks with God face to face as one speaks with a friend.[58] Yet to see God is not attainable – God hides him in a cleft of rock, allowing him to see only his back-parts.[59] For 'truly this is the vision of God: never to be satisfied in the desire to see him'. Moses is taught that he can behold God – simply by following God wherever he might lead, keeping the back of his leader in view and not turning aside.

> The true vision and the true knowledge of what we seek consists precisely in not seeing, in an awareness that our goal transcends all knowledge and is everywhere cut off from us by the darkness of incomprehensibility. Thus that profound evangelist, John, who penetrated into this luminous darkness, tells us that 'no-one has seen God at any time', teaching us by this negation that none – indeed no created intellect – can attain a knowledge of God.[60]

It's as though we struggle up a steep slope to the ridge ahead and arrive at a stage in perfection; we pause, stand over a cliff and feel the vertigo that comes with the realization of God's incomprehensibility; and then the clouds ahead part, and we see another ridge to climb. There has to be eternal progress, because it is impossible to comprehend the infinite. Furthermore, change is constitutive of creaturely being – our nature is essentially changeable: since it is made out of

---

[57] Exodus 34.29–35. [58] Exodus 33.11. [59] Exodus 33.22–3.

[60] *Life of Moses*, as quoted by Jean Daniélou in H. Musurillo, *From Glory to Glory: Texts from Gregory of Nyssa's Mystical Writings* (New York: Scribner, 1961), p. 29.

nothing, it came into being by change. Now to be subject to change is, in a sense, constantly to be born again. So, for Gregory, the important thing about change is that it is the necessary condition for being 'transformed from glory to glory'.[61] On the basis of Philippians 3.13, Gregory coined the word *epektasis* to express a sense of straining forward on the upward climb that never stops: 'Moses, moving ever forwards, did not stop in his upward climb.'

To dismiss all this as allegory is to fail to see that every time we read ourselves into a text, there is a measure of allegory. An exploratory, open-ended approach to scripture and theology alone permits the kind of *theōria* – that 'seeing through' which permits genuine insight – to inspire and transform. So theology is not primarily an explanatory, but rather an exploratory, discipline.

At the same time, however, the fathers' *theōria* was deeply opposed to wild speculations and took place within the context of dogma. 'Dogma' and 'doctrine' are basically the Greek and Latin words for teaching. Much education in human history has been dogmatic, kids learning by rote what their elders pass on from one generation to the next. The early church had a school-like character within the Greek and Roman world,[62] and there were arguments about what teachings this school, as distinct from others, offered to those seeking wisdom. 'Heresy' was a word suggesting alternative 'options'; 'orthodoxy' meant 'right opinion'. For the first time religion became associated with 'correct belief'. Thus the story of early Christianity has become an account of how 'correct belief' triumphed over competing options, and creeds have been interpreted as statements of 'correct belief', to be signed up to if you wanted to belong to the true church. The Reformation reinforced this as articles of belief were drawn up in propositional statements and conformity demanded. Religious teaching became dogmatic in the pejorative sense. The Enlightenment struggle to be free from the constraints of dogmatic

---

[61] 2 Corinthians 3.18.
[62] See my article '*Paideia* and the Myth of Static Dogma', pp. 265–83.

traditions, together with the emergence of scientific investigation of the way things are, has meant that dogma is now viewed negatively, and education seeks to open the mind, to encourage critical engagement, to be suspicious of claims to know the truth in advance. As a scholarly discipline, theology has tended to conform to this general academic ethos: the critic excludes the visionary, the exegete is invited to leave faith outside the door of the lecture room, while the study of religion becomes phenomenological and sociological.

So what is theology? 'Faith seeking understanding' is an answer which encapsulates both the givenness and the invitation to exploration. The fathers remind us that though God-talk is ultimately beyond us, we should be confident about exploring what we have been given, because God really is the same as the God we've learned to know through the *oikonomia*, that is, essentially loving. What we've been given includes the classic creeds and doctrines, particular articulations of what is given in scripture. Many may wish to insist on the historical meaning as a criterion by which anachronistic and inappropriate readings of New Testament theology are to be avoided; but, quite apart from the practical difficulties of ever producing definitive historical meaning, there is no presuppositionless interpretation, and if the New Testament is to be read Christianly, we need to take seriously the hermeneutical principal that the future meaning of the text is as significant as its past meaning.[63] It may be true that only hindsight uncovers the true significance of things, and that a better view emerges from climbing the ladder or ascending the mountain – along with the vertigo of standing on the cliff and attempting to 'see' God in the cloud of the presence. Gregory of Nyssa and others who articulated Trinitarian doctrine were discovering the truth through reading the scriptures and living the life of the church in the Spirit.

---

[63] See 'The Trinity and the New Testament' in Christopher Rowland and Christopher Tuckett (eds.), *The Nature of New Testament Theology*, Essays in Honour of Robert Morgan (Oxford: Blackwell, 2006).

For it is even more important to recognize the doxological origins of the creeds. Though hijacked as tests of orthodoxy, they began life in the context of liturgy, particularly as the confession of faith made by candidates for baptism. Local creeds shared the three-part structure, clauses about God the Father, about the Son of God and about the Holy Spirit, but the word 'Trinity' is not used, and there is no systematic exposition of the doctrine of God as Three-in-One. The essential content of the creeds is a story, and this is an important pointer to their fundamental nature as summaries of the Gospel, digests of the scriptures. As Cyril of Jerusalem put it:

> since all cannot read the scriptures, some being hindered from knowing them by lack of education, and others by want of leisure . . . We comprise the whole doctrine of the Faith in a few lines.[64]

These were to be committed to memory, treasured and safeguarded. The creed was not viewed as some human compilation, but as consisting of the most important points collected out of scripture; it outlined a framework for reading the scriptures and a map for the journey. Christian theology may be exploratory, but the terrain is not uncharted.

For Gregory of Nyssa, the eternal *epektasis*, reaching out and striving forward for what is never fully attained, is the expression of desire and longing. God is beyond us; our presumption is crippled in struggling with God. Yet it is this wound of love which is our salvation:

> From the scriptures we learn that God is love and also that he sends forth His only-begotten Son as his 'chosen arrow' (Isaiah 49.20) to the elect . . . It is a good wound and a sweet point by which life penetrates the soul; for by the tearing of the arrow she opens a kind of door, an

---

[64] *Catechetical Homilies* v.12.

entrance into herself. For no sooner does she receive the dart of love, than the image of archery is transformed into a scene of nuptial joy.[65]

For Gregory, then, the love of God requires receptivity, the abandonment of the desire to possess and control, the acceptance of an eternal longing that can never be satisfied, a wounding with love's arrow that brings fulfilment as well as frustration. For God's generous love reaches out to us in order to transfigure us, and our redemption is worked out in the nitty-gritty of daily care for one another, especially our Lazaruses.

Thus Christian theology becomes the confession in life and worship of Father, Son and Spirit, ever creating and re-creating, ever secretly at work, bringing truth, beauty and goodness to fruition within a creation set free in its otherness for response to the generous love of the Triune God; while the accommodation of the transcendent, divine self to our level is celebrated in constant liturgical re-play, in sacramental *anamnēsis*.

* * *

Palm Sunday sermon

The preacher stands ready to begin. It is Palm Sunday; the congregation has celebrated Jesus' ride into Jerusalem, and the Gospel lection has just been read: Matthew 27.15–26 describes the people baying for Barabbas' release:

So the crowd turns into a mob. Disillusioned and angry, they prefer Barabbas, the freedom-fighter. Peaceful demonstrations turn sour very easily, and it depends which side you're on whether the end justifies the means. We may think Jesus was judiciously murdered after a miscarriage of justice, but the authorities were only trying to keep the peace in a tense situation, as police do everywhere, from Cairo to London.

[65] *On the Song of Songs* 4; ET: Musurillo, *From Glory to Glory*, pp. 178–9.

I once had a sharp reminder that Jesus came into the same awful world we live in. It was on the Golan Heights. The coach had just crawled up from the edge of the Sea of Galilee, now far below. We were to visit the dug-up remains of an ancient town on a kind of high promontory ridge, where we could see a floor mosaic in the foundations of an early church. Setting out on the short walk to the archaeological site, we were warned not to step off the path since the land might be mined. As we arrived at the entry to the site, a Syrian military dugout was pointed out, tucked into the ancient earthwork. Directly below on the shores of the Sea of Galilee was an Israeli kibbutz – no wonder the Israelis were determined to capture the Golan Heights in 1967. You could easily imagine shells being lobbed from up there.

About to return, most of the party were distracted by something, and I found myself alone on that treacherous path. It was the most beautiful spring day. Far over the waters of the lake the afternoon sun was descending beyond Galilee, silhouetting the Mount of Transfiguration. And at my feet, the thick grass covering potential minefields was bright with colourful anemones. 'Consider the lilies,' I thought, 'they neither spin nor weave, yet Solomon in all his glory was not arrayed like one of these.' And suddenly the beauty and tragedy of it all triggered that thought: Jesus came into the same kind of awful world we live in.

Later, in Jerusalem, we visited the Pavement, the ancient stone paving where the soldiers are said to have mocked Jesus; and scratched on the surface were gaming boards, testimony to the boredom of the occupying forces. The whole remembered scene of Jesus caught up in the guards' casual but cruel horseplay coalesced with horrors like Abu Ghraib. Jesus was the victim of group dynamics such as still lead people into perpetrating acts of evil that most of us can barely imagine. He came into the same kind of awful world we live in.

But what we proclaim at this season is that in Christ, God was taking on all the awfulness so as to transform it.

It seems utter foolishness, as Paul said: 'the cross is an offence to Jews and folly to Gentiles'. What we really want is for God to come and sort things out. A colleague at the university once said to me, 'If I were God, I wouldn't let my children do to each other the things they do.' Judged by ordinary common sense, Jesus taught an upside-down way and then took it himself. He didn't ride into Jerusalem on a warhorse and then try to put the world to rights. He said the poor are blessed and taught us to forgive one another seventy times seven. Crazy! Yet, perhaps, the only way to cut through cycles of revenge?

Genesis 45 tells how Joseph disclosed himself to his brothers. The back-story is crucial, of course: jealousy had led to his brothers plotting against him and selling him off to traders *en route* to Egypt; but now Joseph was Pharaoh's powerful administrator, and famine had driven his brothers to seek grain in Egypt. Without any idea who he was, they were dependent on Joseph's response. Furthermore, he'd contrived to make them look like thieves, so as to get them in his power. But now Joseph is overcome by emotion and his mask falls: 'I am Joseph,' he says. 'Is my father still living?' The brothers are understandably so terrified they cannot answer. He calls them close and says, 'I am your brother, Joseph, the one you sold into Egypt! And now, do not be distressed and angry with yourselves for selling me here, because it was to save lives that God sent me ahead of you . . . So then it was not you who sent me here, but God.'

Somehow this extraordinary statement provides a key to the whole narrative of the Bible. This God is one who's let go, allowing the brothers to be free to sin – not a coercing, preventing, intervening God. Yet providentially somehow this same God has enabled a good outcome from that sinful act. This God of the Bible is one who, at the same time, lets things be, yet is always at work, hidden yet active, bringing good things into existence out of chaos and nothingness, and even good effects from evil and sinfulness. To descry God in the mess of history takes prophetic discernment – the traces are never obvious, or discrete from human acts. Yet those with eyes to see may see, rejoice and give thanks.

And the cross is the supreme demonstration of this. Here, God in Christ takes responsibility for the mess we've made, freeing us from the darkness of sin into the glory of new life. Jesus rides into Jerusalem, hailed as the promised Messiah, with the crowd full of hope for liberation from the Roman oppressors, but here is no ordinary king, no idealistic politician or heroic leader determined to sort things. John's Gospel tells how Jesus directly withdrew when, on an earlier occasion, the crowds tried to make him king. No – he's not the kind of leader people want at all. But he is the light of the world, one who, through the passion, submitted to all the evils and horrors of which human beings are capable, indeed entered the depths of our darkness, so as to transform it – for the 'hour of glory' in John's Gospel is the cross. The other Gospels uncover similar themes, as in Matthew and Mark Jesus cries out, 'My God, my God, why hast thou forsaken me?' – sharing the ultimate darkness of God-forsakenness; while in Luke, he demonstrates that other way with his prayer, 'Father, forgive them for they know not what they do.'

Cardinal Newman's great hymn 'Praise to the Holiest in the height' provides a summary of the great over-arching story by which Christians make sense of their lives. Together with Eve, Adam, whose name simply means 'man', represents the whole human race, all gone-wrong, liable to blame everyone but themselves, desperate to find a way out of the consequences of their own actions, to grasp God-like powers to put things right. But, as Paul proclaimed, 'God was in Christ reconciling the world to himself' – as a second Adam, Jesus was victorious over whatever powers of evil have humankind in their grip, and on the cross taught us a different way, the way of generous love. Philippians 2.5–11 sums it all up: Christ didn't grab God-like powers but humbled himself, took the way of obedience to death – even death on a cross; and therefore God highly exalted him.

And the whole point of the passage is that we should have the same 'mind' which was in Christ Jesus.

So to follow Jesus is not just to wave palm branches and sing 'Hosanna', but it is to be changed, taking up the cross daily, so that our own propensities to increase darkness through resentments, disillusionment, frustration, anger and jealousy are transformed into the kind of energy that brings light and love and the fruits of the Spirit into the bits of the world and its history which we inhabit.

Thanks be to God. Amen.

* * *

Postlude

Jesus

> He walked into my home;
>> his eyes pierced
>> my Martha soul.
> He sat and conversed by the fire;
>> his words scorched
>> my Mary heart.
> He bent over the bed;
>> his touch raised
>> my Lazarus smile.
> The broken one he loved
>> beyond us all.

Some Final Observations

> The water-lily flower is closed up tight.
> It is a dark and cloudy day today.
> The big flat leaves are floating, splashed with spray,
> Undulating, trembling at their plight,

Stuck in a watery world disturbed by storms.
But yet a little while, sunshine resumes;
Responding to its warmth and light the blooms
Uncurl and reassert their lovely forms.
Reflecting as a mirror the golden light,
Being conformed to the image of the sun,
Unveiling their inner likeness to its face,
They make the gesture of praise – before my sight
The petalled palms are opened; I too come,
With hands uplifted, grateful for God's grace.

Imagination pierces the drifting mist.
It's nature's bridal veil of intricate lace,
Concealing mysteriously her lovely face.
With sequined teardrops every twig is kissed.
The view's obscured and yet you get the gist
By hints and snatches. Intercession's pace
Mysteriously moves. The hidden base
Of love upholding love is often missed.
Yet providentially coincidence
Unveils in hints and snatches the soft tears
Of caring prayer that kiss each circumstance
With hidden love. And as the noontide nears
The mists begin to lift for all to see
A multitude in prayer eternally.

Imagination contemplates the light.
It's nature's incandescent artistry,
Irradiating sign of Trinity,
From which the eyes must turn – too bright
For mortal view, the dazzling, blinding sight
Is mirrored in a smoky glass, in imagery
Reflecting radiance essentially,
Dispelling darkness and the shades of night.
Here, through the prism, light creates a flame.

423

A candle burns within the human heart,
An image of an image of a name
Unutterable, blazing, whole in part
And part in whole beyond all separation.
The burning God to God makes reparation.

Epilogue

By way of conclusion, I offer a blank verse meditation on Proverbs 7–8, exploring the call of Wisdom as the vocation of the theologian to pursue the life of mind and soul, head, heart and will in union. Its fashioning drew on personal experience and a sense of vocation to church as well as academy, but it is not autobiographical as such. It was composed during a period of convalescence in Scotland, a fact which explains the landscape evoked. I had taken with me John Betjeman, *Summoned by Bells*, to provide a model for versification, the King James Version of the Bible, which influenced but did not determine the language, and Julian of Norwich, *Revelations of Divine Love*, to which, along with other literary and patristic material, allusion is made.

The poem has a patristic flavour: besides adopting the early Christian reading of Proverbs, which identified Wisdom with the Word incarnate in Christ, it works with a highly symbolic set of motifs. It exploits the ambiguities of the word 'conception', and the ambivalences arising from the feminine gender of Sophia (Wisdom) and *psyche* (soul). Analogies and symbols alike are meant to be stretched and shattered by transcendence and otherness, and remain possible only because religious language is necessarily allusive and poetic, while the Wisdom of God is imaged in human life, especially the life and suffering of Jesus.

Sophie's Call

In a long night of loss comes Sophie's call,
Visions in a dark night of passion and loss.

425

She appears lovely in her element.
I see her as the wild order of things.
Her beauty is the strain of a mountain stream,
Filling the conscious mind with unconscious sound,
Intoning the tones of grey-green clouds and rocks
Older than ever ancient sages dreamed.
Sophie's eyes are deep pools of love,
Aged with wisdom, yet dancing with glistening spray
As catching the droplets of light, her youthful hair
Is tossed in the breeze. Ageless is her face.
Her garments fold like the skirts of a mountain-range,
Each ridge itself in colour and form as far
As the eye can see, glinting reflections of light,
Or dark silhouette shapes and slopes rich green,
All colour-woven with delicate alpine flowers
And textured with trees and bracken and scattered stones.
Her silver girdle is water, her necklace and braid
Are showers of rain, her headdress vapoury clouds
Refracting the colour spectrum in rainbow tears.
This wild beauty I see at the heart of things;
Conceived in the mind of the unknown Ancient of Days,
She is the elemental principle,
The underlying pattern beneath the chaos,
The pattern dimly perceived in averages,
In the ecological meshing of natural things.
She's a sparkling fountain playing the tune of life,
Her changeless movements grace personified.
Divine she's drenched in beauty, goodness, truth.
It is her tinkling roar within the soul
That gives the mind its language, and it is
Her wild proportions pouring randomly
That patterns particles in harmony,
In an endless profusion of snowflake symmetries
And biological fingerprints each unique.

So mathematics Sophie's music makes
And beauty measures rationality.

For in the beginning of his ways the Lord
Possessed her. Before the ages, before the earth
She was set up; there were no depths, no springs.
Before the mountains were settled, before the hills,
She was brought forth. When he prepared the heavens
Already she was there; when he measured the deep,
And when he appointed the earth's foundations, she
Was by him, his daily delight, his prentice-boy.
Rejoicing she learned his ways, filling his works.
Sophie is the wild order of things.
Divine wisdom and understanding's in her.
She lies as an only Son at the breast of the Father,
Who succours her life as she snuggles and suckles there.
O Lord our God, how manifold are thy works.
In wisdom, thine offspring, hast thou made them all.

In a dark night, at the window of my house,
I seemed to look through my lattice, there to discern,
Nearby the corner among the youths in the street,
A youngster void of understanding. He heard
The counterfeit Sophie call, then go her way.
At twilight, in the evening, behold in the black
And dark night, I witnessed how he was met
By a woman in harlot's attire, subtle of heart
And loud, at every corner lying in wait.
She caught at him and kissed him, with impudent face,
With seeming goodness, with seeming beauty and truth,
She lured him: 'With tapestry covers my bed is decked,
With carvings and linen of Egypt, with perfumes and myrrh.
So come – till morning let's take our fill of love.
My husband's on a long journey – he'll not be home.'
With much smooth talk she causes him to yield,

427

With much seductive speech she seduces him.
After her he goes straightway, as an ox
Goes to the slaughter or a bird swoops into a snare.
In that dark night of desire I understood
Lust for knowledge, the mock passion for truth,
Pride seduced by pseudo-Sophie's charm.
And I knew her nature, I saw her myth in dream –
How the ghostly image of Sophie had to know
The height and depth of being, the profound abyss,
The infinite resource of divinity,
Incomprehensible, no name, unseen,
The limitless ocean of love beyond all bounds.
Compelled by passion, she had to know the All,
Impelled by lust she grasped at equality
With God, at consummation of desire.
Her sudden fall was quite spectacular,
Like cascades sliding down a precipice,
A streak of white, awesome and beautiful –
As it were, Satan like lightning falling from heaven.
So dreaming a dream, I understood how she,
The dark double of Sophie tempting us,
Came to conceive through the same dark desire
That she induced. And terrible was the birth
Of her jealous offspring, the idol of power and pride,
Inspiring us to act as though divine,
To build our Babels and our atom bombs,
Corrupting science to exploit the earth's
Resources, satisfied with twisted truth
And jaded beauty, and goodness marred and soiled.
For thus deceived, inspired by greatness and power
None can bear too much reality,
The dust and ashes of human dreams and hopes.

Not that it's foolish to follow Sophie's call –
It's not unwise to pursue the truth, to explore,

To long to know, to seek the love of God.
But rushing with all speed after Sophie's song,
With lustful, proud ambition uppermost,
Even the best of us fall into the ditch,
And overwhelmed by the sudden accident,
Thrashing about in the mud, frustrated and cross,
Despairing sink deeper and deeper into the mire,
Fearful we cannot hope to please the Lord.

Then Pseudo-Sophie clothes herself in dreams,
Inspiring a striving spirituality
That seeks to climb the heights to catch a view
Of eternity, the flight of th'alone to th'Alone,
And isolated, looking down on things
Below from a cliff-top vantage-point, to drag
The unwilling body upwards, breathing deep,
One foot in front of the other, pacing the pulse,
Fitting the soul for rigours beyond its reach
By ascetic discipline and abstract thought,
Until by denigration of God's works
The divine being's abstracted to a point,
The blank beginning of things, the One, the Unique
Negation beyond all being, Nothingness.
Reaching the summit dome, weary and lost,
The mud-bespattered seeker cannot find
The final cairn, that elusive perfect ideal.
For thus deceived, inspired by lust to know,
Craving the senseless sensation of ecstasy,
None can bear too much reality,
The dust and ashes of spirituality.

In the dark night of desire, longing for God,
Burning with eros, filled with distrust, dead
In spirit and empty, deserted, lost, betrayed,
Hurt by all the gonewrongness, full of blame,

I knew I was Sophie and pseudo-Sophie was me.
Desperate for proof, impatient with mystery,
Contorted with the pain of 'Why, O why?'
Hearing nothing but nought from the hidden face
Of the deep, seeing nothing but agony,
Perceiving nothing but negativity,
The lust for possession possessed the restless mind,
Banished imagination and poetry.
Like Sophie's ghost, I conceived a monstrous child,
A thought still-born, distinctions dead and cold,
Classifications, prising true from false –
No good in bad, no light in dark, nor hint
Of ambiguity, no boundaries blurred
With wildness, risk or dread uncertainty
But clarification through mental mastery.
Yet elusive is the thought of design like a clock,
Or a formal garden without a weed in place.
My son disappointed my hopes, he failed to mature.
He ruthlessly teased me and hurt me, refusing to be
What to be I would have him be, and it came to pass
In the dark dream of the night, dangerous tricks
And dare-devil exploits, mocking my warnings, tore
At my vitals, and all through the night numb I lay
Longing for comfort, waiting for his return.
The wait was long and fruitless. The way was lost.
Wiser is the foolishness of God.

In the dark night I lie with passion spent,
Unable to conceive, with the womb of the mind
Deadened, beyond emotion, devoid of thought.
Then came another call, loud and clear,
A strange call to a passionless passion unknown,
It's true Sophie's call to love, to pure
Possessiveless prayer, the clean hands of awe –

For doth not wisdom cry, standing atop
High places, or by the wayside and gates of the town?
Doth not understanding raise her voice
At doors and entrances? 'To you, I call:
Understand wisdom, ye simple, ye fools acquire
An understanding heart. Hear, for I
Will speak of excellent things, and from my lips
Will come what is right; for my mouth will speak the truth.
All the words of my mouth are righteousness;
In them is nothing twisted or perverse.
To them that find knowledge, everything's right and true.
Instead of silver, receive instruction from me,
Receive my knowledge rather than choicest gold.
For wisdom is better than rubies and all the things
That may be desired can't be compared to it.
I, wisdom, dwell with prudence and skill.
Counsel is mine, sound understanding and strength.
By me kings decree justice and princes reign.
Riches and honour are mine, durable wealth,
The fruit of righteousness and fear of the Lord.
I shall love them that love me – those that seek
With diligence shall find me, along with the Lord.
For from the beginning I was possessed by the Lord;
At creation I was with him as prentice-boy.
I am Sophie, the wild order of things.

Then I knew that I knew through a glass darkly, in part,
That response to the true Sophie could only mean
A total turn-around, a repentance of mind,
A change of heart, a new and different approach.
But breaking my mind's ambition and heart's pride
Meant ripping out false conceptions, stripping the womb
Of abortive apprehensions, pruning the branch
That from it might issue the fruit of germ received.

No anaesthetic deadened the purging pain.
Then pregnant with possibility, I discerned
That creation emerged where infinity withdrew
Permitting existence other than itself.
In the void creation emerged, in the yawning gap
Of nothingness; and so a gulf is fixed,
A chasm impassable to the finite heart.
No leaping passion can grasp the other side.
But over the waters the Spirit of wisdom broods,
And the voice of Sophie is heard in irregular waves,
In waves of sound as the wind vibrates the trees,
In the haphazard order of breakers on the shore:
The peace of God is a silence full of sounds
Of flowing water, and breeze-played leaves, and song.
To plumb such a silence is quite impossible.
The wildness of Sophie is all you need to know.
For Sophie embodies the presence of God in things.

Where then shall Sophie be found? And where is the place
Of wisdom and understanding? God alone knows –
It's hid from the eyes of the living – it's not in their land:
The sea saith, 'Not in me', and so does the deep.
Yet in nights of trial and pain, the seer may see
Splendid revelations of wisdom divine
And many lovely lessons concerning love.

So Sophie appeared to me as the suffering Christ:
In the labour of love on the Cross, in the sweat and the blood
Was motherhood, pure and divine, giving birth to her child.
At that moment the Trinity filled me with heartfelt joy.
I was overwhelmed with wonder that he, my God,
So holy and awful, could show such love to me.
His love and grace spanned the gulf that seemed so wide.
I had only to wonder, to worship and receive
The wisdom and honesty that acknowledged God's

Greatness, and the sorry smallness of my self.
In his love, he enfolds and embraces, that tender love
Surrounds me, never to leave me, wholly good.
And resting in God's arms I conceive a child,
The overflow of his Spirit of love and mine,
A lustless love-child, fruit of *agape*,
A clear conception of infinite mystery,
Of ultimate One precisely known as Three,
Of divine and human union in personal form
Without confusion, in perfect purity:
In the face of a wounded son smiles the mystery divine
And the face of my half-formed child, reflecting that smile,
Sparks joy in the random wildness and liberty
Of everything the Trinity suffers to be.
The whole of creation is tiny, and only exists
Because God loves it, because he holds it in love
While letting it be, letting it be and be free.
To know the goodness of God is the highest prayer.
Here is the grace which our soul is seeking now
And will for ever seek until that day
When we know for a fact we're wholly united with God.
Our lover desires that our soul should cleave to him.
By grace in the Spirit we gaze eternally
Exulting in that single-minded love,
Incalculable, supreme, surpassing all.

In the wild order of things, there's agony.
There's suffering and pain at the heart of reality.
In Sophie's tears is the passionless passion of love,
A hurt that holds while lovingly letting go.
In Christ the love and tears flow powerfully
As a mountain runnel concentrates its force
Tap-like through the rocks, filling up pools
With bubbling mud-less water, clear and pure.

So in luminous darkness I see Sophie as Christ,
The image of God, the Son at the Father's breast,
The brightness of his glory, his Wisdom and Word.
In him was life, and the life was the light of men.
He came unto his own, who received him not.
The Word was made flesh and dwelt among us, and we
Beheld his glory, full of grace and truth.
No-one has ever seen God, but his only Son
Who lies in the Father's bosom, has made him known.
He was before all things, in him they consist;
In him all fullness dwells, first-born of the dead,
Image of God invisible, head of the Church.
And so my mind is given lucidity
For Sophie's tinkling roar within the soul
Images the rationality
That underlies the wild order of things,
The grand design of life that's Sophie's work,
Like the haphazard colour threads of a tapestry
Or casual streaks of mist stroking the hills.
One eye is focussed by Sophie's kaleidoscope
Which tidies the jumbled litter adrift in the wind,
So that beauty's found in broken odds and ends,
And anecdotal fragments make up truth,
While goodness shadows slivers of dark-coloured glass –
Then Sophie reveals the wild order of love
In the bare flesh and blood of disordered life.
To be immersed in it all with passion and prayer
Must seem the only response to her kind of call.
And then my heart is given purity,
Baptismal immersion in Sophie's pools of love.
And the dark night of passion and desire
Becomes the luminous darkness of mystery.
God's essence cannot be known; the divine works
Are all we can know and all we need to know.

Sophie is God clad in the world and the Word.
Through lust-less passion, sharing the pain of the earth,
The soul may consummate its unity
With all the beauty, goodness and truth of God.
For us and in us and with us Sophie is God.

At dawn as I toss in dreams, as I labour in sleep,
As the first light of the day appears in the East,
The call of Sophie summons me by name.
I seem to rise and go forth, and find myself
Not alone, but people flowing from every side,
So many nations saying, 'Come let us go,
Let's go up to the holy mountain of the Lord.
He'll teach us his ways, and in his paths we'll walk.
His Law will go forth from Zion; his Word will sound
From Jerusalem; into ploughshares they'll beat their swords,
Their spears into pruninghooks; no nation shall lift
Sword against nation; war they'll learn no more.'

So I join the singing throng on the pilgrim way.
Together we start to climb; the way is steep.
Then I see the young begin to help the old,
And the strong to lift the weak – none is let down,
As blind and disabled join on equal terms,
While Sophie goes before as leader and guide,
A pillar of cloud by day and fire by night,
A pioneer tempted and tried at every turn,
Her voice sounding the call to each by name.
Then I feel behind me the power of a mighty wind,
Assisting the upward ascent, thrusting us on
In the ordinary plodding of life or the struggling pain
Of crisis. Here's no flight of th'alone to th'Alone,
But a body composed of many members, diverse
Yet coherent, refreshed by the nectar of mountain streams,
By rests in green pastures beside the still waters,

Where Sophie pauses in her element,
Knitting threads of rain-washed heather-tones
Bright and clear into her tapestry
And mixing the spectrum of rainbow tears in the dark,
Cloudy skyscape, bringing joy to the world.

And the higher we climb, the lighter it gets; yet the light
Is a mist, a deep, dark mysteriousness,
The Cloud of the Presence, made luminous by the sun
Which hidden yet haunts the shrouds of vaporous murk.
Now and again the fog shifts in the breeze,
To reveal glimpses of distant views, ridge
Beyond ridge, crag above crag, snow upon snow,
The beauty grander for being concealed yet revealed,
Imparting trustful longing, confident hope.
From the drifting clouds fall drizzle and sweet showers
That give delight and hurt not; it seems a vast
Ocean envelops the drenched community,
That we're under sea, in a new environment,
The peculiar elemental sea of love.
And the striving goes on, but there's no anxiety:
For the sound of the waters is laughter and sudden smiles
Of unexpected sunlight kiss the waves,
And the marvellous music of God's unending love
Is displayed in the beauty and light of Sophie's face,
A passionate love so deep it broke her heart
In identity with the suffering and pain of the world,
Through identity with the suffering and pain of Christ;
Such a selfless love, such a pain without personal hurt
That its nature is all absorption of others' pain;
A passionless passion, a lust-less love, a sea
So vast it can take the pollution and waste of life
And leech it away on its tide, and children can play
In its waves and ripples, dancing with joy in the sand.

The unknown abyss is beyond passion or change,
Yet all is passion, the boundless love of God,
An overspill of love, as if a dam
Were set to hold it in but over the top
Its richness spills, out and over and on,
Step by step, down irregular rocky stairs,
Dropping and splashing unexpectedly,
Rarely revealing the secrets of its work.

I opened my eyes to find everything ordinary.
Yet the everyday morn was the dawn of a Holy Day:
My heart and mind were healed of their passion and loss.
I was filled with hope, with longing fullness, and God.

Bibliography

Primary sources

Texts and translations

Apostolic Constitutions. Greek text: Marcel Metzger (ed.), *Les Constitutions Apostoliques*, SC. ET: *NPNF.*

Athanasius, *Against the Gentiles – On the Incarnation.* Greek text edited and translated by R. W. Thomson, *Athanasius: Contra Gentes and De Incarnatione*, OECT.

Athenagoras, *Embassy* and *On the Resurrection.* Greek text edited and translated by W. R. Schoedel, *Athenagoras: Legatio and De Resurrectione*, OECT.

Augustine, *Confessions.* Latin text: Luc Verheijen (ed.), *Confessionum libri* XIII, CCL. ET: Henry Chadwick, *Augustine: Confessions*, World's Classics, Oxford University Press, 1992.

  On Genesis. Latin texts: D. Weber (ed.), *De Genesis contra Manichaeos*, CSEL; J. Zycha (ed.), *De Genesi ad litteram liber imperfectus* and *De Genesi ad litteram*, CSEL. ET: Edmund Hill, *Saint Augustine: On Genesis*, New York City Press, 2002.

  City of God. Latin text: B. Dombart and A. Kalb (eds.), *De Civitate Dei*, CCL. ET: Henry Bettenson, in Pelican Classics, Harmondsworth: Penguin, 1972.

Basil of Caesarea, *Homily 8: In Time of Famine and Drought.* Greek text: Migne, *PG* 31.303–28. ET: Appendix to Susan R. Holman, *The Hungry are Dying*, Oxford University Press, 2001.

  Hexaemeron. Greek text: Amand de Mendietta and S. Y. Rudberg (eds.), *Basilius von Caesarea: Homilien zur Hexaemeron*, GCS. ET: *NPNF* and *FC.*

On the Holy Spirit. Greek text: B. Pruche (ed.), *Basile de Césarée: Traité du Saint-Esprit, SC.* ET: *NPNF* and David Anderson, *St Basil the Great: On the Holy Spirit,* Crestwood, NY: St Vladimir's Seminary Press, 1980.

On That Which is According to the Image. Greek text: Alexis Smets and M. van Esbroek (eds.), *Basile de Césarée: Sur l'origine de l'homme: Homélies x et xi de l'Hexaémeron, SC.* ET: Nonna Verna Harrison, *St Basil the Great: On the Human Condition,* Crestwood, NY: St Vladimir's Seminary Press, 2005.

The Letters. Greek text and ET: R. Deferrari, *Basil: The Letters,* 4 vols., *LCL.*

i and ii Clement. Greek text: Kirsopp Lake (ed. with ET), *The Apostolic Fathers, LCL.* ET: Maxwell Staniforth and Andrew Louth (eds.), *Early Christian Writings,* London: Penguin, 1987.

Clement of Alexandria, *Stromateis.* Greek text: O. Stählin, L. Früchtel and U. Treu (eds.), *Stromateis, GCS.* ET: *ANCF* and *FC.*

Paedagogos. Greek text: O. Stählin and U. Treu (eds.), *Protrepticus und Paedagogos, GCS.* ET: *ANCF* and *FC.*

Constantine, *Oration to the Saints.* Greek text: I. A. Heikel (ed.), *Das Leben Konstantins: Eusebius Werke i, GCS.* ET: *NPNF.*

Cyprian, *Epistles.* Latin text: G. F. Diercks (ed.), *Sancti Cypriani episcope opera, CCL.* ET: *ACW.*

On the Lapsed, and *On the Unity of the Catholic Church.* Latin text and ET: Maurice Bévenot SJ, *Cyprian: De Lapsis and De Ecclesiae Catholicae Unitate,* Oxford University Press, 1971.

Cyril of Alexandria, *Commentary on Isaiah.* Greek text: Migne, *PG* 70. ET of selections: Norman Russell, *Cyril of Alexandria,* London: Routledge, 2000.

Commentary on John. Greek text: P. E. Pusey (ed.), Oxford: Clarendon Press, 1872. ET of selections: Norman Russell, *Cyril of Alexandria,* London: Routledge, 2000.

On Worship in Spirit and in Truth. Greek text: Migne, *PG* 68.

Glaphyra. Migne, *PG* 69.16–32. ET of selections: Norman Russell, *Cyril of Alexandria,* London: Routledge, 2000.

Homily 4. Greek text: Migne, *PG* 77.

Cyril of Jerusalem, *Catechetical Homilies*. Greek text: Migne, *PG* 33. ET: *FC*; selections in Edward Yarnold, SJ, *Cyril of Jerusalem*, London: Routledge, 2000.

Ephrem Syrus, *Commentary on Genesis*. Syriac text: *CSCO*. ET: *FC* and Section II in Sebastian Brock, *Saint Ephrem: Hymns on Paradise*, Crestwood, NY: St Vladimir's Seminary Press, 1990.

    Hymns on Paradise. Syriac Text: *CSCO*. ET: Sebastian Brock, *Saint Ephrem: Hymns on Paradise*, Crestwood, NY: St Vladimir's Seminary Press, 1990.

    Church. Syriac text and ET: Sebastian P. Brock and George A. Kiraz, *Ephrem the Syrian: Select Poems*, Provo, UT: Brigham Young University Press, 2006.

Epiphanius, *Panarion*. Greek text: Karl Holl (ed.), *Panarion*, *GCS*. ET: Philip R. Amidon, *SJ*, The *Panarion of St. Epiphanius, Bishop of Salamis*. Selected passages. Oxford University Press, 1990.

Eusebius, *Church History*. Greek text: E. Schwartz (ed.), *Die Kirchengeschichte: Eusebius Werke* II, *GCS*. ET: G. A. Williamson, *Eusebius: The History of the Church from Christ to Constantine*, rev. edn, A. Louth, Harmondsworth and Baltimore: Penguin, 1989.

    Demonstration of the Gospel. Greek text: I. A. Heikel (ed.), *Die Demonstratio evangelica: Eusebius Werke* VII, *GCS*. ET: W. J. Ferrar, *The Proof of the Gospel*, 2 vols., London: SPCK, 1920.

    Life of Constantine. Greek text: I. A. Heikel (ed.), *Das Leben Konstantins: Eusebius Werke* I, *GCS*. ET: S. G. Hall and Averil Cameron, *Eusebius: The Life of Constantine*, Oxford: Clarendon Press, 1998.

    Preparation of the Gospel. Greek text: K. Mras (ed.), *Die Praeparatio evangelica: Eusebius Werke* VII, *GCS*. ET: E. H. Gifford, *Eusebii Pamphili Evangelicae Praeparationis Libri* XV, Oxford University Press, 1903.

Evagrius, *Praktikos*. Greek text: A. and C. Guillaumont, *Évagre le pontique: Traité pratique ou le moine* I & II, *SC*. ET: Robert E. Sinkewicz, *Evagrius of Pontus: The Greek Ascetic Corpus*, Oxford Early Christian Studies, Oxford University Press, 2003.

Gregory of Nazianzus, *Orations*. Greek text in Migne, *PG* 35 and volumes of *SC*. ET: Selections in *FC*.

    Oration 14. Greek text: Migne, *PG* 35.857–909. ET: Brian E. Daley, *Gregory of Nazianzus*, London: Routledge, 2006.

Theological Orations. Greek text: P. Gallay and M. Jourjon, *Saint Grégoire de Nazianze: Discours théologiques (27–31), SC.* ET: F. W. Norris, with F. Williams and L. Wickham, *Faith Gives Fullness to Reasoning: The Five Theological Orations of St Gregory Nazianzen,* Supplement to *VC.*

Gregory of Nyssa, *Works.* Greek text: W. Jaeger *et al.*, *Gregorii Nysseni Opera,* Leiden: Brill, 1960–. ET of selections: H. Musurillo, *From Glory to Glory: Texts from Gregory of Nyssa's Mystical Writings,* New York: Scribner, 1961.

On Loving the Poor. ET: Appendix to Susan R. Holman, *The Hungry are Dying,* Oxford University Press, 2001.

On the Making of Humankind. Greek text: Migne, *PG* 44. ET: *NPNF.*

On Virginity. ET: *FC.*

Life of Moses. ET: *CWS.*

On the Soul and the Resurrection. ET: Catherine Roth, *On the Soul and the Resurrection,* Crestwood, NY: St Vladimir's Seminary Press, 1993.

Great Catechism. ET: J. R. Srawley, *The Catechetical Oration of Gregory of Nyssa,* London: SPCK, 1917.

The Beatitudes. ET: *ACW.*

On the Song of Songs. ET: Casimir McCambley, *St Gregory of Nyssa: Commentary on the Song of Songs,* Brookline, MA: Hellenic College Press, 1987.

Hermas, *The Shepherd.* Greek text and ET: Kirsopp Lake (ed.), *The Apostolic Fathers,* 2 vols., *LCL.*

Irenaeus, *Against Heresies.* Text: A. Rousseau and L. Doutreleau (eds.), *Irénée de Lyon: Contre les hérésies, SC.* ET: *ANCF* and *ACW.*

Demonstration of the Apostolic Preaching. ET: John Behr, *St Irenaeus of Lyons: On the Apostolic Preaching,* Crestwood, NY: St Vladimir's Seminary Press, 1997.

Jerome, *Epistles.* Latin text: I. Hilberg (ed.), *Hieronymus: Epistulae, CSEL.* ET: *ACW.*

John Chrysostom, *Homilies on 1 Corinthians.* Greek text: Migne, *PG* 61. ET: *NPNF.*

On the Incomprehensibility of God. Greek text: A. M. Malingrey, *Jean Chrysostome: Sur l'incompréhensibilité de Dieu, SC.* ET: *FC.*

Julian of Norwich, *Revelations of Divine Love.* ET: Clifton Wolters, Harmondsworth: Penguin, 1966.

Justin Martyr, 1 *Apology*. Greek text: M. Markovich (ed.), *Iustini martyris apologiae pro Christianos*, *PTS*. ET: *ACW*.

   Dialogue with Trypho. Greek text: M. Markovich (ed.), *Dialogus cum Tryphone*, *PTS*. ET: *FC*.

'Macarius', *Spiritual Homilies*. Greek text: H. Berthold (ed.), *Makarios/ Symeon: Reden und Briefe*, 2 vols., *GCS*. ET: *CWS*.

Nemesius, *On the Nature of Humankind*. Greek text: M. Morani (ed.), *Nemesius: De Natura Hominis*, Leipzig: Teubner, 1987. ET: W. Telfer, *Cyril of Jerusalem and Nemesius of Emesa*, *LCC*.

Origen, *Against Celsus*. Greek text: P. Koetschau *et al.* (eds.), *Origenes Werke*, *GCS*. ET: Henry Chadwick, *Contra Celsum*, Cambridge University Press, 1965.

   On First Principles. Text: P. Koetschau *et al.* (eds.), *Origenes Werke*, *GCS*. ET: G. W. Butterworth, London: SPCK 1936, reprinted Gloucester, MA: Peter Smith, 1973.

   Commentary on John. Greek text: E. Preuschen (ed.), *Origenes Werke*, *GCS*. ET: *ANCL* additional volume.

Socrates, *Church History*. Greek text: G. C. Hansen (ed.), *Sokrates: Kirchengeschichte*, *GCS*. ET: *NPNF*.

Sozomen, *Church History*. Greek text: J. Bidez and G. C. Hansen (eds.), *Sozomenus: Kirchengeschichte*, *GCS*. ET: *NPNF*.

Tatian. Greek text edited and translated by Molly Whittaker, *Tatian, Oratio ad Graecos and Fragments*, *OECT*.

Tertullian. Latin texts: E. Dekkers *et al.* (eds.), *CCL*.

   Against Praxeas. Latin text and ET: E. Evans, *Tertullian's Treatise against Praxeas*, London: SPCK, 1948.

   On the Resurrection of the Flesh. Latin text and ET: Ernest Evans, *Tertullian's Treatise on the Resurrection*, London: SPCK, 1960.

   Against Marcion. Latin text and ET: E. Evans, *Adversus Marcionem*, *OECT*.

   On Monogamy, On Chastity. ET: *ACW*.

   Against Hermogenes. ET: *ACW*.

   On Fasting, On the Veiling of Virgins. ET: *ANCL*.

   On the Soul. ET: *FC*.

Theodoret, *Church History*. Greek text: L. Parmentier and F. Scheidweiler (eds.), *Theodoret. Kirchengeschichte*, *GCS*. ET: *NPNF*.

Theophilus, *To Autolycus*. Greek text edited and translated by Robert M. Grant, *Theophilus of Antioch Ad Autolycum, OECT*.

Compendia

Boss, Sarah Jane (ed.), *Mary: The Complete Resource*, London: Continuum, 2007.

Hennecke, E., *New Testament Apocrypha*, 2 vols., W. Schneemelcher (ed.), ET: R. McL. Wilson, London: Lutterworth, 1963–5.

Outler, Albert C. (ed.), *John Wesley*, Oxford University Press, 1964.

Robinson, James (ed.), *The Nag Hammadi Library in English*, Leiden: Brill, 1977.

Stevenson, J. (ed.), *A New Eusebius: Documents Illustrative of the History of the Church to AD 337*, London: SPCK, 1957.

Whaling, Frank (ed.), *John and Charles Wesley: Selected Writings and Hymns, CWS*, Mahweah, NJ: Paulist Press, 1981.

Secondary sources

Ayala, Francisco J., *Darwin's Gift to Science and Religion*, Washington, DC: John Henry Press, 2007.

Baptism, Eucharist and Ministry (Faith and Order Paper No. 111, the 'Lima Text'), Geneva: WCC, 1982.

Barnard, L. W., *Athenagoras: A Study in Second-Century Christian Apologetic*, Paris: Éditions Beauchesne, 1972.

Barton, John, *The Nature of Biblical Criticism*, Louisville, KY and London: Westminster John Knox, 2007.

Barton, Stephen C. and David Wilkinson (eds.), *Reading Genesis after Darwin*, Oxford University Press, 2009.

Beattie, Tina, *Rediscovering Mary: Insights from the Gospels*, Tunbridge Wells: Burns and Oates, 1995.

Beeley, Christopher, *Gregory of Nazianzus on the Trinity and the Knowledge of God,* Oxford University Press, 2008.

Behr-Sigel, Elisabeth, *The Ministry of Women in the Church*, ET: Stephen Bigham, Crestwood, NY: St Vladimir's Seminary Press 1999; previously Oakwood Publications 1991; original French, Paris: Les Éditions du Cerf, 1987.

Benko, Stephen, *The Virgin Goddess: Studies in the Pagan and Christian Roots of Mariology*, Leiden: Brill, 1993.

Beste, Jennifer Erin, *God and the Victim: Traumatic Intrusions on Grace and Freedom*, Oxford University Press, 2007.

Birdsall, J. Neville, 'Diatessaric Readings in the *Martyrdom of St Abo of Tiflis?*' in E. J. Epp and G. D. Fee (eds.), *New Testament Textual Criticism*, Essays in Honour of Bruce M. Metzger, Oxford University Press, 1981, pp. 313–24.

Boff, Leonardo, *Praying with Jesus and Mary*, ET, Maryknoll, NY: Orbis Books, 1983/2005.

Børresen, Kari Elisabeth, 'God's Image, Man's Image? Patristic Interpretation of Gen. 1,27 and I Cor. 11,7' in Børresen (ed.), *The Image of God: Gender Models in Judaeo-Christian Tradition*, Minneapolis: Fortress Press, 1995.

Bourke, Joanna, *What it Means to be Human: Reflections from 1791 to the Present*, London: Virago, 2011.

Braaten, Carl E. and Robert W. Jenson (eds.), *Mary: Mother of God*, Grand Rapids, MI: Eerdmans, 2004.

Brakke, David, *Athanasius and Asceticism*, Baltimore: Johns Hopkins University Press, 1995.

Brock, Sebastian, *The Luminous Eye: The Spiritual World Vision of St Ephrem*, Rome: CIIS, 1985, republished Collegeville. MN: Cistercian Publications, 1992.

Bronowski, Jacob, *The Ascent of Man*, London: BBC Publications, 1973; paperback London: Macdonald Futura, 1981.

Brook, Peter, *The Empty Space*, London: Penguin Modern Classics, 2008 (first published 1968).

Brown, David, *The Divine Trinity*, London: Duckworth, 1985.

Brown, Peter, *The Body and Society: Men, Women and Sexual Renunciation in Early Christianity*, London: Faber and Faber, 1989.

Called to Love and Praise, Peterborough: The Methodist Church, 1999.

Cassidy, Sheila, *Confessions of a Lapsed Catholic*, London: DLT, 2010.

Chadwick, Henry, 'Eucharist and Christology in the Nestorian Controversy', *JTS* NS 2 (1951), 145–64.

Clark, Elizabeth A. (ed.), *Women in the Early Church*, Wilmington, DE: Michael Glazier, 1983.

Coulson, John, *Religion and Imagination: In Aid of a Grammar of Assent*, Oxford University Press, 1981.

Creel, Richard E., *Divine Impassibility*, Cambridge University Press, 1986.

Crouzel, Henri, *Théologie de l'image de dieu chez Origène*, Paris: Aubier, 1955. *Origen*, ET: A. S. Worrall, Edinburgh: T&T Clark, 1989.

Crowder, Colin, 'Humanity', in Adrian Hastings, Alistair Mason and Hugh Pyper, *The Oxford Companion to Christian Thought*, Oxford University Press, 2000, pp. 311–14.

Cupitt, Don, *Only Human*, London: SCM Press, 1985.

Daley, Brian E., *The Hope of the Early Church*, Cambridge University Press, 1991.

Dalrymple, William, *From the Holy Mountain*, London: HarperCollins, 1997.

Davidson, Martin, *The Perfect Nazi*, London: Penguin, 2010.

Dawkins, Richard, *The Selfish Gene*, Oxford University Press, 1976. *The Blind Watchmaker*, Harmondsworth: Penguin, 1988. *The God Delusion*, London: Bantam, 2006.

de Waal, Frans, *The Age of Empathy: Nature's Lessons for a Kinder Society*, London: Souvenir Press, 2009.

Delcogliano, Mark, 'Eusebian Theologies of the Son as the Image of God before 341', *JECS* 14 (2006), 459–84.

Dennett, D., *Darwin's Dangerous Idea: Evolution and the Meaning of Life*, New York: Simon and Schuster, 1995. *Consciousness Explained*, Harmondsworth: Penguin, 1992.

Dillistone, F. W., *The Christian Understanding of Atonement*, Welwyn: Nisbet, 1968.

Dillon, John, *The Middle Platonists*, London: Duckworth, 1977.

Drioton, Etienne, 'La Discussion d'un moine anthropomorphite Audien avec le patriarche Théophile d'Alexandrie en l'année 399', *Revue de l'Orient Chrétien* 20 (1915–17), 92–100, 113–28.

Dunbar, Robin, *How Many Friends Does One Person Need? Dunbar's Number and Other Evolutionary Quirks*, London: Faber and Faber, 2010.

Dunbar, R. E. M. and Louise Barrett (eds.), *The Oxford Handbook of Evolutionary Psychology*, Oxford University Press, 2007.

Eagleton, Terry, *On Evil*, New Haven: Yale University Press, 2010.

Edwards, Mark, *Origen against Plato*, Aldershot: Ashgate, 2002.

Edwards, Ruth, *The Case for Women's Ordination*, London: SPCK, 1989.

Ehrhardt, Arnold, *The Beginning: A Study in the Greek Philosophical Approach to the Concept of Creation from Anaximander to St John*, Manchester University Press, 1968.

Eliot, T. S., *Murder in the Cathedral*, London: Faber and Faber, 1935; 1982 reprint.

Fiddes, Paul S., *The Creative Suffering of God*, Oxford University Press, 1988.

Fitzgerald, Allan D. (ed.), *Augustine through the Ages: An Encyclopedia*, Grand Rapids, MI: Eerdmans, 1999.

Forbes, Christopher, *Prophecy and Inspired Speech in Early Christianity and its Hellenistic Environment*, Peabody, MA: Hendriksen, 1997.

Ford, David (ed.), *The Modern Theologians: An Introduction to Christian Theology in the Twentieth Century*, Oxford: Blackwell, 1997.

Gavrilyuk, Paul, *The Suffering of the Impassible God: The Dialectics of Patristic Thought*, Oxford Early Christian Studies, Oxford University Press, 2004.

Gebremedhin, Ezra, *Life-Giving Blessing: An Inquiry into the Eucharistic Doctrine of Cyril of Alexandria*, Uppsala: Borgstroms, 1977.

Gleick, James, *Chaos: The Amazing Science of the Unpredictable*, London: Heinemann, 1988.

Golitzin, A., 'A Testimony to Christianity as Transfiguration: The Macarian Homilies and Orthodox Spirituality', in Kimbrough Jr (ed.), *Orthodox and Wesleyan Spirituality*, pp. 129–56.

'Temple and Throne of the Divine Glory: "Pseudo-Macarius" and Purity of Heart, Together with Some Remarks on the Limitations and Usefulness of Scholarship' in Luchman and Kulzer, *Purity of Heart*, pp. 107–12.

Goulder, Michael, *Incarnation and Myth: The Debate Continued*, London: SCM Press, 1979.

Graef, Hilda, *Mary: A History of Doctrine and Devotion*, London: Sheed and Ward, 1963/5, reissued 1985.

Grant, R. M., 'Athenagoras or Pseudo-Athenagoras?', *HTR* 47 (1954), 121–9.

Hanson, R. P. C., *The Search for the Christian Doctrine of God*, Edinburgh: T&T Clark, 1988.

Hardy, Daniel W. and David F. Ford, *Jubilate: Theology in Praise*, London: DLT, 1984.

Harrison, Nonna Verna, *God's Many-Splendored Image: Theological Anthropology for Christian Formation*, Grand Rapids, MI: Baker Books, 2010.
'Gender, Veneration and Virginity in Cappadocian Theology', *JTS* NS 47 (1996), 38–68.

Hart, David Bentley, 'The Mirror of the Infinite: Gregory of Nyssa on the *Vestigia Trinitatis*' in Sarah Coakley (ed.), *Re-Thinking Gregory of Nyssa*, Oxford: Blackwell, 2003, pp. 111–31.

Haught, John F., *God after Darwin*, Boulder, CO: Westview Press, 2000.

Hawking, Stephen and Leonard Mlodinow, *The Grand Design: New Answers to the Ultimate Questions of Life*, London: Bantam Press, 2010.

Heine, R. E., *Perfection in the Virtuous Life*, Cambridge, MA: Philadelphia Patristic Foundation, 1975.

Heyes, Cecilia M., and Bennett G. Gale, Jr., *Social Learning in Animals: The Roots of Culture*, San Diego, London, etc.: Academic Press, 1996.

Heyes, Cecilia M. and Ludwig Huber (eds.), *The Evolution of Cognition*, Cambridge, MA: The MIT Press, 2000.

Hollenweger, Walter J., *The Pentecostals*, London: SCM Press, 1972.

Holman, Susan R, *The Hungry are Dying*, Oxford University Press, 2001.

Holmes, Richard, *The Age of Wonder: How the Romantic Generation Discovered the Beauty and Terror of Science*, London: Harper Press, 2008.

Hopko, Thomas, *A Manual of Prayer and Praise to the Theotokos*, rev. edn, Otego, NY: Holy Myrrhbearers Monastery, 2004.

Jaki, Stanley L., *Creator and Cosmos*, Edinburgh: Scottish Academic Press, 1980.

Johnson, Steven, *Emergence*, London: Penguin, 2001.

Kaufman, John, 'Becoming Divine, Becoming Human: Deification Themes in Irenaeus of Lyons', Dissertation for the Degree of PhD, MF Norwegian School of Theology, Oslo, 2009.

Keating, Daniel A., *The Appropriation of Divine Life in Cyril of Alexandria*, Oxford University Press, 2004.

Kelly, J. N. D., *Early Christian Doctrines*, 2nd edn, London: A&C Black, 1960.

Kelsey, David, *Eccentric Existence: A Theological Anthropology*, 2 vols., Louisville, KY: Westminster John Knox Press, 2009.

Kimbrough, S. T. Jr (ed.), *Orthodox and Wesleyan Spirituality*, Crestwood, NY: St. Vladmir's Seminary Press, 2002.

Knox, R. A., *Enthusiasm*, Oxford University Press, 1950.

Koen, Lars, *The Saving Passion: Incarnational and Soteriological Thought in Cyril of Alexandria's Commentary on the Gospel according to St John*, Uppsala University Press, 1991.

Küng, Hans, *The Church*, London: Burns and Oates, 1968.

Lampe, Peter, *From Paul to Valentinus: Christians at Rome in the First Two Centuries*, ET: Michael Steinhauser, ed. Marshall D. Johnson, London: Continuum, 2003.

Lane, Nick, *Life Ascending: The Ten Great Inventions of Evolution*, London: Profile Books, 2009.

Laurance, John D., *'Priest' as Type of Christ, the Leader of the Eucharist in Salvation History according to Cyprian of Carthage*, New York: Peter Lang, 1984.

Limberis, Vasiliki, *Divine Heiress. The Virgin Mary and the Creation of Christian Constantinople*, London: Routledge, 1994.

'Resurrected Body and Immortal Flesh in Gregory of Nyssa' in *Jesus Christ in St Gregory of Nyssa's Theology*, Minutes of the Ninth International Conference on St Gregory of Nyssa, Athens 7–12 September 2000, Athens: Eptalophos, 2005, pp. 515–28.

Lennox, John C., *God's Undertaker. Has Science Buried God?* Oxford: Lion, 2007.

Lienhard, J. T., *Contra Marcellum: Marcellus of Ancyra and Fourth-Century Theology*, Washington, DC: Catholic University of America Press, 1999.

Lindars, Barnabas, *The Gospel of John*, New Century Bible, London: Oliphants, 1972.

Louth, Andrew, *The Wilderness of God*, London: DLT, 1991.

Luchman, Harriet A. and Linda Kulzer (eds.), *Purity of Heart in Early Ascetic and Monastic Literature*, Collegeville, MN: Liturgical Press, 1999.

Macfarlane, Robert, *Mountains of the Mind: A History of a Fascination*, London: Granta, 2003.

The Wild Places, London: Granta, 2007.

Malik, Kenan, *Man, Beast and Zombie: What Science Can and Cannot Tell us about Human Nature*, London: Phoenix, 2000.

Markus, Robert, *Saeculum: History and Society in the Theology of St Augustine*, Cambridge University Press, 1970/88.

Mary: Grace and Hope in Christ, ARCIC Agreed Statement, Harrisburg/ London: Moorhouse, 2005.

May, Gerhard, *Creatio ex Nihilo: The Doctrine of 'Creation out of Nothing' in Early Christian Thought*, ET: A. S. Worrall, Edinburgh: T&T Clark 1994; original German edn, 1978.

McFadyen, Alistair I., *The Call to Personhood: A Christian Theory of the Individual in Social Relationships*, Cambridge University Press, 1990.

McGilchrist, Iain, *The Master and his Emissary: The Divided Brain and the Making of the Western World*, New Haven and London: Yale University Press, 2009.

McGuckin, John A., *St Gregory of Nazianzus: An Intellectual Biography*, Crestwood, NY: St Vladimir's Seminary Press, 2001.

McIntyre, Alasdair, *Dependent Rational Animals: Why Human Beings Need the Virtues*, London: Duckworth, 1999.

McLeod, Frederick G., SJ, *The Image of God in the Antiochene Tradition*, Washington, DC: Catholic University of America Press, 1999.

Merton, Thomas, *Elected Silence: The Autobiography of Thomas Merton*, London: Hollis and Carter, 1949.

Middlemiss, David, *Interpreting Charismatic Experience*, London: SCM Press, 1986.

Midgley, Mary, *Beast and Man: The Roots of Human Nature*, Sussex: Harvester, 1978; rev. edn, Abingdon: Routledge, 1995; reissued 2002, reprinted 2010.

Moltmann, Jürgen, *The Crucified God: The Cross of Christ as the Foundation and Criticism of Christian Theology*, ET: R. A. Wilson and John Bowden, London: SCM Press, 1974.

Mühlenberg, E., *Die Unendlichkeit Gottes bei Gregor von Nyssa*, Göttingen: Vandenhoeck and Ruprecht, 1966.

Murphy, Nancey, *Bodies and Souls, or Spirited Bodies?* Cambridge University Press, 2006.

O'Neill, J. C., 'How Early is the Doctrine of *creatio ex nihilo*?' *JTS* NS 53.2 (2002), 449–65.

Ouspensky, Leonid and Vladimir Lossky, *The Meaning of Icons* rev. edn, New York: St Vladimir's Seminary Press, 1982.

Pailin, David A., *A Gentle Touch: From a Theology of Handicap to a Theology of Human Being*, London: SPCK, 1992.

Pannenberg, Wolfhart, *What is Man? Contemporary Anthropology in Theological Perspective*, ET: Duane A. Priebe, Philadelphia: Fortress Press 1970; German original 1962.

Pattison, Stephen, *Shame: Theory, Therapy, Theology*, Cambridge University Press, 2000.

Peacocke, Arthur and Ann Pedersen, *The Music of Creation*, Minneapolis: Fortress, 2006.

Plested, Marcus, *The Macarian Legacy: The Place of Macarius–Symeon in the Eastern Christian Tradition*, Oxford Theological Monographs, Oxford University Press, 2004.

Polkinghorne, John, *One World – The Interaction of Science and Theology*, London: SPCK, 1986.

Prior, Colin, *Scotland: The Wild Places*, London: Constable, 2001.

Quarmby, Katharine, *Scapegoat: Why we are Failing Disabled People*, London: Portobello Books, 2011.

Quasten, J., *Patrology*, Utrecht and Antwerp: Spectrum Publishers, 1963.

Rees, Martin, *Before the Beginning: Our Universe and Others*, London: Simon and Schuster, 1997; The Free Press, 2002.

Robertson, J. M., *Christ as Mediator: A Study of the Theologies of Eusebius of Caesarea, Marcellus of Ancyra, and Athanasius of Alexandria*, Oxford University Press, 2007.

Ruether, Rosemary Radford, 'Misogynism and Virginal Feminism in the Fathers of the Church' in Ruether (ed.), *Religion and Sexism: Images of Woman in the Jewish and Christian Traditions*, New York: Simon and Schuster, 1974.

Ruse, Michael, *Can a Darwinian be a Christian? The Relationship between Science and Religion*, Cambridge University Press, 2001.

Sanders, E. P., *Paul and Palestinian Judaism*, London: SCM Press, 1977.

Sargant, William, *Battle for the Mind*, London: Doubleday, 1957.

Sewell, Dennis, *The Political Gene: How Darwin's Ideas Changed Politics*, London: Picador, 2009.

Sorabji, Richard, *Emotion and Peace of Mind: From Stoic Agitation to Christian Temptation*, Oxford University Press, 2000.

Spencer, Nick, *Darwin and God*, London: SPCK, 2009.

Spoerl, Kelley McCarthy, 'The Schism at Antioch since Cavellera' in Michel R. Barnes and Daniel H. Williams (eds.), *Arianism after Arius: Essays*

450

on the Development of the Fourth-Century Trinitarian Conflicts, Edinburgh: T&T Clark, 1993.

Stannard, Russell, *The End of Discovery*, Oxford University Press, 2010.

Steenberg, M. C., *Of God and Man: Theology as Anthropology from Irenaeus to Athanasius*, London: T&T Clark, 2009.

Stewart, Columba, *'Working the Earth of the Heart': The Messalian Controversy in History, Texts, and Language to* AD *431*, Oxford: Clarendon Press, 1991.

Introduction to Harriet A. Luchman and Linda Kulzer (eds.), *Purity of Heart in Early Ascetic and Monastic Literature*, Collegeville, MN: Liturgical Press, 1999, pp. 1–16.

Swanson, R.N., (ed.), *The Church and Mary*, Studies in Church History vol. XXXIX, Woodbridge: Boydell Press, 2004.

Tallis, Raymond, *Michelangelo's Finger: An Exploration of Everyday Transcendence*, London: Atlantic Books, 2010.

Aping Mankind: Neuromania, Darwinitis and the Misrepresentation of Humanity, Durham: Acumen, 2011.

Tanner, Kathryn, *Christ the Key*, Cambridge University Press, 2010.

Taylor, Charles, *A Secular Age*, Cambridge, MA: Harvard University Press, 2007.

Taylor, John H., *Spells for Eternity: The Ancient Egyptian Book of the Dead*, London: British Museum Press, 2010.

Thompson, Ross, *Holy Ground: The Spirituality of Matter*, London: SPCK, 1990.

Thurston, Bonnie Bowman, *The Widows: A Women's Ministry in the Early Church*, Minneapolis: Fortress Press, 1989.

Tilby, Angela, *The Seven Deadly Sins: Their Origin in the Spiritual Teaching of Evagrius the Hermit*, London: SPCK, 2009.

Torjesen, Karen Jo, *When Women were Priests*, San Francisco: HarperCollins 1993.

Torrance, T. F., *Divine and Contingent Order*, Oxford University Press, 1981.

Trevett, Christine, *Montanism: Gender, Authority and the New Prophecy*, Cambridge University Press, 1996.

Trevor, William, *Love and Summer*, London: Viking/Penguin, 2009.

Trigg, Joseph W., *Origen: The Bible and Philosophy in the Third-Century Church*, London: SCM Press, 1983.

Turcescu, Lucian, 'Modern Misreadings of Gregory of Nyssa' in Sarah Coakley (ed.), *Re-Thinking Gregory of Nyssa*, Oxford: Blackwell, 2003, pp. 97–109.

Vanier, Jean, *Visages de Marie*, Paris: Nouvelles Éditions Mame, 2001.

    Drawn into the Mystery of Jesus through the Gospel of John, Toronto: Novalis, 2004.

von Balthasar, Hans Urs, *Presence and Thought: An Essay on the Religious Philosophy of Gregory of Nyssa*, ET: Mark Sebanc, San Francisco: Ignatius Press, 1995; French original 1988.

Ward, Keith, *Defending the Soul*, London: Hodder and Stoughton, 1992.

Warner, Marina, *Alone of All her Sex: The Myth and Cult of the Virgin Mary*, London: Weidenfeld and Nicolson, 1985.

Weil, Simone, *Gateway to God*, ed. David Raper London: Collins/Fontana, 1974.

Wiles, Maurice, *God's Action in the World*, London: SCM Press, 1986.

Wilken, Robert, *Judaism and the Early Christian Mind: A Study of Cyril of Alexandria's Exegesis and Theology*, New Haven: Yale University Press, 1971.

Williams, A. N., *The Divine Sense: The Intellect in Patristic Theology*, Cambridge University Press, 2007.

Williams, Rowan, *Why Study the Past?* London: DLT, 2005.

Wilson, E. O., *Sociobiology: The New Synthesis*, Cambridge, MA: Harvard University Press, 1975.

Wijngaards, John, *The Ordination of Women in the Catholic Church: Unmasking a Cuckoo's Egg Tradition*, London: DLT, 2001.

Wisdom, John, 'Gods', originally published in *Proceedings of the Aristotelian Society*, 1944–5, reprinted in John Wisdom, *Philosophy and Psychoanalysis*, Oxford: Blackwell, 1953.

Women Bishops in the Church of England? A Report of the House of Bishops Working Party on Women in the Episcopate, London: Church House Publishing, 2004.

Wright, M. R., *Cosmology in Antiquity*, London and New York: Routledge, 1995.

Yong, Amos, *Theology and Down Syndrome: Re-imagining Disability in Late Modernity*, Waco, TX: Baylor University Press, 2007.

Zachhuber, J., *Human Nature in Gregory of Nyssa: Philosophical Background and Theological Significance*, Leiden: Brill, 2000.

Zahl, Simeon, *Pneumatology and Theology of the Cross in the Preaching of Christoph Friedrich Blumhardt: The Holy Spirit between Wittenberg and Azusa Street*, London: T&T Clark, 2010.

Zalasiewicz, Jan, *The Earth after us*, Oxford University Press, 2008.

Zizioulas, John D., *Being as Communion*, London: DLT, 1985.

Author's previously published studies to which reference is made, listed alphabetically

*Items marked with an asterisk are republished in the Variorum Collected Studies Series, *Exegesis and Theology in Early Christianity* (Farnham: Ashgate Variorum, 2012).

'A cloud of witnesses' and 'Two roots or a tangled mass?' in John Hick (ed.), *The Myth of God Incarnate*, London: SCM Press, 1977, chapters 2 (pp. 13–47) and 5 (pp. 87–121).

*'Adam and Anthropos: A Study in the Interaction of Science and the Bible in Two Anthropological Treatises of the Fourth Century', *VC* 37 (1983), 110–40.

*'Allegory and Atonement', *Australian Biblical Review* 35 (1987), Special Issue in Honour of Professor Eric Osborn, 107–14.

*'Allegory and the Ethics of Reading,' in Francis Watson (ed.), *The Open Text*, London: SPCK, 1993, pp. 103–20.

Biblical Exegesis and the Formation of Christian Culture, Cambridge University Press, 1997.

Brokenness and Blessing: Towards a Biblical Spirituality, Sarum Theological Lectures for 2004, London: DLT, 2007.

Can These Dry Bones Live? London: SCM Press, 1982.

'Christian Scripture and the "Other"' in Michael Ipgrave (ed.), *Scriptures in Dialogue: Christians and Muslims Studying the Bible and the Qur'an Together,* a record of the seminar 'Building Bridges' held at Doha, Qatar, 7–9 April 2003, London: Church House Publishing, 2004.

'Christology and Creation: Towards an Hermeneutic of Patristic Christology' in T. Merrigan and J. Haers (eds.), *The Myriad Christ*, Leuven University Press, 2000, pp. 191–205.

*'"Creatio ex nihilo": A Context for the Emergence of the Christian Doctrine of Creation', *SJT* 44 (1991), 139–51.

*'Creation and Human Being: The Forging of a Distinct Christian Discourse', *SP* 44 (2010), 335–48.

Encounter with Mystery: Reflections on L'Arche and Living with Disability, London: DLT, 1997.

*'Exegetical Method and Scriptural Proof: The Bible in Doctrinal Debate', *SP* 24 (1989), 291–304.

Face to Face, London: Epworth, 1985; revised and enlarged, Edinburgh: T&T Clark, 1990.

'From Analysis to Overlay: A Sacramental Approach to Christology' in David Brown and Ann Loades (eds.), *Christ: The Sacramental Word: Incarnation, Sacrament and Poetry*, London: SPCK, 1996, pp. 40–56.

From Nicaea to Chalcedon: A Guide to the Literature and its Background, London: SCM Press, 2010.

*'From Suspicion and Sociology to Spirituality: On Method, Hermeneutics and Appropriation with Respect to Patristic Material', *SP* 29 (1997), 421–35.

'God's Image: "The Elephant in the Room" in the Fourth Century?', *SP* 50 (2011), 57–71.

'Hermeneutical Questions: The Ordination of Women in the Light of Biblical and Patristic Typology' in Ian Jones, Janet Wootton and Kirsty Thorpe (eds.), *Women and Ordination in the Christian Churches: International Perspectives*, London: T&T Clark, 2008.

'Inner Struggle: Some Parallels between the Spirituality of John Wesley and the Greek Fathers' in Kimbrough Jr, (ed.), *Orthodox and Wesleyan Spirituality*, pp. 157–72.

'John Chrysostom on I & II Corinthians', *SP* 18 (1986), 1.349–52.

Meaning and Truth in 2 Corinthians, with David Ford, London: SPCK, 1987.

*'Naked or Clothed? Eschatology and the Doctrine of Creation' in Peter Clarke and Tony Claydon (eds.), *The Church, the Afterlife and the Fate of the Soul*, Studies in Church History 45, Woodbridge: Boydell and Brewer, 2009.

*'On *Episkopos* and *Presbyteros*', *JTS NS* 45 (1994), 142–8.

*'*Paideia* and the Myth of Static Dogma' in Sarah Coakley and David Pailin (eds.), *The Making and Remaking of Chrisian Doctrine*, Essays in Honour of Maurice Wiles, Oxford: Clarendon Press, 1993, pp. 265–83.

'Presbyteral Ministry in the Catholic Tradition or Why Shouldn't Women be Priests?' London: The Methodist Sacramental Fellowship, 1994.

*'Proverbs 8 in Interpretation (2): Wisdom Personified' in David F. Ford and Graham Stanton (eds.), *Reading Texts, Seeking Wisdom*, London: SCM Press, 2003.

'Songs without Words: Incorporating the Linguistically Marginalized' in Stephen Burns, Nicola Slee and Michael N. Jagessar (eds.), *The Edge of God: New Liturgical Texts and Contexts in Conversation*, London: Epworth Press, 2008.

The Art of Performance: Towards a Theology of Holy Scripture, London: DLT, 1990.

'The Church and Mary', *Ecclesiology* 5 (2009), 272–98.

'The Critic and the Visionary', Inaugural lecture, University of Birmingham, 1987; reproduced in *SJT* 41 (1988), 297–312.

*'The God of the Greeks and the Nature of Religious Language' in W. R. Schoedel and Robert Wilken (eds.), *Early Christian Literature and the Greek Intellectual Tradition*, Festschrift for R. M. Grant, Théologie Historique 53, Paris: Éditions Beauchesne, 1979.

The Making of the Creeds, London: SCM Press, 1991.

'The Materialism of the Christian Tradition', *Bulletin of the Methodist Sacramental Fellowship* No. 138 (Epiphany 2011), 4–10.

'The "Mind" of Scripture: Theological Readings of the Bible in the Fathers', *International Journal of Systematic Theology* 7 (2005), 126–41.

'The Pastorals and the Ethics of Reading', *JSNT* 45 (1992), 105–20.

'The "Penultimate" Nature of the Church – the *Eschaton* Is Not Yet!' in Kimbrough Jr, (ed.), *Orthodox and Wesleyan Ecclesiology*, pp. 199–211.

The Theology of the Pastoral Letters, Cambridge University Press, 1994.

'The Trinity and the New Testament' in Christopher Rowland and Christopher Tuckett (eds.), *The Nature of New Testament Theology*, Essays on Honour of Robert Morgan, Oxford: Blackwell, 2006.

'*Theotokos*: Mary and the Pattern of Fall and Redemption in the Theology of Cyril of Alexandria' in William McLoughlin and Jill Pinnock (eds.), *Mary for Earth and Heaven: Essays on Mary and Ecumenism*, Leominster: Gracewing, 2002, pp. 340–54.

*'*Theotokos*: Mary and the Pattern of Fall and Redemption in the Theology of Cyril of Alexandria' in Thomas G. Weinandy and Daniel A. Keating (eds.), *The Theology of St Cyril of Alexandria: A Critical Appreciation*, London: T&T Clark, 2003, pp. 55–74.[1]

'Towards Transformational Reading of Scripture', with Jean Vanier, in Craig Bartholomew, Scott Hahn, Robin Parry, Christopher Seitz and Al Wolters (eds.), *Canon and Biblical Interpretation*, Bletchley: Paternoster Press, 2006.

'Typology' in Stanley E. Porter, Paul Joyce and David E. Orton (eds.), *Crossing the Boundaries*, Essays in Biblical Interpretation in Honour of Michael D. Goulder, Leiden: Brill, 1994, 29–48.

'University Sermon for the Tercentenary of the Birth of John Wesley', *Epworth Review* 31 (2004), 44–51.

[1] Despite the identical title, this and the previous essay are not the same, though there is some overlap.

Index

Arian, controversy 162, 166, 170, 173, 240, 332, 386, 411
Aristotle 56, 112, 114
Arius 154, 165, 324, 333, 386, 408
Ark (of the Covenant) 330, 340
arrogance 204
Artemis (Diana) 220, 349
Arthur (Young) x, 10–11, 44, 66, 68, 82, 107, 108, 128, 129, 138, 176, 178, 179, 181, 190, 219, 224, 228, 246, 247, 248, 282, 284, 285, 287, 292, 357, 358, 383, 385, 404
artist 103, 146
arts 183, 192, 250
Ascension 339, 360
ascent 72, 217
ascetism 14, 71, 72
Asclepius 251
Aseity 385
Askēsis 38
Assurance 299
Asterius 164, 165
Atasnassova, Antonia 335
Athanasius 153, 166–70, 172, 173, 221, 239–42, 324, 336, 386, 387, 408, 409, 411, 417
Athenagoras 53, 95, 96, 99, 277
Atonement 42, 182, 202, 204, 230, 235–50
Audians 154, 156
Augustine of Hippo 32, 48–50, 52, 53, 58, 59, 60, 61, 62, 71, 73, 74, 75, 78, 80, 81, 99, 102–5, 108, 109, 110, 111, 129, 131, 132, 133, 134, 135, 136, 153, 182, 186, 225, 232, 254, 305, 339, 351, 383
Aulén, Gustav 241, 243, 247
Australia 353
authority 110, 112, 243
autism 192, 229
autonomy 108, 181, 223
Awe 191
Ayala, Francisco 64, 67
Azusa Street 270

Babel 205, 231, 254, 278, 428
Babylon 231, 352
balance 68
Bampton Lectures 403

baptism 152, 155, 161, 219, 220, 226, 267, 326, 328, 353, 417
baptism, infant, 226
Barbara June, SLG x
Barnard, L.W. 95
Barrett, Louise 126
Barton, John 24–5, 51
Barton, Stephen 48
Basil of Caesarea 10, 11, 12, 13, 14, 18, 44, 46–7, 49, 50, 53, 58, 59, 61, 62, 70, 71, 72, 73, 74, 75, 78, 134, 150, 160, 317, 348–50
Beattie, Tina 338
beauty, the beautiful 6, 61, 71, 72, 73, 77, 78, 81, 101, 102, 105, 107, 116, 119, 132, 133, 134, 135, 141, 172, 173, 298, 426
Beeley, Christopher 396
beginning 163
begotten 408
behaviour 114, 126
Behr, John 158, 204
Behr-Sigel, Elisabeth x, 324, 325, 326, 329, 330
being 176, 399
Benko, Stephen 332, 333, 334
Berthold, H. 294
Beste, Jennifer Erin 230
Betjeman, John 425
Bevenot, Maurice S. J. 343, 344
Bible, scripture 4, 5, 7, 10, 11, 32, 33, 35, 87, 114, 117, 157, 166, 206, 209, 214, 217, 223, 231, 235, 241, 262, 268, 274, 275, 284, 296, 305, 318, 324, 325, 331, 333, 341, 346, 353, 371, 373, 378, 397, 407, 408, 410, 411, 412, 417, 420
biblical criticism 22
Big Bang 51, 52
biochemistry 130
biology 126, 127
Birdsall, J. Neville 236, 237
Birrell, Ian 226
bishops 213, 316, 318, 319, 320, 321, 345, 346, 347, 352
Black 175
blasphemy 247
blessing 205
blood 221, 316, 401